Secrets of Self-Employment

Secrets of Self-Employment

SURVIVING AND THRIVING
ON THE UPS AND DOWNS OF
BEING YOUR OWN BOSS

SARAH AND PAUL EDWARDS

A JEREMY P. TARCHER / PUTNAM BOOK
published by G. P. Putnam's Sons
New York

Most Tarcher/Putnam books are available at special quantity discounts for bulk purchases for sales promotions, premiums, fund-raising, and educational needs. Special books or book excerpts also can be created to fit specific needs. For details, write or telephone Special Markets, The Putnam Publishing Group, 200 Madison Ave., New York, NY 10016; (212) 951-8891.

■   ■   ■

A Jeremy P. Tarcher/Putnam Book
Published by G. P. Putnam's Sons
Publishers Since 1838
200 Madison Avenue
New York, NY 10016
http://www.putnam.com/putnam

Library of Congress Cataloging-in-Publication Data

Edwards, Sarah (Sarah A.)
    Secrets of self-employment: surviving and thriving on the ups and downs of being
    your own boss / Sarah and Paul Edwards.
        p.   cm.
    Rev. ed. of: Making it on your own. 1991.
    Includes index.
    ISBN 0-87477-837-9
    1. New business enterprises. 2. Self-employed. 3. Success in business.   I. Edwards, Paul,
date.   II. Edwards, Sarah (Sarah A.), Making it on your own.   III. Title.
HD62.5.E393   1996
658'.041—dc20   96-12715 CIP

Printed in the United States of America
10 9 8 7 6 5 4 3 2 1
This book is printed on acid-free paper. ∞

"Twelve Characteristics of Tough-Minded Optimists" is reprinted with permission from *The Power of Optimism* by Alan Loy McGinnis. New York: Harper and Row, 1990.

Book design by Lee Fukui

Acknowledgments

OUR GRATITUDE GOES FIRST to the men and women we meet in our workshops, on-line, and whom we interview on our radio and television shows for their insights and experiences in being self-employed. The reaction of our readers to the first edition of this book, published as *Making It on Your Own,* validated our belief in the need for a book of this kind and inspired us to go farther in providing tools and resources for coping and becoming victorious over the confusion, doubts, and concerns that come with separating yourself from a paycheck and job. That we have sought to do with additions in this edition.

We especially appreciate the team of remarkable men and women at Tarcher/Putnam who make publishing this series of books as much of a joy as writing and publishing can be for people like us who would rather talk than write. Robert Welsch, who had the vision for a series of books, deserves special mention as does Jeremy Tarcher, who grasped that vision. We thank our editors, Irene Prokop and Rick Benzel. To Coral Tysliava, Tricia Martin, Jennifer Greene, Lisa Russell, and Paul Cohen, we express our deep thanks for not only doing their jobs well but doing them cheerfully.

Contributing significantly to this book were Sheila Syracuse, our assistant, and Barrie Jaeger, who painstakingly researched and verified the *Where-to-Get-Help Resource Directory.*

Contents

Introduction

IF YOU WERE AN OLYMPIC ATHLETE, enthusiastic audiences would cheer you on to great feats. Your coaches would encourage, prod, and guide you to success. If you were part of a top sales team for a leading company, you'd attend regular seminars and training programs presented by experts who would charge you up and build your skills and confidence.

But if you are one of today's growing number of self-employed individuals, or want to be, who cheers you on? Who picks you up? Who gives you the boost you need? Chances are you have to do most of that for yourself.

Your family, friends, and colleagues may think you're crazy to go out on your own, even though they may wish they could do it themselves. They may be telling you that what you're doing isn't practical, and when problems arise they may not be sympathetic. After all, what can you expect when you don't play it safe?

Even if those around you are understanding and supportive, you may hesitate to discuss your concerns with them. They may, unintentionally, show their support in less-than-helpful ways like sending you a want ad for what they think could be a good job for you or suggesting another line of work you could pursue. Sometimes it's even hard to share the excitement of your victories. Your success may be a reminder to others of what they wish they were doing.

If you've had any of these experiences, you're certainly not alone. All people who set out on their own feel the isolation of taking a road less traveled. Even though that road is taking you toward your dreams and the journey is exciting, it can also feel long and bumpy en route. That's why we wrote this book. It's the collective voice of thousands of people like you who have left the familiar comforts, bothersome discomforts, and newfound insecurities of a salaried job to venture into the unfamiliar but enthralling world of being your own boss.

If making it on your own feels something like running a marathon, and many would agree it is, then this book is like a crowd of enthusiastic fans lining the road, cheering you on, shouting out encouragement along the way. These fans have run the race themselves, so you'll hear them calling out the precise words you need to hear at the very moment you need to hear them.

We've written this book because we've been there. We've felt both the exhilaration and the apprehension of leaving behind what seemed like the security of a paycheck to pursue our ideas and manifest our dreams. We've lived through the lean years; we've felt the pain of Heartbreak Hill. But we also know the tremendous joy and satisfaction that come from knowing you've made it—that you've done what you set out to do and accomplished what others told you could not be done.

Over the past years, through our seminars, the thousands of interviews and conversations on the Working from Home Forum on CompuServe Information Service, and our television and radio shows, we've met and shared journeys with thousands of others who have undertaken the challenge to make it on their own, sometimes by choice, and sometimes as a result of an unexpected crisis. In the process we've found that success or failure on your own is no accident. Those who succeed approach the challenges with a different attitude and react to them in a different manner from those who don't.

Success is much more than simply knowing the basics of business start-ups and having a positive attitude. While having a positive attitude is important, very important, success also means knowing what to do with negative attitudes (both yours and others'), and what to do when the bills exceed the business. It's knowing when to invest money you don't have so that you will ultimately have it. It's knowing when to persist and when to change. It's knowing what to do and what to think when the money runs out. In many ways, how you respond and handle what seems like the negative aspects of being on your own is even more important than how you handle the opportunities and the routine aspects of making it.

We wrote this book to address the most common questions and challenges we and other self-employed people encounter . . . after all, the basic how-to-start-a-business details—like selecting your business, writing your business plan, getting your business license, and getting your marketing under way—are taken care of. Since the release of *Making It on Your Own* in 1991, we've received many deeply touching letters from people who tell us this book is much more than they expected. They tell us it's unlike any other resource they've found and that they are grateful that finally someone understands and is willing to talk about what they've been too afraid or too embarrassed to ask. From these letters, we realized this book is actually about the "secrets" of being self-employed. It's about the many, many things no one ever talks about, the things most business books, seminars, and courses leave out. It's about the things you'd rather not find out through humiliating mistakes or painfully long struggles, the many subtle and not-so-subtle challenges that arise without warning, and the delightfully clever options that can get you over, around, or under any of these obstacles.

So, we changed the title of this new edition to *Secrets of Self-Employment*. As before, throughout the book, you'll gain the experience of people who've done what others told them couldn't be done: people like Ellie Kahn, who earns a living creating videos that document family and corporate histories; people like Liz Danzinger who gets to stay at home to raise her four young children while she works twenty-five hours a week and earns more than she did at her full-time editorial job; people like the photographer Dean Tucker, who turned his hobby into a business by traveling across the country doing multimedia presentations; people like the comedian Kevin Hughes, who found a unique and profitable way to earn over one hundred thousand dollars a year by making people laugh, both on college campuses and in his own workshops for couples. And people like Robbie Bogue who turned losing his job into a better life than he'd ever imagined.

At one time, ventures like these might have been considered impractical, yet now they are thriving. Was it easy? Of course not. Most of these people started on a shoestring. They all had doubts. They all had challenges. But was it worth it? These individuals and those whose lives are improved by their services answer with a resounding *yes!*

It's from such experiences and those of other successful self-employed individuals, that we've learned the many practical "secrets" you'll find throughout the book to meet the most challenging demands of being your own boss. Through the secrets gleaned from such experiences, you can learn how to proceed with confidence, how to overcome financial difficulties, how to remain relaxed and positive under the pressure of deadlines, how to keep your energy up and perform in the midst of crises—and how to position yourself to recognize and seize opportunities while keeping the wolves at bay.

These are the prerequisites for directing your own future that anyone can master. For years, we've been asked what kind of people are able to make it on their own. Can anyone do it, or are there certain characteristics someone must have in order to succeed? Over and over again, we've replied that you can make it on your own if you have a strong desire and the willingness to learn how to become a goal-directed, self-motivated person.

But let's face it: most of us were not taught how to be goal-directed, self-motivated people. We're given far too few opportunities to think for ourselves, to take the initiative, to run with our own ideas, make mistakes, and learn from them so we can get where we want to go. For most of our lives, the rules, the expectations, and directives of parents, teachers, and bosses have defined so much of what we do and how we can do it.

As a result, many people who set out on their own don't feel at first that they have what it takes; and yet they succeed, nonetheless, because everyone can become goal oriented and self-motivated. In fact, going out on your own provides the perfect opportunity to develop these abilities. And actually that's what this book is about: how to develop the attitudes, skills, and confidence of a self-motivated, goal-directed person who accomplishes whatever you set out to achieve on your own.

We've found that these attitudes and skills will enable you not only to survive on your own, but to thrive. They will enable you to do the three things that can assure your success:

1. How to develop a new, self-reliant mindset. As you may already have discovered, working successfully on your own requires a new mental outlook. You need to think about yourself, your work, and your life in a new way as you leave behind the traditional world of the paycheck and enter a world in which you must rely upon yourself to produce the income you need to live well.

In part one of this book, "Making the Mental Shift from Payroll to Profit," we outline the secrets to making vital and sometimes surprising mental shifts being on your own requires. You'll learn how to leave the paycheck mentality behind forever and permanently adopt a successful self-supporting orientation. In fact, you may find yourself unfit to ever be someone's underling again.

In this section, you'll also learn the reasons some self-employed individuals succeed where others fail. You'll discover how most of the failures can be averted. And you'll learn the difference between today's new breed of self-employed individuals and the classical entrepreneur of the past. You'll understand why much of the business advice you've received has not been as useful to you as you might have liked. And, best of all, you'll discover why your chances of success are greater today than ever before.

2. How to put your show on the road. We all have dreams of how we'd like to spend our lives. We know how we'd like things to be. But to make it on your own, you have to take the next step. You have to know where you're going and set your life up so you'll get there. You have to take charge and start directing the many things that need to be done so that you're running your life instead of it running you. You must literally have the time of your life.

We're sure you didn't go out on your own to spend most of your time serving as the secretary, receptionist, salesperson, bookkeeper, and cleaning service. But these tasks do need to be done, and you're probably the one who will have to do them. In part two of this book, "Managing Everything That Needs to Be Done," you'll discover the secrets of how to get organized so your business can essentially run itself while you spend most of your time earning a living doing what you do best and enjoy most.

You'll learn how to take strategic advantage of technology and support services and make marketing yourself and your work a part of what you're already good at. You'll also learn tactics for how to turn around slow times and make the most of limited resources.

3. *How to literally become your own boss.* When you're self-employed, you've got to manage yourself to make sure that you do what you need to do and get where you want to go. You've got to literally be your own boss, motivating, inspiring, and preparing yourself to function at your peak as you ride the emotional roller coaster of being on your own. You can't let the ups and downs get you down. You have to direct and guide yourself through whatever challenges and problems arise along the way.

Part 3, "Becoming the Boss You've Always Wanted to Have," is a mini-course in how to assume the role of effectively managing yourself. You'll learn the secrets of how to deal with common motivational issues like staying focused, handling rejection, giving yourself ample time off, and performing well under the pressure of deadlines, setbacks, and having too many things to do. You'll learn what to do when you don't know what to do and how to respond when you feel like quitting. You'll find guidelines for dealing with some of the most difficult issues self-employed individuals encounter—like not being taken seriously, running out of money, and not having enough clients or customers.

And you'll learn the secrets of how to deal with many things you'll rarely hear anyone talk about—such as what to do when you don't want to do what you know you need to do, what to say when business isn't so good, and survival strategies for overcoming crises we hope you'll never have to face. But if you do, you'll be better prepared to respond with confidence. And we'll talk about another ingredient of making it on your own that's rarely discussed—living well with success. You may have noticed that sometimes "successful" people aren't happy people. In fact, sometimes success itself becomes overwhelming and demanding. Instead of feeling fantastic, you can become enslaved to your success. So in the closing section of this book, "Enjoying Your Success," we talk about the unexpected aspects of achieving your goals and what's involved in making sure your success turns out to be worth all the time and effort it takes to achieve.

Since the first edition of this book, the information revolution has literally exploded with new resources. Not only are there many more books that will be helpful to your success, there are audiotapes and videotapes, newsletters, CD-ROMs, software, organizations, and on-line resources that can help you succeed. So, in this new edition, we've expanded and updated the annotated resource lists at the end of most chapters to incorporate resources from all these media, including the Internet, using the following icons.

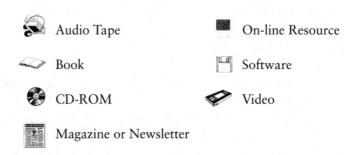

	Audio Tape		On-line Resource
	Book		Software
	CD-ROM		Video
	Magazine or Newsletter		

As with our first edition, rather than list tons of resources on every possible subject, to save you time and energy, we've reviewed and screened those we've selected to include only what we consider to be among the best. We've also focused on resources you'd be unlikely to find elsewhere along with "classic" sources of information on a subject, which are identified with an asterisk (*).

We've also added an appendix: "Where-to-Get-Help Resource Directory," where you'll find a list of the agencies and organizations in your state that are available to assist self-employed, home-based, and very small businesses. Again, rather than simply listing all possible organizations and agencies, we've called to talk with the agencies you see on standard generic resource lists and screened them to assure that, at the time of this writing, those we've included do, in fact, strive to address the needs of self-employed individuals, not just larger small businesses.

Essentially, we've designed this book to help you make a revolutionary shift in the way you look at yourself and your work. As you read through it, we feel certain you'll begin to see more clearly than ever before that your fate does not depend on chance, the whims of others, or even the ups and downs of the economy. Indeed, you'll undoubtedly come to believe ever more strongly that you hold the power to create your own future and the quality of your life. We look forward to your thoroughly enjoying amazing results from making it on your own—results that will surprise even your in-laws!

I

MAKING THE MENTAL SHIFT FROM PAYROLL TO PROFIT

■

Can success change the human mechanism so completely between one dawn and another? Can it make one feel taller, more alive, handsomer, uncommonly gifted, and indomitably secure with the certainty that this is the way life will always be? It can and it does. MOSS HART

Have you ever noticed the transformation that takes place when someone becomes a champion? One day they're struggling to get to the top of their game. They clutch in the clinch. They *almost* make it. They're inconsistent—brilliant at moments and disappointing at others.

And then one day, after dogged determination and much effort, they do it. They get a perfect ten. They win the title. They break a record. They take the gold medal. And somehow, almost miraculously, at that point they *become* a champion. They step onto the field with a different gait. They project a new aura of confidence. They begin thinking and walking and talking like a champion. Something has shifted. And everybody knows it.

For me, Sarah, going out on my own was just like that. One day I was working for someone else, dreaming about being my own boss, about writing books and doing many things I'd always wanted to do. Then one day I couldn't wait anymore and I did it. I quit my job. I went out on my own. It was exciting and exhilarating—at first. I was like the rookie on opening day basking in the cheers of the crowd. Then came the next day and the next day and so on, and soon I realized what it meant to have stepped into the big league.

Suddenly I was called upon to *be* far more than I had ever been before. I was called upon to *do* far more than I had ever done before. There was so much I had not expected. So much I didn't know. I was playing with the pros. It was faster and harder than I had ever imagined. I loved it . . . but I felt small, inadequate, confused, and scared. Still, I was determined and committed: I wanted to make it. We both did. We'd gone out on our own at the same time, and we wanted to succeed.

That's when we became interested in studying champions. Not just the champions we see in sports, but people in all walks of life who are thriving on their own, doing work they've chosen to pursue. We wanted to think and walk and talk like those champions. We needed to know what enabled them to thrive while others seemed to struggle and flounder or even give up. We were determined to discover how these highly successful individuals have such seeming good fortune while others with similar tales, experience, and capability never make the shift.

It's tempting to think that the successful self-employed individuals are the lucky ones, the ones who had more money to begin with, the ones who knew more of the right people. Yet as we looked deeper into their stories, we found that those are rarely the real reasons some people thrive on their own, while others don't survive.

The business journals will tell you that the most common reasons for business failure are undercapitalization, poor business management, unfavorable economic conditions, and lack of business experience. But how can that be? Haven't you heard or read about people who went out on their own with no business experience whatsoever, some without even a high-school diploma, and were able to turn $65 into a six-figure income? We've not only heard about such individuals, we've met them. We've also met people with virtually unlimited funds and extensive business experience, Ph.D.'s and M.B.A.'s, whose ventures never got off the ground.

Of course, the opposite is true as well. We've talked with people who had limited funds and experience and fell flat on their faces, while others have thrived with ample funds and strong academic or business backgrounds. Furthermore, each of these varied outcomes has occurred under identical economic conditions.

So what makes the difference? The fact that we can't find an easy answer to why some people succeed while others don't is the very reason so many people fear going out on their own. It's this lack of clarity that keeps so many of us chained to a paycheck or questing after one. It's this lack of certainty that sometimes makes being on your own more of an ordeal than a dream come true.

After talking with tens of thousands of people who are successfully making it on their own, we've found that the reasons some people fail, or barely survive, while others thrive are usually not the ones we read about or even the ones people talk about when asked why they've met with success, disappointment, or failure. Basically, the reason people have a hard time making it on their own, or fear they will, is that most of us have had virtually no preparation for how to be our own boss. In fact, what we are taught about how to succeed in life is often diametrically opposed to what we need to do if we're going to succeed on our own.

From the moment we're born, we're busy learning how to do what we're told. We're fed on schedule—told when and what to eat. Before long the teacher takes over where our parents left off, and by the time we get out of grade school we're masters at taking orders and following rules—or at breaking them. We've learned how to get in line, be quiet, speak only when called upon, and raise our hands if we need to go to the bathroom. In the process, we've been prepared to become good workers. Or we've rebelled against this regimentation and learned to become terrible workers.

Once we graduate from school, our employers quickly step into the role once played by our parents and teachers. We're still expected to show up on schedule, eat on schedule, and work on schedule. We're still basically expected to stay in line and do what's asked of us.

These lessons over our lifetime have prepared us perfectly for what we call the *payroll mentality*: come to work on time, work hard, do a good job, do what the boss or the job description says, and in return you'll receive your paycheck on a regular basis. Today, of course, lots of people who have been following these rules are not getting their paycheck. Instead they're getting downsized, right sized, merged, and purged. And it's no wonder many of us feel angry, disillusioned, and determined to take charge of our lives by going out on our own.

The minute you leave the job to go out on your own, you're free from all the regimens that have shaped your life since childhood. You can do anything you want. No one will tell you when to get up, when to eat, when—or if—to take breaks, how long to work, where to work, or even whether to work. There aren't any rules. Or at least there's no one to oversee whether you follow any particular rules. And even more important, there's no paycheck! There's only the *prospect of profit*. Suddenly the whole world works differently. In fact, we've found a dozen fundamental mental shifts you need to make in how you think about yourself, your work, and your life if you want an income to materialize in place of the missing paycheck. Each of these mental shifts is diametrically opposed to the way we've been trained to think from the time we were born. Is it any wonder we're often uncertain how to proceed?

In this section, we'll outline these twelve mental shifts and demonstrate how, in reality, the reasons for success or failure on your own are not in your bank balance . . . or on your résumé. They're in the way you think about yourself, and your work. Undercapitalization, lack of experience, setbacks due to unfavorable economic conditions—these are all situations that almost *everyone* faces at one time or another on their own. The problems someone has in responding to these challenges are the visible *symptoms* of the *real* ailment: trying to produce a profit with a payroll mentality. Responding to these challenges successfully requires a new set of attitudes, a new set of beliefs and actions . . . that are quite distinct from how we used to respond to problems in school or on the job.

In fact, if you think and make decisions like an employee, being on your own becomes an *agonizing* experience. The characteristics that make for a good employee are often the exact opposite of those that make for successful self-employment. But, of course, the habits of bad employees won't work either. And to make matters worse, when someone goes out on their own, much of the standard advice they get about how to proceed isn't particularly helpful. Not even all the positive thinking in the world can get people through treacherous waters they're totally unprepared to navigate.

That's another reason people sometimes don't thrive on their own—much of the traditional information that's available about how to become your own boss doesn't really apply to today's new breed of independent workers. It doesn't address the needs of the majority of today's twenty-four-million-plus professionals, freelancers, home businesses, craftspeople, consultants, and contract workers whose numbers continue to grow every day. And much of what we need to know is never discussed at all!

Throughout this section, we'll talk candidly about many things that are rarely talked about. You'll find new tools and new ways of thinking that will enable you to make it on your own with a confidence and certainty that wasn't possible in the past. It's truly a whole new world—one in which your chances to enjoy the freedom and success of making it on your own have gone up dramatically.

You'll see how increasing numbers of people of all ages from all walks of life are literally making it on their own. They're carving out new understandings, new tools, and new attitudes that are making it possible for anyone who sincerely wants to follow in their footsteps to do so with a certainty and confidence that hasn't been possible until recently.

1

We're Not Taught to
Make It on Our Own

*There are so many places I wouldn't have gone, so many
people I wouldn't have seen and met, so many expeditions I
wouldn't have led, if I had only known in advance what I
was to experience.*

DOUCHAN GERSI, EXPLORER

MOST OF THE PEOPLE going out on their own today are, like us, a new
breed of entrepreneurs who are faced with making up their own rules and discovering their own new and different ways of earning a living.

When we began feeling the pressures of being a two-career family, we had
no intention of becoming entrepreneurs or starting a business. We simply
wanted a better way of life. And we were amazed at how dramatically the
quality of our lives improved once we were out on our own. Suddenly we had
time for each other, for our son, and even for regular exercise. Our stress level
went down immediately. Simultaneously, however, we realized that in our
search for a better life we had unwittingly become entrepreneurs . . . people
who, as the dictionary reminds us, have created a commercial endeavor that
requires considerable initiative and risk!

We knew, however, that we were not what you think of as classic entrepreneurs, turn-of-the-century capitalists like Henry Ford and John D. Rocke-
feller. We weren't even like today's high-profile entrepreneurs such as Steven
Jobs, Bill Gates, Donald Trump, and Harvey MacKay. We weren't captains of
industry seeking to build a financial empire. Although we were plenty ready
to take the initiative, we weren't that interested in taking risks. Nor did we
want to build an organization.

I, Paul, had already headed up an organization. And I, Sarah, been part of a very large one. We didn't want to duplicate those experiences. We wanted the financial comfort and security of a good job along with the independence and freedom of being our own boss doing work we found rewarding and living life more on our own terms.

Later, in interviewing people for *Working from Home,* we met thousands of others like ourselves who are self-employed but do not fit the classic entrepreneurial profile. Like us, these new entrepreneurs are highly motivated to be their own boss. They have good ideas and valuable skills and talents, and are willing to work hard. But they're not prepared to run a business, nor are they particularly interested in doing so.

Today's new entrepreneurs are professionals, artists, and service providers—from accountants to video producers, from computer consultants to public-relations specialists, from caterers to designers and writers, from plumbers to publishers, from word processors to inventors and toymakers. Most of us have wondered at times if we were suited to be on our own. We don't always do well on those self-scoring quizzes you see in popular books and magazines that tell you if you're suited to be an entrepreneur. Nonetheless we—and literally millions of others—are making it on our own. Personally, we've been self-employed for many years, and we're pleased to say you don't need to be an entrepreneur in the classic sense to survive and thrive on your own.

TODAY'S NEW INDEPENDENT WORKER: A NEW BREED OF ENTREPRENEUR

The classic entrepreneur loves the business of business. He or she probably had a lemonade stand and paper route as a child and by high school or college was running one or more sideline businesses to help pay expenses. For this classic entrepreneur, business is like a game; money is the scorecard. Making deals and living with the uncertainty and experimental nature of business are exciting. The classic entrepreneur moves eagerly from venture to venture, loving the business of doing business.

Chances are if you're reading this book you don't fit that profile. You're probably one of the emerging new breed of entrepreneurs who, like us, are setting out on their own in order to have greater control over their lives, to work on their own terms in their own way. Many of this new breed are women or men who wish to earn enough to have a good standard of living and still be at home to raise their children. Others are seeking a viable way to stay in or move to a desirable locale or to pursue their preferred career.

For the new breed of entrepreneurs being in business is more a means to an end than an end in itself. And for this reason we call them *propreneurs*—

individuals engaged in a business enterprise not for its own sake, or even for the profits per se, but for a purpose beyond the enterprise.

Propreneurs want to create a livelihood for themselves that enables them to do more meaningful work, enjoy life more while doing what they know how to do best, and do it the way they want to do it. They're more interested in doing the work of their business than in running a business. Here's some examples of what we mean.

Chellie Campbell is a classic entrepreneur. She took a job as a bookkeeper and, seeing the potential for bookkeeping services, proceeded within two years to buy out the owners of the business. She wasn't particularly interested in doing bookkeeping herself. In fact, she immediately hired other bookkeepers to do the bookkeeping so she could go out and get more business. Soon she had sales personnel to do that as well so she could spend her time overseeing the business. She plans to expand her company to several locations throughout her local metropolitan area and perhaps someday across the country.

Georgia Graves, on the other hand, is a propreneur. When her daughter was born, she didn't want to place her baby in day care and resume commuting each day to the downtown accounting firm where she worked as a bookkeeper. She loves doing bookkeeping, especially helping people manage their money. So she had no intention of giving up her career. In fact, with the new baby, she and her husband needed her income more than ever because they had just moved from their rented apartment into a new house. Georgia believed her chances for any substantial salary increase on her job were small. Opening a bookkeeping service of her own was a way for her to do what she loves without having to leave her young daughter, and still make more money than she did on salary. "I work when I want, as much as I want, and I love what I do," she says. "I have the best of both worlds."

When Georgia gets more business than she can handle herself, she farms it out to other freelancers in the area. As soon as possible she plans to hire an administrative assistant to help her manage the business side of her work. "The better known I become for doing a good job for my clients, the higher the fees I can command. And that's the way my business will grow."

Ron Andrews is a classic entrepreneur. He always wanted to run his own business, and after many years as a corporate executive he decided to search the marketplace to identify a good business opportunity. Based on his research, he decided to buy a dry-cleaning company. By hiring the right people, he got his first location running well and decided to open a restaurant. We asked him why he chose dry cleaning and he said, "Why not? The cash flow's great and it's all a game. It doesn't matter to me what the business is as long as it's legal and profitable."

For the propreneur, however, the nature of the business is often the main motivation. For example, Ed Crystal is also a propreneur. After thirty years of doing other work, he decided to do what he'd always wanted to do—pursue a career as an artist. He was able to do this after all those years because he and his wife opened a picture-framing business. The flexibility and profits of running this business have provided him with the opportunity and the economic security to begin painting and to open a gallery of his own.

Donald Marrs is a propreneur. Donald was working as the creative director at one of the country's largest advertising agencies when he realized he was writing ads for cigarettes, junk food, gas-guzzling cars, and other products he not only didn't use but didn't believe in. After considerable soul-searching, he left the agency and opened his own company, where he works with clients whose products he believes are making a positive contribution to life. He's written about his decision in his book *Executive in Passage*.

Callan Pinckney is also a propreneur. She began teaching classes to show people how to exercise safely, spurred on by her anger at the many exercise programs on the market that she believes can actually hurt people. From this passion have come three best-selling books and three megahit videotapes on her exercise methods.

Kathryn Dager is another propreneur. A manager for a large retail chain, she became disheartened by what she saw as a declining level of customer service. She was encountering an entire generation of young people who, having grown up in a self-serve society, had never actually experienced service. So she opened a customer-service training firm, which helps retail stores to recruit and train service-oriented personnel. Her company, Profitivity, has grown by leaps and bounds, and she offers her programs nationwide.

Like Ed, Donald, Callan, and Kathryn, many of today's new propreneurs would continue doing the type of work they do even if they won the lottery. Sometimes they can't imagine ever retiring from their work. They may foresee the themes of their work changing, but the work they do is for life. It's almost like a mission or a calling.

In other cases propreneurs see business as a means to truly excel in the career they love. Mike Greer, an instructional designer, was frustrated by the bureaucratic inefficiencies of the educational-design companies he worked for. He felt like he was getting in only five good hours of work a day; the rest of the day was spent hassling with office politics. He also knew his employers were billing his time out at nine times his hourly rate. He was confident he could do a better job on his own and charge substantially less. And he was right. After creating I.D. Network he tripled his income, although he was charging his clients substantially less. He was still working only five hours a day, but the rest of the day was his own.

Chris Shalby, a marketing consultant who created Bottom Line Communications, puts it this way: "If you work for a corporation, your idea may never get heard, or will be so watered down by the time you get approval to do it that it's not your idea anymore. My employer's attitudes were that if their PR personnel were really that good, why would they be here?" So now he's not. "In your own business," he says, "you can actually see your ideas come to life."

As you can see from these examples, the classic entrepreneur—the one for whom most business courses and books are written—wants to work on the business; the propreneur wants to work in the business. Which are you? Take this simple quiz and find out.

Are You an Entrepreneur or a Propreneur?

Which of the following statements best describes you?

1. A. I always wanted to run my own business.
   B. I never actually wanted to run a business, but I want to be my own boss.

2. A. I set up lots of little businesses to earn money when I was young.
   B. As a young person, I had an allowance and took various jobs.

3. In going out on my own:
   A. Any business venture would be just as good as another so long as it was legal and profitable.
   B. I would only pursue an independent career that involves something I like doing and find meaningful.

4. In describing my career would say, primarily:
   A. I'm a businessperson.
   B. I'm someone who does the type of work I do (for example, an artist, accountant, programmer, word processor, doctor, consultant, editor, etc.).

5. If I could hire someone to work for me, the first person I would hire is:
   A. Someone who would help provide the product or service, so I could spend more time developing and running this business.
   B. Someone who would help run the business side of my work, so I could spend more time providing my product or service.

The more A's you chose, the more like a classic entrepreneur you are. If you chose more B's, you're more like a propreneur.

One of the simplest tests of whether you're an entrepreneur or a propreneur at heart comes at the time when your business grows to the point where you have to decide whether to expand or consolidate. For example, as

Howard Shenson grew increasingly successful with his seminars and books on how to become a consultant, he moved his office away from home and began adding employees. A true entrepreneur would be riding high on such growth. Each expansion would be more invigorating. But for Howard, the larger he grew, the less rewarding his work became. "I was spending more time managing and less time creating. And that wasn't enjoyable to me," he told us. So, he decided to pull back on the growth of his business and returned to being essentially a sole practitioner. He continues to prosper, and he's much happier.

Propreneurs often respond to growth in this way. They like success, but they don't want hassles and complications. They don't like the pressures of management and weighty payroll responsibilities. They like making money, but they also want to enjoy their work and the freedom being on their own offers.

Patricia Lineman felt that way. Eight years ago she lost her job when the company she was working for closed down. Having worked her way to the top in that company, she didn't think another company would give her the same authority, money, and responsibility she had grown accustomed to, so she decided she would have a better chance on her own. She found a need and filled it. She founded Patricia Lineman and Associates and began consulting with apparel-manufacturing firms on negotiating collections. Within the first month she had five clients, and her business grew rapidly from there.

Soon she had grown from running a one-person home business to managing a ten-employee office. Although she says she had to try growing a big company, now she's back to working by herself from home. She preferred working personally with her clients to managing an organization. "This is where I make the most money and this is where I'm happiest," she told us. "I also serve my clients better. I can say that unequivocally, and they feel that way, too. I serve fewer, but I serve them better."

Howard and Patricia are proof that you can succeed gloriously on your own without becoming a slave to your business. If you're like most propreneurs, chances are you went into business so you could take charge of your life and you want to keep it that way. Fortunately you can. You don't have to choose between being on your own and having a life of your own. But you will need to take a different approach to earning a living than you would as either an employee or a traditional business.

BEING SELF-EMPLOYED REQUIRES A DIFFERENT APPROACH

Since a propreneur is more interested in and better prepared for working *in* the business, certain aspects of the work that the classic entrepreneur finds exciting and enjoyable can be uncomfortable and even intimidating for today's propreneur. Notable among these are selling, negotiating a deal, projecting profits and losses, managing cash flow, financial planning, and marketing. Yet without these functions there is no work.

Here's a case in point. A man came to us for a consultation with this dilemma. An excellent management trainer, he had become frustrated with having to spend 50 to 60 percent of his time on the job dealing with administrative trivia and office politics. He wanted to spend his time training and making a positive difference in people's lives. After much inner conflict, he decided to leave his job to establish a training and consulting firm of his own.

One year later, however, he was despondent. He was having to spend 50 to 60 percent of every week finding, negotiating, and administrating opportunities to do a day or two of training here and there. He never had enough business and was on the verge of giving up the idea of being on his own and taking another job.

To make matters worse, the business books and courses he turned to for help focused on how he could master the intricacies and complexities of marketing, negotiating, and other business strategies so he could grow into an even larger, more profitable business. For him, however, learning and implementing these strategies just meant more time away from doing what he wanted to do—management training.

What he needed, like most propreneurs, was not more business textbooks but practical ways to streamline the business side of self-employment so he could profitably pursue his work which he does so well and enjoy the independent life he desires.

In short, making it on your own today involves leaving behind both the payroll mentality and the classic approach to doing business. If you're a classic entrepreneur, you'll probably have an easy time adjusting to the freedom and flexibility of being on your own. You've probably been operating outside the paycheck mentality all along. For you, though, the challenge of becoming successfully self-employed will lie in mastering the self-discipline that's required to pursue your goals and satisfy your customers.

If you're one of today's new propreneurs, you're probably already a disciplined and focused worker. Your challenge may well lie in becoming comfortable with the ambiguity and flexibility of having so many options and leaving behind the security and certainty of a regular paycheck. For you, succeeding on your own will mean learning as much as possible about running your independent career as a business . . . but doing so in a way that leaves you free to do what you enjoy, do best, and want most from life. And whether you're an entrepreneur or a propreneur, that's what this book is designed to help you do.

2

Making the
Mental Shift to
Independence

It often happens that I wake up at night and begin to think about a serious problem and decide I must tell the Pope about it. Then I wake up completely and remember that I am the Pope. POPE JOHN XXIII

HAVE YOU EVER NOTICED how eagerly we seek the thrill of the new and the novel while tenaciously clinging to the familiar. We seek freedom. We want to be in charge. Like a small child who begs to take the wheel of the family car, we yearn to be in the driver's seat. And the moment we go out on our own, we've done it. We're behind the wheel. But are we in command, or will we career wildly into oblivion?

That's the fear most people have when they say good-bye to the security of a paycheck. Often we feel little more prepared to assume full responsibility for our destinies than a small child would feel taking the wheel of a moving car. All the thousands of self-employed individuals we've talked with found being on their own to be filled with surprises—some big, some little; some delightful, others dreadful. Confronted with such unfamiliar circumstances, most people try to turn the novel into the known; so it's only natural for us to want to operate from the paycheck mentality, which has been familiar to us for so long.

Once we have the chance to be on our own, we may try very hard to run our lives in much the same way we did when we were on the job. But that's like trying to drive a car from the passenger's seat. From over there it looks easy. It's hard to imagine all the complications that can arise once you actually take the steering wheel of a moving car in your hands.

I know I, Sarah, certainly experienced this. When I went out on my own I was at once confident and uncertain. I boldly declared what I was going to do. I read everything I could, talked to everyone I knew, took several courses. I was sure of myself—until things didn't go according to plan. I'd been told to develop a business plan. This plan was my security. It showed me exactly how many clients I would need each week and told me exactly how much I needed to charge per hour. I established my business name, obtained my business license, set up my bank account, printed my cards and letterhead, and even prepared my first brochure. I had been told how to announce the opening of my practice, and I followed the guidance I'd received and my plan to the letter.

Then I waited for the phone to ring. It didn't. The only business call I got those first two weeks was a wrong number. That was when I realized there was more to this than anyone had mentioned. The next few years were not pleasant ones. The shift from having a position of influence where I wielded the power and authority of the federal government to being a sole practitioner on my own was a jolt. I went from feeling powerful to feeling powerless. The logical and dependable world I knew had given way. I was no longer being controlled, but I was not yet in control.

Not everyone faces such a crisis of expectations so immediately. But once we leave the familiar world of having a job, at some point we are usually confronted with having to make an adjustment in how we approach earning a living. For Charles Cannon the crisis came after what looked like a great start. Charles's medical-billing business took off quickly. He was a stunning success within a year. He, too, did everything he was told. He, too, thought he had done it right. Then his major client suddenly decided to go elsewhere. He came close to bankruptcy.

William Sayer's computer-consulting business took off right away, too. He had two major clients lined up even before he left his job. He, too, thought he'd done it right—so much so that he took out a handsome profit at the end of his first year and went on a long-earned vacation. When he returned, however, he discovered that in having completed his major projects, he was out of work. It took him over three months to secure his next project.

These setbacks were unnecessarily devastating for the three of us and probably occurred in the first place only because we were each still viewing the world from a paycheck mentality. We expected life to work the way it had when we were employed. We thought if we followed directions carefully, we would succeed. But sooner or later, operating from a paycheck mentality can make being self-employed a confusing, frightening, and pressure-filled experience. And business decisions based on fear and doubt made under the pressure of imminent failure only make matters worse.

Fortunately, once you realize you have to approach living on your own in a fundamentally different way, the challenges will push you, as they did each of us, to adopt a new profit perspective. And from this perspective, what has been confusing will become clear, what has been dreaded will be welcomed, and what seemed impossible will become manageable.

By making the following twelve mental shifts, you'll avoid many of the more painful adjustments to being on your own. Instead, you can begin today

Twelve Mental Shifts for Moving from Paycheck to Profit Thinking

1. From Pipe Dreams to Practicalities: Adopting a New Concept of What's Possible

2. From Certainties to Possibilities: Establishing a New Definition for Security

3. From Outer Support to Inner Trust: Finding a New Sense of Direction

4. From Conforming and Waiting to Creating and Initiating: Reaching a New Understanding about How Things Happen

5. From Rules to Results: Discovering a New Way to Know How Well You're Doing

6. From Mastery to Marketing: Using a New Approach to Making an Impression

7. From Rights to Responsibility: Taking a New Attitude for How to Get What You Deserve

8. From Job Title to Charisma : Developing a New Source of Power

9. From Covering to Capitalizing: Assigning a New Role to Mistakes

10. From Playing It Safe to Keeping Options Open: Setting a New Standard for When to Say Yes

11. From Earning to Spend to Spending to Earn: Making a New Relationship with Money

12. From "Help Me" to "How Can I Help?": Creating a New Basis for Building Alliances

to ease your transition from payroll to profit. And once you make these mental shifts and leave behind the paycheck mentality, you'll emerge like a champion, with a new ability to take whatever comes along in stride, turn challenges to your advantage, and make what seemed difficult look easy. You will no longer be an employee trying to be on your own. You will have made the mental shift you see reflected in the champion's face, gait, and demeanor. You will have shifted permanently from a *paycheck* to a *profit* mentality, and you will be empowered.

Traits Propreneurs Share Throughout Time

Dr. Barrie Yeager's review of the literature on self-employment shows that successfully self-employed individuals share common traits throughout history. These traits are usually passed down through the deeds, beliefs, and teachings of their families or other significant adults they grew up with. But they can be acquired as well. Here's our synopsis of those traits and how you can develop them if you haven't inherited them yourself:

1. **Being independent is part of the kind of person you think you are,** should be, or would like to be. If that doesn't describe you, experiment with thinking of yourself as someone who's self-employed. If you like how it feels, keep imagining it and sooner or later you may no longer feel satisfied with yourself until you've become the person you're aspiring to be.

2. **The work you do or want to do is rewarding, satisfying, and enjoyable** in and of itself. If it isn't, you can begin searching for work that would meet these criteria. When you find it, you'll know because you'll want to stay up late, get up early, and sneak away to fit it into your day. You'll start feeling impatient and restless until you can begin doing it.

3. **The thought of being autonomous is appealing,** even if somewhat frightening or challenging. If not, start making and following through on small autonomous decisions, like "Today, I'm going to make a purchase without consulting anyone" or "Tonight I'm going out to a movie alone." See how you feel about taking autonomous action. You may grow to like it.

4. **Work is a way to serve others and thus is enjoyable.** If you've never thought of work that way, watch how work can benefit others and imagine enjoying the positive effect of your work. See how that makes you feel.

5. **Being on your own leads to goals you're highly motivated to achieve.** We all have different priorities and goals during different periods of our

MENTAL SHIFT #1. FROM PIPE DREAMS TO PRACTICALITIES: ADOPTING A NEW CONCEPT OF WHAT'S POSSIBLE

> *We were wild with joy because tomorrow we would leave the*
> *known world behind. What a wonderful feeling. To be able*
> *to decide your own life and destiny, obeying without limita-*
> *tions your own mysterious calls, and dreams and passions.*
>
> DOUCHAN GERSI, EXPLORER

Most of us have grown up in an era when aspiring to go out on your own wasn't considered to be economically viable. But that hasn't always been so.

lives. When being on your own meets key personal goals, you'll find doing it much easier than when your goals lie elsewhere.

6. **Each person has their own standards of what it means to be responsible and to do a good job.** Start defining what you would expect of yourself. How do you know if you've done a good job? You can begin exploring what clients and customers expect in your field and, when the time comes that you won't tolerate less than that from yourself, you'll find working on your own easier.

7. **Working hard is enjoyable.** This doesn't mean you have to like doing difficult, unpleasant things you don't want to do. It means putting concentrated time, energy, and effort into doing sometimes challenging and difficult things that are compatible with goals you have freely chosen. To test out how much you enjoy working hard, think of things you like to do (golf, chess, gardening, tennis) and evaluate whether you enjoy the challenge they present. If you don't, it may be that you haven't yet found things that challenge and engage you enough to enjoy working hard for.

8. **What's started should be completed.** If once you've set a desired goal and started toward it you don't feel compelled to finish it, start experimenting with pushing through to the finish. You may find you enjoy the sense of satisfaction that comes from following through enough to want to make it a habit.

9. **If you're going to do something, you might as well do it right.** If you have a tendency to do the minimum necessary, but would like to be your own boss, experiment with going the whole nine yards. Try giving 100 percent to some small task you enjoy. Give it your all; don't hold back anything. See how that feels. You may find that the pride you feel in a job well done will push you to want to make doing your best a regular habit.

In fact, self-employment has a long and rich history in this country. It has been an integral component of the American Dream. Researcher Dr. Barrie Jaeger, author of *The Meaning of Work for the Self-Employed,* reports that as early as the sixteenth century, most industries in this country arose from self-made individuals whom Benjamin Franklin called "parvenue." These parvenues were not captains of industry. They sound, instead, very much like today's propreneurs, right down to preferring the work they did to operating a business and building support networks of stable clientele so they could stay small, one-person operations. They shared the same traits as successfully self-employed individuals have throughout history. (See pp. 16–17)

But while such self-reliance and independence have been part of our nature throughout the history of our country, the opportunities for succeeding on your own have not. In 1870, self-employment hit a high. Eighty percent of the American workforce was self-employed. But with the full flowering of the Industrial Revolution that figure dwindled to a low of 6.7% by 1970 and '71. So until recent years, financial realities forced most people to forgo any ideas of owning their own business. The practical concerns of supporting oneself and one's families dictated that most people work for someone else, doing something more "realistic" than striving to be their own boss. Only a few very talented, determined, and well-placed individuals could make it on their own.

But times have changed again. Now the practical concerns of supporting ourselves and our families are shifting. Economic, technological, and cultural forces are converging not only to support and encourage you to take your economic future into your own hands but, in some cases, to demand that you rise to the challenge and assert your independence by creating your own job and becoming your own boss. In fact, today even those who are looking for a job are being taught to think, and act, like their own boss. So in deciding to venture out on your own, you are no longer going against the tide. You are riding an entrepreneurial wave of rising proportions. So, the first mental shift you need to make to succeed on your own is to adopt an entirely new concept of what's practical.

The Force Is with You

To borrow a famous line from the classic movie *Star Wars,* the force is with you now as you set out on your own. What we're doing today will be even more commonplace in the future: the day will come when as many as half of all individuals will be self-employed. So although you are on your own, you are not alone in your endeavors. You are taking part in epochal changes that are altering forever the way we live and work. You are in the right place at the right time, and you're better positioned to succeed as your own boss today than at any other time in history.

Self-employment began to rise in the 1970s and has taken a sharp turn upward since 1987. Today a new business begins every twenty-three seconds. Almost 3,800 new home-based businesses start every day. At that rate, a new home business began somewhere in America just since you started reading this chapter!

According to research firms like Find/SVP and Link Resources, fourteen million people are making it on their own from home. And these numbers are growing at a rate of over 7 percent a year. Even the number of people successfully earning a living on their own in the arts is growing. The futurist John Naisbitt has identified independent artists—actors, directors, authors, dancers, choreographers, designers, musicians, composers, painters, photographers, and so on—as one of the nation's megatrends.

As technology continues to be more affordable, more powerful, and yet smaller, the Electronic Industries Association tells us that 54 percent of U.S. households already have a home office, a fact that opens the door for more and more of us to start earning a living on our own if we wish. And while the number of people going out on their own is going up, so is their success rate. While 50 percent of small businesses as a whole are still in operation now after five years, analysis of data from several sources shows that 75 percent of home businesses are still in business five years after opening their offices.

Such a low failure rate is not as surprising as it might seem. Other research shows that our perceptions of there being such a high failure rate among the self-employed are based not upon the numbers of people who actually get started in a business of their own but on the large numbers of others who take several steps toward independence but never really get under way. As major changes in our society line up to support those who want to venture out on their own and as more people learn how to do it successfully, increasing numbers of ventures will survive and thrive. In fact, we think it's time as far as self-employment is concerned to stop referring to the high business failure rate and refer instead to the business success rate.

You Have Profit Potential

In the industrial age, money was the most important resource needed to succeed in a business of your own. Large amounts of money were required to set up and operate large facilities and meet large payrolls. A business might have to operate for years before the owner made a return on the investment needed just to open the doors that first day.

In this information age, however, you are your most important resource and your time, your skills, your knowledge have profit potential. You can become your boss with little or no added costs. By working from your home you can keep your costs down to little more than your basic living expenses. Like so many self-employed individuals we meet, with the right know-how you can turn a profit quickly and more easily than your larger competition. And because you are working alone on your own, or with a small number of employees, you have the flexibility to respond quickly to fluctuations in your market and redirect your efforts in more profitable directions when needed.

As an employee, every hour you work, you're earning money for someone else. You are an expense. Obviously every employer wants to keep expenses down. That means keeping your salary down. The day you went out on your own, however, you instantly became an asset—the principal asset of your business. As long as you keep your costs down, everything else you earn is yours to keep and there is no arbitrary ceiling. The sky is the limit. You are limited only by your own time, energy, creativity, know-how, and willingness to do what it takes. Properly positioned, you can actually make more than you would ever be able to as an employee doing the same work.

Eleanor Duggan is a good example of what's possible. She was making $32,000 working for a market-research firm. When she asked for a raise, the president told her she was making enough money for a woman her age. At the suggestion of her accountant, she decided to go out on her own. From her very first year, she was working to full capacity. Seven years later she was making $700,000 a year.

Even two generations ago, success was highly dependent upon such factors as where you went to school and who your parents were. Most of what you knew was learned either at home or in school. Whatever you got there usually set the course for what you could achieve over the remainder of your life. Today, however, virtually anything you need to know in order to do virtually anything you want to undertake is available to you through an ever-growing wealth of books, tapes, workshops, seminars, public-education programs, consultants, and training programs. And all this information is available anytime you need it.

So becoming your own boss is no longer a pipe dream. The tide has turned. Instead of pushing against you, it is carrying you forward. In today's economy making it on your own is a practical and possible choice, and sometimes a necessity.

MENTAL SHIFT #2. FROM CERTAINTIES TO POSSIBILITIES: ESTABLISHING A NEW DEFINITION FOR SECURITY

The best way to predict the future is to invent it.
ALAN KAY, SCIENTIST

As an employee you *receive* a paycheck. As long as you show up and do what you're told, your paycheck arrives automatically. It's a certainty you come to rely upon. But when you're on your own your profit is *created*, not received. On your own, nothing arrives except the bills. You have to create any money you receive. You don't even get a chance to work unless you generate the opportunity to do so. But as we said, the possibilities for what you can generate are unlimited.

This shift from the certainty of a paycheck to the ambiguity of the opportunities is probably the most difficult mental shift people have to make when venturing out on their own. It stops more people from following their dreams and sends more people back to a job than any other aspect of being on your own.

As S. H. Dewhurst has said, "One of the toughest lessons in life is learning to expect the unexpected." And after all, receiving a paycheck has been a culturally ingrained symbol of security. The nation still trembles as our major corporations continue to announce significant layoffs. A shiver still goes down the spine of an entire community when a major employer relocates.

Perhaps, other than the fear of death, there is no greater fear than unexpectedly losing one's paycheck. Yet today it has become commonplace, and to reclaim the sense of security you once felt in a job and to enjoy being your own boss, you must cast off this deep-seated fear and replace it with anticipation of the many possibilities of self-generated gain. Making the following shift in perspective can help you do this.

Security Is an Illusion

Increasing numbers of people who have been merged, purged, laid off, and otherwise downsized realize that a paycheck no longer provides security. When translator Jim Waldron started out on his own, for example, he realized that when you're employed, your fate is in the hands of one person— your supervisor. He told us, "A decision by one person can put you on the street. But in your own business, every one of your customers has to fire you before you're out of income." This one shift in the way he thought about his work gave him the sense of security he needed to make friends with the ambiguity of being on his own.

Karen Rubin had held more than 120 jobs during her thirty-five years, but she had never been fired for poor performance. She decided that working for herself couldn't possibly be any less secure than her own job history. So, she created Organizers Extraordinaire and helps her clients organize their lives and offices. She has been in business almost ten years now and is making over $40,000 a year.

As Jim, Karen, and thousands of others are finding, perhaps the sense of security we feel with a paycheck has become more illusion than reality, more historical than actual.

Ambiguity Is Our Only Hope

On the other hand, consider this. Ambiguity—the sense of not knowing what lies ahead—is actually the only context in which we can create a future different from our past. When everything is certain, there can be only what has been. But ambiguity by definition means that anything is possible.

A beleaguered but undaunted actor once wrote a telling dramatic scene that captures the sense of hope and anticipation she and many others feel in deciding to choose the ambiguity of making it on their own. In this scene, a young actor is living in near-poverty, waiting on tables and going out for auditions every day, trying to break into show business. Her brother drops by to invite her to a family gathering. The brother, who drives up in a Mercedes and is dressed in expensive clothes, begins chiding the actor for living such a meager existence. "Why don't you stop all this and come work for me at the used-car lot?" he asks. "How can you live like this?" The actress replies, "Look, things may not be so great for me right now, but I know that any day can be my big break and all this will change."

Few people who work at a job can say that. On your own, if you keep working toward your goals, you always have the possibility of creating a new future, one that is more satisfying and rewarding than the present.

The Ultimate Security

There's nothing more rewarding or more empowering than knowing that you can support yourself by creating something valuable from nothing. Former Miss America Debra Sue Maffit captured the sense of power that making it on your own can provide when she told us, "If I lost everything today I wouldn't be afraid, because, having [been successful] once, I know I could do it again."

But when you look at the calendar and don't see any appointments for the next month, or you see the balance of your checkbook dropping and there are no checks in the mail, or you notice that the phone hasn't rung all day—that's when the ambiguity of being on your own can be disconcerting. But this is true only if you're looking at these events from a paycheck mentality that says you have to know in advance exactly how much is coming in on what day. To work confidently with the ambiguity of no paycheck you have to change your money clock. Here's what we mean by that:

Changing Your Money Clock

When Robbie Bogue lost his job to downsizing, like most of us, he'd been working at a job for some time. Over the years both he and his family had become used to orienting their purchasing decisions to the first and the fifteenth of each month when his paycheck arrived. "We might be eating weenies and beans on the fourteenth," Bogue remembered, "but we knew we'd always have groceries tomorrow." Then, he started his own marketing consulting firm. Suddenly he was self-employed. "Out of habit we all were still operating on the first and the fifteenth of the month clock," he told us. The kids still expected their allowance. He and his wife were still expecting to pay their bills and make needed expenditures on the same schedule they were so familiar with. But, when Bogue was working on his own, the money wasn't necessarily in the bank on the first and the fifteenth.

Did that mean his business was a failure? "No," he decided. "It meant we had to find a new way to keep score." He and his family had to change their money clock. Instead of measuring success based on how much money they had in the bank on the first and the fifteenth, they had to start viewing success in terms of how much marketing activity Robbie was initiating every day and every week.

Bogue found that the marketing activities he undertook . . . like sending out mailings, giving away samples, attending networking meetings, and making follow-up calls . . . were directly related to how much income would be coming in three months hence. "I discovered I can predict within $500 what my cash flow will be in the next 120 days by adding my monthly postage bill to my monthly phone bill and multiplying by 30.2."

So, Bogue advises, "Get your family involved, including your kids, especially if they're teenagers. Tell them about this shift in the money clock. Then just as when parents ask their children around the supper table, 'How was school today?' your family can ask you, 'How was your marketing today?' And if you've gotten behind, he suggests, sometimes they can all get involved and help out . . . stuffing envelopes for mailings, making copies, assembling samples, etc., Robbie says, "This way everyone realizes the money will still be there on a schedule, but just a different one—one based on what you do!"

Trust Is a Decision; You Can Put It Where You Want To

So as you can see, the decision to trust yourself and your ability to support yourself is exactly that, a decision. As the weeks and months go by, if you refuse to be immobilized by fear and doubt and continue doing everything you know how to do to succeed, despite your fears and doubts, you will discover *the ultimate security*—the knowledge that you can and will make it on your own.

And that's the second mental shift you need to make to succeed on your own. You need to adopt a new definition of security, one that's based on knowing that your security lies in continuing your own quality effort. And once you make that shift, you'll find that ambiguity becomes a comfortable and loyal companion, reassuring you each and every day that anything can happen.

MENTAL SHIFT #3. FROM OUTER SUPPORT TO INNER TRUST: FINDING A NEW SENSE OF DIRECTION

Destiny is not a matter of chance, it is a matter of choice; it is not a thing to be waited for, it is a thing to be achieved.
WILLIAM JENNINGS BRYAN

Being able to relax into the ambiguity of not knowing exactly when, or how, or if you will have a profit from your efforts requires finding a new locus for your trust. To the extent that we've learned to trust that a paycheck will arrive, we've learned to look outward for our direction and sense of security. We've come to put our trust in the system, in the powers that be. And, of course, the reverse is true as well. We put the blame on external factors when things go wrong. We find fault in others and expect them to make it right!

Looking outward for our source of direction and support goes back to trusting our parents to protect us—or at least believing that they should protect us. In the past, we transferred this expectation to our employers, believing that they should provide for and guide us, that we're entitled to a job and a paycheck or some other source of income. In fact, many people still feel angry that they can no longer count on an employer to provide them with the security of a good-paying job.

But making it on your own means leaving that mindset behind forever. Ultimately the power to determine the future of our lives always rests with us. As George Bernard Shaw observed, while people are always blaming circumstance for their lives, "the people who get on in this world are the people who get up and look for the circumstances they want, and, if they can't find them, make them." Nowhere is this more true than when you're working for yourself.

When you're on your own, no one owes you anything, no matter how nice you are or how good you are at what you do. No one is there to rescue you. Whereas a boss might take pity on you, customers won't. People don't buy products or services from a sense of pity or guilt, or even fairness. They buy based on competence and the results they receive. No one is looking to give you a break. Your raise becomes effective when you do.

There's No One to Blame

In other words, you need to adopt a new sense of direction, one in which the source of power in your life shifts from external factors to an internal one. Here's how one woman told us she ultimately made this shift: "I didn't go out on my own by choice. I got laid off and couldn't find a job, so I thought, Why not start my own business? But whenever business was slow, I got scared. I wanted to blame someone for it. I wanted to blame the economy, I wanted to blame my competition. I even tried to blame my customers. I felt like they weren't appreciative enough of all the work I was doing or they would send me more business. I felt so angry at them that I finally recognized how ridiculous I was being. Of course it wasn't their job to keep me in business. It was my job to make my business work. From that point on, when I got scared I stopped fretting. Instead, I'd roll up my sleeves and start working to get more business. After a while I could see that my own efforts paid off and I knew I was truly the source of my own security."

So succeeding on your own means learning to trust yourself to be able to respond effectively to real needs of others in order to achieve your goals. It's learning to know what you want and trust that you will come through for them and for yourself. Once your sense of security no longer lies with forces outside yourself over which you have little or no control but shifts to within yourself, many other things will shift inward as well. You will no longer feel dependent on outside sources for approval to feel good about yourself. You will no longer feel compelled to struggle for control over everyone and everything around you. Instead, you feel confident that you can utilize your experiences in your life to create what you need. You become less afraid of what life will bring and more excited about what you can make from it.

But you may say, "How do I know I can count on myself? How do I know I'll come through?" And the answer is, You don't. You'll have to learn to tune in to your own desires, your interests, and your preferences so you can literally manage yourself. We call this developing your self-management muscle. That's the one that's located somewhere between your brain and your bottom. But like building any other muscle, your self-management muscle takes time to develop. You have to give yourself time to learn how to manage yourself, and you have to believe that ultimately you and yourself will make a great team.

Trust Comes from Experience

Often parents think children are either trustworthy or they're not. But that's not the case. Those who become trustworthy are those who are already trusted and called upon to live up to the trust others put in them. If you believe in yourself long enough and lovingly enough, you will become someone you know you can count on.

Succeeding on your own is somewhat like planting a garden. A farmer can dream of a great garden, but it will remain a dream until he or she gets out there and starts the backbreaking work of planting and tilling the soil. And despite all these efforts, for a long time there's no evidence that all the work is paying off. The ground looks as barren as ever. Then one day, green shoots break through the soil. But even then, the farmer cannot lean back and count the money. The tender shoots must be nurtured to maturity. Only later in the season does he or she get to harvest the crop.

So it is with your own ventures. You can't become impatient with either the farmer or the crop. You've got to give yourself and your crop a chance to grow. You've got to stay at it every day. And, as the freelance photographer Charles Berhman found, having to count on yourself can actually be freeing. Charles worked full-time as an engineer for fifteen years while he built his business on the side as a photographer. He told us, "Your paycheck is tied to what someone else wants you to do. Your success is being rated by someone who doesn't even know what you can do. On my own, I have the satisfaction of knowing that any progress I make in the business is because of what I do."

Developing the Self-Management Muscle

On the job you get sick leave, vacation time, coffee breaks, quarterly performance evaluations, periodic pep talks and a social support system from fellow workers. And, of course, the boss is always there to keep you on your toes . . . be it with a word of advice, a pat on the shoulder, a look, or that tone of voice that sets you straight. Although these incentives don't always do the job, they are designed to keep workers on their toes and raring to go. And the better management is, the better the morale.

On your own, you don't get any of these perks . . . unless you give them to yourself. So that is what you need to do. You need to know what will motivate you and keep you on track. You literally have to become your own boss. You have to become your own daily cheerleader, colleague, disciplinarian, mentor, coach, best friend, and trainer—so that you work at your best and produce good results for yourself. You'll have to charge yourself up and keep yourself motivated. You have to reward yourself, reprimand yourself, and promote yourself regularly.

And while this is an unfamiliar role for most of us at first, you are nonetheless in the ideal position to keep your morale and your energy at their peak, because you get to create your own working conditions. When you work, where you work, and how you work can all be exactly the way you need them to be to perform at your very best.

So, how satisfied are you with the working conditions you've set up for yourself? Do you like the boss you've become? Are you pleased with the perks you're providing yourself? Do you give yourself enough time off? Do you let yourself get away with too much? Have you set up enough contact with others? These are the kinds of questions that will assist you in developing your self-management muscle.

Take a moment to list the qualities of the kind of boss you'd like to work for and make note of the type of working conditions such a boss would pro-

Twelve Ways to Keep Yourself Charged Up

1. Surround yourself with positive, successful colleagues, clients, and friends. Their attitudes and energy will rub off on you.

2. Join or create a weekly networking group with whom you can support and share successes.

3. Join or create weekly electronic coffee breaks with friends and colleagues on the telephone or on-line.

4. Give yourself a break . . . in fact, several breaks. Research shows that a short break every forty-five minutes increases productivity.

5. Take a vacation . . . or several minivacations . . . once a year, even if you don't feel like it, especially if you don't feel like it. Set aside funds to cover the costs of these breaks.

6. Give yourself an office with a window, or as close to it as you can get. Set up a nourishing home/office environment with good light, positive colors, relaxing and upbeat background music, comfortable and functional furniture, and appealing artwork or scenic views from your windows.

7. Set goals, and be clear about what you expect of yourself. Expect the best.

8. Compliment yourself liberally whenever you do things, even little things, that make you the kind of person you want to be.

9. Do regular performance reviews. Does your performance match your goals?

10. Notice immediately when you don't live up to your expectations, but don't berate yourself or dwell on it. Simply remind yourself of what you expect and affirm that you know you can and will improve.

11. Greet your negative feelings as valuable messengers that bring you clues as to the actions you need to take. If you're overwhelmed, recognize that you need to get help or take on smaller tasks one step at a time. If you're anxious, identify what you need to do to reassure yourself.

12. Follow the advice of the psychologist Shad Helmstetter: to get in a good mood fast—smile. Or as Famous Wally Amos says, "Find the humor in every day. If you're getting ready for bed and you haven't laughed yet, just start laughing." Because as Norman Cousins pointed out to us, "I have never seen anyone in a good state of belly laughter who was also panicky."

vide to assist workers to function optimally. Then list the qualities of the kind of boss you'd most dread working for and the working environment that kind of boss would provide. How do you stack up? Give yourself a report card as your own boss. And do so periodically.

For more information on developing your self-management muscle so you can make sure you'll be able to count on yourself to do what you most want to do, see part 3, Becoming the Boss You've Always Wanted to Have.

Mental Shift #4. From Conforming and Waiting to Creating and Initiating: Reaching a New Understanding about How Things Happen

What is really important is not so much what work a person does, but what he perceives he is doing it for.
WILLLIS HARMAN, FUTURIST

Being on your own is the ultimate act of creativity. As bookkeeper Chellie Campbell says, "I was an actress, a singer, and a dancer before I started my business, and I've never had to be so creative in my life as in running my business. It has called upon every ounce of creativity I possess. Every day I know I can create the day the way I want it. I am totally the master of my own fate. I can look at the success I've created and say, 'I did that!'"

Many self-employed individuals talk about the surprising sense of control that comes from knowing that you can use your raw talents and ideas to create a product or service or experience that others find so valuable that you can support yourself comfortably from it.

In essence, making the switch from being bossed to being the boss forces us to stop dreaming and waiting for what we want, or blaming others for the fact that we don't have it. It forces us to stop doing what we've always been told to do, the way we've always been told to do it, and start finding ways to do what we want to do. It forces us to stop waiting for the conventional solutions to provide us with opportunity and start initiating and creating our own opportunities. Haven't most of us been dreaming and waiting for a long time? Hasn't it been a world of someday it will be great? Being on your own is your chance to turn someday into today.

Give Yourself the Break You've Been Waiting For

Greg Blanchard, a singer and actor, is an example of how you can, and indeed need to, make your own breaks. When Greg read that the producers of the musical *Les Miserables* were coming to Los Angeles to hold an open call for their upcoming production, he decided to try out even though he'd had little professional musical experience. And of course he wasn't the only one to respond to the open call that day. In fact, by the time he got there the line of hopefuls was so long that officials had closed the line, feeling certain they had more prospective talent than they would ever need.

Not willing to let this stop him, however, Greg struck up a conversation with the doorman and suggested that he create a backup list just in case there was a need for additional people at the end of the day. The guard agreed, and of course Greg's name was at the top of that list. When by 7:30 that evening everyone in the original line had been seen and there were still roles to fill, the producers turned to the backup list. Greg had his chance to sing for them and ultimately got a leading role.

Debbie Fields of Mrs. Fields Cookies had to use a similar bit of initiative to get her cookie company off the ground. She was convinced her cookies would be a hit, despite others who bet she would never make it. So you can imagine her horror when halfway through the first day she opened her store, no one had even come in the shop. But again she wasn't willing to let fate take its own course. She loaded up a tray of cookies fresh from the oven and began walking up and down the sidewalk, giving out cookies to everyone she met. Before long, a trail of people were following her and the wonderful smell of her cookies back to the shop like children following the Pied Piper.

You Can Make the Magic

We've heard literally hundreds of such stories. After losing his job, the engineer Payne Harrison dug in and wrote an unsolicited novel, *Storming Intrepid*. Although Harrison had never written before, it became a best-seller. The comedian Michael Colyer performed on the street for five years before he won the Star Search Competition. The singer Terry Bradford tried out for Star Search five years in a row before he had a chance to appear. He went on to become a $100,000 Male Vocalist Champion. When Leroy LoPresti left his job as a corporate executive, he had to travel all over the country to find the financial backing he needed to do what he'd always wanted to do—build his own airplanes. But he found the money, and in 1989 the LoPresti Swiftfury Piper made it to market. He sold over five hundred planes in the first year! The playwright David Steen got so tired of waiting for someone to see the value of a play he had written that he produced it himself and received immediate critical acclaim.

Each of these people persevered. They didn't wait. They kept putting in the time, doing what it took to do what they wanted to do. You never know how long it will take or which effort will be the one to do the trick, but as the singer Kenny James told us, "Success is like a grocery line. If you stay in line long enough, your turn will come."

Mental Shift #5. From Rules to Results: Discovering a New Way to Know How Well You're Doing

You have to listen to your heart. Sometimes you'll be right. Sometimes you'll be wrong. You can't be perfect, but you can be and do whatever you want.
HEIDI MILLER OF HEIDI'S FROZEN YOGURT

Contrary to what most business books, courses, and consultants claim, we've discovered there are no fixed rules for succeeding on your own. There is no right way. No one knows the answer. Books, courses and consultants relate many impressive success stories, but their most notable feature is how dramatically contradictory these stories are. Our own experience in interviewing thousands of successfully self-employed individuals is equally spiced with glowingly contradictory stories. Again and again we find there are many right ways to succeed. And many wrong ways. And the *right* way for one person is the wrong way for another.

For example, Paul Moreno, the founder of Los Angeles's first radio guide, told us, "Having a solid business plan was one of the keys to our success. We would recommend it as a must for any new business." On the other hand, Hal Schuster, who founded Pioneer Press, a $5-million-a-year home-based publishing house, told us that one key aspect of his success has been that he's never limited himself by having written a business plan.

Both these people have been successful. Their way works for them. Take almost any aspect of business and you'll find many similar polarities. Some people tell us they were able to make it because they started on a shoestring and didn't waste any money up front. Other people say their success was the result of investing everything they had up front and not skimping on anything. Some people tell us the Internet is a fabulous source of business, while others claim it is a waste of time. Some people tell us pricing low is the best way to start. Others say the one thing they learned is never to price low.

The contradictory advice is so abundant it could be enough to drive you nuts if you didn't know that making it on your own is an experiment.

Making It on Your Own Is an Experiment

While there is no predetermined right way to do it, the process of *discovering* what works can lead to otherwise unimagined success. This one fact is at the heart of every decision and every action you will take, from marketing your business to pricing your product or service. The key word is *experiment*—an act that's undertaken to discover something unknown.

But experimenting is something most of us haven't had much opportunity to do since childhood. In becoming "good" employees, most of us have learned carefully over many years to follow the rules and do what we're told. In fact, at the beginning of the Industrial Revolution, employers were concerned that the average man and woman would never be able to hold a job. They feared most people wouldn't be disciplined enough to carry out the same procedures day after day, precisely as specified over and over again. In fact, Sunday school classes were started to help people learn disciplined work habits following set rules and procedures.

And most of us have learned these habits well. But now, on your own when there are no procedures, no fixed rules to follow, you must be more innovative, more flexible, more exploratory. In fact, rigid conformity to procedures can defeat your success. But usually experimenting to find what works feels unfamiliar and makes us feel insecure, especially since we know that at the same time, we must be focused and follow through to achieve our goals. But that's the challenge. We must learn to have the flexibility to pursue a focus by creating structures that both support our goals and enable us to go with the flow.

From this perspective, you needn't become distressed about the array of conflicting business advice you encounter. Consider it to be a cafeteria of solutions others have found. You can select from among various approaches and experiment yourself. Try one thing and then another; follow your hunches, test, evaluate, and redirect until you find a way that works.

There Is No Right Answer Until You Find It!

In the book *Are You Happy?* NBC's *Today* show weatherman Willard Scott told television talk-show host Dennis Wholey that he spent weeks agonizing over why his talk-show pilot didn't succeed. He kept asking himself, "What is wrong? What am I doing wrong?" Finally, he concluded the only thing he was doing wrong was trying to figure out why he'd failed instead of moving on to try something else.

Once you're on your own, you're in that same boat every day. You have to just move on. There is no right answer until you find it! It can be frustrating to have done everything that you've been told to do and tried everything everyone else you know has done and still not get the results you want. But it just means you need to try something else. Often the solution for you is something no one else has tried. And the only way to find it is to move on.

In moving on and trying another approach . . . and another and another . . . you'll ultimately find the answer. Sometimes years later you can look back and see what went wrong, but that's only because you found what went right.

The Lack of a Clear Path Is Never a Sign to Turn Back

Seeing no clear path is simply a signal to look with new eyes, to improvise, to double your determination, to find another possible route. Often the reason you can't see where you're headed is because you haven't gotten to the corner yet.

Succeeding on your own means being willing to let go of the idea that there is a set of rules or procedures you can follow. Because despite efforts by some to make it into a simple and orderly procedure, going out on your own remains an experiment, a process that shows you the way only as it unfolds. The rule book, employee manual, and job description must become things of the past. In their place, you'll find the confusion and frustration that are always involved in exploring and experimenting. But you'll also have the joy and elation of discovering what combination of efforts will produce the profits that will support you from this point forward.

No matter how hopeless the search appears, you never need to give up the experiment you've begun, because each renewed effort brings you closer to the results you seek. If you feel as if you don't know exactly what you're doing, that's normal. If you feel as though you don't know which way to go, that's normal. If you are puzzled by the results you get at times, that's normal. That's what it feels like to experiment. It means you don't know. You're seeking to discover.

To make it on our own, we need to shake the expectation that we're supposed to know what we're doing each step of the way. People who fear taking a step until they're certain it's the right one are destined to step only where they've already been. When you're going along a new path with many turns, you never know what lies ahead until you get to the next one. As you've undoubtedly already discovered, there is no straight line to success. The path to making it on your own is filled with many twists and turns. And confusion is normal. But as long as you know where you're headed—that is, as long as you know what you want to accomplish—and stay focused on that, while remaining flexible as to how you'll get there—before long, you'll know if you're still on course and can adjust accordingly.

No Results—No Reward

When working on a payroll, you're not encouraged to experiment. You're supposed to do what you're supposed to do. And if it doesn't work, you'll still get paid because you were just doing what you were told. But not so in venturing out on your own. On your own, you don't get paid until you deliver the results. No results, no reward. You've always got to be looking at the *results* you're getting and adjusting your behavior accordingly.

When I, Sarah, was a little girl, one of my household jobs was to dry the dishes after dinner. Of course, as a ten-year-old I always had a hundred other things I would rather do. So I'd hurriedly wipe the towel over the dishes exactly as I'd been shown to do. When my father went to put them away, however, he'd say to me, "These dishes aren't dry." And I would defiantly respond, "Well, I dried them!" So night after night he would remind me, "Sarah, you haven't dried the dishes until they're dry."

So it is with running your own business. Whatever you're trying to do, you haven't done it until the results are in. You need to experiment until you discover what particular combination of your skills and abilities, at what price, will be valuable to what group of people within the context of the prevailing economic realities.

Let the Results Be Your Guide

Since you can't be certain about your results, since you can't know for sure ahead of time just what the winning combination will be, all you can do is keep moving in the direction you want to go and keep your eye on your results, trying out and testing first one thing and then another. Ultimately you'll find a combination that produces the desired results for both you and your clients or customers.

Sandra McKnight is a good example. As a speech coach, she had been advised that telemarketers would be the ideal market for her voice seminars. So she approached one telemarketing company after another. Yes, she discovered, they could benefit from her services, but their personnel were paid so little that simply replacing them was deemed more cost-effective than training those who needed improvement. This approach simply wasn't getting results. So she tried another and another and finally found one that worked—helping people with foreign accents communicate more clearly.

Ellie Kahn had a similar experience. Initially she planned to do audio and video biographies with the elderly. Although families were enthusiastic about her service, too often they couldn't afford to hire her. Again, she just wasn't getting the results she needed. So she began to consider alternatives, trying first one thing and then another until she decided to focus on producing institutional biographies, documenting the history of companies and organizations. Sure enough, that worked.

We're not saying you shouldn't plan. There's nothing wrong with having a plan. But first you must have a clear outcome in mind. Your outcome serves as your compass. The plan must be flexible. As the home-based publisher Hal Schuster told us, "I have a clear idea of where I want to go with my business and some ideas about how I'm going to get there. But I can't pin down exactly how I'll do it because the variables are always changing and I have to be flexible enough to respond."

A plan is simply one possible route for getting from where you are to where you want to be. It's only as good as the results it produces. So never think you need to stick rigidly to a plan if it isn't working. Try out the approaches and methods others have tried, but realize that you're experimenting. When one approach doesn't work, you haven't failed; you're just one step closer to knowing what will work. You've simply got to follow your results.

MENTAL SHIFT #6. FROM MASTERY TO MARKETING: USING A NEW APPROACH TO MAKING AN IMPRESSION

Ultimately, customers are your only source of funding.
TIM MULLEN, CATALOG PUBLISHER

Having enough people to buy what you have to offer week after week, month after month, and year after year is the premier element for making it on your own. And the one magic word that can put you in charge of having all the work you need is *marketing*. Marketing refers to all the activities involved in making sure the people who need or want what you have to offer know about you and are motivated to choose to work with you.

It's an unfamiliar concept to most salaried individuals. Frankly I, Sarah, admit I didn't know what marketing meant when I went out on my own. I knew it meant more than going to the grocery store, but I wasn't sure just what. On the job, doing a good job is what matters most. But on your own, while doing a good job is vital, unless people know what a good job you can do, you don't get the job.

But that does not mean that you have to develop a supersales personality or learn how to hype yourself and your work. Quite the contrary. We find that many successfully self-employed people not only don't have a sales personality, but also have little or no sales experience and may not even like selling as we commonly think of it. What they do have, though, is what we call a *marketing mindset*. They're willing and eager to find ways to let others know about what they do and how they can help, serve, improve, or make life better for those they work with.

In other words, they think about what they're doing from the viewpoint of the people who need it. Having a marketing mindset means focusing not only on having a high-quality product or service, but also on how what you offer is unique, what benefits it provides, and how you can spread the word about these benefits to those who need them.

You Have to Toot Your Own Horn

In her book *Skills for Success,* Adele Scheele writes about two kinds of people: sustainers and achievers. Sustainers are the people who do a good job and hope someone will notice. They tend to complain a lot about being passed over for promotions and other opportunities in favor of people who don't do as good a job as they do. Achievers, on the other hand, also do a good job, but they make sure people know about it. They call attention to their work because they believe they can make an important contribution. Scheele claims that most people are sustainers. And that's not surprising. It's an integral part of the paycheck mentality we've grown up with. We learn not to brag, not to toot our own horn, not to call attention to ourselves. Our work is supposed to stand on its own.

To make it on your own, however, as W. S. Gilbert of Gilbert and Sullivan said, you've got to "blow your own trumpet or, trust me, you haven't a chance!" You have to brag; you have to call attention to yourself, or at least to your product or service. No matter how good you are, if you don't market yourself, so few people will know about your work that it will stand on its own—alone. And what a waste! Here you are with all your talents, abilities, education, and experience. And there are people and companies that need what you can do. You owe it to yourself and those who need you to make sure people know what you can do to improve their lives and make a better world. That's what marketing will do for you.

And while marketing yourself does not mean you have to use a lot of hype or become a slick sales personality, it does mean you have to develop a high profile, and do it in a particular way.

Toot About What You Can Do, Not Who You Are

When people with a paycheck mentality attempt to promote themselves, they usually think *résumé* and talk about their credentials. They're used to having to prove to the powers that be that they have earned the proper credentials to be competent at what they do. When they go out on their own, they attempt to use this same approach to market their products and services. And then they wonder why others with less experience and offering less quality somehow manage to get more business.

Here's why. Once you're on your own, people are much more interested in what you can do for them than in the details of how and why you can do it. Just look at the descriptions that follow and see which appeal most to you.

Mastery Mindset	**Marketing Mindset**
1. "I'm a board-certified gynecologist. I studied at Yale University and did my internship at Cedars-Sinai. Now I'm in private practice in Beverly Hills."	1. "You know how so many women suffer from severe PMS? Well, I'm a gynecologist and I specialize in helping women find ways to eliminate their symptoms of PMS."
2. "I am a graphic artist. I work in all media. I can do line drawings, airbrush, computer-aided design, color separations, and advertising mechanicals."	2. "You know how many small businesses have limited budgets for designing their advertising and promotions but they still need to look professional? I'm a graphic artist and I design brochures, flyers, logos, cards, and stationery that look expensive, but aren't."
3. "My company is Laser New. We restore laser-printer cartridges using a new patented process that seals in toner using an air-pressure system developed in Europe by a leading physicist."	3. "You know how the cost of supplies can add to your overhead and eat into your profits? Well, our company, Laser New, takes your used laser-printer cartridges and makes them as good as new within twenty-four hours for almost half the price of buying a new one."

As you can see, developing a marketing mindset is simply a matter of shifting your focus from how you do what you do to the benefits of what you do. Here are six key steps you can take today to make that shift:

1. Describe what you do in fifteen words or less and what makes it unique or special.

2. Identify specifically who needs what you offer. Make a list of several types of individuals or companies.

3. Write down ten ways these people or companies will be better off as a result of what you do.

4. Make a list of ten ways you could let these people know about the benefits of what you offer.

5. Read, look, and listen every day for any clue that someone needs any of the benefits you offer and follow up on any sign of potential interest.

6. Read, look, and listen every day for any opportunity to let people or companies know about the benefits of what you offer.

Coleen Springer used a process similar to this when she decided to begin selling her artwork. Coleen works in soft pastels, and her pieces are very calming. The goal of her art is to bring a sense of peace and harmony to those who view it. So she asked herself, "Who especially needs the kind of work I do? What can I do for them? How can I let them know about my art?"

Here's her list:

WHO?	BENEFITS	HOW TO REACH THEM
Drug rehab centers	Calms and relaxes people	Send a mailing offering a free trial exhibit
Prisons		
Tax offices	Creates a more pleasant atmosphere	Speak or write an article for trade associations about the effects of art
Dental offices		
Hospitals	Makes the office more attractive	
Therapists' offices	Can be customized to existing decor	Donate an exhibit and get press coverage
Pain centers		
Doctors' offices	Sends message that you care how people feel	Offer a referral fee to sales reps who call on these people
Beauty salons		
Lawyers' offices		

Coleen was particularly intrigued with the idea of placing her art in dental offices, so she started with that market. She joined the local chamber of commerce and met several dentists. From them, she learned that the local dental college was sponsoring a symposium on dental phobias. Her next step was to contact the person planning the symposium and offer to do a presentation on the use of art to reduce anxiety. She also offered to provide an exhibit of her art at the registration table.

At the symposium she met several dentists who were interested in her work and followed up to offer them a trial exhibit. At the symposium, she also overheard someone talking about a chronic-pain center that was opening soon. She contacted the developer and offered to volunteer to work with the designer. Ultimately she was commissioned to do the art for the center. She also realized that perhaps she could help the designer get business with other health centers, and they soon agreed to refer business to each other.

Most of the other artists Coleen meets don't have a marketing mindset. So, they're amazed at how well she's doing. Most are still working at low-paying day jobs, creating their art in the wee hours of the night and trying to get a gallery exhibit. Very few people ever see their work. Some, however, seeing Coleen's success, are starting to think about who specifically would benefit from their work. They're beginning to shift to a marketing mindset.

For more information about marketing your business, see "The Critical Mass Marketing Alternative to Having to Constantly Sell Yourself" in chapter 4 and "Diagnosing What You Need to Do to Get More Business" in chapter 7.

MENTAL SHIFT #7. FROM RIGHTS TO RESPONSIBILITY: TAKING A NEW ATTITUDE FOR HOW TO GET WHAT YOU DESERVE

The choices we make dictate the lives we lead.
WILLIAM SHAKESPEARE

There's no use campaigning or complaining about your rights when you're on your own. You have to take responsibility and stand by your work, for better or worse. In fact, excuses don't work anymore . . . if they ever did.

On past jobs you may have had a certain degree of leeway to goof off, take off, or knock off. Until you really messed up, you'd probably still have had your job even if you gave less than 100 percent. Of course, with recent shifts in our economy, this is usually no longer true even on the job. And it certainly isn't true when you're on your own.

Your clients and customers will cut you very little slack. In other words, if you don't deliver you won't get paid. You won't get repeat business or referrals. On your own, there are no workers' rights. You can decide what you can do and what you can't do and what you are willing to do and what you're not. But then, we have to be responsible for doing whatever we need to do to achieve what we agreed to.

No Explaining or Complaining Allowed

Let's face it, even if your clients and customers are kind and compassionate people, they're not interested in your problems! They've hired you to solve one of theirs, not add to them. Without knowing it, for example, each of the following self-employed individuals could be well on his or her way to losing a client. And when they do, they'll probably wonder what went wrong, because, after all, they were working hard to accommodate their clients' needs under difficult circumstances.

"The reason you're having that problem with your hair," the hair stylist told his client, "is because you have an unusual neck line and your hair is very fine. Also, it's been processed a lot. So it's very difficult to style the way you want it."

"I'm trying to sing the jingle the way you want it," the voice-over artist told her client after several takes, "but, you see, you've written this rather fast here and I have to breathe at this particular interval and the product name has so many syllables it's slowing me down."

"I'm sorry that this brochure is late," the desktop publisher told his client, "but my baby-sitter got ill and now there's no one to take care of the baby, so I'm getting behind."

"I would have had that banner ready for you today as promised," the sign maker told her client, "but I'm installing some new software and my computer froze. So now I have to have this consultant come over and so I've gotten behind."

A woman who's having her hair cut doesn't want to hear that she has "problem" hair. The advertising agency producing a commercial doesn't want to hear that their client's product name has too many syllables. The professional who needs his brochure or banner for a trade show that starts tomorrow doesn't want to hear about your child-care problems or your computer breakdowns.

So, if you want to keep your clients and customers happy and have them come back again and again and send everyone else they know to you, you can't complain and explain. You've got to keep your mouth shut and figure out how to meet their needs to make their lives easier. But, what do you do when a client's situation makes serving their needs more difficult than you expected? And what do you do when life intervenes to make it difficult or even impossible to deliver on what you have promised? Here are some ideas.

1. Try to uncover the full scope of the work you'll be asked to do before quoting a price or promising a delivery date. Don't be so eager to take on a job that you leap into it without looking. Explore the possible complications or complexities while you're discussing what the project will involve. If what's needed is beyond the scope of what you can do confidently, refer them to someone else without hesitation and be sure the person you're referring to knows the source of the referral, so he or she can refer to you in return when appropriate.

2. If a project is especially complex or time-consuming, factor these complexities into your pricing and tell your clients up-front how much time you'll need. Should they tell you that someone else has offered to do it for much less or much more quickly, that's your chance to shine. That's the perfect moment to demonstrate your expertise. You can demonstrate your understanding of the complexities involved and the quality of work demanded. You can describe how you plan to address these complexities and how other standard services don't address such issues. The hair stylist, for example, can point out that he intends to begin a conditioning program to balance the pH level of the client's hair and has a special plan for adding volume to it.

3. *If an unexpected problem develops, take full responsibility.* If at all possible, figure out on your own how you will solve the problem without having to burden the client about it. If your computer crashed, for example, get an overnight service to come in and fix it. If supplies weren't delivered, drive across town and pick them up yourself. Your client doesn't need to know about these complications. Solving such problems yourself so you can still deliver for your client as expected may increase your costs, but consider it an investment in your future and your reputation. Consider it part of your learning curve, and plan to build the possibility of such costs into your future fee schedule.

4. *If an unavoidable problem or delay occurs that will prevent you from doing what the client is counting on, notify the client immediately.* Apologize and let them know precisely how you will be handling it. Do not overexplain and complain and certainly don't implicate them in the problem. No comments like "Well, if your specifications weren't so complex, this wouldn't have happened." Always be willing to offer some type of compensation for the inconvenience your problem has caused the client. You might offer a discount or credit. Or if the problem is sufficiently severe, you may have to swallow hard and provide, or redo, the work at no cost. Again, it's your reputation and future success of your business that are at stake.

Just think, for example, about your own reaction if, having received poor service at a restaurant, the manager came over to apologize and offered dessert or the entire meal on the house. You're more apt to be forgiving and come back again.

Of course, when during the process of a project, a client requests new or additional things be done outside the scope of what was originally agreed upon, then it is appropriate to renegotiate both the time and costs involved. But otherwise, do whatever you need to do to show your clients they can count on you to solve, not add to, their problems. And when you do, you'll be their hero, and you'll get to enjoy all the well-earned rewards you deserve.

MENTAL SHIFT #8. FROM JOB TITLE TO CHARISMA: DEVELOPING A NEW SOURCE OF POWER

*I don't like work—no one does—but I like what is in work—
the chance to find yourself.*

JOSEPH CONRAD

Going out on your own is incredibly empowering, because suddenly you are totally in charge of your life. No one can tell you what to do or how to do it. And that usually feels great. But consider this: while no one can tell you what to do, you can't tell anyone else what to do, either.

A job gives you a certain degree of authority—perhaps not a lot, but within the purview of your job description and your position within the organization you can get people to do what you want them to do because of the authority your job carries with it. The company you work for also provides you with a certain amount of authority, maybe even purchasing or hiring power. People may take your calls, answer your letters, agree to meet with you, or involve you in various activities because of the *position* you hold. This is what Dr. Eric Berne, the developer of the psychological theory Transactional Analysis, called *position power.* And to the extent that you have it, you can open doors and get things done.

The moment you go out on your own, however, the only authority you have is whatever authority you can command through your own personal power. This sudden loss of automatic authority can be an incredible shock to anyone who's had even a small degree of position power. It can be especially disorienting to someone who's had a considerable amount of authority within an organization.

I, Paul, had been the chief executive officer of a research-and-development foundation affiliated with the famed Menninger Clinic. Before I left to go out on my own I had two full-time administrative assistants and a staff of professionals working for me. I, Sarah, was an administrator for a federal agency, personally responsible for a six-figure budget and overseeing hundreds of thousands of dollars in federal grants. Needless to say, we both commanded a comfortable degree of authority because of our positions.

But, the day we said good-bye to our paycheck, we also said good-bye to all that authority. We no longer had the power of the United States government or a research organization behind us. We had no secretary to screen calls, no administrative assistant to handle details, no one to get paper clips or even to clean up the office. But even more disheartening, when we placed calls people didn't necessarily know who we were anymore. When the secretary heard our name, we'd be asked, "Who? Will he know what you're calling about?" You undoubtedly know what that feels like. Suddenly we were nobody—or anybody.

What were we to do? The same thing we each must do on our own—reach down deep within ourselves and call forth the *personal power* we each have within us. *Personal power* is a source of power that comes from knowing who you are as a person, not as a job title or a role. It's the power that comes from believing in yourself and your talents. It's the power that comes from knowing that you are *somebody* in and of yourself.

You can hear it in people's voices. You can see it in the way they walk and carry themselves. You can see it in the way they dress. It is not based on age, although the older you are the more opportunity you've had to recognize and develop it in yourself. It is not just based on how much money or education you have. Money and education are other sources of power we tend to rely upon, and certainly personal power can be used to make money and is enhanced through knowledge and education. But personal power arises from the confidence and assurance that, despite any difficulties, life will work and respond to us.

Personal power is also called *charisma,* a personal quality that gives an individual a commanding influence or authority. And it's actually more powerful than any other source of power. It's a kind of presence that people stop and take note of. Once you own your personal power, you carry with you all the authority you need, regardless of your position or worldly circumstances.

Most of us are never called upon to develop this quality within ourselves because we can lean upon the other sources of power that are provided to us through our roles and job descriptions, but also because working within an organization doesn't usually encourage the development of personal power. In fact, organizations usually have room at the top for only a few people with personal power.

Feeling powerless and having no other form of power to grab onto, however, is one of the best and surest ways to bring out our charisma. In this sense, one of the greatest benefits of being self-employed is that it calls upon us to tap into and develop this inner source of strength. After having to start his business from scratch twice, wellness-research consultant Dean Allen would agree. He told us, "For anyone who wants to truly fulfill their potential, being on your own is the only way to go." Whereas it took Dean three years to turn a profit the first time around, he was booked to capacity within four months when he started over in a brand-new community following a coast-to-coast move. His growing sense of personal power made the difference.

The surest route to developing your personal power quickly is to identify clearly the type of person you want to be and start thinking and acting as if you were that person. Start being someone you admire, someone you respect, someone you know you can count on. Of course, becoming that person may take some time or it may already come naturally to you.

You can begin, however, at any time, by asking yourself, "What would someone I most respect and admire do in this situation? How would such a person deal with these circumstances?" Then do that. If you can't pull it off at first, that's all right. Who can do something perfectly the first time? No one expects a new employee to perform like an old-timer. So, if you keep aiming toward becoming the confident and effective person you want to be, you'll bring that person out in yourself. And you'll feel, if you don't already, something like this:

"When I was a young person I used to look at all the beautiful people who were so successful and happy. Life seemed to work for them so effortlessly. Not that they didn't have any problems, but their problems didn't seem to interfere with their ability to live with gusto. I, on the other hand, suffered through whatever I achieved. Even when things were going well, I was too busy dreading the doom the next moment might bring. I felt like someone who'd been dealt an adequate hand in life but didn't know how to play the game.

"When I first went out on my own, it was worse than ever. At least on my job I was somebody. It said so right on my name badge. Now all I saw were closed doors that I'd have to open somehow. I felt like a teenager again, sitting on the sidelines feeling like a total klutz, wishing I could be part of the 'in' crowd. But this time I wasn't a teenager. I decided to go after those doors, and one by one I found a way to open them and my business started to grow. The more it grew, the better I felt about myself. I was pleased to discover what I could do!

"One day I was sitting in a business meeting across from a large plate-glass panel, and reflected there in the glass was a roomful of successful, competent people, the kind of people I'd always looked up to and admired—the beautiful people. All of a sudden I realized that one of those people was me. I had become the person I wanted to be."

For more information on how to develop your personal power, see "Making Sure You're Taken Seriously" in chapter 7.

MENTAL SHIFT #9. FROM COVERING TO CAPITALIZING: ASSIGNING A NEW ROLE TO MISTAKES

The way to succeed is to double your failure rate.
THOMAS WATSON, FOUNDER OF IBM

Remember when you were a little kid and you tried to cover up your mistakes so your parents and teachers wouldn't see them? Remember the little white lies you told so you wouldn't get caught for doing something you shouldn't have done? Most of us just love to hide our mistakes, and we love to hide from our mistakes.

Looking good and covering up mistakes becomes a habit many of those around us may conspire to help us maintain. Parents, teachers, and bosses hate mistakes, so they may look the other way. Our paycheck mentality reinforces this habit. It says you've always got to look good. You're supposed to have the right answers and do the right thing. Most people believe that's what they were hired for. They fear they'll get in trouble or even lose their jobs if they make a mistake. So they do whatever they can to cover up and play down their errors.

On your own, however, covering up your mistakes can get you into a lot more trouble than making them. While results are your guide, mistakes can be your best friend. They can let you know when you're off course, before it's too late. It's been reported that the way NASA mission control keeps its rockets on course as they travel through outer space is by noticing when they're off course. So it is when you're on your own: there's nothing wrong with being wrong unless you ignore it or stick to it. Mistakes simply tell you when you need to correct your course.

There's Nothing Wrong with You

After hearing us talk about this needed mental shift, a guidance counselor came up to us and said, "I wish someone had told me about the value of making mistakes when I first went out on my own. I know I'm good at what I do, but even though I've been doing everything I thought you're supposed to do as a freelancer, it's just not working. I've been thinking there must be something wrong with me. I guess the only thing wrong is that I haven't been trying other ways to do it." He was quite relieved.

A husband and wife we'll call Jean and Shaun were not so fortunate. They started a business providing referrals to all types of independent maintenance personnel like carpenters, plumbers, rug cleaners, and so on. After considerable investigation and advice from several consultants on how to structure their business, they wrote a detailed business plan based on charging each freelancer a moderate fee to be listed with the service and charging the person who called to get a referral a small fee, as well. On paper it looked very profitable. Their advisers suggested they follow this plan for at least the first year.

They had no difficulty getting the maintenance personnel to sign up and pay the fee, but most of the people calling for the service didn't want to pay for a referral. This became apparent within the first few weeks of doing business. But to restructure their business plan would have required a major hike in their listing fee. That would have involved changing all their promotional materials and telling everyone they'd already contacted about the new policy.

They didn't want to admit they'd made a serious and costly mistake. So they tried to keep up a front and look good—and didn't make it through the first year.

Success Is More Important Than Being Right

It goes to show that when you're on your own, success is more important than proving your point. Maybe people should have been willing to pay for referrals, but they weren't. Maybe the plan should have worked, but it didn't. Naturally, it's difficult to admit you're wrong, especially if you think it means you are less of a person or that you're a failure. But ask yourself this: Would you rather be right or achieve your goals? Of course, we're not talking about ethics. There never need be a business reason to compromise your ethics. We're talking about the ability to admit you made a mistake about what you thought would work.

Once you get out on your own you need to develop an entirely new relationship with the idea of failure. In past generations, people tended to think that if they failed in business, that was it. Often they never tried again. Today, we've realized that usually the most successful people are also the ones who have made the most mistakes. In her study of the lives of successful people, for example, Adele Scheele, the author of the book *Skills for Success,* observed that mistakes and even failures are characteristic of successful people.

Many successful people, like motivational speaker and author of the best-selling book *Chicken Soup for the Soul,* Mark Victor Hanson, claim that their biggest failure was the turning point for their ultimate success. Academy Award–winning actor and director Kevin Costner claims, "I've always gotten fueled by my disasters." Thomas Edison had five thousand failures before getting a working lightbulb. That's one failure a day for over thirteen years! In this sense, it appears that failure is a prerequisite for success.

So whenever you make a mistake or suffer a setback that you're tempted to view as a failure, look at it in terms of how it can be a springboard to your success. Make a list of the benefits you can and will get from this experience. Of course, at first you won't feel like doing this because we have been conditioned since kindergarten to dread the thought of failure. When we were growing up it was called flunking. But to succeed, you can't let failure stop you. The only way you can flunk now is if you quit at something you still want to do. You need to think of failure as a friend that's showing you the way to success.

As private-practice consultant Gene Call puts it, "I view what I do as practice. I'm always looking for a way to make it better. If I send out a mailing and it doesn't get a response, it's not a failure; it's a challenge to my creativity."

Make Your Mistakes Where They Won't Hurt

Since mistakes are inevitable, especially in the beginning, arrange whenever possible to make your mistakes where they won't hurt you. Get the bugs out of your operation by doing trial runs. Then you can actually enjoy making mistakes, because you'll be able to find and correct them before they can do you any harm. For example, don't try out a new speech on a group that could make or break you. Volunteer to do it before a supportive group of friends or an appreciative community group.

Experience makes you effective, and experience is built on a history of corrected mistakes. That's why it's said that "practice makes perfect." You get perfect by making mistakes at times when it doesn't matter. You'll find further information about how to deal with the feelings arising from setbacks in chapters 5, 6, and 7.

What to Do When You Make a Mistake

Dos	Don'ts
• Compliment yourself for your courage and ingenuity in trying what you did.	• Dismiss it as unimportant, unchangeable, or something you can't handle.
• Remain confident in your ability to excel.	• Berate yourself.
• Resolve not to repeat the same mistake.	• Blame anyone: yourself, someone else, or something else.
• Take responsibility for what you did. There's almost always another chance.	• Try to ignore or overlook mistakes.
	• Decide to give up.
• Do any necessary damage control.	• Expect sympathy.
	• Make excuses.
• Do what you can to make it right.	• Repeat the same error.
• Apologize if others were involved.	• Avoid trying again for fear of repeating the error.
• Learn everything you can from it.	• Use it as evidence that you can't or won't succeed.
• Try again immediately, but do it differently.	• Worry endlessly about where you went wrong.
• Feel confident you won't have to make that mistake ever again.	

Mental Shift #10. From Playing It Safe to Keeping Options Open: Setting a New Standard for When to Say Yes

Stress comes from doing less than you can.
Jim Rohn, Motivational Speaker

On the job, one of the things you learn fast, if you didn't already know it, is to never, ever take on more work than you can deliver. When you agree to take on something for the boss, he or she expects you to do it, and you will be in hot water if you don't. On your own, however, the opposite is often true. You've got to generate two, three, four, or more times as many prospects for work as you could possibly handle, because only a small percentage of these prospects will actually turn into business. You always have to generate more potential work than you can actually do.

When Jeannette Monroe opened her consulting business for dental offices, she was delighted at the response she got to her initial calls and mailings. Many dentists were interested in having her come in and set up a more efficient administrative office. After talking with three or four dentists who seemed particularly interested, she realized that if they each hired her, she wouldn't be able to serve them all, so she decided not to follow up with any others who had expressed interest.

One snag after another, however, delayed a final decision from these dentists. Weeks turned into months and she still had no contract for any actual work. She was without a paying client. Only after this painful experience did Jeannette realize that her paycheck mentality was on the verge of putting her out of business. She quickly began contacting as many dentists as she could and eventually did get her first client. Of the first four dentists she spoke with who were *so* interested, only one ever actually hired her, and that was over a year later.

Francis Dole created a line of handcrafted antique model cars. He thought they would make ideal gifts. But when we met him he was discouraged. A manufacturer's representative he'd been talking to for some time was interested in his line of cars but kept dragging her feet about whether she would actually carry them. During this time, Francis hadn't contacted any other reps because he was still negotiating with her. So there he was, dead in the water as weeks turned into months. Essentially he had given up his power and put the fate of his business in her hands. Of course, we advised him to tell her that while he hoped she would decide to work with him, in the meantime, he would be talking with other reps. Actually that speeded up her final answer, which turned out to be a "no."

A Deal Isn't a Deal Until It's Done

Opportunities that don't materialize can be disappointing and discouraging—but only because our payroll mentality creates unrealistic expectations. When your boss tells you to do something, the decision is made, and even if it's delayed, you still get paid. But not so when you're on your own. Decisions can literally take from days to weeks to years. We've worked to get contracts that weren't signed until more than a year after the initial contact. We've also had companies change their mind on contracts that were all but signed after nine months of discussions.

In other words, when you're on your own, you need to say yes to every desirable possibility that comes along and continue generating as many such opportunities as you can until you have actual cash in hand or a contractual agreement signed on the dotted line. You always have to leave your options open.

Of course, it's important not to imply that you will be available when you know you won't or that you can do something you can't, but you can always let prospects know about your timetable as your situation changes. And keep in mind that if you do get more business than you can handle at one time, you can refer it out or bring on associates. In fact, it's a good idea to line up reliable high-quality backup in advance, because you never know when you'll suddenly have more than you can handle.

MENTAL SHIFT # 11. FROM EARNING TO SPEND TO SPENDING TO EARN: MAKING A NEW RELATIONSHIP WITH MONEY

Throw your money in the direction you want to go and the rest will follow.

DAVID BEAIRD, FILM DIRECTOR

"I lost my job two months ago and now I'm out of money, so I guess I should start a business."

"I don't have money for marketing, so how can I get business?"

"I don't have any money to do it the way I should, so will this do?"

"I've spent all my money on setting up my office. Now how do I get some business fast?"

Unfortunately these questions are like a litany of the paycheck mentality. We hear them often. They arise from not knowing that on your own you have to think about money in new terms. When you live on a paycheck, your income is fixed by what your job pays. Although you can hope for an annual salary increase or a promotion that keeps up with or ahead of inflation, the amount of money you receive each week is relatively set. Therefore you must try to live within your means. If you spend what you don't have, you go into debt. And most Americans do. They go into debt to purchase things they'll enjoy like furniture, clothing, travel, gifts, and so on. They hope to get out of debt by gradually paying off these purchases over time. This approach works reasonably well for most salaried individuals. Once you're on your own, however, if you operate on these paycheck principles, you'll most likely run into financial problems for four reasons:

1. You have to support your business before it will support you. Starting a business venture is like raising a child: you have to support it until it can support itself. There isn't usually an immediate source of steady income; it's more likely to be an immediate source of steady expenses. Sometimes the expenses are low and the financial investment you need to make may be small. Peggy Glenn, for example, started a secretarial service with only $65. But Peggy had just walked out on her job in frustration, and that $65 was a stretch for her. At other times, the investment required is larger. Herb and Linda Schultz, for example, invested $5,000 to purchase a rug-cleaning franchise. Tina Linert invested $20,000 in specialized typesetting equipment.

So as a rule of thumb, if you're completely out of money, the best route to a full-time income fast is to get some type of job. In fact, the best time to go out on your own is from the security of a steady job. And if you have a job, the best advice is to keep it. Let the job finance your start-up investments and provide you with the time to begin laying a foundation for going out on your own. If you don't have a job and you don't have any money or any immediate business on hand, consider getting a full-time, part-time, or temporary job while you launch your independent career. There's nothing worse than having to start a business from scratch with bill collectors hounding you.

2. You have to spend money to make money. Susan McNeil is a good example of someone whose paycheck mentality prevented her from making it on her own. Susan was tutoring foreign executives about American customs. Most of her initial clients came to her from the company where she used to work. After a few months, however, all the foreign executives from that company had completed her program and she realized she would have to start marketing to other companies.

Since she'd started out on a shoestring, she didn't have $500 in the bank to have an attractive brochure printed and mailed to a select number of companies. She didn't have the $250 she needed to join a local business organization where she could make key contacts. She didn't have the money to buy a laser printer. She kept saying, "I'll do that as soon as I get the money." Instead she hand-lettered some materials on cheap paper and delivered them in person to several companies. As you might imagine, she didn't get any business.

Of course not. No company would take someone seriously who solicits a $250 workshop with a twenty-five-cent flyer. She thought she couldn't afford to do it right. Actually, she couldn't afford to do it wrong. Her company was going down the drain and she believed it was because she didn't have enough money. She needed to borrow the money or barter to produce the brochure, buy the laser printer, and join the networking organization. She needed to invest in at least one of these things.

Whenever you hear yourself say, "I need to do that, but I don't have the

Credit Sources

Here's a list of several credit sources you can use to invest in your success:

Credit Cards. One or two credit cards that you use exclusively for business purposes can provide you with the funds you need to do what you need to do to get more business coming in.

A secured credit card. If you have no credit and no credit cards, you can build a credit history by using a secured credit card like the one offered through the First National Bankcard Center ([800] 552–9895)

A loan from friends or relatives. You can show friends and relatives exactly how the money you are borrowing will generate ample money to repay their loan.

A personal bank loan. Some banks are now making consumer loans available to small businesses.

Microloans. The Small Business Administration and other private organizations have created lending programs that enable self-employed and small-business owners to obtain character-based loans from several hundred to over fifty thousand dollars. (See the appendix for microloan programs in your area.)

A line of credit. Some banks are making consumer lines of credit available to small businesses. A line of credit enables you to borrow only what you need up to a specified limit. In partnership with Wells Fargo Bank, the National Association of Women Business Owners has established a one-billion-dollar loan fund to provide unsecured lines of credit to women business owners. (For membership information, contact NAWBO, 1337 K Street NW, Suite 637, Washington, D.C. 20910 301/608–2590.)

money" or "That's what I should do, but I can't afford it," take note: *You are operating from a paycheck mentality!* To make money, you have to invest money, but there is usually a creative way to get the money you need, especially if you can show yourself and the source of potential funds how what you will do with the money will pay for itself in an immediate return.

For example, if you can make a sale and produce a purchase order for it, your supplier may extend you the credit you need to fulfill the order. To make it on your own, you have to shift your thinking from *How can I get the money I need?* to *How can I generate the money I need?*

3. The money you spend needs to make money. While Susan didn't have money to buy a laser printer or to produce a brochure, she did spend several hundred dollars on clothing her first year in business. She felt she needed to look the role of a professional. And indeed she did, but the attractive business suits she bought didn't make any money for her. A sales letter printed on a laser printer with an attractive brochure, sent to the proper places and followed up with phone calls, could have paid for itself, and the suits, too, from the business it would have generated.

Developing a profit mentality involves thinking about how you can invest whatever money you have in activities that will produce more money. Money spent wisely on marketing, for example, can multiply itself. Money spent on products you have or could get orders to sell at a higher price will immediately multiply itself. Money spent on producing a workbook with valuable information people will pay for can multiply itself.

When a couple we'll call Charles and Rose started their training firm they invested their personal savings and retirement funds in a luxurious office, elegant stationery, the most advanced equipment, and a lavish open house to announce their business. All these things were, although important, not income generators. As a result they were out of money the day they started, and unfortunately it took too long to get business without any marketing budget. Their business closed before their first anniversary. Had they started their business from their home, however, and invested their savings in simple but attractive stationery and more basic equipment, they could have used the bulk of their funds to live on while they marketed their business.

When the film director David Beaird moved from Shreveport, Louisiana, to Los Angeles to make movies, everyone told him he was wasting his time and the little money he had. They said he wouldn't even get a foot in the door. And sure enough, when he began approaching studios, all the doors were closed. His strategy, however, was to take the little money he had and rent a theater where he could put on a play he'd written. Not only did the play provide a limited source of income; the theater also served as a place where he could teach acting classes, from which he could earn some money and draw talent for the play. The play also served as a magnet to attract agents, backers, studio executives, publicity, and exposure.

And sure enough, he secured a backer to finance his first movie and then a second one, and finally he was placed on the directors' list of a major studio. This all came from investing the money he had in something that would produce the results he wanted.

So before you spend a cent, ask yourself, "How will what I'm doing with this money bring money back to me multiplied?" For additional ideas on how to generate more business when you need it, see "What to Do When You Don't Have Enough Money" in chapter 7.

4. You have to believe it's okay to have money. Are you ashamed to make a profit? This may seem like a strange question, but are you sure you're comfortable with financial abundance? Surprisingly, some people aren't. According to the *Random House Dictionary*, simply defined, "profit" means to "benefit, gain, or earn from one's efforts." The opportunity to profit, that is to benefit from our efforts, is at the heart of a free-enterprise system. Yet we often hear self-employed individuals make disparaging comments like these about others who are successful: "So and so is just out to make a profit." "Boy, I bet he's making a killing on that!" or "I'm not out to make a profit; I just want to do a good job."

Such comments may help explain why so many self-employed people chronically undercharge. They also suggest why so many self-employed people actually forget to factor a "profit" into their fees. And they shed a bright light on why some of us can barely get by from month to month. In other words, for some *profit* is a dirty word. Some people are actually embarrassed to profit from their efforts. Beliefs like these can unintentionally keep you from becoming as successful as you'd like to be.

Historically, the "robber barons" of the Industrial Age may have tainted the word *profit* for some of us. Negative feelings about "profit" linger from decades of bitter wage wars between labor and management. But clearly, in today's evolving Information Age, if you are to create a good lifestyle for yourself and those you love by working on your own, you must begin to see profit in a new light. We need to think of it as our reward for making some valued contribution to the lives of those we serve.

So, you must proudly charge what you know you're worth and make sure what you provide is well worth the price. In turn, you must gladly pay a good fee for the high-quality information, products, and services that enable you to achieve your goals and dreams. And, if you are to feel good about profiting from your good work, you must feel pleased to see others profit from theirs as well. It's true: the more you give, the more you can receive. But the opposite is true as well: the more you receive, the more you can give.

What You Think About Money Matters

When you're self-employed, the way you view money often determines how much of it you'll have, how difficult it will be to obtain, how you'll feel about the amount you make, and even how successful your business will be. Unfortunately, negative attitudes about money can prevent you from making as much of it as you might want. Here are eight dysfunctional attitudes about money, the myths that underlie them, the negative results they produce, and how you can both know if you have these attitudes and what you can do to turn them around.

1. Money Is Everything

Myth:	Signs:	Negative Results:	Needed Mental Shift:
Money buys everything: love, success, happiness.	Obsessing and worrying about how much or, more likely, how little money you have	• Poor decisions made out of fear • Failure to focus and niche your business • Inability to enjoy progress toward your goals	Money is a resource; it's not how much of it you have but how you use what you have that matters.

2. Money Is Evil

Myth:	Signs:	Negative Results:	Needed Mental Shift:
Money is the root of all evil.	Believing that people who have lots of money are ripping other people off Feeling ashamed, guilty, or tainted for making too much or too little money	• Chronic undercharging • Limited or marginal success • Feeling unsatisfied with whatever you achieve	Money is your reward for making a positive contribution to the lives of others.

3. Money Is Embarrassing

Myth:	Signs:	Negative Results:	Needed Mental Shift:
Money is a private matter; it's no one else's business.	Feeling uncomfortable asking or talking about money.	• Unclear contracts • Misunderstandings about fees and payment schedules • Collection problems	In doing business, people want and expect you to talk openly, clearly and comfortably about money.

4. Money Is a Mystery

Myth:	Signs:	Negative Results:	Needed Mental Shift:
Money is the result of luck, chance, or other forces over which an individual has little control.	Thinking money matters are complex and confusing; feeling uninterested, avoiding or ignoring money issues	• Feeling resentful of others' success • Money problems from not balancing your checkbook, keeping track of invoices or payments, not making tax payments, etc. • Never feeling secure or in control	Money is the return on activities you put in motion. It's a barometer that lets you know how you're doing and if you need to do something else.

5. Money Is Automatic

Myth:	Signs:	Negative Results:	Needed Mental Shift:
Money grows on trees.	Expecting to have money materialize from whatever you do and feeling puzzled and confused if it doesn't	• Frustration that your business doesn't "take off" • Feeling angry that you're not doing as well as others or as expected • Low self-esteem, diminishing self-confidence	Realizing that you need to plan, market, negotiate, invoice, track, and sometimes collect the money you earn from doing what others view as good work.

6. Money Is Hard to Come By

Myth:	Signs:	Negative Results:	Needed Mental Shift:
People don't like to part with their money.	Feeling that getting people to pay you and meet your price is like pulling teeth	• Undercharging • Resorting to manipulative selling • Adversarial financial negotiations • Feeling antagonistic toward your clients	People gladly pay for things they find valuable and worthwhile.

7. Money Comes from Misery

Myth:	Signs:	Negative Results:	Needed Mental Shift:
You shouldn't get paid for doing something you enjoy.	Feeling as if you never get to do the kind of work you really want to do or doing what you love as a "starving artist"	• Undercharging • Difficulty asking for money if you enjoy the work • Making whatever work you do difficult and unpleasant	People will gladly pay you for doing something you enjoy as long as it meets their needs, too.

8. Money Is Limited

Myth:	Signs:	Negative Results:	Needed Mental Shift:
There's not enough money to go around, so you've got to grab as much as you can and hold on to whatever you get.	Feeling highly competitive, hoarding money, spending as little as possible, agonizing over every purchase, feeling guilty when you spend money and thinking you lose whenever a competitor gains	• Your business can't grow. • Without spending money for useful services, equipment, and supplies, doing business becomes more difficult than need be. • You don't get to enjoy the fruits of your labor.	There's plenty of money to go around, and money spent wisely comes back to you multiplied.

So, get rid of your negative attitudes about money you earn honestly by meeting the needs of others. But give yourself the time you need to succeed.

Success Takes Time

It's amazing what we expect of ourselves. Most people who go out on their own anticipate they'll hit the pavement running. Often limited start-up funds demand that we began making a profit or at least break even almost immediately. But we forget that sometimes large corporations must run in the red for years before they become profitable. There's always a learning curve. That's why athletes go into training before competition. That's why stage productions have rehearsals. Since we're generally so poorly prepared to become our own boss, don't you think we, too, should plan for the inevitable learning curve of launching a new venture?

Sometimes what's called undercapitalization or mismanagement is actually the result of having too long a learning curve. On the payroll, you usually have the luxury of some on-the-job training. If you don't know what to do, usually someone will instruct you or provide training; or at least you can earn a salary while you learn on the job. Not so in your own business. There's no profit until you produce it. Nobody else pays for you to learn.

On a salaried job, getting your paycheck is only indirectly related to whether any actual income comes in from what you do during that particular week. In other words, if you are doing a research study for your employer, any income generated from the results of that study may be years away. Or if you are conducting in-house training for a company, the income the training will ultimately produce for the company will depend on whether the participants use the skills you taught them to boost their performance at some unspecified time in the future. Even if your students never do improve their performance and thereby the company never does profit from that training session, you will still have received your paycheck for having conducted it.

On your own, however, if you take six weeks to do a market-research study, there's no income. If you attend a training program to build your skills, you don't make any money that week. If you take off to learn a new software package, no one else pays the bills. Going out on your own can be very much like being the mother bird who must push her baby out of the nest so it can learn to fly. You've pushed yourself out of the secure nest of a paycheck. You've given yourself the opportunity to learn to fly. Just like the young bird, you have all the necessary equipment you need, but you've got to give yourself the time to learn to use it.

Fortunately, you can build a financial net for yourself so that, should you fall before you can get your wings under you, you can simply start again. You owe it to yourself to have a clear-cut source of income sufficient to survive on while you learn to fly. Such a cash cushion will make your inevitable learning curve less painful. We recommend a cushion for three to nine months of income.

At the same time, you can put yourself on a steady diet of consultants, tapes, books, workshops, and seminars in the particular areas of expertise you need. These will help shorten your learning curve. Ideally you will take advantage of as many of these resources as possible before going out on your own. But those who are most successful on their own always stay one step ahead of their next challenge by continuing to learn.

Finding a Cash Cushion

There are many ways to build up a cash security blanket. Here are just a few:

1. Start your business on the side while you still have a job. When it gets going, then you can leave the job.

2. Take a part-time job that will cover your basic expenses while you get your business under way.

3. Do temporary work until you have enough money coming in from your business.

4. If you're living with a partner, cut expenses and live off one salary while you start your business.

5. Use your savings or other sources of income—like retirement funds, a sabbatical, divorce settlements, or an inheritance—as a cushion.

6. Take out a second mortgage on your home or arrange to get a consumer line of credit such as some banks are now offering to very small businesses that enables you to borrow if, and only if, you need to. These loans are backed up with the equity in your home or other assets.

MENTAL SHIFT #12. FROM "HELP ME" TO "HOW CAN I HELP?": CREATING A NEW BASIS FOR BUILDING ALLIANCES

There are no passengers on spaceship Earth. Only crew.
BUCKMINSTER FULLER

We believe that success is always a joint venture. You can't do it alone. And you don't need to. Seeking out and asking for help when you need it are basic to success at anything you do. Just because you're on your own doesn't mean you have to do everything yourself. In fact, research shows that those who are most successful on their own make heavy use of consultants, mentors, and experts. They are willing to pay for the information and expertise they need. They also hire people to help them carry out aspects of their business they know little about or are too busy to handle.

Sandra McKnight is an excellent example of how successfully self-employed individuals surround themselves with the expertise and support they need. When Sandra decided to work for herself as a speech and diction coach, she realized she didn't know a thing about business. So she began taking classes and talking with other professionals who were in private practice.

"I don't feel like I'm in business by myself," she told us. "Although I started out alone, I now have a marketing expert to guide me, whose courses I've taken and who I can call whenever an emergency arises. I have a sales trainer, a lawyer, an accountant, and a lot of friends who are self-employed. I'm an expert at what I do and that's my part, but I feel like this is their business, too. I'm on my own but I'm not alone. My success is their success."

Sandra's attitude illustrates a significant mental shift you need to make in building alliances and gaining support once you get out on your own. It's a shift many people miss as a result of their paycheck mentality. In many ways the payroll system resembles the family structure in which siblings compete for favors and attention from their parents. On the payroll, employees often compete with one another in a similar fashion, trying to impress their boss and win his or her favor and support. On your own, however, building alliances and contacts is not usually a matter of winning someone's favor. It's more a matter of doing someone a favor.

Sandra, for example, didn't approach her mentors and advisers with her hand out. In some cases, she went to them with cash in hand, willing to pay for their expertise. At other times she exchanged services or otherwise discovered how she can reciprocate to help those who help her succeed as well. And in all cases she came across as a competent professional, someone who has much to offer.

A marriage and family counselor we'll call Mark also needed help to get his private practice under way. But his payroll mentality prevented him from getting the support he needed. He was hoping to get referrals from pediatricians. He had contacted several, telling them about his special methods for helping children deal with the traumas of divorce. "I tried to impress them with what I could do," he told us. But in each case he got a cold shoulder, even though he was certain many of the doctors' patients would benefit from his services.

Since we knew a pediatrician, we suggested he contact her. Several weeks later we ran into that pediatrician and asked if Mark had contacted her. "Oh yes," she said in an exasperated tone. "I get one of those calls almost every day." Curious, we asked what type of calls she meant. "Oh," she explained, "someone who calls to tell me what a great job he or she could do for my patients. I guess they see my practice as a happy hunting ground."

We asked her if she ever needed to refer a child out for counseling. She told us, "I refer out a lot. But I'm not a referral agency. I refer to my colleagues, other professionals who consider me to be part of their team. We refer to each other."

Over the years, we've heard many similar stories. But here's something you can do to make sure you don't inadvertently fall into this version of paycheck thinking. The moment you think about something you need that someone else could provide, immediately ask yourself, "What can I do for them? How could I help them?" But, you may argue, "I'm just starting out, or I'm just a . . . How could I help them?" But don't believe it! You have something valuable to offer. That's why you're on your own.

Let's take Mark as an example. Yes, he was just starting his practice, so he didn't have a lot of patients yet whom he could refer to a pediatrician, although he will when he's successful. But he does need to have pediatric backup right now in case an emergency arises with a future patient. And he does have a special approach to helping children deal effectively with divorce. So he could print up a small booklet for divorcing parents on how to help their children accept the changes of divorce and provide these booklets free of charge to pediatricians for their waiting rooms.

In fact, before doing the booklets Mark could call pediatricians and tell them about his plans for the booklet and ask what information their clients would most like to have. Or he could print up a booklet for his future clients on what to ask their pediatrician when their child has physical symptoms during the process of divorce. Again he could quote or feature local pediatricians in his booklet.

Mark could also interview pediatricians for an article he would write about the role of the pediatrician in helping families handle divorce. The article could feature and quote leading pediatricians in the community. Or he could pull together a panel of pediatricians to speak about the health implications of divorce to the local chapter of marriage and family counselors. The possibilities are endless, once he shifts his thinking from "How can I get them to help me?" to "How can I help them?"

This one shift transforms you from a beggar, supplicant, indigent, or struggling newcomer into a professional colleague who brings a lot to offer. The more you get going for yourself, the more people want to be part of what you've got going. As we said before, business is not charity. Doing business is about benefiting from helping others benefit. So ask for help by finding ways to help. For additional information about getting help when you need it, see chapter 4.

With a New Outlook It Gets Better and Better

If you've already had concerns about making it on your own, this chapter may make success sound like an awful lot more work. And it's true: at first, making it on your own may feel like you're pulling a very large wagon up a very long, very steep hill. Actually, however, it's like riding a bicycle. At first, you've got to exert considerable energy just to get it going, but it gets better. Once you get started it gets better and better. You can stop pumping so hard and ride along, only occasionally having to pump up your efforts to keep yourself moving.

Like riding a bicycle, the initial effort to get yourself under way on your own is usually considerable. It may consume you day in and day out for months or even years. It may seem that everything that could possibly go wrong does, along with a thousand other things you would have thought could not possibly happen. During the initial start-up period, people sometimes feel that this isn't what they bargained for. You may ask yourself, "Who needs this?" And the answer, of course, is no one . . . except those who want to succeed at what they've set out to do.

On a job, your job description limits your turf and defines what you can and cannot be called upon to do. When pressed to go beyond the limits of what you normally do, you can justifiably say, "That's not my job." Although people sometimes find these turf boundaries restrictive, such limits nonetheless help make a job more manageable. They also seem only fair because no matter how much harder you work, you still get paid the same. And once people see that you're a hard worker, they'll probably give you more to do.

When you're on your own, of course, having people bring you more work to do is exactly what you want, but suddenly there's no job description to protect your sanity. Suddenly everything is your job. You may be called upon to do anything at any moment. There probably won't be any average day at first. As the free-lance publicist Kim Freilich points out, "You no longer have to just be good at what you do; you have to be good at everything."

Even if you do hire help, ultimately you're still responsible. Your client doesn't care if your supplier was late or your child was ill or your secretary made a mistake. You have to handle whatever comes up. As Cindy Butler, a professional shopper and fashion consultant, discovered in running her business, Gone Shopping, "If you don't do it, it won't get done." Even though the more you're able to do the more you get in return, this demand for versatility and unlimited accountability usually seems overwhelming at first.

But have you ever noticed that human beings are experts at turning the novel into the mundane? We're like vacuum cleaners; we devour experience. We take in and process everything new we come in contact with and quickly turn it into the ordinary. Remember, for example, how complex learning to drive seemed the first time you got behind the wheel? But after only a few months, what could have been more ordinary than driving somewhere? You didn't even think about it anymore. We talk, eat, put on makeup, plan the day, listen to the news . . . all while driving.

So it is with being on our own. When unfettered by the limitations of job descriptions and organizational rules and regulations, most people find they can gradually take on more and more with less and less stress. Because you work when you want to, the way you want to, it's most likely that you'll find ways to become optimally efficient. What once took days eventually takes only hours. What was once difficult becomes easy.

Success Creates Its Own Momentum

In other words, you won't have to continually put up with the incredible level of exertion that going out on your own requires at first. Success begets success. You'll discover that the more you do, the more you can do. The more you can do, the more you get to do. You'll surprise and delight yourself. It's a delicious circle: the more you do to get work, the more work you get; the more work you get, the better your work gets; the better your work gets, the more work you get—and so on and so on.

If you have something to offer that people need and you make sure they know about you, the day will come when suddenly, like magic, your business will click in and take on a life of its own. When that breakthrough comes, you will be able to catch your breath and your business will keep running. In fact, the more efficient you become, the less and less time you will spend to earn more and more. If you wish, you may even find the time and energy to take on and create other things with the funds generated from your business.

Earlier we mentioned how the artist Ed Crystal has been able to do that with the picture-framing business he started. Once he got the business going, he could afford to spend several days a week pursuing his lifelong desire to be an artist. Ultimately his framing business provided the funds to open an art gallery showcasing his paintings.

When we first went out on our own, we agonized over the tremendous amount of effort that went into submitting just one proposal or getting just one newspaper article written about us or stimulating even one person to take our calls or write just ten pages for an article. There were times we thought we must be crazy to think this business would work. It didn't seem cost-effective. It didn't seem practical. It didn't seem worth the effort. All that kept us going was how much we wanted to accomplish our goals. There was certainly no indication we ever would.

But each year it became easier, and then one day we reached a turning point, a breakthrough. We noticed that our phone was ringing regularly through no direct effort of our own. People were eager to take our calls. We could prepare a proposal in no time flat. And while our first book took four years to write, we wrote three new books in one year. We had generated so much momentum from those years of effort that we were sailing along—riding the wind, so to speak. We had crested the hill, and it was all downhill on the other side.

On your own, you'll find that your rewards increase in direct proportion to your cumulative effort. It's just the reverse of being on a job. As an employee, you get a reward immediately whether you produce much or not. Your salary carries you through the learning curve. But then no matter how much you produce ultimately, you run into a limit on what you can get in return.

On your own, while the initial efforts are great, the initial rewards are small. No one carries you through the rough times, but once you've made it, there's no limit to what you can reap from what you've produced. There is no glass ceiling, no plateau, no salary scale.

And ultimately, as a result of your sustained effort over time, your business will become what we call self-sustaining—operating under its own momentum. At that point, you'll be able to stop pumping so hard and coast for a while. In "Does It Have to Take So Long and Be So Hard?" in chapter 7, we talk about what determines when you can anticipate that this breakthrough will occur. Until then, give yourself a chance to get there.

The Suffering Is Temporary

So, rest assured that you won't have to keep pedaling madly year after year after year, although some people mistakenly do this. They think that since it took so much effort to get going, you can't ever let up, but actually as the business develops, little by little you can begin allowing the business to carry you and itself.

You will need to pay attention to the momentum at all times, of course—because, again, just as in riding a bicycle or driving a car, when the momentum begins to wane, or as you approach a hill, you'll have to start pedaling again. You'll have to put on the gas. Not doing this is another way people get in trouble. They get used to things sailing along and forget that they're still the engine that drives the business. If you catch the slowdowns soon enough, however, you won't need to exhaust yourself to get things moving again. A little bit of effort will be all that's required to keep you going at a reasonable, steady pace.

Once you've made these twelve mental shifts from a paycheck mentality to a profit mentality, you'll find that making it on your own is no longer an illusive glimmer to long for or struggle through. It's reality to enjoy now—for you and for millions of others. You can breathe easily. From this perspective, you can see where you're going. You're ready to take charge with confidence and move forward step by step in the direction you want to go.

MANAGING EVERYTHING
THAT NEEDS TO BE DONE

———————————— ▪ ————————————

We are told that talent creates its own opportunities. But it sometimes seems that intense desire creates not only its own opportunities, but its own talents.   ERIC HOFFER

A s your own boss you no longer have a job: you've got three jobs. You've got to get the business, do the business, and run the business. And heaven help the person who tries to do each of these as the full-time job it could easily become. To survive and thrive on your own, you've got to make time for everything that needs to be done and still have some left over for yourself.

Is it any wonder that managing everything that needs to be done is one of the top problems self-employed individuals mention year after year? Their concerns range from making sure they get to work and making sure they stick to business to being able to stop working at a reasonable hour with the work always beckoning to be done.

Nonetheless, while doing it all may seem impossible, it can be done. Thousands of successfully self-employed people are not only finding the time and energy to do it, but they're enjoying themselves in the process. In fact, some are even working fewer hours than when they were on a paycheck. Judy Wunderlich, for example, wanted to stay home to raise her two small children. She was able to make $200,000 a year working twenty-five hours a week in her home-based employment agency for graphics personnel. And you may recall that the instructional designer Mike Greer ended up making three times the money he earned working for someone else while working three fewer hours each day.

How is that possible? That's what this section is about. You'll discover you can have the time of your life and to some extent even get your business to run itself.

3

Having the Time of
Your Life

Never before have we had so little time in which to do so much.
FRANKLIN D. ROOSEVELT

TO HAVE THE TIME of your life. Isn't that what we all want . . . to feel that we own the time that constitutes our lives? In many ways, your time is your life. What you do with your time is what you do with your life. In this sense, being on your own is the greatest gift you can give yourself. Because the moment you step into the world of self-employment you own your time.

What you do with every minute of your day is up to you. Of course, strictly speaking that's always true. But having a job is like putting a mortgage on your time, and thereby on your life. With a job, you've agreed to be some specific place doing some specific thing for the bulk of your waking day, five or more days a week.

While you might think financial gain is the primary reason people choose to become their own boss, research shows that the majority of self-employed individuals don't go out on their own for the money. According to a poll by United Group Information Services, only 3 percent of small-business owners do what they do for financial gain. The other 97 percent say they're on their own because they want to be in charge. In other words, it's more freedom, not more money, that lures us away from the paycheck.

Our research also shows that *freedom* is the number-one reason people decide to go out on their own and is what they enjoy most about being their own boss. And it's no wonder freedom plays such a role in why we want to be on our own. Louis Harris Associates reports that leisure time in America shrank from 26.2 hours a week in 1973 to only 16.2 hours. Almost a third of the people in the survey feel rushed on a daily basis while two thirds feel rushed at times. Even weekends are no longer our own. An R. H. Bruskin survey of 1,008 people found that the typical adult spends fourteen weekend hours on chores. And, according to Bruskin, nine out of ten people feel no more energetic on Sunday evening than they did on Friday evening. One result of these time pressures is that increasing numbers of Americans are stressed out. *Prevention Magazine*'s "Prevention Index" claims that 63 percent of Americans suffer from frequent stress—up from 55 percent.

But, you may be wondering, is it *really* any better when you're self-employed? After all, there's more to do than ever. Actually, we find the successful self-employed individual works sixty-one hours per week. That's about equivalent to the workweek of many corporate workers. So, does that mean we're simply trading one set of time pressures for another? Have we simply escaped from one taskmaster to become indentured to another—our own work?

The good news is that for most people the answer is no! Self-employed individuals who work from home, for example, free up at least four weeks a year that they once spent stuck going to and from work in rush-hour traffic. This extra time acts like a cushion. Even though many self-employed individuals continue to grapple with managing their time, they tell us they are still less stressed than they were when they were employed.

They claim, and research confirms, that the more control you have over what you do and how you do it, the less stress you experience. So even though your days may be as high pressure and full as ever, because what you do with your life each day is now up to you, your situation no longer feels impossible or hopeless. Time pressures become a problem to solve, not a burden to bear.

And that's what this chapter is about. It's about claiming your time once you're your own boss so you can take charge of what you do with your life. It's about knowing what you're doing so you can direct yourself competently and thereby use the precious hours of each day in the ways you wish. It's about acquiring a new attitude toward time, an attitude you couldn't have when your time was mortgaged to someone else. It's about approaching time as a resource you can draw upon and spend as you choose, not as a constraint you have to live with or an enemy you must struggle against. This chapter is about learning to enjoy the newfound freedom of being on your own.

MAKING TIME FOR IT ALL

The happy person is one who sees all things as possibilities.
LEO BUSCAGLIA

"I just don't have the time!" How often do you say that, even now—or especially now—that you're on your own? In the fast-paced high-pressure world of supporting ourselves, even though we are now free to use our time as we choose, it may still be hard to find time to be with the ones we love, to create the true masterpieces that live in our hearts, or to pursue the dreams tucked away in our souls. After all, now we have to do it all, even down to getting the paper clips and dusting the filing cabinets. It's easy to simply impose the same inflexible deadlines and rigid time pressures on ourselves as were once imposed on us by our employers. Why do we do that?

Often it's simply a matter of conditioning. It's the same reason that a seven-ton eleven-foot-tall circus elephant stands passively chained to a small metal stake in the ground. Although such a powerful creature weighs about as much as a Greyhound bus and most certainly could easily pull up the stake, it doesn't even try to break loose. Because it learned at a very early age, when it was much smaller, that no matter how hard it tugged and pulled on the chain, it wasn't strong enough to get away. So eventually it stopped trying to get free . . . forever.

This is the same conditioning process that limits the way we spend our time once we finally get out on our own. We become so accustomed to believing that we have to let our work and other obligations run our lives that even when we're free to run things the way we want, we continue to let force of habit call the shots.

Another reason we don't take charge of our time is that on our own, we may be even harder on ourselves than any boss would be. Driven by fear of failure or blind ambition, you may find yourself enslaved to the tyranny of the clock, working into the wee hours of the night and right on through the weekend. I know that I, Sarah, certainly did. I was terrified that I wouldn't have enough clients, so to quell my fears I just kept working. I thought somehow if I worked unceasingly I'd have to succeed. It was actually years before I realized—thanks to a dear friend and colleague named Richard Nadeau—that I would be just as successful working more reasonable hours.

When Richard went into private practice as a psychotherapist, he, too, worked madly to assure his success, cramming his days with clients, his nights with groups, and his weekends with workshops. But eventually he began talking about his growing unwillingness to work morning, noon, and night. He began setting limits on the number of hours and days he would work. He told me he wasn't willing to give up his life for success.

"When I first went out on my own," he recalls, "I had a feast-or-famine attitude. I think sometimes we're like petrified little children. There's this fear that if we say no we'll be out of business the next day. My great terror was that all my clients would conspire to cancel their appointments at one time. I feared that somehow these thirty unrelated individuals who didn't even know one another would all decide to cancel. It was ridiculous, of course. But I used to have to take out my appointment calendar regularly just to check out the objective reality and assure myself that I wasn't going into Chapter Eleven."

I had the good fortune to watch Richard summon the courage to cut back his time and see him become even more in demand. I watched him raise his fees so he could work fewer hours. I watched him pass up lucrative opportunities to do workshops so he could enjoy more free time. And I liked what I saw. While he was working less, he was earning more. I became committed to doing the same. And while it was frightening at first, I gradually developed an entirely new outlook on time that has truly put me in charge of my life. We invite you to consider adopting this new outlook on time yourself.

A New Outlook on Time

Instead of thinking of time in terms of twenty-four-hour blocks into which we can never quite fit everything that needs to be done, what if we approached it as an endless, flowing supply that never runs out? Actually, there's always plenty of time. Time is a bountiful resource! We have all the time in the world. In fact, as long as we live, all we have is time. Every day, every minute, we get more of it . . . no matter what we did with our previous allocation. Time is totally democratic. Every day everyone gets a fresh supply. Whether we waste it, savor it, manage it, or invest it, we still get a steady flow of time. And once you're on your own, your time is like a brand-new shopping bag you receive every morning. As you shop your way through the day, you can fill your bag with all the good things you like, taking some of this and some of that, sampling whatever seems most valuable or most enjoyable to you.

But, you may say, that's not how my day goes! It's true that sometimes you get up in the morning only to discover that your bag is already filled with the leftovers from yesterday. Or perhaps you awaken to find that someone else has filled your bag with things *they* want you to do. Or maybe, you've accepted a standing order, so you wake up to the same, dull routines every day.

Or if you approach time like a cafeteria line and take some of everything, you'll undoubtedly live with a chronically overstuffed day. And if you're willing to take potluck, you can end up not liking a lot of what is dumped into your life. But now that you're on your own, you're in a position to be the one who decides how your day goes. You, and only you, decide who puts what into your day. If you don't like what gets in, you can dump it out and say, "No more!" You can take charge and put first things first.

It's as simple and as difficult as that. While there's an endless supply of time, it can't be preserved. You can't make more. You can't buy more. What you waste or invest poorly is lost forever. As teacher Marva Collins tells her students, "This day has been given to you fresh and clear to either use or throw away."

For Naomi Stephan, a career counselor, this discovery came early one morning: "When I first went out on my own, I used to answer the telephone at every hour of the day and night. Then one morning I woke up and realized I don't have to answer the phone whenever it rings! I went out and bought a two-line phone, and now I put on the answering machine when I don't want to be interrupted!" You can do the same with any aspect of your work and your life. You can start living according to your priorities.

Putting First Things First

Decide what you want, decide what you are willing to exchange for it. Establish your priorities and get to work.
H. L. Hunt, Founder, Hunt Oil Co.

If life is a vast ocean and time is the vessel in which we journey through life, how would you describe your journey now that you're on your own—or about to be? Are you traveling at the helm of an ocean liner in command of the seas on a clearly charted course? Or are you on a sailboat drifting about on the winds of life—as the wind blows, so your day goes?

We've found that the more successful you become, the more challenging managing the varied aspects of your journey through time becomes. At times we've felt as if we were traveling in a leaky rowboat, pushing and pulling, struggling and fighting against the impossible demands of time. Sometimes we've felt as if we weren't even in the boat anymore but were hanging onto the sides trying to ride out each day's storm.

Perhaps you've felt like that at times, too. Because everything is up to you, it feels as though everything needs to be done right now. This is especially true when you're first getting started or when things are more difficult to get under way than you anticipated. But it's also true no matter how successful you become. How do you put first things first when everything seems to need to come first? Where do you begin? What can be done later? And what doesn't need to be done at all?

"Sometimes there's so much to be done that I just don't do anything!"

one person told us. We know that feeling. But there is one overriding princi-ple that can get you out of this dilemma again and again. This one principle puts you in charge. When we follow this principle, things work. When we don't, life gets out of hand again.

The first person to uncover this principle was the nineteenth-century economist Vilfredo Pareto. Pareto found that a small proportion of any ac-tivity produces a majority of the results. His discovery is now called the 80/20 Rule or the Pareto Principle, and if you apply this rule to your life, you will have much more of everything you want and much less of everything you don't. Examples of this 80/20 Rule abound in every aspect of life. Think about this: Don't you wear 20 percent of your clothes 80 percent of the time? Don't 20 percent of the people in your life create 80 percent of your prob-lems? Don't 20 percent of your calls or letters or projects produce 80 percent of the results? Don't you use 20 percent of your files 80 percent of the time? That's the 80/20 Rule at work, and it applies to virtually everything you do.

In other words, for better or worse about one fifth of everything in your life produces about four fifths of the results. That means a lot of what we think we need to do doesn't need to be done. It means that if we can identify what works in our lives, what produces the results we want, we can let go of the rest. We can get more of what we want and less of what we don't for much less time, money, and energy.

Do you find that hard to believe? We did. But two things happened in our lives that convinced us it just might be true. First, when we decided to go out on our own, we wanted to work from home instead of renting office space for our respective businesses. At the time, however, we were living in a 750-square-foot apartment. So working from home meant we'd have to move into larger quarters. We bought a new house and began packing. Our son's room was filled with toys, most of which he no longer played with, so we planned to give away many of his older toys. But he threw a fit over each toy we planned to discard. Each one was a special treasure he *had* to keep.

So we devised a plan. We packed all the older toys into a very large box, and when we moved we put that box in the basement of our new home, as-suring him that any time he wanted those toys, he could always go down and get them. Guess what? Two years later that box had yet to be opened.

We thought, as perhaps you are thinking, "Well, that's just kids, right? Adults have surely outgrown something like that!" But we couldn't overlook this as a childish phenomenon. It was too similar to something that had hap-pened to me, Sarah, two years before we moved. I was working as a special-ist for a federal child-care program when our agency was moved from one office building to another. I carefully boxed up all the outstanding stacks of material on my desk: correspondence, in-house memos, phone messages, pro-jects I was working on, and so forth. These papers were so important to me at the time that I decided to transport this box to the new office building in my own car.

As in any office move, things became pretty hectic, so when I got to my new office, I set the box in the corner while I addressed the urgencies of the moment. I told myself I would get to them as soon as possible. Well, two years later, when I was clearing out my office to go out on my own, I found that box, packing tape still carefully sealed. Over that time, no one had called or written or dropped by to ask me about any of what I had thought to be such important matters addressed in those materials.

Interesting, isn't it? In reality, we simply don't need to attend to much of what comes into our lives. Of course, there are many things that we do need to focus on, but they are the few—the vital few—among the trivial many. As self-employed individuals we truly don't have the luxury of relating to the trivial many. We can't earn a living and succumb to bureaucratic inefficiency. In fact, our ability to streamline and do things efficiently is what enables us to survive and thrive. It gives us the edge to get things done more quickly and proficiently than the larger bureaucratic organization.

Quadruple Your Results Following the 80/20 Rule

Just imagine your life without the 80 percent of things that are bogging you down and leading you nowhere. Just imagine what it would be like if you could identify the 20 percent of things in your life that provide you with 80 percent of your satisfaction and results. What would happen if you were doing *those* things 80 percent of your time? It would be like finding six extra hours a day! Three extra file drawers! A gigabyte of additional memory for your computer! And perhaps a 25 percent increase in your income!

That's exactly what happened to us when we decided several years ago to 80/20 our lives. We sat down and asked ourselves, "Which of our efforts provide us with 80 percent of our enjoyment in life? Which efforts produce 80 percent of our profits?" Slowly, piece by piece, we began eliminating the unrewarding 80 percent of hassles and trivia that used to fill our lives.

We had a gigantic garage sale to free our home from the many things we owned but rarely used. We emptied our closets of clothes we rarely wore. We cleared out our overstuffed file cabinets. We reorganized our business to focus only on those aspects we found rewarding and profitable. We began spending more time with the people who support and nurture us.

We began to truly put first things first in our lives, and in so doing we traded in the leaky rowboat we'd been clinging to for a gleaming ocean liner, and we took the helm. Subsequently, we've discovered that most of the successful self-employed people we interview have also learned to apply the 80/20 Rule, although they don't always call it that.

For example, the career counselor Naomi Stephan told us she found being on her own a real juggling act until she started to ask herself, "What is the core of my business? What am I in business to do? What has always brought me the most business?" She decided that was what she needed to concentrate on. Wellness researcher Dean Allen finds things work best when he follows one simple rule: "I don't plan anything I don't want to do, and I don't do anything I don't want to plan."

Chellie Campbell, owner of Cameron Diversified Management, told us, "I've gotten to the point now that I only do those things that are income producing or fun—preferably both. For example, I don't have time for negative, difficult clients. I only work with positive, bright people who also want to be successful and therefore don't have time for hassles."

Perhaps when you were working for a paycheck you couldn't run your life like that. Your job was to handle whatever came across your desk. But now that you're on your own, you can absolutely make room for those things that work and drop out those that don't. The three things we did to 80/20 our lives are listed below. Since we've taken these steps, our business and our income have increased, yet we have more free time and we're certainly enjoying our lives more.

How to 80/20 Your Life

Work on purpose. What motivated you to go out on your own? What do you want to accomplish? Why are you doing all this? Whether it's to be with your children, become a millionaire, or express your creative instincts, your reasons give purpose to your day, and this sense of purpose can enable you to know where you're going and to put that first in your life.

Clear out your backlog. If your desk, files, cabinets, and calendar are filled with things that don't relate to your purpose, you won't have the time or the space to put first things first. Therefore, once you know your purpose, and before you take another step, you must clear the other things out of your life to make room for what matters most.

Schedule for results. Once you know where you're going and you've cleared the way, setting goals will take you where you want to go, but only if you bring them down to the minute. Leaving your goals on a notepad in a drawer somewhere puts them out of sight and out of mind. You've got to get them onto your calendar and let them become the focus of what you do every day.

Working on Purpose

Nothing can resist a human will that stakes its heart upon a purpose.
BENJAMIN DISRAELI

If there's no one expecting you to get to work, if there's no job description or company policy prescribing what you're to do and when, if there's no guarantee of a paycheck—then why get up and get to work on any particular day? Why today? Why not some other day? Or sometime later today? How do you decide what to do when you can do anything you want, and when do you start when there's no particular time to start? When do you quit if you can quit anytime you want to, especially if you're the only person who'll know when you're goofing off.

Clearly, when you're on your own, if you want to get any work done, you've got to want to do it. You have to want to do it badly enough that you actually will, because no one else is going to make you do it. In other words, you've got to have a compelling reason to do it. There has to be some purpose for doing it. Otherwise you probably won't get around to it.

I (Sarah) remember when I was working for the government, that I used to wake up in the morning and begin mentally planning my day while I was getting ready for work. Usually I looked forward to getting a lot done. Anticipating all the things I would accomplish felt good. But before I knew it, the day was over and I was wondering where it had gone. Somehow I never got around to most of the things I planned to do—the things I most wanted to do. I was always getting sidetracked by other people's demands and expectations. And that didn't feel good. My life was moving, but not in the direction I wanted it to. Weeks melted into months, months into years. And although I'd done many things, I hadn't done what I wanted to do.

When I went out on my own I thought things would be different. After all, now I was my own boss. I could call the shots! I was surprised that somehow I still found myself at the end of the day not having done most of the things I'd intended to do. I still wasn't directing my life toward what I wanted to accomplish. I was still responding to the events of the day, and those events were determining the course of my life. I was disappointed and frustrated because my own agendas still seemed to end up on the back burner. I wasn't working on purpose.

The Power of Knowing Why You're Doing What You're Doing

Until recently it made little sense for most people to spend much time dwelling on the inner purpose of their lives. Their options were more limited by the circumstances of their birth and upbringing. In fact, having deep personal desires often simply led to a life of frustration and disappointment because most people were destined to lead "realistic" lives. Today, however, that has changed. Now we have the opportunity to pursue our inner callings. In fact, if we listen carefully, we each have something we're working toward in this life, some reason for our being here, something that calls on us to use our unique talents and skills to the fullest. We call this reason for being our life purpose.

Having a chance to pursue your life purpose may be the reason you decided to go out on your own in the first place. In talking with other proprietors and entrepreneurs, we find that often their decisions to go out on their own arose from an inner sense of needing to make a change so that their lives would be more fulfilling and rewarding. Usually it's this sense of purpose that propels them to work long enough, hard enough, and eagerly enough to make it. Just knowing what you want to get away from is not usually enough; you have to know what you're working toward.

And even then, once you get out on your own the pressures of self-employment can divert you once again from doing what you intend to do with your life. Surprisingly, however, getting clear about your purpose is the most powerful self-management tool available to you.

Knowing what you want to do and how you want to do it need not lead to frustration, as it did in the days when someone else was directing you. In fact, now that you're on your own, in order to put first things first in your life, you have to know what you want to come first. You have to commit yourself to putting it there. Defining what you intend to do in your life and how you want it to be is no longer a luxury. It's a survival tool.

Without such clarity, on your own you'll probably always have a hard time with time. You'll have a hard time with choices. You won't know what needs to be done today and what can wait until tomorrow. You'll agonize over what to keep and what to throw away. You'll be confused about which advice to follow, whose demands to respond to, which role to play, what direction to take.

When you're living your life in accord with a sense of inner purpose, however, not only will you find making decisions much easier; you'll also feel a greater sense of gratification and fulfillment from everything you do, even the more unpleasant aspects of being on your own. You'll feel that you're making a difference, a contribution.

Without a sense of purpose, you may feel that you're spinning your wheels, going nowhere. You have nothing to aim for. And when you aim at nothing, you hit it every time. Keeping your purpose clearly in mind, however, gives you something to get out of bed for. It keeps you going when things get rough. As the philosopher Friedrich Nietzsche said, "He who has a why can bear almost any how." Working on purpose also provides the foundation for setting goals and priorities and for making critical choices throughout the day. You'll be astounded at what you'll be able to do and how quickly it will get done. We certainly were.

Up until the time we clarified and committed ourselves to our purpose, we had been going in many directions, searching for what would pay off. We'd try first one thing and then another. We kept thinking that if we could just get something profitable under way we'd be able to pursue what we really wanted to do. Once we got clear, however, on what that was—that is, once we knew our purpose—that's when our efforts really began to pay off. The results were dramatic. Suddenly we knew which projects to pursue and which to pass by. We knew which expenses would be worthwhile and which would not. We knew what needed to take priority on any given day.

Within one year we accomplished more than we had in the previous seven years we'd been out on our own. In a year of working on purpose, we completed three books, designed three seminars, and produced a line of audiotapes—all because we began working on purpose. Now at the end of each day, we usually have the wonderful feeling of knowing that we like where we are, that we're getting where we want to go, and that we'll love it when we get there. You can feel that way by working on purpose.

Three Steps to Getting on Purpose

If you don't feel that you're working on purpose, you can start today. You can start working *with intention,* with a desired end result in mind. You can begin to live your life by design as opposed to by accident, deliberately as opposed to by happenstance, with determination and resolve instead of from circumstance. Doing so will give new meaning and significance to what you do and to those things you must endure along the way.

Commit, or recommit, yourself to finding and relentlessly pursuing your life with purpose in mind. Chances are you already know what the greater purpose of your effort is. It may be something you've been wanting to do since your childhood. Perhaps it's what you've always been good at or what you've done in whatever spare moments you've had. It's probably related closely to the reason you've decided to go out on your own.

If you don't immediately know what will give purpose to your work, all you need to do is listen closely to your inner desires and dreams. They are like a beacon leading you directly to what you need to be doing not only to find fulfillment in your work but also to guarantee your financial success. Ask yourself the following three questions and listen patiently and quietly for the answers.

1. What would you be doing if you could do anything you wanted to without concern for the money it would produce? At the heart of this question lies the secret to your ultimate success. At first it may appear that your answer has nothing to do with your work. Like Bill Jack you may say, "I'd just like to play tennis all day." Or like Rita Tateel you might say, "I'd love to watch TV, go to the movies, and give parties." Or perhaps like Geneen Gardner you'd say, "I'd travel throughout the world." Or, as Janet Belinkoff might say, "I'd just spend my time playing with animals."

Just think about this. When Bill Jack asked himself this question, he was suffering from cancer. He didn't know how much more time he had to live. He decided he was going to do only work he found gratifying, so he quit his management position and began teaching tennis. Fortunately, he recovered from his illness, and his purpose became to teach others to enjoy the sport he finds so fulfilling.

When Rita Tateel asked herself what she would do if she could do whatever she wanted to do, she decided to open Celebrity Source, a company providing celebrities for fund-raising events. She now finds that "ninety percent of what I enjoy outside of work is now part of my work, even watching TV and going to parties." And yet her work is important. She helps many worthwhile charities obtain hundreds of thousands of dollars each year.

When Geneen Gardner asked herself what she loved doing most, she shifted the nature of her business to organizing and conducting educational travel tours. She took groups to the Soviet Union before glasnost and continues to conduct tours that bring people from foreign cultures closer together. When social worker Janet Belinkoff began feeling burned out on her job, all she wanted to do was play with animals. Now she and her husband own and operate a successful pet-sitting service.

These propreneurs are but a few of the many who have discovered that maximum performance comes from maximum enjoyment. So if you're in a business that doesn't relate to what you most want to do, begin rethinking and refocusing your business to be more in line with what will give meaning and purpose to your work. You'll be surprised at how much more easily you'll be able to motivate yourself and how quickly your success rate will rise.

And that's not all. Once you're working on purpose and you're doing what you really want to do, anytime you don't know what to do, anytime you feel like quitting, anytime you're tired and discouraged, anytime you wish there were someone to tell you what to do—all you need to do is remind yourself of why you're doing all this and you'll find the inner wisdom, resolve, and desire you need to continue.

In his book *Creative Work* Edmond Bordeaux Szekely quotes Patanjali, the founder of the ancient Indian practice of yoga, as saying "When you are inspired by some great purpose, some extraordinary project, all your thoughts break their bonds: your mind transcends limitations, your consciousness expands in every direction, and you find yourself in a new, great, and wonderful world. Dormant forces, faculties, and talents become alive, and you discover yourself to be a greater person by far than you ever dreamed your-self to be." If you're not sure what your life purpose is and what kind of work would help you pursue it, refer to our book *Finding Your Perfect Work*, listed in the resources at the end of this chapter.

2. What's the point of what you're doing? Why does what you do for a liv-ing matter? This is certainly a good question to ask in order to successfully market your business. But it's also at the heart of knowing the purpose of your work. If your work doesn't matter, why should you get up and do it? Why should you undertake all the challenges involved? Whatever your rea-son for being in business, it needs to matter—to you—and to your clients or customers. It needs to make a positive difference both to you and to others.

At first you might think, "Oh, I just do . . ." But if you have any clients and customers now, or if someone has ever paid you to do what you do, it means that what you're doing does matter to someone. It's important to them or they wouldn't be paying you their hard-earned money. Your work doesn't need to be glamorous or extravagant to be important. Peggy Glenn *just* did typing for her customers. But they were so pleased with her work that they brought her flowers and candy for doing a good job for them on time. Chel-lie Campbell *just* does bookkeeping, but her service gives the business owners she works with a restful night's sleep knowing their finances are in order. She's even rescued some clients from the brink of financial disaster. James Mc-Callister *just* cleans carpets, but the carpets he cleans not only make a differ-ence in the quality of life for his customers, they also affect the bottom line of these business establishments by making them more presentable.

Think about how what you do has an impact on the lives of those you work with and how those results have an impact on the world. Don't be con-cerned about becoming too grandiose in understanding your purpose. Al-though what you do may seem small at first, as you think more about it, never forget it's all the little things that collectively shape life's ultimate reality.

3. Why is it important that you're the one who's doing what you do? Why should someone turn to you instead of to someone else who does something similar? This is another important question to ask in order to market yourself successfully. But it's also an important question for clarifying your purpose. Your background, skills, talents, aptitudes, and personality are unique. No one else has exactly what you have to offer. In an industrial society, manu-facturing processes were built around being able to stick somebody at any given work station. But even in industry today, management has discovered, sometimes painfully, that one body cannot necessarily be replaced by another. The skill, experience, know-how, and makeup of each human being is unique; each individual can contribute something that no one else can in quite the same way.

There is no future in any *job*. The future is in the *person* who holds it. This is particularly true in today's information and service society, where what you're most likely selling is your unique expertise. For example, Sarah's unique gift may well be her enthusiasm. She has the ability to see the big picture of what could be and to get people excited enough about what's possible to get busy creating it. Paul has an ability to analyze and make sense out of complex and apparently contradictory information. He can make useful what might otherwise be intimidating.

Bill Jack knows how to make learning tennis fun. Rita Tateel is an expert at linking up people who need help with one another. Geneen Gardner can make the foreign and unfamiliar seem both exciting and safe. Janet Belinkoff can make friends with animals and put them at ease. Chellie Campbell can take the stress out of financial management.

Knowing what makes what you do unique clarifies and validates your role on this journey called life. So think of your work as the role you're uniquely qualified to fill on this voyage. With that in mind, you'll be prepared to make clear goals, set priorities, reach decisions, and design strategies with greater ease. You'll be able to fill your day with those things that will help you accomplish your dreams.

Using a Purpose Poster to Stay on Track

> *Examine yourself; discover where your true chance of great-ness lies. Seize that chance and let no power or persuasion deter you from your task.*
> SCHOOLMASTER IN *CHARIOTS OF FIRE*

Okay! You know what you want. You know where you're going. But it's still easy to get off track, isn't it? Some days make your head spin so fast you can't even remember your Social Security number, let alone the reasons you're doing what you do.

So how do you keep on track when all around you is going haywire? We had to face that question when we were writing our first book, *Working from Home*. Like so many people, we had to sandwich the dream for our book between the many other things we were doing to earn a living. There were interruptions galore. At times we began to fear the book would never be finished.

To help myself stick to business, I, Sarah, hung a sketch of the book jacket behind my computer, so I was looking straight at it while I worked. As interruptions and distractions arose, I would see that sketch and know that I had to continue writing no matter what was going on around me or that jacket would never have a book in it.

That sketch kept us on track. And sure enough, as you might imagine, once we completed the book and Sarah took down the book jacket, the distractions of the day took charge once again.

That's when we realized the value of having a Purpose Poster, a picture you can hang up in your work space that displays your goals and dreams in living color. And that's just what we decided to create for ourselves. We had an artist design a poster that reminds us moment by moment of where we're headed. At that time, we'd recently moved from Kansas City to the Southern California megalopolis. We were strangers in a strange land. But we wanted to live by the ocean and find friends in Los Angeles with whom we could share our work and our lives. We'd written one book, but we wanted to write others. And we wanted to speak on radio and television and before large groups of people to spread the word about becoming your own boss and taking charge of your life from the comfort of your own home.

We had no idea how these things would come to pass, but we had them all illustrated on our poster anyway. They certainly didn't occur overnight and there were even times when we wondered if they would ever happen, but now as we look at that poster, most of the things on it are a regular part of our lives. We live two blocks from the ocean; we can see it from our balcony. That's the power of visualizing what you want and always keeping your ultimate goals in the forefront of your mind.

Think about what you're working toward. What does success look like for you? Visualize it as if it were already reality. See it right now in your mind's eye. Imagine it in full detail. What does it sound like? What does it feel like? How would you describe it to someone? Keep that image in mind and write it out or sketch it on a sheet of paper you can hang above your desk. Or clip pictures from magazines that capture the essence of your image and create a montage.

Whatever you're seeking to accomplish by being on your own, your mind will go toward whatever's in front of you. So create your own Purpose Poster to remind yourself of what you're doing all this for.

CLEARING OUT THE BACKLOG

It's easier to win than to worry. The mind is like a calculator;
it has to be cleared of all previous problems before you can
solve a problem with it. Worry jams up the mechanism. We
can't solve our problems unless we clear our minds.
EARL NIGHTINGALE, SPEAKER AND BROADCASTER

Before you can work on your purpose, you've got to make room for those things that matter most. That means clearing ample time, space, and energy for them. If your desk, your file cabinets, your calendar, and your mind are stuffed with many competing and trivial concerns, end up operating on the Hope System—that is, "I hope I'll get to that," "I hope I'll get that done," "I hope I'll fit than in," and so forth.

Isn't that too often the way the day goes, juggling many little but seemingly important balls and dropping a few along the way—a call that doesn't get returned, a letter that isn't sent, a missed meeting, a misplaced file, to-do and must-do lists scattered here and there? Our experience is that worrying about all the things you have to do and whether you'll get them done is one of people's biggest time wasters.

We call all the incomplete minutiae that clog up our time, our space, and our minds the *backlog*. And often it's this backlog that keeps you from doing what you want to do and getting where you want to go. In fact, research shows that 64 percent of us wish our offices were more organized and one in four of us wastes twenty minutes a day looking for misplaced items. That's thirty-one eight-hour days—a full month! According to Lisa Karanek, author of *Organizing Your Home Office,* we could save an hour a day just by cleaning out our files twice a year and keep piles from sprouting up.

So, until you can clear out the piles, the files, and "to dos" that make up the backlog you're juggling, how can you possibly get around to using even the most basic time-management principles? Here are some ideas for how to do that, fast:

1. Clear your mind with an Everything List. There is no way you can concentrate on what you need to do at any given moment if you're simultaneously trying to keep track of all the other things you could, should, and ought to be doing. To literally clear your mind, sit down and make up a list of *everything* you think you need to do—everything, from sending a birthday card to your aunt to calling your lawyer to cleaning out your file cabinets to sending a thank-you note for a recent referral.

The purpose of this list is not to overwhelm you. Rather, it's to give you a place where you can store all the things you're trying to keep track of. We suggest keeping it in a daily planner or personal organizer, either in paper or electronic form. (See "Use a personal organizer to make time" on page 84.) At least once daily, while you're making plans for the day, review your Everything List. Cross off or delete items that have been completed, and put the important or urgent tasks from your list onto your schedule for the day. If you feel overwhelmed by looking at your Everything List, don't panic. Just remember there will never be time for everything on your list, but there will always be time for the most important things.

2. Throw out everything you don't need. And the time to do that is right this minute, right now, today. Begin with your Everything List. Cross off or delete those things you don't really need to do—those things that make no contribution to what you want to create in your life. Ask yourself, "What benefits will doing this provide me or my clients? What will happen if I don't do this?" If there seems to be no gain from doing it and no major loss from not doing it, forget it. If, however, you still want to do it, you can. You're the boss. So leave it on your list.

Then move to your closets, desktop, drawers, and filing cabinets. If you don't use it and won't use it, lose it. Again, ask yourself how the contents contribute to what you want to accomplish in life. What benefits will keeping each item provide? What will happen if you don't keep it? Be ruthless. You owe it to yourself! This is your life. It should be filled with those things that nurture, assist, support, reward, and fulfill you and make a positive contribution to your life.

If you can't stand to throw away some things you no longer want or need—or if you don't have the time to go through all the piles and files you've accumulated—you can still clear the backlog out of your life. You can do as we did for our son: put these things—whatever they might be—in one or more large boxes in the attic, garage, basement, or even in an off-site storage locker. After several years, discard the contents of any boxes you haven't opened. We've often done this ourselves with books we were afraid to part with—and we rarely opened the boxes we put them in.

3. Start afresh with a time and place for everything. Once you've cleared your mind, calendar, closets, file cabinets, drawers, and desk of the backlog, you'll have more room for the important things in your life. If you designate a specific time or place for each of these things, you'll find managing your work much easier. There will be no need for stacks and piles to build up. You'll be able to put your finger on everything you need to locate. Things will get done routinely in a timely manner.

You may even see your profits go up. That's exactly what happened when an advertising executive came to us for a consultation on how to boost his sales. He came in feeling frustrated by how he never seemed to be able to get the solid base of sixteen accounts that he needed to make his income goals. He had a good marketing plan and was good at sales, so we decided to ask him about his accounting system. We wanted to know if he had a ledger for his accounts. He didn't. He just kept track of each account individually. So, we suggested that he set up a ledger with eighteen rows and bill, record transactions, and track the status of each account weekly.

To his amazement, within no time he routinely had eighteen accounts. "When I made a physical space for the accounts I wanted," he recalls, "and had to look at them weekly, the missing ones were constantly staring me in the face. I began talking with others about having openings for another client. Actually, I don't know exactly what happened; I just know that now I have eighteen steady accounts. Maybe I should set up a ledger for twenty and see what happens!"

To get results like that for yourself, here are several ways you can make sure you have a time and place for everything that matters most to you.

4. Use a personal organizer to make time. Using a personal organizer or time planner is an invaluable way to make sure you have time for everything you want to do in your life.

Paper organizers come in various sizes: pocket, purse, or notebook. We recommend one with a loose-leaf binder like *DayRunner, Harvard Planner,* or *Filofax* so you can remove and add pages as needed. We also recommend selecting one you can conveniently carry with you to meetings and appointments. Available in office-supply and stationery stores, such planners have customized pages you can mix and match to meet your needs: month-at-a-glance, week-at-a-glance, and daily calendars; addresses and phone numbers; goals sheets; project sheets; and notes.

Or use your computer to organize your day with software like *Lotus Organizer, Ecco Pro and Ecco Lite* by Netmanage, or *Ascend* by Franklin Quest. Make sure the program you select has all the same elements you'd want in a paper system: a place to write and plan goals, a place to set up your Everything List, and, of course, daily "to-do lists," and a calendar. If you choose to run your life from your computer, you can still take your schedule and plans with you wherever you go by printing them out or by using a personal digital assistant like Apple's *Newton,* Sony's *Magic Link,* or Sharp's *Wizard.* These are the electronic equivalent to paper organizers like the *DayRunner, Daytimer,* or *FiloFax.*

Place all important tasks, appointments, meetings, events, and activities on one master calendar in whatever personal organizer you're using, including those related to your personal and social time. People often reserve their calendars for business-related activities only and wonder why their private life suffers.

For example, if you want to exercise daily or every other day, reserve time on your calendar for it. If you want to spend time with your children each day, reserve time for it. If you want to pay bills, catch up on filing, learn a new software package, or read a book, don't leave these to chance: put them on your schedule, too. Of course, you can always move them if necessary. But make sure you do move them, not cancel them. In other words, place them on your calendar for another time, and be careful about making too many exceptions.

5. Set aside a time each day to plan your day in your personal organizer. Either first thing in the morning or last thing in the evening, plan how you will allocate your time for the upcoming day. You'll notice that those things that you make room for in your day are the things that will get done. You'll get results in those areas of your life that you invest time and energy in. The areas of your life you don't invest in will usually deteriorate.

For example, if you don't have enough business, review your calendar. Notice how much time you've invested in the past month in getting new business. If your relationships aren't working, review your calendar. Look to see how much time and energy you've invested in building the relationships you want. If you have trouble with cash flow, look at your calendar. How much time have you invested in billing, managing, and tracking your funds? If your health is suffering, review your calendar. How much time have you spent relaxing and taking care of yourself?

If you make room for these activities on your calendar and invest concentrated time and energy in them, you'll see them grow and develop in direct proportion to the investment you make. You will get the results you want!

6. Establish an activity center for key tasks, and keep everything related to these tasks in that place. Did you know corporate executives waste an average of forty-five minutes every day looking for things they can't find? It's true, and they usually have secretaries to help them keep track of things! But as self-employed individuals, who usually must organize and keep track of everything ourselves, we can't afford to spend time like this each day trying to find things.

There's nothing more frustrating than trying to find something you need and know that you have . . . somewhere. But usually, the primary reason desks, floors, closets, countertops, tables, and drawers get buried in piles of random stuff you can't find when you need it is that there's not a *place* to put these things when they come into your office or your life. When you don't have a place for things, you don't know what to do with them when they arrive. And too often you don't have time to figure out what to do with them. And when you don't know where something belongs, no matter where you put it, out of sight will be out of mind. As one person told us, "Once I put something in a file, it's lost forever."

If, however, you have one, and only one, place for everything you need to keep track of, and that one place is where all the other things like it are located, then putting things away and getting them back out when you need them becomes quick and easy.

Four Essential Activity Centers

One way to make sure there's a place for everything, so you can keep it in its place, is to organize your office into activity centers. Think of the primary activities you carry out each week and establish a center or work space where you carry out those activities. Then keep all materials and supplies related to that activity in that same work area. Such a center need be nothing more than a particular drawer or shelf. Or, depending on how much material and activity is involved, it could be an entire table, separate desk, or even portion of a room. Here are examples of several key centers most self-employed individuals need in order to make sure everything has a place.

1. A *telephone work center*. Have a place near your work phone where you keep your card file of names and addresses, answering or voice-mail machine, and all phone messages. You might locate this area on your desk or next to your computer. We have an answering pad by the phone on which we record all phone messages. This pad is invaluable for making sure we don't misplace calls to be made, dates, addresses, and other data people give us over the phone.

2. A *mail center*. Have a place where you process all your mail. Here you can have a bin or box in which to place incoming and outgoing mail. Here you can keep stationery, envelopes, stamps, cards, publicity materials, and anything you need to mail out regularly. This area might be on a worktable, on top of a cabinet near your desk, or in a desk drawer. We have our mail center on a worktable in a walk-in-closet-sized storage room off the loft where we have our desks. There, in addition to the things already mentioned, we also keep items like a postage meter, mailing and shipping envelopes, overnight-delivery materials, and a paper cutter.

3. A *money-processing center*. If you want to make sure you have enough money, you have to mind your money. That means having a time and space for processing your financial transactions such as making deposits, invoicing, bill paying, and keeping bank records. We have set aside a drawer in our office for all our bank records and a file drawer for all current tax records. There we keep deposit materials, checks, receipts, bills to be paid, and bills that have been paid.

We also recommend computerizing your financial records. In chapter 4 we list software that can help you streamline financial-management tasks like billing, inventory, cash flow, accounting, and so forth.

4. *Filing centers*. If you have a place for each file and a file for each type of written material you need to keep, you'll have no need for piles. Actually, filing cabinets should be called retrieval cabinets, because the goal of filing is to put something where you can find it when you need it. To keep your desk and other surfaces clear and still have quick access to what you need, create three filing areas:

IMMEDIATE FILES. Keep files you refer to daily or are working on currently within arm's reach—in a file drawer in your desk, a movable filing cart placed beside your desk, stack trays on your desk, or a nearby bookcase or credenza.

CURRENT FILES. Files that you use on a weekly or monthly basis can be kept in a filing cabinet in a closet or nearby storage area. These include your current client files, financial records, and relevant subject-area files.

ARCHIVES. Materials that you are keeping for reference or for purposes of documentation can be kept in remote locations out of your immediate office area such as a basement, attic, or garage. We call this filing area deep storage. Financial and tax records from previous years, completed projects, and other materials you are either required to keep or might otherwise have to reconstruct should be kept there.

We've found that clearing out the backlog of your concerns, files, and piles to make time and space for more of what you want in life works miracles. Actually it's in accord with a major law of physics: nature abhors a vacuum. If you continue holding open time and space for the most important things in your life, there will be less and less room for those things you don't find rewarding because you'll attract more and more of the things you've made room for. You'll have made room to expand and grow in the directions you desire.

SCHEDULING FOR RESULTS

If you don't know where you're going, you'll probably end up someplace else.

YOGI BERRA

Once you know where you're going and you've cleared the way, setting goals can help you get there, but only if you bring them down to the minute. Leaving your goals on a notepad in a drawer somewhere puts them out of sight and out of mind. You've got to get them onto your calendar and let them become the focus of what you do every day.

Nothing happens until you create a space in your day for it, and that's what a schedule is for. Your schedule, if you make and follow one, carves out time for the things you want in your life. You can think about your schedule for the day as a table with a limited number of chairs. Each chair can either be reserved for an honored and cherished guest or be left open, to be filled on a first-come, first-serve basis. Of course, as with any dinner party, the guests at the table determine how much you enjoy the meal. So although in business there will always be periodic surprise guests, you want to make sure that for the most part, the party goes according to your invitation list.

Undoubtedly you've already heard about the importance of setting goals if you want to succeed. Brian Tracy, motivational speaker and author of *The Psychology of Success*, says, "Goals are dreams with a deadline." Goals bring your intentions to life. In fact, a University of San Francisco study has clearly demonstrated that the highest indicator of success is the passion to pursue well-defined goals. But just setting goals is not enough. A study on goal setting sponsored by the Ford Foundation showed that:

- Twenty-three percent of the population has no idea what they want from life and as a result they don't have much.

- Sixty-seven percent of the population has a general idea of what they want but they don't have any plans for how to get it.

- Only 10 percent of the population has specific, well-defined goals, but even then, seven out of ten of those people reach their goals only half of the time.

- The top 3 percent, however, achieved their goals 89 percent of the time. That's an .890 batting average. What any baseball player wouldn't give to hit that well!

Like us, the researchers wanted to know what accounted for the dramatic difference between that top 3 percent and the others. They found that of all the possible variables, the only difference between the top performers and the rest was that the top 3 percent wrote down their goals.

Operating from Goals

If you want to increase your chances for success and up your batting average, you have to do more than just set goals. You need to write them down and then bring them to life. Making up a list at New Year's and then forgetting about it won't get you nearly as far as incorporating your goals into each and every week. If you can see them on your calendar and make room for them on your schedule, you'll get where you want to be much more quickly. Here are six steps for turning goals into reality.

1. Define specific goals. Goals are a target for you to shoot at. They enable you to know where you're going, how you'll get there, and when you'll arrive. The more specific you can be and the more urgency you give them, the better. Set goals in terms of measurable results you're committed to achieving. For example, don't set general goals like "I'll have a successful desktop publishing business" or "This week I'll get more clients." Be specific.

- "By December 31, I will have produced $65,000 in income from my desktop publishing service."

- "By next month, I will have two new contracts of more than $4,000 each."

- "This month I will interview five product reps and select one to represent me."
- "This week I will make twenty sales calls and sell $2,000 worth of products."
- "I'll finish thirty pages of the report this week."
- "I'll have my newsletter in print by April 1."

Such specific goals enable you to know what you have to accomplish by what date. If you miss the target, however, don't despair. You haven't failed; you just haven't succeeded yet. Simply aim again until you hit the bull's-eye.

2. Write your goals down. Create a separate file on your computer or electronic organizer for listing your goals. Or list them on a separate page in your personal organizer. Or write them on three-by-five index cards you can carry in your calendar or wallet. Under each goal, list all the tasks you will need to perform to reach that goal and cross these off as you finish them.

3. Keep your goals in your line of sight. Remember, the mind goes toward what's in front of it. So don't bury your goals somewhere and look at them once a year. Carry them with you. Post them above your computer. Hang them on the wall behind your desk. Have them printed on your calendar.

4. Review your goals daily. Refer to your goals when planning your schedule and constructing your daily to-do list. Don't let a day go by without taking some step toward your goals. In fact, make sure you take several steps toward your goals every day by putting key tasks on the calendar. I, Sarah, like to see my goals at the top of my daily "to do" list. I find that even though I'm usually looking at the same goals each week, having them in front of me keeps them on the top of my mind.

5. Do a daily goal check. At the end of each day, ask yourself, "What have I done today to achieve my goals?" Don't be satisfied with excuses and rationalizations. Even if it means staying up late or missing out on an evening of TV, agree not to go to bed without having taken at least one step in the direction you're headed. This will be a real motivation for making sure you take steps toward your goals during the workday.

6. Create goals for all aspects of your life and career. One common way to sabotage goals is to set them for only one aspect of your business or your life. For example, as self-employed individuals we not only have to conduct the business; we also have to get the business and run the business. If we concentrate on only one of these vital aspects, the business will ultimately become lopsided and suffer. Therefore, set goals each week or month for the following:

- What business you will actually do—how many clients, projects, or portions of projects you will complete
- What marketing efforts you will undertake—how many networking meetings, sales calls, thank-you notes, ad campaigns, or mailings you will attend to
- What administrative tasks you will complete—when you will do the filing, bookkeeping, purchasing, and invoicing

Don't forget to include your personal, social, and financial goals. If the only goals you make are work related, don't be surprised if your health, relationships, and personal well-being suffer. We get results in those areas of our life that we invest time, energy, and money in. Spending time with friends and family, relaxing, meditating, learning, and nurturing and entertaining ourselves are equally important to our success. Your goals could include:

- Meditating daily
- Going to the gym three times a week
- Enjoying a family outing each week
- A romantic evening on Friday nights
- Dinner with friends twice a month

Bringing Goals into the Moment

> *Even if you're on the right track, you'll get run over if you just sit there.*   WILL ROGERS

Having a clear purpose for your work, setting specific goals, and having good ideas for what you want to accomplish will get you on track, but ultimately the best measure of your effectiveness is how quickly you can turn your ideas, goals, and dreams into reality. And that's a matter of what actually makes it off your schedule and into the events of your day.

Here are three ways to make sure you bring your goals into the moment.

1. Prioritize your daily to-do list. Based on your goals, as you list the things you need to do each day, put them through the 80/20 Test. Mark each item *A* or *B*. *A* is for the items that produce 80 percent of our results—the truly essential, important, or urgent activities. *B* is for everything else—the trivial, insignificant, and extraneous.

Screen your *A* list again. Are there some items on this list you can do without? Are they truly essential, or do you only think they are? Post your *A* list on your desk, phone, drafting table, or computer while you work. Resolve to work until you complete as many *A* tasks as possible. Sometimes there's only one big item. Usually there are one big one and four or five little ones.

2. *Stick to your priorities.* The most common time wasters are procrastination, interruptions, emergencies, not being able to find the information you need, mismanaged meetings, unnecessary phone calls, trying to do everything yourself, and overworking. As you've undoubtedly discovered, if you allow them to, these activities can eat up 80 percent of your time while producing only 20 percent of your results. To make sure this doesn't happen, identify which activities are your biggest time wasters. What sabotages your plans? What gets you off course? For a week, keep a log of the activities that get you off course, and pinpoint the 20 percent that cause 80 percent of your problems. Then take action. Once you recognize the culprits, you're halfway to eliminating them.

For example, if you have a client who calls you endlessly with one headache after another, maybe you need to summon up the courage to refer this client elsewhere. If you find yourself driving an hour each way to an office, maybe you should move your office home. If your kids intrude too often into your workday, maybe you need to arrange for child care for part of each day. If the paperwork involved in being a corporation or having an employee is taking up too much of your time, maybe you need to operate as a sole proprietor or subcontract your work.

Do whatever it takes to stick to those things that produce your best results. Schedule the *A* events of your day during your high-energy peaks. Reserve more taxing activities for time blocks when you're fresh. Leave less demanding tasks for off-hours. Set up a system to touch any piece of incoming paper only once. Screen your calls, and return them during a specified time block. Put up a Do Not Disturb sign. Say no politely but firmly. And build in time for the few but unavoidable emergencies that will still arise. Then, when the time comes, close the door on work.

3. *Focus your efforts.* Since you undoubtedly will have multiple *A* items on your list, focus your energy by grouping the things you need to do into effective time blocks. Put similar tasks together and schedule these blocks rather than putting random activities on your calendar throughout the day. For example, you might set aside a time when you make all your phone calls. Or do your paperwork in one block. Cluster meetings and appointments back-to-back. Run all errands on one trip.

Scheduling your day with activity blocks instead of sprinkling various types of activities throughout the day saves you time in getting out and putting away materials. It cuts down on interruptions and helps people know when it's best to reach you. And best of all, because each type of activity demands its own mindset, working in activity blocks helps you concentrate and stay focused. And be sure to remember to include a block of time each day for your personal life.

HAVING TIME FOR YOUR PERSONAL LIFE

Downtime can be very uplifting.
                              CLIFF MANGAN, PH.D.

If you tend to overwork and therefore have difficulty making time for the personal aspects of life, treat your personal time with the same discipline and dedication with which you approach your work. For example, develop the habit of putting personal and social free time on your calendar just as you would an important work activity. When business-related tasks are proposed for those times, you can then rightly say you're already booked for that time—because you are.

You are as important as your work. In fact, as the source of your work, you're the most valuable asset of your business. As such, your well-being is vital to your success. You need to be healthy, happy, rested, and nourished. What kind of breeder would run a prized racehorse day in and day out without rest? What race driver would allow his or her multimillion-dollar car to go without regular maintenance? What kind of boss works his or her employees morning, noon, and night? Would you want to work for someone who has no respect for your personal life? Isn't that part of why you wanted to work for yourself? Would you drive someone who was working for you that hard? Why do it to yourself?

Of course, there are exceptions. There are times when you must put in long hours. But unless that's the way you honestly want to live your life, don't let fear or drive make you into the kind of management that incites a strike. Ultimately that's what our bodies do for us when we overwork. They get sick. Often illness is the body's way of going on strike.

That's what happened to a very successful independent insurance broker who came to consult with Sarah. He was one of those people who, obsessed with work, drive themselves fourteen hours a day for weeks on end. Periodically he would collapse in exhaustion, unable to work at all for days or even weeks. During that time he'd lie in bed feeling weak and drained, chiding himself for leaving his clients and projects hanging in midair. Finally he'd recover enough to get back to work and start the cycle over again. His periodic illnesses forced him to cancel important appointments and miss many deadlines, and he would feel compelled to make up for these inconveniences to his clients by working even harder, which would ultimately put him back in bed again. In his desire to do the superhuman, he had actually become unreliable.

When he came to talk with Sarah, his hope was that she would help him to work harder so he could be more reliable. Instead, she helped him recognize the overwork/collapse pattern he was living out again and again. Once he realized that if he had a boss who drove him that hard he'd certainly quit (and probably file a workmen's-compensation claim, too), he applied the same remarkable determination that had driven him to overwork to maintaining a more realistic work schedule. To his surprise, he got just as much done over a six-month period and still had time to fall in love, enjoy weekends and evenings with his lover, and even take regular three-day weekend trips.

Needless to say, this is an extreme example. But it illustrates how we can in fact have it all, but only if we make room for it all. Once we're on our own, it's actually our own excesses that create the illusion that there isn't enough time to balance our lives.

Why wait until you get sick to make sure you have time each day to relax and enjoy the personal aspects of your life? Pretend you are your own labor union. What bargain can you strike with yourself? When the time comes to close the door on work, you must simply stop wherever you are. Isn't that what you would do if you'd scheduled an appointment with a VIP client? Would you stand that client up? Would you keep him or her waiting? Of course not. Well, don't put your life on hold, either. Don't stand yourself up.

MAKING TIME TO WORK AS MUCH AS YOU WANT TO

> *I regard myself as . . . one of the happiest men on earth because I've been doing what I like all my life.*
> ASHLEY MONTAGU, ANTHROPOLOGIST

But what if you're one of those people who *want* to work all the time? Many people who go out on their own love what they do so much that they want to do it morning, noon, and night. They eat, sleep, drink, and breathe their work. If they were left on their own, their life would become their work and often does. If this describes you, you probably feel energized by your work and have little interest in finding free time. Instead you probably feel pressured and beleaguered by the demands of others in your life who are always trying to pry you away from your work. Perhaps you feel guilty for not spending more time with your family and friends.

But remember this: On your own, you are in charge of your life. Don't turn your family and friends into the thorn in your side that your boss once was. You get to decide who sits at your dinner table, so to speak, and what goes onto your plate each day. If you want to work morning, noon, and night, it's truly your choice. But is that really what you want? And is it actually working for you? Are you healthy? Are you producing the quality of work you want to be producing? Are you enjoying it? Or are you driving yourself out of fear, anxiety, obsession, or to escape other things in your life that aren't working? If so, an honest assessment of your situation will probably show that the quality of your work and the quality of your life would be far higher if you were to relax a little.

If, however, you are in fact enjoying your work and you find it rewarding, fulfilling, and energizing to work constantly and to allow it to consume your time, then the truth is there's room for little else in your life. You will do yourself a favor by taking the time to explain this honestly to the others around you. Tell them what your work means to you and how you feel about it. Often when people know what they can expect and understand the significance of it, they are willing to support you, even if they would prefer to spend more time with you.

A child, for example, whose single parent must work at two jobs to support the family may not like having so little time with his parent, but he will probably understand that the lack of attention he gets is actually coming from love and is not a sign that he is unimportant, unworthy, or unlovable. A child whose parent could easily spend more time with him, however, might feel that he's not loved. From his perspective what else could it mean? He may think there must be something wrong with him—or with you, the parent. But once the child understands why what you do is so important to you, he may feel proud of your work and of you, even though he sees very little of you. This can also be true of spouses and friends.

If you are *fully* present for children or loved ones at those times when you are available, this will help, too. If by the time you get to them you're exhausted and grumpy, that will only compound the problem and increase their disappointment and dissatisfaction. Of course, simply taking them for granted when you are free will, too. But if they know you are delighted and pleased to be with them in the time you do have, and you make sure to be available at the times that are most important to them, everyone will be more supportive. Doing this, however, means you have to free yourself from any guilt you may be feeling about working so much, because feeling guilty about not being more available will only put further distance between you and the others in your life when you are together.

You will certainly enjoy life more if your partner and friends are supportive and excited about your work. But they will be able to feel this way only if you help them understand what your work means to you and to those you serve. If, after you've done this, they still don't and won't support you, perhaps you will be better off coming to a parting of the ways and developing other relationships that are more compatible with your goals and life purposes. In building new relationships, be sure to let others know from the start what they can expect from you in terms of time.

Interruption Busters

1. Put on the answering machine or engage an answering service or voice mail so you can devote large blocks of uninterrupted time to your work. Set up a time later in the day to return phone calls and deal with other matters that arose during these periods.

2. Free the majority of your week for uninterrupted work by setting aside a day or half a day to handle all the administrative aspects of your business. Set up a special file or in box for all the matters you must address that day.

3. Hire a full- or part-time assistant or outside business services to do whatever aspects of your work you can afford to delegate.

4. Set up your office and the business side of your work so that they will run themselves as much as possible. Chapter 4 outlines how you can use routines, technology, and creative approaches to free yourself to do what you do best and enjoy most.

Sometimes it's not just friends and family who try to take us from our sacred work. Often it's the administrivia of being on our own that prevent us from getting anything done. We resent the constant intrusions of phone calls, piles of mail, urgent letters from the IRS, bank statements that need justifying, and on and on. Isn't it amazing how such minutiae can devour your day? Above is a list of things you can do to protect and preserve your ability to work, with uninterrupted abandon.

As you can see, it is possible to set up your life so what needs to be done will get done and still have time and energy to enjoy your life. Being self-employed gives you the flexibility and control to take charge of your time and your life. So go ahead: have the time of your life!

RESOURCES

PUTTING FIRST THINGS FIRST

Executive in Passage. Donald Marrs. Los Angeles: Barrington Sky Publishing, 1990. The autobiography of a highly paid advertising executive who encounters a crisis of consciousness when he discovered that his job is at odds with his personal values and ethics. It outlines how he came to establish and operate a business that integrated his values and his career.

Finding Your Perfect Work. Paul and Sarah Edwards. Los Angeles: Tarcher/Putnam, 1996. This book helps you discover what you really want in life, set your goals and priorities, and find a self-employment career suited to what will support you in living in accord with your desires.

House As a Mirror of Self: Exploring the Deeper Meaning of Home. Clare Cooper Marcus. Emeryville, CA: Conari Press, 1995. This fascinating book allows you to explore your home (and we believe the same could be done in terms of your office) as a way to understand what's in your life and how to clear away what you don't want and make space for more of what you want.

*The Path of Least Resistance. Robert Fritz. New York: Fawcett Columbine, 1989. The underlying thesis of this book is that we have the capacity to create new structures in our lives that will take us precisely where we want to go.

Rainbow Rising from a Stream, The Natural Way to Well-Being. New York: Morrow, 1992. A useful collection of exercises, stories, and fables that guide you to accept your imperfections, define your purpose, and get on with your life.

Reevaluating Your Life. Mark Oechsli. Niles, IL: Nightingale-Conant. (800) 525-9000. A six-tape audiocassette program and workbook outlining ten steps to developing a master plan for your life.

Simplify Your Life: 100 Ways to Slow Down and Enjoy the Things That Really Matter. Elaine St. James. New York: Hyperion, 1994. A user's manual for how to unwind from feeling overextended, overworked, and overcome. This book can help you set your priorities to improve the quality of your life. Like us, your solutions and conclusions may be different from St. James's, but this book can help clarify what matters most to you, so you can 80/20 your life.

CLEARING OUT THE BACKLOG

Getting Organized. Stephanie Winston. New York: Warner, 1991. Increase your efficiency. Learn to cut through confusion and take control of your life by getting organized.

*A classic.

~~~ **Organized to Be the Best.** Susan Silver. Los Angeles: Adams Hall, 1995. Designed for the busy professional, this "Bible of Organization" provides information about specific organizing products and software as well as handy 800 numbers that positively organize you for action.

~~~ **Organizing Your Home Office for Success.** Lisa Kanarek. New York: Plume, 1993. This guide provides information and time-saving tips on all aspects of home-office management including how to get started, where to put supplies and equipment, and ideas on storing and filing and choosing office products that fit personal needs.

🎧 **Visualizing Is Realizing.** Mark Victor Hanson. Mark Victor Hansen & Associates. (800) 433-2314. This eight-audiocassette album shows you how to visualize your future success so that where you're going matters more than what you haven't done, haven't got, or haven't said.

SCHEDULING FOR RESULTS

~~~ **The Celestine Prophecy.** James Redfield. New York: Warner, 1993. Embedded in this best-selling mythical novel is a useful paradigm for understanding family and interpersonal dynamics that explains how we inadvertently solicit unwanted reactions from loved ones instead of the support and understanding we need.

~~~ **Embracing Each Other.** Hal Stone and Sidra Winkelman. Novato, CA: Nataraj Publishing, 1989. (415) 899-9666. If you're having trouble getting loved ones to understand your work needs, this is the best book we've seen on understanding and healing problem relationships.

🎧 **First Things First.** Stephen R. Covey, A. Roger Merrill, and Rebecca R. Merrill. Niles, IL: Nightingale-Conant. (800) 525-9000. A six-tape audio program for structuring your time around what's truly important to you.

~~~ **Love Is the Answer: Creating Positive Relationships.** Gerald Jampolsky and Diane Cirinsione. New York: Bantam, 1994. Often loved ones want to support us in our new goals when we become self-employed, but their fears and our own get in the way. This book provides seven steps to creating positive relationships and fifteen lessons for transforming fear into love.

🎧 **The New Dynamics of Goal Setting.** Dennis Waitley. Niles, IL: Nightingale-Conant. (800) 525-9000. A six-tape audiocassette program on how to stay focused on your goals, shape your life, and thrive on challenge.

Unlimit Your Life: Setting and Getting Goals. Dr. James Fadiman. Berkeley, CA: Celestial Arts, 1994. Not only does the book cover the basics of setting realistic goals, it also explores overcoming the forces that prevent us from carrying them out, including improving low self-esteem, building better relationships, and changing disfunctional habits.

TIME MANAGEMENT

How to Stay Up No Matter What Goes Down. Sarah Edwards. Here's How (Box 5091, Santa Monica, CA 90409), 1988. This audiocassette album provides practical daily messages for getting organized, sticking to business, and living your life on purpose.

Master Strategies for Higher Achievement. Brian Tracy. Niles, IL: Nightingale-Conant. (800) 525-9000. A six-cassette audiotape program for identifying and achieving your goals.

The Now Habit: A Strategic Program for Overcoming Procrastination and Enjoying Guilt-Free Play. Neil Fiore. New York: Tarcher/Putnam, 1988. A comprehensive system for overcoming the causes and eliminating the effects of procrastination.

Personal Time Management. Brian Tracy. Niles, IL: Nightingale-Conant. (800) 525-9000. A fifty-five-minute video program for how to overcome procrastination, get started, and become more productive by developing a blueprint for your day.

Time Management for Dummies. Jeffrey Mayer. Foster City, CA: IDG Books, 1995. Practical ideas for saving time while you're on the phone, making decisions, doing correspondence, traveling, using a computer, and more.

Winning the Fight Between You and Your Desk. Jeff Mayer. New York: Harper Business, 1993. How to use your computer to get organized, become more productive, and make more money.

Working from Home. Paul and Sarah Edwards. Los Angeles: Tarcher, 1994. In Parts 4, "Managing Your Home Office," and 5, "Managing Yourself and Others," this book provides practical advice for getting organized, managing your time, information and money, dealing with feeling isolated, handling relationships when you're self-employed, child care, and getting help when you need it.

4

Getting the Business to Run Itself So You Can Do What You Do Best

The last thing I get to do is sing. Lou Rawls

How much of your time do you actually spend doing the parts of your work that you enjoy and find rewarding? Like the singer Lou Rawls, do you find that your work is the last thing you get to do? If so, you are paying a high price for the privilege and freedom of being your own boss. Instead of having the time to enjoy the work you do, you may feel more as if you're struggling to hold down several part-time jobs—spending hours as a receptionist answering the phones and responding to mail; hours as a salesperson finding leads, making presentations, and closing sales; hours as a file clerk and administrator keeping records, filing, billing, collecting, and getting in supplies; even hours as a housekeeper or janitor keeping the home and office presentable.

And, worst of all, you don't even get paid for doing these jobs—they're your overhead! Unfortunately, such administrative aspects of being on your own can easily consume a disproportionate amount of your energy and eat into your actual income-producing time. Some self-employed individuals spend 40 percent of their time marketing or selling themselves and 25 percent of their time administering their business. That leaves only about a third of your time to actually do the work you went on your own to do. It also means you have to either charge more or earn less, because you've got to live off what you make in that vital third of your time.

But what if you could reduce the time you need to spend marketing and running your business? What if you could set up the business side of what you do so that it essentially runs itself? That's what this chapter is about. There are actually many simple things you can do to shrink the most time-consuming, non-income-producing aspects of being on your own. In this chapter we'll address how you can position yourself so that instead of having to go out and get business, ample business will come to you in the course of the work you do. We'll show you how technology can streamline otherwise tedious and time-consuming administrative tasks; how you can create routines so you can take care of details automatically; and ways to avoid unnecessary make-work so you can double up what you're doing and more than double your results. And we'll provide guidelines for how to decide when it's time to call in or send out for help.

Of course, if you're a one-person operation, chances are you can't literally get your business to run itself entirely on its own. In other words, you probably won't be able to become an absentee business owner. But most likely that's not why you went out on your own anyway. What you can most certainly do is create a momentum that will enable your business to become self-generating and self-sustaining. You can literally get the world around you—your daily operations, your industry, your clients and customers—working for you.

Nine Principles for Getting Things Working for You

Imagine this: You're working on a rewarding project. It keeps you busy, and it pays well. Throughout the project you get frequent requests to work on other projects. You consult your timetable and begin filling in your calendar. Before you know it, you're booked for the next few months and then for the next year. Invoices go out; checks come in.

Or perhaps you're selling a product and you get your first large order. Soon more orders are coming in and your accounts begin renewing orders automatically. Whereas you once had to make several phone calls, meet with buyers, and send volumes of follow-up correspondence to get an order, now buyers are calling you for information. Purchase orders come in; products and invoices go out; checks come back.

That's what we call *momentum*—that is, an impetus that accelerates seemingly under its own power. The more momentum your business generates, the less effort you need to expend to keep things going and the more the details and administrivia of doing business become automatic and routine, freeing you to enjoy the excitement, drama, and challenge of doing rewarding work. That's the way it's supposed to work.

If you're continually struggling and suffering on your own, that is not normal. That's not par for the course. It's not all you can expect! If you're just beginning, then yes, a considerable degree of extra effort may be necessary. For heaven's sake, do not think that's what being on your own has to be. That's only what it's like when you're starting out or if you're doing it the hard way.

You can think of yourself as a novice training for a long-distance race. At first, your steps may be labored and you feel short of breath. But as you continue to work out each day, your stride becomes steadier and your pace picks up. You go longer and farther with less effort; no more straining and huffing and puffing. Going the distance becomes second nature. That's the way you want your business to develop. You want to reach a stride that will provide you with the momentum to carry you through the race and over the finish line.

Here are nine key principles for building ample momentum to keep you going with less effort.

1. Commit to having things work smoothly and easily. Don't settle for a difficult, complicated life. No matter how long it takes, don't accept difficulty as your way of life. Identify the administrative things that take up inordinate time and energy and resolve to find ways to streamline them. Don't assume overwork and struggle are just the price you have to pay for being on your own. Although sometimes you may have to pay a stiff price at first, if you demand more out of life, you're much more likely to find a way to make it work the way you want it to.

2. Adopt technology that will help you work more quickly and easily. We're in the midst of an unprecedented technological revolution. There is more technology available to improve our lives today than any of us can absorb. If you're a technophobe, give it up. Embrace new technologies that will make your life work better. It's getting easier every day, and there are plenty of resources to help you learn to use the equipment you need.

Later in this chapter we'll introduce you to what we consider to be the ideal technology for someone who's self-employed. But we can't begin to mention all the specialized technology that's available for your particular field. You'll find news about these technologies in trade journals from your field and by talking with colleagues and friends. When you see or hear about innovative new technology, keep an open mind. Say yes to it mentally. Avoid the temptation many of us have to immediately think, "Oh, I don't need that" or "That wouldn't work for me" or "I can't afford that." Usually we can find a way to do whatever we decide we need to do.

Often equipment will actually pay for itself directly with increased savings or sales. Operating your own copy machine, for example, can cost less in a few months than driving to and from a copy store and paying print-shop prices for each copy. A laser printer can pay for itself in what you save on the cost of typesetting your newsletter. A fax can pay for itself in overnight-delivery fees and speed all forms of communication with clients and suppliers, including billing. A computer and printer can enable you to do your own direct-mail campaign in half the time and can pay for itself in increased sales from the additional mailings you send out. If you receive a lot of mail, an electronic letter opener can free your time for billable activity. And if you send out a lot of mail, a postage meter can more than pay for itself.

Sometimes technology will pay for itself indirectly, by increasing the value of your product or service sufficiently that your sales or prices can go up, or by giving you a professional image that gets you in the door so you can line up more business or by saving money better spent elsewhere. An ergonomically designed chair, for example, can save you discomfort, lost productivity, and physical therapy.

Such cost savings and increased sales make strategic equipment an investment you can't afford not to make, and well worth buying on credit if you don't have funds to pay up front in full. And, of course, the cost of your business equipment is tax deductible.

3. Get help. As we said before, although you're on your own, you don't have to do everything yourself, even if you can't afford to hire full-time or even part-time employees. Many of your biggest time-consuming tasks can be done by contracting for outside help on a project-by-project basis. Bookkeeping, public relations, filing, mailing-list management, newsletter preparation, housecleaning, and even sales are all functions that many people find can be cost-effectively done by hiring someone else on an as-needed basis.

People frequently tell us they can't afford to hire outside help. But sometimes you will actually save money by hiring someone else. On the following page are some rules of thumb for deciding when and if it's time to hire out. Whenever you identify something that is taking up time you could be spending more profitably and pleasantly, think about how you can find someone else to do it for you more quickly and cost-effectively. Ask yourself if there's a service that could do this more cheaply. Then think of how to make sure the work you pay others to do can directly or indirectly pay for itself in increased income. In other words, amortize the cost of hiring staff or services just as you would your equipment.

4. Use OPE—Other People's Energy. Hiring help is not the only way to get others to work for you. There are many creative and mutually beneficial ways to get customers, clients, colleagues, suppliers, gatekeepers, and mentors to work for you as well. Why not do joint mailings with others whose products or services are compatible with yours? Or arrange to slip your materials in with someone else's mailings? With the proper incentives and information, a few highly satisfied clients can become an extension of your sales effort. You can offer discounts, free services, or even finder's fees to people who bring business to you.

When to Hire Help

1. It's time to hire help if it would free you to use your time to do or get income-producing work that exceeds the cost of the help. For example:

   - Hiring someone to design and send out a direct-mail piece that will generate more income for you than the cost of the help to produce it

   - Hiring a publicist to do public relations so you can take on an added project that will more than cover the fee of the publicist

   - Hiring a computer consultant to set up and install your computer when trying to learn to do it yourself will eat away hours of billable time

2. It's time to hire help when the cost of hiring a staff person would be self-liquidating. In other words, when the person's activity would generate as much income as, or more income than, you would have to pay him or her. For example:

   - Hiring someone to sell your services

   - Hiring a service to take your calls when losing one call because no one was there to answer a potential customer's questions would more than pay for the service

   - Hiring someone to publish a newsletter for you that will draw in more business per issue than it costs to produce the publication

3. It's time to hire help when paying someone else would cost you less than doing it yourself. For example:

   - Contracting out to print one hundred copies of a ten-page project report instead of hand-feeding your copy machine

   - Hiring someone to oversee the production of a brochure that would cost you more to subcontract to multiple individuals

4. It's time to hire help when you're bringing in enough income that you can cover the costs of hiring help to increase the quality of your life. For example:

   - Hiring someone to clean your home/office

   - Hiring someone to do your filing

Cross-referring clients with other professionals can also be a low-cost, time-saving marketing method. For example, if you do accounting, your clients may need legal services at times and you can arrange to cross-refer to an attorney, who will in turn send you his or her clients when they need an accountant. You can do the same with your suppliers.

Speech and diction coach Sandy McKnight made creative use of OPE when she arranged with a temporary-help service to offer a free introductory seminar on accent reduction. Since the seminar would attract needed new personnel to the service, the service owners agreed to provide the space and pay for an ad promoting the seminar. They also agreed to mail a flyer to all their existing temporary staff. At the free seminar, Sandy enrolled those who wished more assistance in an ongoing seminar for which she split the profits with the agency.

In such an arrangement, everyone wins. By offering something its competitors don't offer, the agency gains a competitive edge and attracts new personnel. The participants get good information, and Sandy gets to fill her seminars without any out-of-pocket advertising costs. She calls this arrangement value-added marketing and plans to make as many such arrangements as possible.

Often, even when speaking for free before a professional or community group, you can get the organization to publicize you and your appearance by sending a news release to the local media. You can also request that the organization enclose some of your materials with its meeting announcements. Or you can volunteer to do work for a trade association in your field in exchange for piggybacking on association mailings and being featured in a special article in the association's newsletter.

Also, building a relationship with one or two well-placed gatekeepers (people who can unlock opportunities for you), can save you hours of marketing. For example, an interior designer might get most of his business from one prominent architect. A commercial real-estate agent can be a source of business for a cleaning service. So identify who comes into regular contact with people who need your service and see how you can work cooperatively to save each other time and money.

5. Use experts. British prime minister Benjamin Disraeli once said that, all other things being equal, the person who succeeds will be the person with the best information. Just one key piece of information can save you hundreds to thousands of dollars and hours, months, or even years of time, not to mention safeguarding you from the agony of painful mistakes. In fact, a Dunn and Bradstreet study found that 92 percent of business failures could be traced to the lack of some type of knowledge or how to apply that knowledge.

When any aspect of your endeavor isn't working for you as well as you'd like, don't accept defeat. Nothing is inevitable. Don't even accept marginal results. Seek out the specialized information you need to get the results you want. This is the Information Age. Information is available on almost any subject you need. You can read, attend seminars, and use consultants who specialize in helping people accomplish what you need to do. Someone, somewhere, knows about something that can help you. In the appendix: "Sources of Help," you'll find a variety of sources of help that are available in your state to assist self-employed individuals and small businesses.

Here's an example of what we mean. The owner of a gift-basket business knew that being able to take MasterCard and Visa would increase her sales, but every bank she approached turned down her request for merchant status because she ran her business from home. Through the Working from Home Forum on CompuServe Information Service, however, she discovered a list of companies that broker merchant status for home-based businesses. And sure enough, now that she can offer credit, her business has increased without her having to spend more than a modest amount of additional time or money.

This is just one example of how seeking out the key information and expertise you need can make your life simpler and increase your success. The reference librarian at your local library may be able to direct you to the information you need as well as sources of information for finding books, tapes, and seminars. Professional associations are also often a rich source of information. They're a particularly valuable source for finding reliable consultants.

Through the Internet or on-line services like CompuServe and Microsoft Network, you can locate a vast array of information from getting credit reports to finding the names of corporate personnel to call or sending marketing materials to.

Specialized on-line forums or news groups offer a wealth of information, too, as well as access to experts. You'll find attorneys, accountants, market-

Your Personal Information Network

- Accountant or tax adviser
- Information researcher
- Investment counselor
- Marketing and advertising specialist
- Professional organizer
- Computer consultant
- Insurance agent
- Lawyer
- Public-relations specialist

Ask Your Way to Success

Success is clearly a joint venture, a team effort. You can't achieve it alone. But sometimes it feels lonely along the road to your goals. How would you like to have a team of experts, mentors, guides, and well-wishers to assist you along the way? Sound good? Well, you may be surprised to discover that there are plenty of such supporters who could be at your beck and call.

In fact, as author and motivational speaker Brian Tracy says, you can ask your way to success. There are always people who are complimented by your asking for their help. There are, however, certain rules for attracting benefactors into your life. Here are a few we've learned.

- **Admit you don't know.** Too often we think we have to put on the appearance that we know it all. And even worse, sometimes we even fool ourselves into thinking it's true. In reality there's always something new to learn from life and from others. The pace of change is accelerating rapidly, and there are more scientists and specialists breaking new ground than at any other time in history. It's not a sign of weakness to admit you don't know. It's a sign of strength to approach life as a lifelong learner, curious and eager to know more. So routinely take note of areas of your work or business that you would like to learn more about.

- **Go to the source.** Once you identify something you need to know more about, go to those people who are clearly the authorities in that area. Identify who has the talents, expertise, and know-how you need. Start there. If they can't help you, they'll probably know someone who can.

- **Be specific.** Gatekeepers and mentors are eager to help, but they can help you only if they know what you need. So do your homework before

ing experts, and many other professionals who will gladly provide advice and information. (See Resources at the end of this chapter for key on-line resources)

Or, if you'd rather have someone else find the answers for you, information brokers are another resource you can turn to for strategic information. They specialize in finding difficult-to-locate information for a fee.

We urge you to build your own personal information network of experts whom you can call on when you need assistance. Build relationships with reliable professionals from the list in the box on page 105. The best way to find such professionals for your support team is by networking with others in your field or community. Or you can refer to the resource list at the end of this chapter for national professional organizations that can refer you to professionals among their membership.

you ask for help. Such people are intrigued and challenged by intelligent and well-thought-out questions. And when you don't know what you need, ask: Where should I go to find out what I need to know to do this successfully?

- **Be willing to pay.** People are flattered when you ask for their help, but if what you need requires more than a phone conversation or guest lunch, offer to pay for the expertise. If you have the right person, it's worth every penny. Most certainly plan to pay whenever the help you need is what the person does for a living.

- **Accept the help you're offered.** One of Sarah's mentors told her recently that he was glad to see she was using his advice. He said he often hesitates to take the time to share his expertise with others because while many people seek his advice, few actually use it. Is it any wonder that 20 percent of all medical prescriptions are never filled? If you respect someone enough to ask for her help, at least give her advice a try. Most certainly don't take up his time listing all the reasons his advice won't work for you.

- **Express appreciation.** For heaven's sake, make it a point to thank the people who help you. Isn't that one of the major reasons people help one another? Everyone likes to be appreciated. We all want to know we've made a difference.

- **Pass it on.** Circulate what you learn. When you find out about something that could be helpful to others, pass it on. We all grow from what we know. As Jesse Jackson said, "You aren't known for what you know; you're known for what you teach."

6. Find the little things that make a big difference. Don't overlook asking for or lining up help to deal with the little hassles in your life, too. A study at the York University in Toronto points out that everyday annoyances like noise, traffice jams, or difficult customers may account for more long-term chronic unhappiness than major life traumas. During major traumas, we're more likely to seek and receive support from others, but we're more apt to think we must put up with or endure life's many mundane little irritations.

Often in working successfully on your own, though, it's the little things that make the biggest difference. Little things that don't cost much and aren't terribly glamorous or exciting can often simplify your day and make your life a lot easier. Many of these lifesavers don't make it onto the list of must-haves in setting up an office. In fact, they're easily overlooked. They may be things you never think of or just never get around to doing anything about.

Little Things That Make a Big Difference

A cordless phone. Have you ever noticed that whatever document you need to refer to while you're on the phone always seems to be in another location? A cordless phone frees you from the ball-and-chain effect of a standard phone. You can go to and from files and bookcases and from one room to another while talking on the phone. You can continue your phone conversation while you answer the door as clients or deliveries arrive. And of course if you're working on tasks in an area away from your desk, you can take the phone with you and answer incoming calls without having to drop what you're doing. They're also great for those moments when the dog is scratching noisily to be let out while you're talking to a key client. A mute button that cuts off unwanted noise helps at moments like those as well.

A telephone headset. If you spend much time talking on the phone, a headset is a lifesaver, and specifically a neck saver! Rather than trying to cradle the phone on your shoulder while you take notes or enter text, you can have both hands free to write or do other tasks while you talk. This is particularly handy when you've been put on hold. Instead of getting aggravated about the delay, you can go on about your work while you wait. Plantronics headsets, for example, are comfortable and provide satisfactory incoming and outgoing voice quality. Headsets come in both corded and cordless models.

A copyholder. What contortions we go through to enter text or numbers from a paper copy into a computer! We crook our necks. We prop up the paper on the monitor—but, of course, it falls over and we lose our place. A copyholder ends all this needless frustration. They come in many styles, from freestanding magnetic or clip-on desktop models to flexible arms that attach to your monitor. Legal-sized and extra-wide holders for spreadsheets are available, too. Copyholders range in price from under $3 to $150 for an electric model that advances your copy as you work. A new version, the Copy Hinge from West Manufacturing, holds paper with a roller grip rather than a clip hinge, making it possible to insert and remove pages with only one hand and to display more than one page at a time.

Grammar-checking software. Certainly nothing makes a worse impression in business correspondence than poor grammar. But bad grammar is like bad breath: you don't know you have it until someone points it out—and usually no one does. Fortunately, grammar-checking software can save you the embarrassment. You can quickly and routinely run your documents through a grammar checker right along with your spell checker. We use Reference Software's *Grammatik,* which lists for $99 but can be bought by mail order for as little as $47.

A digital postage scale. How much time do you waste waiting in line at the post office? Somehow the lines are always longest just when you're most pressed for time. A digital postage scale makes meeting the pickup deadlines easy and saves you hours every month by enabling you to weigh and stamp all your outgoing mail yourself. There's no more waiting in line. To determine the correct amount of postage, request a booklet on rates and fees from the U.S. Postal Service, and keep a supply of stamps in many denominations on hand. And don't forget to keep a supply of overnight-mail envelopes and stamps handy, as well as forms for certified and registered mail. Having to go to the back of the line to fill out a form can be double punishment. Costs for digital postage scales begin about $100.

Preinked and customized stamps. Customized preinked stamps are neat and make a more reliable impression than the old ink pads. We have ones reading First Class, Priority, and Fourth Class Mail. You can also get them made for your return address, your signature, and to designate particular actions taken.

Plastic silverware trays. Usually desk drawers are better suited for sweaters and underwear than for the many little things we need to keep in them. More likely than not, when you open your desk drawer it's all there in a hodge-podge—pens, pencils, Post-it pads, paper clips, rubber bands, scissors, stapler, and so on—that you have to rummage through every time you need something. Happily, plastic silverware trays fit perfectly in desk drawers and provide an excellent place for keeping everything neatly in sight and at your fingertips.

Plastic stacking trays. If you can't find the top of your desk, plastic stacking trays can clean up desktop clutter in a snap, and they're only two to three dollars apiece. They're also ideal for storing documents you use too frequently to be constantly filing. Unless you are diligent about weekly filing, however, we advise against using them as to-file piles. They work best as handy receptacles for work in progress.

A good way to identify the little things that will make a big difference in your day is to notice the reoccurring irritants and the repetitive tasks you find most frustrating. Periodically, for example, we keep a Daily Irritant List. Rarely is it major issues that are eating away at our peace of mind and productivity. One time, problems with a chronically malfunctioning fax machine came out on the top of the list. We decided to replace it. Over another time period, not being able to find things in our files topped our Daily Irritant List, so we decided to get help from a professional organizer. The last time we kept the list, deciding to network our computers resolved a nagging irritant we'd been living with. Since one of us has a color ink-jet printer and the other has a laser printer, we were forever having to shift files to floppy disks in order to print them out on each other's printers. Now it's a snap.

To rid your life of such irritants, keep your own Daily Irritant List. Undoubtedly, tasks that frustrate you over and over again are irritating to others, too, so chances are someone has created something to help. Why suffer? Visit office-supply stores and browse through mail-order catalogs such as those from Reliable and Quill. You'll be surprised at the little things that have been developed to make your working life easier, more convenient, and more comfortable. A few of our favorites are listed on the following pages. (See also *Creating a Supportive Work Environment* on page 170.)

7. Work smarter, not harder. Hard work is often the result of allowing simple details to pile up. So don't make extra work for yourself. In other words, running an office is like doing the dishes: the longer you wait to do what needs to be done, the more elbow grease it takes to do the job. Consider the following ways we make extra work for ourselves:

- If you don't create a pile, it doesn't have to be filed.
- If you don't accumulate a bunch of receipts, they don't need to be sorted.
- If you collect when you deliver your service, you don't have to bill or invoice.
- If you send out timely invoices, it's less likely you'll have to spend time collecting.
- If you handle a complaint now, you won't have to call back later.
- If you order enough, soon enough, you won't have to run out in the middle of a project to get needed supplies, only to find that they're out of stock and an inconvenience has become a crisis.

As a general rule, when it comes to handling the details of being on your own, what you can do in a minute now can take you an hour later.

8. Set up routines to take care of details automatically. Whenever something needs to be done routinely or repetitively, the first thing to ask yourself is how you can get it to happen automatically. This applies to most aspects of business: marketing, billing, inventory, filing, cleaning, ordering, and so on. There's nothing like a routine to make things happen automatically. Routines enable you to make a habit of taking care of minutiae in the quickest and least intrusive way. Once established, they enable you to take care of many details without even thinking about them.

Essentially, having a routine means having a regular time, space, and manner for handling something. Here are several routines that most self-employed individuals will find helpful. Have a standard time, place, and procedure for:

- Processing the mail
- Filing receipts
- Balancing the checkbook
- Taking orders or phone calls
- Making follow-up marketing calls
- Sending out thank-you notes
- Reading newspapers, journals, and newsletters
- Filing and cleaning up work in progress
- Ordering supplies
- Running business errands

Each of these activities is easy to put off until tomorrow. They're easy to forget about and lose track of. But they also take much less time to do routinely than after they've piled up. And usually if you have no routine for these activities, you fall behind in doing them. Then they back up and ultimately bury you.

Although routines are often considered to be restrictive and dull, they actually free us to attend to more important matters. Routines are like the boiler room of your office. You want them to remain in the background and just keep chugging away while you go about your business.

To create useful routines, identify the details you need to handle regularly and assign a convenient time and place to do them. Then commit to following your routines diligently for at least six weeks. If you find yourself avoiding or resenting your routines, it's a sign that either the ones you've established aren't functional or you need additional help to manage them because they're taking up too much of your day.

9. Piggyback activities. The more business activities you bundle into any one effort the better. For example, you can avoid doing a special mailing if you put sales promotional materials and reorder forms in every product order or invoice you send out. You can avoid extra phone calls if you keep a list by your telephone of things you want to pass on to people who call you.

With every business activity you undertake, get in the habit of asking yourself how many uses you can make out of it. If you're traveling to Houston for a conference, for example, think of the networking contacts, sales calls, or media appearances you can make while you're there. If you're speaking before a trade group, what materials can you distribute to those in attendance? Which key individuals can you invite to hear your presentation. What media coverage can you get? If you have a meeting in a particular area of the city, what other errands could you run in that vicinity while you're there?

We have become adept at piggybacking activities. If we're making a speech, for example, we might have it taped to use as a demo for getting future speeches; we'll have the tape transcribed and then edit it into an article or handout; we'll collect names from the audience to call for future interviews; we'll conduct on-the-spot market research by asking key questions of the audience. Everything you do holds a wealth of potential piggybacking opportunities. If you're going to do something, why not make the most of it?

Making Light Work of the Most Time-Consuming Tasks

It will probably take you some time and energy to set these principles in motion in your work, but once they're operating, the momentum they create will free you to do more of what you want to do. You'll be able to make more money doing it. And you'll have more time to enjoy yourself in the process. So begin with the one idea from this chapter that could save you the most time, money, and energy. Implement that idea, and then with the extra time you save, do the next one and the next, until things are running themselves with just a little help from you.

When you start to apply these principles, you'll find they can help you make light work of the two most time-consuming and unpaid aspects of being on your own: marketing and administering your business. Let's take a further look at how.

THE CRITICAL-MASS MARKETING ALTERNATIVE TO HAVING TO CONSTANTLY SELL YOURSELF

Marketing can make a small business large.
JAY CONRAD LEVINSON

Basically there are two ways to get work for yourself: go out and get it, or get it to come to you. The first is faster, but much more time-consuming and energy intensive. On your own, time is money and you're not getting paid while you're drumming up work. So if you want your time and energy free to earn money and enjoy your life, you're better off using methods that will bring work to you with the smallest investment of your time and energy.

That's what Critical-Mass Marketing can do for you. Ultimately it can produce a steady stream of business with virtually no extra effort on your part. And it works especially well for people who don't have the time or inclination to sell themselves in the traditional ways. It may initially be slower and more indirect than more traditional approaches to getting business, but it does work. And once it gets under way, it leaves you free to do the work it brings in for you to do.

Critical-Mass Marketing is a strategy that involves giving yourself and your work a sufficiently high profile that your name becomes a powerful magnet that draws business opportunities to you. The goal is to create a situation whereby whenever someone needs what you offer, he or she will think about, hear about, read about, or otherwise be directed to you! Here's an example of how it works.

Helen Berman decided to become a consultant and sales trainer for the publishing industry, but the competition was tough. There were already a number of well-known consultants serving this industry. So how was she to break in? She knew that calling a list of thousands of potential customers would be very costly both in time and in money. The people on that list didn't know about her or her training programs, so she'd have to place lots of calls to make any sale.

So instead, she used Critical-Mass Marketing. She began building a high profile for herself and her programs that would cause interested, qualified individuals to identify themselves to her. Then when she contacted them, they would already know who she was and be motivated to talk with her. This way the same number of calls would lead to many times more sales.

Having researched what the hot sales topics would be, she contacted meeting planners for upcoming conferences in the publishing field and proposed that she provide seminars that addressed these topics using her sales methods. She got several bookings. Simultaneously she began calling the trade magazines in the field to explore writing a sales column for them. Soon she was writing a column for *Folio,* the publishing industry's leading trade magazine.

From attendees at her workshops and contacts made as a result of her column, she identified potential clients who would immediately recognize her as a credible professional. She contacted them by phone and mail, and soon her training calendar begin filling up. By the following January, Helen was booked ahead for the entire year.

You've heard the saying "Success attracts success." Critical-Mass Marketing operates on that principle. It assumes that if you create enough momentum around yourself and your work and then follow through by providing a top-quality service or product, your success will grow.

Thirty-five Ways to Get Business to Come to You*

Word-of-mouth

1. Networking
2. Mentors and gatekeepers
3. Volunteerism
4. Sponsorships
5. Charitable donations
6. Referrals
7. Business name
8. Letterhead and business card
9. Product packaging
10. Point-of-sale display

Public Relations

11. Writing articles
12. Letters to the editor
13. News releases
14. Speeches and seminars
15. Publicity:
    Newspaper
    Magazine
    Radio and TV
    Business and trade publications

Direct Marketing

16. Sampling
17. Incentives
18. Discount pricing
19. Contests and giveaways
20. Newsletters
21. Circulars and flyers
22. Trade shows and exhibits
23. Sales seminars
24. Demonstrations
25. Direct mail

Inventive Advertising

26. Classified ads
27. Business directories
28. Yellow Pages advertising
29. Bulletin boards and tear pads
30. Your own radio show
31. Your own TV show
32. On-line networking
33. Fax
34. Direct-response ads
35. Card decks

*Reprinted from *Getting Business to Come to You,* by Paul and Sarah Edwards and Laura Clampitt Douglas.

Boldly Standing Out from the Crowd

Another way of thinking about this approach to creating opportunities for yourself is to remember that people are attracted to bright, shiny, moving objects that stand out from the crowd. That was what Helen Berman was able to make herself into. In a short period of time, she was able to catapult herself to a level of prominence that a traditional lower-profile approach would have taken years to achieve. She went from seeking business to being sought after.

Here's another example of Critical-Mass Marketing. You may recall that when the aspiring movie director David Beaird went to Los Angeles, everyone told him Hollywood didn't need another director. And indeed he found the studio doors closed tight. Having taught acting and built a theater company in Chicago several years before, however, he decided to use that experience to get into film directing. He rented a theater and began teaching acting classes there on Monday evenings. Soon he put on a play he'd written, starring students from his classes. He then invited the press and industry representatives to see it. Many liked it. It received several drama awards from a local trade paper. The momentum was building. Based on the response to his play, he was able to attract backing for a low-budget film.

Although the film was never distributed, he did get to show it at the Cannes Film Festival and received some attention. That led to further backing. After his second low-budget film he reached his critical mass and was placed on the directors' list for a major studio. Three years later, he finished the film version of the original play he had put on at the theater. It's called *Scorchers*. It stars Faye Dunaway and after having been released in movie theaters it's available now on video. David was able to create the critical mass he needed to leap to a level of success that might have taken many years to accomplish via more traditional routes.

Becoming Self-Generating

One of the most rewarding aspects of using Critical-Mass Marketing is that it's like riding a bicycle: once you get the momentum going it enables you to go further faster with less and less effort. Activity you generate develops a life of its own, and you find that not only do you have to call fewer people, but a growing number of people are calling you. Efforts from months and years ago continue to bear fruit. We still get calls from articles that people clipped five years ago. That's why we use the term *critical mass*. Once you achieve it, the momentum will keep your business going, and growing.

Making Your Marketing Efforts Self-Liquidating

Critical-Mass Marketing has other advantages as well. Most self-employed individuals have limited marketing funds. But they do have a strong need to generate income. Critical-Mass Marketing not only enables you to produce revenue to pay for itself; it can also be a potential profit center.

Sometimes, for example, Helen is paid to make presentations at the trade-association meetings where she markets her programs. Or she may be offered a free booth at a convention. Even when she is simply reimbursed for her expenses, most of her marketing costs are being paid for. Sometimes she's paid to write for trade magazines and journals. But even if she contributes an article for free, she can arrange to barter for ad space in exchange for her article.

By like token, David can charge for his acting classes and thereby cover the cost of the theater through which he is able to promote his work. Charging admission to the play also helps offset his marketing costs.

Letting Your Work Market Itself

Another advantage of Critical-Mass Marketing is that instead of spending your time selling and/or learning to master traditional marketing methods, you can market yourself by simply doing what you do. In both her articles and presentations, for example, Helen is using the very skills she teaches in her sales-training program. So when people see what she's doing and say "I wish I could do that," she can reply "You can. I'll teach you." Likewise at the theater, David is demonstrating his writing and directing skills. And since that's what they love doing and they're good at it, marketing becomes fun as well as profitable. To start producing these dramatic results for yourself, here's how you can begin using Critical-Mass Marketing as a springboard to a new level of success.

Four Steps to Building Your Critical Marketing Mass

1. *Identify your unique advantage.* To call attention to yourself and your work, you have to distinguish yourself from the crowd. You need to find and highlight what makes you extraspecial. And everyone is special in some way. For Helen it was her proprietary sales methodology. For David, it was his ability to stun and startle an audience with a very low budget. Although there may be many others who provide a product or service similar to yours, no two businesses are the same. Each word-processing service can have its own personality. Each PR firm can have its unique advantages. What do you do that's unique to you?

A good way to identify your unique advantage is to research your competition. Read their literature, study their advertising. Ask your customers and clients about their previous service providers. Find out what they liked and didn't like about the service they received. You'll soon begin to recognize that indeed you do have your own modus operandi. And that's what you want to highlight. That's what makes you distinctive!

2. *Find a platform to show off your unique advantage.* Helen's platform was annual trade meetings and her column for *Folio*. David's was the small theater he rented. Teaching trade-school classes was the platform for the programmer James Milburn.

Milburn began his career as an accountant, so he understood what small-business people needed in customized software. He spoke their language and could get the computer to speak it, too. But how was anyone else to know he was any different from any other programmer? He showed them by offering low-cost classes in custom programming for small businesses. These classes became his marketing platform. Some of his students soon learned how difficult programming customized software could be, and they knew they didn't want to do it themselves. Since they could see that Milburn understood their needs, he got all the business he needed.

Free consultations for corporate employees became the platform for Teri Goehring. An image and color consultant, Goehring offers image seminars for corporation employees during the lunch hour and sells products to those who attend. The Science of Mind Church became a platform for Jerry Florence. Instead of waiting for a record company to produce his first musical album, he produced it himself and sold copies at church performances. Within two years he'd sold over thirty thousand copies and was booked to sing concerts across the country. For Bill Vick, it was the Internet. Vick operates an executive-recruiting firm and by being among the first to offer his services online, he's become a leader in his field.

Think of where you could demonstrate what you have to offer on a regular basis to those who need it.

3. Give away samples. Although their marketing became self-liquidating, all the people we've talked about so far began by giving away samples of their services. Helen spoke for free at first. David's theater barely broke even in the beginning. James offered his valuable expertise for only a small fee. Jerry's first appearance was free, and often at first he sang for a small fee, but each time he sang the ranks of his loyal fans grew and each time he sold more tapes.

Here's another excellent example of how initially giving away your services or products can help you reach critical mass. When Ted Laux began his book-indexing service with a TRS Model I, he looked through bookstores for books that didn't have adequate indexes. To demonstrate how much more effective these books would be had the publishers used his services, he indexed the books on his own and sent copies to the publishers. Several liked the results, and Ted was in business. His indexing software was his unique advantage, and the postal service became his platform for showing off just what he could do.

So find a way people can sample what you offer. Give them a chance to become excited about what you do and start spreading the word.

4. Showcase what you offer in as many media as possible. The more avenues you can use to demonstrate your unique advantage the better. Although Helen began with trade conferences and a column, she has gone on to produce audiotapes and write many magazine articles. Her next project is a book. Teri has expanded her image demonstrations to trade shows and radio. Jerry has developed a video and holds concert series.

Begin thinking of the many avenues open to show off your work. Where could you speak about your subject? Where could you offer seminars or do demonstrations? What trade shows might you exhibit at? What magazines, newsletters, or newspapers could you write for or arrange a feature story in? How could you use radio or television? After demonstrating her techniques repeatedly on a local television morning show, bridal-makeup artist Sally Van Swearington has opened two new studios. Florida financial consultant Brian Sheen has built a thriving practice from his own radio talk show. By making use of prominent listings in women's business directories and personal networking, Roseann Higgins of Phoenix, Arizona, has established a high profile for herself and turned her business, S.P.I.E.S, Single Professionals Introductions and Event Services, into a model of success. She's become known as the "romance headhunter."

Such results are not unusual. These are examples of what you can accomplish with a concentrated effort sustained over time. If you start now, find your platform, and expand from it into as many arenas as you can, you can develop similar results. It's what happens when you shift your focus from merely surviving project-by-project to thriving on an abundance of work.

Using this approach, you'll be able to generate enough momentum to leap to a new level where everything occurring around you begins working in your favor. Once your efforts reach a critical mass, you'll find yourself accomplishing much more with much less effort.

For more information on how to develop your marketing mindset and tools, we recommend reading our book *Getting Business to Come to You* and using *The Business Generator,* which are listed in the Resources section at the end of this chaper.

USING TECHNOLOGY TO REDUCE ADMINISTRIVIA

Technology is the great equalizer. It gives the small the power of the large.   PAUL AND SARAH EDWARDS

Twenty years ago, the information you needed to take advantage of the latest modern technology was expensive, time-consuming, or nonexistent. Just one generation ago, Sarah's father had to travel from Kansas City to New Jersey and spend an entire summer there learning how to computerize the billing for his company. Installing their computer system cost tens of thousands of dollars and took several consultants over six months to accomplish. Today that entire billing system could be run on a personal computer with off-the-shelf software her father could either install himself or hire a consultant to set up within a few days to a week.

Today there's a wealth of relatively inexpensive, increasingly small office technology that can free you from the headaches of handling the business side of your work so you can spend your time getting paid for doing what you enjoy. And this new technology, which can be used at home or in a car or van, is increasingly easy to use. Often you can simply turn it on and put it to work doing the things you hate to do or don't like taking your time to do—tasks such as billing, balancing your bank account, invoicing, keeping up your mailing list, taking messages, keeping track of key information, and so forth.

Equipping the Ideal Do-It-Yourself Office

When you're trying to get your work done, having to constantly stop what you're doing to play the role of clerk and gofer can be demoralizing. You can start to feel like a second-class citizen. Having to take out a half hour to drag yourself over to the print shop in the rain to make just one copy that has to go out today, begging friends to print out a proposal for you on their computer so it won't look like schlock, paying $12.50 every time you have to send something overnight, having a client tell you your answering-machine message sounds like you're drunk, or, worst of all, getting a chance for some really good work only to have the client ask you to fax him or her something, and you don't have a fax—well, it's embarrassing, time-consuming, and demeaning.

You deserve better. You owe it to yourself and to your work to equip your office in a manner that will support you like the professional you are and aspire to become. Fortunately, you can equip your office so that everything around you works just as it would for the CEO of a well-run corporation. Below is our list of the ideal equipment for a single-person office and how each piece of technology we recommend can take the drudgery out of being your own boss. By shopping carefully you can purchase some combination of all this equipment for under $3,000.

1. A personal computer that is quick and expandable. A computer is the single most versatile and valuable piece of equipment you can own. It's a staff in a box. It can be a secretary, bookkeeper, receptionist, file clerk, business consultant, financial analyst, tax preparer, graphic designer, and print shop all rolled into one. It can save you hours of time, tons of money, and much misery, yet to date less than half of home-based businesses have one. On page 122 are fifty things a computer can do for you.

By shopping carefully you can buy a fast, powerful, and expandable one bundled with basic software for about $1,500, plus the cost of your printer and any additional software. That means your computer can pay for itself quickly in reduced costs and increased productivity. Over 70 percent of self-employed individuals now own and use a computer. So, even if you have a high-touch/low-tech business like plumbing, carpentry, psychological counseling, family day care, or tutoring, we urge you to invest in a personal computer to help you run your business. At a bare minimum we recommend using a computer to run the following aspects of your business:

- Word processing. Do all your sales letters, correspondence, flyers, reports, proposals, invoices, statements, and so on.

- Bookkeeping. Keep track of your income and expenses. Balance your bank account, get instant reports on how you're spending your money, and tally expenses quickly for tax purposes.

- Contact management. Develop a mailing and contact list and keep it up-to-date so you can announce new services or products, run specials, send out newsletters, invitations and news releases, and carry out other marketing activities quickly and easily.

You may not be able to start doing all these tasks on a computer at once. In fact, we've read that those who are using computers are using only 20 percent of the capability of the software they use. So we recommend starting with the task that is taking up the most time and/or the one that's the most frustrating. Once you've computerized that task, you can move on to the next most time-consuming or aggravating one.

To identify our most frustrating tasks, we periodically keep track for a two-week period of every daily irritation that disrupted and disturbed our ability to work effectively and prioritized the equipment we wanted to add to our home office based on what would eliminate the most prevalent hassles. That's how we decided to get a business card scanner. With a card scanner, like *CardScan* which you can get for under $200, you can scan all the business cards you collect directly into contact management software. After scanning in the paper card, you'll have an actual graphic image of the card in your computer, and the key information like name, address, and phone number will be automatically picked up and transferred into the contact management software like *ACT*.

Other computer-based time-savers to consider include:

- File-management software. Studies show we waste more time looking for things we can't find than doing anything else. And what's more frustrating than not being able to remember what you named a particular file you created six months ago? File-management software solves this problem. It enables you to search through your hard disk and locate files with any key word or phrase you can remember from inside the file you need to find. Today such software is built into your operating system or your can use separate software with additional capabilities like Norton *Navigator*.

• Desktop publishing software. You can create your own marketing materials by using desktop publishing software to design and print your own business cards, brochures, letterhead, newsletters, flyers, and postcards. If you use a laser-quality printer and the templates that are built into software like *Microsoft Publisher, QuarkExpress* by Quark Inc., and Corel's *Ventura,* your self-made materials can look highly professional while saving you both the time and money of having to go elsewhere to have them designed and printed.

• Presentation software. If you need to give sales presentations, speeches, or seminars, presentation software will allow you to create professional-quality overheads and handout materials that would once have cost hundreds, if not thousands, of dollars in outside services to produce. Programs are Microsoft's *PowerPoint, Freelance Graphics* by Lotus, and *Harvard Graphics* by Software Publishing Corporation.

• Phone-dialer software. Using phone-dialer software, with a few keystrokes of your computer, you can dial any phone number that's stored in your computer—all clients and prospects, even thousands of them. And if you need to locate an out-of-town address or phone number quickly, a CD-ROM like *PhoneDisc Powerfinder* instantaneously gives you access to residential and commercial telephone numbers from the nation's Yellow Pages. And additional products like *CompuPhone* and *Cyberphone* by Prometheus can turn your computer into a telecommunications center, combining fax, modem, speakerphone, voice mail, and dialer all in one.

• Time and expenses software. Packages such as *Timeslips* and *Time-Tracker* can streamline your billing by automatically keeping track of your time and then creating your invoice without any additional calculations. *Timeslips Remote* lets you collect and edit time and expense information on the road.

We've listed several resources at the end of this chapter that spell out in detail how to purchase, set up, and learn to use a computer to carry out the administrative aspects of your business, along with specific software packages that can do these tasks for you. For assistance in shopping for or expanding your computer equipment and software you can refer to Chapter 8 of *Working from Home.*

Finally, once you're using a computer regularly to do the most crucial aspects of your work, make it a point to go beyond the bare minimum of what your software can do. Explore and adopt useful new aspects periodi-

Fifty Jobs Today's Home Office Technology Can Do for You

1. Business planning
2. Market research
3. Market forecasting
4. Cash-flow projections
5. Financial planning
6. Project management
7. Newsletter layout
8. Brochure layout
9. Logo design
10. Graphs and charts
11. Slides and overheads
12. Letters, reports, and other documents
13. Business forms
14. Library searches
15. Find and merge files
16. Place phone calls
17. Answer your phone
18. Record phone messages
19. Set agendas
20. Receive mail instantly
21. Send mail instantly
22. Send faxes of bills, invoices, and marketing materials
23. Receive faxes
24. Locate resources
25. Track your schedule
26. Store, locate, and search for information
27. Record notes
28. Outline projects, articles, and reports
29. Manage telemarketing efforts
30. Build mailing lists
31. Keep mailing lists up-to-date
32. Serve as a tickler system
33. Be an electronic Rolodex
34. Network coast to coast
35. Personalize mass mailings
36. Record keeping
37. Run a PR campaign
38. Check writing
39. Bookkeeping
40. Accounting
41. Balance your bank account
42. Tax planning
43. Tax preparation
44. File your tax return
45. Budgeting
46. Keep time and expense records
47. Billing
48. Invoicing
49. Inventory Control
50. Print labels

cally, and be sure to get the newest versions of your software, because each new release is usually updated with new features that can make your work easier in some way.

2. A laser-quality printer. A laser printer is to other printers what a computer is to a typewriter. Laser printers are faster, more versatile, and QUIET. They shoot out your documents in seconds in a wide variety of type styles and sizes, and you can be talking in hushed tones nearby and hardly know they're printing.

But best of all, owning a laser printer goes a long way toward addressing the number-one concern of self-employed individuals who work from home: the need to project a professional image. If you select a decent laser printer, the documents you produce may be indistinguishable from those coming from a Fortune 500 company.

Although once priced beyond the reach of most self-employed individuals, laser printers are no longer expensive. Every year they come down in price. At the time of this writing, you can get an adequate laser printer for under $600. This is another item of equipment that will pay for itself quickly. Bios, handouts, newsletters, flyers, reports, presentations, media materials— virtually anything you want printed—come out camera ready, to use as is or to have professionally printed or copied. For further assistance in selecting your printer, see Chapter 8 in *Working from Home.*

3. A copy machine. For as little as $300, you can buy a personal copy machine today the size of a briefcase. Not only can these personal copiers produce better-looking copies than you'll get at most copy stores for less money; a copier costing about a $700 can make reductions and enlargements. And think of how quickly your copy machine will pay for itself. How long does it take you to go out to the copy store? How far do you have to drive? How long do you have to wait for your copies? How many phone calls will you miss while you're gone? How quickly will you be able to make needed copies when the machine is on hand? This one purchase will save you innumerable hours and endless frustration. For the features to look for in a copier, see Chapter 8 in *Working from Home.*

4. A two-line telephone. A two-line telephone provides you with a wealth of options for simplifying your life. It enables you to have separate lines for incoming and outgoing calls. This means you can place calls and still leave your incoming line open to receive others without the inconvenience of *call waiting,* which is unquestionably disruptive and highly irritating to some callers. The incoming line can also roll over to an answering machine if you are on the other line.

Alternatively, if you work from home, you can use one line as your personal line and the other for your business calls. Another advantage of a two-line phone is that one of the lines can be used for fax or modem transmission, although if you use these features frequently, you really should have a separate third line dedicated just to fax and modem use. And, of course, a two-line phone saves precious desk space and reduces the cord jungle around your work space.

5. An answering machine or voice mail. A good answering machine is a must; voice mail is even better. Voice mail turns your telephone into an answering machine, a switchboard, and a phone-mail system like those you encounter when calling many large companies today. In addition to simply recording a caller's message when you're away, it also records messages while you're talking on the phone. Voice mail can give the caller a number of other options, too. For example, it can relay a specific prerecorded message about your product or service and provide directions or instructions for placing an order. If you are talking on another line, it can tell callers you're busy and take their messages or switch them to another line. So it becomes another alternative to call waiting. Voice mail can also be used to take dictation and act as a calendaring system as well as a directory that enables you to call in and obtain phone numbers when you're away from the office. Or it can be used to automatically fax back frequently requested information, like price lists, order forms, directions, etc.

Most local telephone-operating companies are now offering voice mail through their regular phone service for a low monthly charge. The Bogen *Friday,* selling for under $300, is an answering machine with voice-mail features. Or you can set up your own voice-mail system on your computer using a product like the Prometheus *CyberPhone* described above. It sells for between $100 and $300, depending on the model you need. Chapter 8 of *Working from Home* summarizes many additional telephone services that can help to make sure your clients and customers can reach you anywhere anytime. And new services are being added every day. So, to find the best solu-

A Unique Telephone Solution

How would you like a twenty-four-hour-a-day telephone receptionist without having to pay someone a salary? If you are willing to have an electronic receptionist, an electronic personal assistant can be yours from a service like Wildfire (1-800-WILDFIRE). Train your assistant to recognize your voice to do things for you like remind you of calls you want to make and to actually place the calls. As a receptionist, an electronic assistant will screen calls, forward them to you, and while you are on calls "whisper" to you the names of new callers, enabling you to put the person you are talking to "on hold." Unlike with call waiting, you decide if you want to place the incoming call on hold. Most amazingly, Wildfire sounds like a person you want to hear from and she's at your beck and call. All you need to do is say her name.

tions for you, call your phone company's small-business or home-business consultant.

6. A fax machine or a fax board. With a fax you can send a page of text over phone lines in only twenty seconds. That beats any overnight-delivery service or same-day messenger service for a fraction of the cost! But that's not all. Think of the time a fax can save you. You don't have to put your mail in an envelope, address it, stamp it, and get it to a mailbox. You just push a button and it's on its way.

Just think what that means. How much more quickly an invoice can be paid. How many hours—and how much pressure—that saves you when meeting a deadline. How much simpler it becomes to resend something some-one claims he or she never received. And you can get a thermal-paper fax machine for under $200 dollars and a plain-paper fax for as little as $500.

Even faster is a fax board, which turns your computer into a fax machine. With a fax board in your computer, you can send and receive material through the phone line directly. You don't even have to print it out; you can also edit it and send it back without ever printing it out. Another advantage is that you can print out anything you've received through your fax board on your printer and thereby avoid having a separate fax machine.

The only drawback to a fax board is that you can send only materials that you have in your computer. That rules out sending newspaper clippings, magazine articles, and so on, although you can receive such materials through your fax board. Personally, we have both a freestanding fax machine and a fax board and find the flexibility of having them both to be worth the invest-ment. For further information about shopping for fax capability, see Chapter 8 in *Working from Home*.

7. A high-speed modem. Used with communications software, a modem turns your computer into a library, telephone, and store front to the world. With a modem you can gain access to a significant amount of the information that's been published in the last fifteen years and some that's available only on-line. You can do market research, check stock prices, find venture capital, locate personnel, investigate companies, and use the processing capabilities of main-frame computers.

By using the Internet and on-line services like CompuServe, you can also send mail, market your business, sell your products and services, do banking, shop, pay bills, get airline schedules, and make reservations—all without leaving your desk.

Today you will not want to get less than a 28.8-baud modem.

8. Integrated equipment. One of the most cost-effective ways to quickly ob-tain most of the equipment we've just described is to get as many of them as possible all in one. Computers have long been able to house modems, faxes,

"What I've Gotten On-line"

We asked people on the Working from Home Forum on CompuServe to tell what they had gotten as a result of their on-line participation. Here are some of the responses:

"I found insurance coverage. . . . something I could not find locally."

"I learned how to bid my first big freelance job, and what to charge per hour."

"I have made many contacts for potential business. . . ."

"I keep in touch with colleagues around the world."

"I obtained a Visa merchant account that works well."

"Odd props for video shoots."

"A page from the N.Y. Yellow Pages."

"Interviews in major newspapers and magazines."

"Respect and recognition from local colleagues."

"Friends in foreign cities."

"Local work-at-homers whom I never would have met elsewhere because neither I nor they ever leave our homes!"

"Significant advice about a problem employee—something I was extremely reluctant to discuss with local friends because they all know who this employee is."

"Connected with a marketing company in Milan, Italy, who translated, produced, and so far sold 100,000 copies of my organizing tips booklet."

"Found a video producer for my newest product, a video on office organizing."

"Was approached by a published author in Oregon to co-author a book."

"Have been referred business."

"Found promoters around the country and in Canada."

"Had speech drafts critiqued."

"Have made personal and professional friendships."

". . . emotional support. It's no exaggeration to say the friends I made literally saved my life."

"I discovered that my 'career' was—for me, at least—something I really didn't want to do, but had merely settled for."

and voice mail systems and many manufacturers offer computers with these components. In addition, companies like Canon, Hewlett-Packard, Panasonic, and Xerox have integrated equipment that serves as a printer, fax, modem, and copier. Xerox's *WorkCenter 250,* for example, has five functions in one package. It's a laser-quality printer, plain-paper fax, copier, scanner, and PC fax, all for under $700. And the best thing about this product is that if one function breaks down, the others don't. And they will replace it within twenty-four hours, so you're not stranded without equipment that's vital to your business. Xerox calls this their While You Sleep service guarantee. Even the keyboard now does double duty. Compaq's Scanner Keyboard enables you to scan documents such as business cards, receipts, and photos and with accompanying software, retrieve them within seconds.

If you take a few minutes to identify the tasks that take you the most time and cause you the most frustration, chances are the equipment we've described or other technology can simplify, streamline, and automate what you need to do. You'll find a wealth of information about the latest equipment and software for today's home and small office in the magazines listed in the resource list at the end of this chapter.

Breaking Down Myths and Resistance to Technology

While technology can never make up for a poor product or service or for bad business decisions and poor management practices, we can say with certainty that as a general rule those who take advantage of what technology has to offer are apt to be more successful on their own than those who try to muddle through by doing everything the old-fashioned way. Technology clearly gives you the power to accomplish much more with less effort.

Yet we do encounter people who for one reason or another resist investing time and energy to bring their offices up to the level of sophistication better equipment could help them achieve. Here are several common myths and sources of resistance and how we and others have gotten past them.

1. I don't need that. In truth, one of us has said this about nearly every piece of equipment we listed above. I (Sarah) was much slower to adopt new technology than Paul was. At first, I didn't think we needed a computer. We had a Selectric typewriter, and that was enough for me. But within two weeks of Paul's talking me into our buying a computer, I found I couldn't live without it. Now I'm as eager as Paul to explore new technology.

If you have an "I don't need that" attitude toward any particular piece of technology, at least allow yourself to take a serious look at how your competition is using it. Whenever you hear yourself saying "I don't need that," erase that thought and replace it by asking this question: "What could this do for me?" See if you're missing out and making your life harder than it needs to be.

2. It's too complicated. I'm not mechanical.   If you're someone who thinks of yourself as low tech, we have good news for you. Much of the equipment we recommend is no longer complex and difficult to use. Using a two-line phone, an answering machine, voice mail from the phone company, a personal copier, or a personal fax is no more difficult than using a toaster. So if technology is intimidating to you, start with these. And if you have any difficulty or need moral support, ask for help from a friend or colleague who's already using one.

Even computers and copiers are available in models that are simple to get up and running. Many software packages have become intuitive or have a tutorial that walks you through using them. Most hardware and software companies have customer support phone service to troubleshoot for you. Low-cost seminars are available in most communities for you to learn about major software programs and how to get on-line. If you still have resistance to getting a computer, hire a consultant to walk you through selecting, setting up, and learning to use one, or use a service like Action Trac, which for a $190 annual fee will walk you through any computer problem twenty-four hours a day. Located in Lancaster, California, Action Trac's unlimited friendly phone is available worldwide (800/443-7117). Today using a computer is like driving a car. Just as you don't have to be a mechanic to drive a car, you don't have to be a programmer or techie to master a computer.

3. I can't afford that.   In regard to technology, it's particularly easy to think that the price tag will be too high. Many people are not aware of how dramatically the prices for the items we've described have dropped and continue to drop. Since they first came onto the market, their prices have been going down at the rate of about 20 to 30 percent a year.

By shopping carefully you can purchase all the equipment we've mentioned for the ideal small office/home office in some combination for under $3,000. If your money situation is tight, however, or nonexistent, consider using a separate credit card for financing equipment purchases. Purchase one item at a time on that card, beginning with the one that will pay for itself most quickly. And, remember, since small office equipment (up to $17,500) and even interest on business debt is tax deductible, Uncle Sam can even help pick up part of the tab.

We found that for less than the cost of producing one set of overhead transparencies for a workshop we could buy a good-quality color printer that we've used for years. It paid for itself on the first job. A consultant we know found that once she purchased a laser printer, she was able to get a book contract—with an advance—that had been eluding her for years. A carpenter was able to take on two extra clients a month in the time he previously spent doing his accounts by hand and, thus, was able to pay for his computer and software within six months.

To get her business under way, typesetter Tina Linert leased her specialized equipment, as did Dorothy Baranski when she opened DorBar Executive Services. Others have had customers purchase the equipment they needed and then leased it back from them. One woman brought in a partner who financed the equipment so she could expand her video-production business.

Gloria Parks was especially eager to start a desktop publishing business, which, of course, depends entirely upon having a top-of-the-line computer system. She had just lost her job unexpectedly, however, and had neither the credit nor the cash to purchase the system she needed. At first the situation looked hopeless. But then she had an idea. She approached several print shops that were not yet providing desktop publishing and told them that if they would purchase the equipment, she would handle all their desktop-publishing needs and make payments on the equipment from the revenue. It worked. One shop had been wanting to add desktop publishing for months, and this idea saved them the expense of hiring additional staff.

Recently even major banks like Bank of America are beginning to make small consumer-type loans to small and home-based businesses. But if you can't find the funds to purchase the equipment you need, another way to finance it might be through one of the microloan programs that are now available in many communities throughout the country. These are loans based on your character, available through local organizations funded by the Small Business Administration and other private sources. Here are several examples of people who have used microloans to finance their equipment.

When Kevin Chubb of Conway, New Hampshire, got custody of his two little boys after his divorce, he knew he would have to change his line of work. He was an international offshore oil driller working twenty days on and twenty days off. In looking for alternatives that would allow him to be home with his kids, he decided to turn his lifelong hobby of doing crossword puzzles into a business.

Using an old 8088 computer, Chubb designed his own software to create his first puzzles. But he needed $500 to print up sample puzzles that he could take to publishers. He got the money he needed through a microloan from a program called Working Capital. The samples provided him with the exposure he needed to sell his first puzzle to Mensa, and that led to additional puzzles. The Pacesetter Puzzle Company was born and Chubb paid back the loan in six months. He says, "It wasn't hard to get the loan." He just showed the ten-person lending group one of his puzzles. The group not only approved the loan; they each wanted a copy of the puzzle!

Chubb soon realized, however, that if he wanted to continue he would need to upgrade his computer. So he borrowed another $1,000 through his Working Capital lending group to make the initial payments on a more powerful one. Now his company is almost a full-time business, and he serves as the treasurer for the lending group.

Single parent Pam Jorgensen was working in her chosen field as an architectural designer when she decided she wanted to go out on her own. She opened PJ's Designs from her home in Long Beach, California, moonlighting at first and then going full-time three and a half years ago. She's been designing renderings for real estate companies, materials for advertising agencies and menus for restaurants ever since. She also creates murals for homes.

Before long, however, she got fed up with middle-of-the-night trips with her young children to the copy store and decided she needed to get a loan to purchase a copy machine. She approached the local Chamber of Commerce for ideas about where she could obtain a loan. While they were skeptical about her chances of getting such a loan from traditional lenders, they referred her to the Coalition for Women's Economic Development where, after graduating from the required six-week course on how to run a successful business, she was able to obtain a $1000 microloan.

"It's true what you hear," she reports. "The more equipment you have, the more you can expand." After having gotten her loan in November, she has gone from needing business to needing some time off. And although Jorgensen could have taken a year to pay off her loan, her business grew so quickly that she paid it off by March. Then she decided to borrow an additional $2,500 to purchase a laser printer and have her car repaired so she can reliably travel to and from her clients' locations without worrying about breakdowns. (For more information on microloans in your area, refer to the resources directory in the appendix.)

So, as you see, there are many ways you can afford to get the equipment you need. And, if you're thinking this all sounds good but you can't afford to hire the consultant you'd need to help set up and use your new equipment, that too need not be expensive. You can get a referral from the store where you buy your equipment, from a college or university, or your peers. We've found excellent, very reasonably priced assistance in these ways.

Cutting Down on Cleaning Up

Technology can also help you cut down on the time involved in cleaning up. You can free your time and energy for more important tasks and still keep your home/office professionally neat and clean by using labor-saving appliances. We've actually found, however, that many time-consuming cleaning tasks are unnecessary if you don't make the mess in the first place. Here are several ways you can keep your home office clean without taking up your time.

60-Second Cleaning Secrets

1. Dirt that doesn't get through the door doesn't need to be cleaned up. Good-quality mats at the door and covered or elevated entryways keep dirt, mud, and water out.

2. Well-insulated doors and weatherproofed windows let in less dust.

3. Using liquid-soap dispensers instead of bars of soap prevents soap-scum buildup on sinks.

4. Deep sinks prevent splattering.

5. Brushed brass plating on faucets doesn't show spots that must be polished.

6. A shower stall or tub wiped down immediately stays clean.

7. Mildew doesn't grow as much in well-lighted bathrooms with plenty of air circulation.

8. Food doesn't get caked on dishes that are washed right after they've been used.

9. Laundry folded when it comes out of the dryer usually doesn't need ironing.

10. Clothes hung up at the moment you take them off don't get piled up to be put away.

11. Magazines and newspapers read or skimmed, clipped, and filed when they arrive don't accumulate into a major catch-up project.

12. Receipts filed when you return from the store don't pile up for sorting.

13. Semigloss latex enamel paint and vinyl wallpaper don't spot, and they are easily cleaned.

14. Fabrics treated to resist stains are easier to clean and need cleaning less often.

15. Neutral colors for all surfaces are easier to clean than dark or white ones.

16. Installing tile with dark grout saves hours of bleaching and scrubbing.

17. Streamlined furniture and fixtures don't collect dust and dirt the way ornate ones do, and they can be cleaned more quickly.

18. Plenty of storage units—drawers, racks, cabinets, and closets—prevent messes by providing places to put everything away in, on, or under.

You'll find more tips on messes that don't need to happen in some of the books listed in the resource list at the end of this chapter.

You're the Boss

The next time you start to feel as if your business is running you instead of the other way around, *stop,* take a break, and ask yourself what you need to do to turn the tables. You're the boss. By applying the basic principles we've outlined in this chapter, you should be able to decrease the time you have to spend running your business. Once you get the most time-consuming aspects of marketing and administration operating automatically in the easiest, most efficient ways, you'll find that you can concentrate your energy on your work, your health, and your quality of life.

RESOURCES

FINDING INFORMATION

Business Almanac and Sourcebook. Seth Godin, editor. New York: Houghton Mifflin, 1996. More than 4,000 associations, organizations, and companies listed including technical support numbers for software manufacturers. Useful for businesses of all sizes, including the self-employed.

The Internet and Other On-line Services are the doorway to virtually any information you could need from both public and private sources. For example:

> **Better Business Bureau Directory.** Lists the addresses and phone numbers of Better Business Bureaus in the U.S. and Canada. **http://www.cbbb.org/cbbb/bbb-dir.html**

> **Department of the Treasury.** Provides tax forms and answers most frequently asked tax questions from small and home-based businesses. Includes access to their small-business newsletter. **http://www.ustreas.gov/treasury/bureaus/irs/fwforms.html**

> **Home Business News.** This bimonthly newspaper provides information for home-based business owners and people in transition from working for others to self employment. **http://www.gohome.com**

> **Homeworks.** Our Internet site provides weekly updates of text, audio and video excerpts from our books, tapes, newsletters, our Q&A *Home Office Computing* column, radio and television shows on topics of interest to self-employed individuals, home businesses, and small business pro-

fessionals such as trends, pricing, marketing, tips for succeeding in specific businesses, and new technology. Also includes links to other "hot" sites. http://www.homeworks.com

Internet Patent Searching System. This Internet site allows you to search for patents and also provides lists of news on patents. http://sunsite.unc. edu/patents/intropat.html

IRS Home Page. Since the Government Accounting Office reports only 8 percent of calls to IRS get through during tax time, this site is helpful. It includes 600 tax forms and publications, a summary of changes in tax laws and answers to most frequently asked questions. http://www.irs. ustreas.gov

The SBA Online. Provides very detailed information on services and information available through the SBA, including a downloadable outline for a business plan. SBA Online also offers information via E-mail for 14 cents per minute at (900) 463-4636 and a help line at (202) 205-6400. http://www.sbaon-line.sba.gov

The challenge, of course, in using the wealth of information available on-line lies in finding it. So here are several services that can direct you to Internet sites that provide information on virually every topic imaginable:

■ **InfoSeek.** One of the best on-line search sites; allows you to search by words and get lists and links to Internet sites that use this term. http://www. infoseek.com

■ **The Prentice Hall Directory of Online Business Information 1996–1997.** Christopher Engholm and Scott Grimes. Englewood Cliffs, NJ: Prentice Hall, 1996. The complete what, where, and how guide to 1,000 on-line business sources, 1,000 descriptive reviews, including a five-star rating system that evaluates each source. The directory comes with a free CD-ROM with immediate Internet access and is compatible with Windows 95 and all Windows-based platforms.

■ **Yahoo.** The consummate place to search for other Web sites which you can do by topic. http://www.yahoo.com

GETTING HELP, FINDING SUPPORT, LOCATING EXPERTS

Professional Associations. To build your professional support network, you can get referrals to individuals in your areas by contacting the following national trade and professional associations:

American Bar Association. 750 N. Lakeshore Dr., Chicago, IL 60611 (800) 285-2221.

Association of Independent Information Professionals. 245 5th Ave, Suite 2103, New York, NY 10016 (212) 779-1855.

Independent Computer Consultants Association. 11131 South Towne Square, Suite F, St. Louis, MO 63123 (800) 774-4222.

The Institute of Certified Financial Planners. 3801 E. Florida Ave, Suite 708, Denver, CO 80210 (800) 282-7526.

International Association of Business Communications. 1 Halladie Plaza, Suite 600, San Francisco, CA 94102 (415) 433-3400.

International Association for Financial Planning. 5775 Glenridge Dr. NE, Suite B300, Atlanta, GA 30328-5364 (404) 395-1605.

National Association of Enrolled Agents (NAEA). 200 Orchard Ridge Dr., Suite 302, Gaithersburg, MD 20878 (301) 212-9608.

National Association of Insurance Brokers. 1300 I St. NW, Suite 900 East, Washington, DC 20005 (202) 628-6700.

National Association of Professional Organizers. 1033 La Posada Ave., Suite 220, Austin, TX 78752 (512) 454-8626.

Public Relations Society of America. 33 Irving Pl., New York, NY 10003 (212) 995-2230.

Business Organizations. Many national organizations have been created to serve self-employed individuals. In addition to this list, see the Appendix for state Home Business Associations. There are also a variety of networking organizations with local chapters in most cities across the country. The primary purpose of these organizations, which are also included below, is to help members to get business.

American Association of Home-Based Businesses. P.O. Box 10023, Rockville, MD 20849 (202) 310-3130, (800) 447-9710: **Internet Site** http://www.aahbb.org

American Business Women's Association. P.O. Box 8728, Kansas City, MO 64114-0728 (816) 361-6621.

Association of Enterprising Mothers. 914 South Santa Fe, Suite 297, Vista, CA 92084 (619) 598-9260, (800) 223-9260.

Business Network International. 268 S. Bucknell Ave., Claremont, CA 91711 (800) 825-8286. A nationwide networking organization. **Internet Site** http://www.bninet.com

Independent Business Alliance. 111 John Street, 27th Floor, New York, NY 10038 (212) 513-1446, (800) 450-2422.

International Association of Home-Based Businesses. 8333 Ralston Road, Suite 4, Arvada, CO 80002-2355 (800) 414-2422 [800-41-IAHBB].

Leads Club. P.O. Box 279, Carlsbad, CA 92108 (619) 434-3761. A nationwide networking organization. **Internet Site http://emanate.com/ leadsclub**

National Association of Certified Home-Based Businesses. 801 W. Mineral Avenue, Littleton, CO 80120-4501 (800) 867-5293.

National Association for the Self-Employed. P.O. Box 612067, Dallas, TX 75261 (800) 232-6273. **Internet Site http://www.nase.org**

National Association of Women Business Owners. 1100 Wayne Ave., Suite 830, Silver Spring, MD 20910 (301) 608-2590.

National Black Chamber of Commerce. 2000 L Street NW, Suite 200, Washington, DC 20036 (202) 416-1622.

National Federation for Independent Business. 53 Century Blvd., Suite 300, Nashville, TN 37214 (800) 634-2669.

National Home Office Association (NHOA). 3412 Woolsey Drive, Chevy Chase, MD 20815 (301) 652-1667. **Internet Site http://www. nhoa.org**

National Indian Business Association. 1605 Carlisle NE, Suite A-1, Albuquerque, NM 87110 (505) 256-0589. **Internet Site http://niba. aol.com**

Small Business and Home Office Association International. 1765 Business Center Drive, Suite 100, Reston, VA 22090 (703) 438-3060.

The United States Chamber of Commerce. 1615 H Street NW, Washington, DC 20062 (202) 659-6000. Many Chambers now have small-business and home-business sections or forums. **Internet Site http:// www.uschamber.org**

U.S. Hispanic Chamber of Commerce. 1030 15th St. NW, Suite 206, Washington, DC 20005 (202) 842-1212. **Internet Site http://www.ushcc.com**

U.S. Pan Asian American Chamber of Commerce. 1329 18th St. NW, Washington, DC 20036 (202) 296-5221.

Women in Franchising. 53 W. Jackson St., Suite 205, Chicago, IL 60604 (800) 222-4943.

■   **America Online.** 8619 Westwood Center Drive, Vienna, VA 22182 (800) 827-6364. AOL has over fifty clubs, forums, and interest groups including ones for professions and organizations. To find a list of these networks, select the Directory of Services and review the list. AOL also has help for small businesses through the Small Business Center. For more information about AOL, you can read *How to Use America Online,* by Elaine Madison. Emeryville, CA: Que, 1995.

■   **CompuServe.** 5000 Arlington Centre Blvd. P.O. Box 20212, Columbus, OH 43220 (800) 848-8990. CIS is home to over four hundred forums where people with similar needs and interests communicate via computer. Our forum, the *Working from Home Forum,* is an example. We've operated this online community since 1983. You can get information resources and support from the forum libraries or by leaving messages on the bulletin board for the over 50,000 members, who include many business experts in fields like legal, tax, and marketing as well as other self-employed individuals who will share their wealth of experience. And you can share your expertise with others as well. To visit, enter CompuServe; our address is Go Work.

There are two ways to peruse the list of other CIS forums. Every year *CompuServe* magazine publishes a complete list of forums, or to find a list of on-line press Ctrl+G and type Forums in the text box. You can also search for forums by topic. For more information about using the resources of CIS, you can read *CompuServe for Dummies,* by Wallace Wang. Foster City, CA: IDG Books, 1995.

■   **Internet News Groups.** At the time of this writing the Internet offers over ten thousand special-interest groups, called news groups, on all varieties of topics. Using Yahoo and InfoSeek you can search for comments on these news groups related to your topic of interest. And there are sites like Ohio State's site (**http://www.cis.ohio-state.edu/hyptertext/faq/usenet/FAQ-List. html**) where you can review frequently asked questions for the most popular news groups. Here's a variety of ways to find a list of news groups. On Usenet you can click on "Search All News Groups" and then find out about groups of interest by clicking on "Read My News Groups." Web browsers like Netscape have a button for finding listings of news groups. And some Web sites list the location of related news groups. Some groups of interest to self-employed individuals are **alt.biz., alt.biz.misc.,** and **misc.entpreneur.** For more information about using the Internet, you can read *The Internet Trainer's Guide,* by Diane K. Kovacs. New York: Van Nostrand Reinhold, 1995.

■   **Microsoft Network.** 1 Microsoft Way, Redmond, WA 98052 (206) 882-8080. MSN has BBSs on a wide variety of topics. To review BBSs you can visit, click on the categories button where you'll find a choice of topics like Business and Finance, Science and Technology, and Education and Reference. Chose the category you wish to explore and open a folder to see the

BBSs available in that category. Under Home and Family, for example, you'll find the Work at Home Dad newsletter and Small Office Home Office. For more information about using MSN, you can read *Microsoft Network Tour Guide,* by Jan Weingarten and Phil James. Research Triangle Park, NC: Vantana, 1995.

Prodigy. 445 Hamilton Avenue, White Plains, NY 10601 (800) 776-3449. The Home Office and Entrepreneurs' Exchange are two bulletin boards on this service where self-employed professionals can network.

Creating Community Anywhere: Finding Support and Connection in a Fragmented World. Carolyn R. Schaffer and Kristen Anundsen. New York: Tarcher/Putnam, 1993. Guidelines for how to find emotional encouragement and practical support wherever you are from contact with others in person, on-line, in organizations.

How to Avoid Housework. Paula Jhung. New York: Fireside, 1995. A self-proclaimed slob shares practical tips, hints, and secrets she's learned for maintaining a spotless home by barely lifting a finger. Includes guidelines for if, when, and how to have household help and for dealing with guests.

How to Build a Network of Power Relationships. Harvey Mackay. Niles, IL: Nightingale-Conant. (800) 525-9000. This six-tape audio album provides tips for developing people-skills and communication techniques for building mutually supportive business and collegial relationships.

How to Interview and Hire the Right People. Stephen Carline. CareerTrack, 3085 Center Green Dr., Boulder, CO 80301, 1995. You'll learn how to develop a job description and advertise it, evaluate resumes, and negotiate the employment agreement. Available in audiocassettes and/or a video set.

Make Your House Do the Housework. Don Aslett and Laura Aslett Simons. Cincinnati: Writer's Digest Books, 1995. A must for anyone who wants to do less housework. It is filled with practical suggestions for preventing your home from getting dirty.

Teaming Up: On Your Own, but Not Alone. Paul and Sarah Edwards and Rick Benzel. New York: Tarcher/Putnam, in press. This book describes twelve ways self-employed individuals are creating collaborative relationships to work more successfully, including networking, affiliations, cooperatives, partnerships, and virtual corporations.

TELEVISION

How to Succeed in Business, CNBC, airs Saturday and Sunday mornings.

Bloomberg Small Business, with syndicated business columnist, Jane Applegate, USA Network, airs Saturday mornings.

Working from Home with Paul and Sarah Edwards, seen weekly on the Home and Garden Television network. For availability in your area call your local cable company, or take a look at This Month's Videobyte on the Edwardses' Website, **http://www.homeworks.com**

RADIO

Working from Home is heard weekly on Business News Network, Sundays at 10:00 P.M. Eastern, 7:00 P.M. Pacific. You can listen live on the Internet via Real Audio at **http://www.cfra.com** or tune in to the radio station nearest you. For an on-air consultation, call in during the live broadcast hours at (800) 730-8836.

GETTING BUSINESS

The Business Generator. Paul and Sarah Edwards. Niles, IL: Nightingale-Conant. (800) 525-9000. Or on CD-ROM from Info Business (801) 221–1100. A comprehensive marketing program that includes a videotape, *Top of the Mind Marketing,* the book *Getting Business to Come to You,* and *The Marketing Partner,* a workbook for identifying which marketing activites are best suited to you and your business and a unique marketing system for making sure you're initiating and following through on enough marketing activities to get and keep business coming to you.

Getting Business to Come to You: Everything You Need to Know About Public Relations, Advertising, and Sales Promotion for the Small and Home-Based Business. Paul and Sarah Edwards and Laura Douglas. Los Angeles: Tarcher, 1991. Introduces no- or low-cost marketing methods used by successful self-employed propreneurs and provides practical information for how to do them yourself without having to spend your time selling. Also includes lists of many valuable marketing resources.

Getting Business to Come to You. Paul and Sarah Edwards. Niles, IL: Nightingale-Conant, 1995. A six-tape audiocassette program that outlines the five habits involved in doing Critical-Mass Marketing so you can get business coming to you instead of having to continually spend your time trying to get enough business.

◅▻ **The World's Best-Known Marketing Secret: Building Your Business with Word-of-Mouth Marketing.** Ivan Misner, Ph.D. Austin, TX: Bard & Stephen, 1994. The basics of of getting business from referrals, networking, and relationship building.

Using Technology

Home Office Computing Magazine. Scholastic Inc., 730 Broadway, New York, NY 10003. A gold mine of information about how to succeed on your own including reviews of the latest software and equipment as well as articles on marketing and other business-management skills.

◅▻ **Making Money with Your Personal Computer.** Paul and Sarah Edwards. New York: Tarcher/Putnam, 1995. Part 3 of this book, "Using Your Computer in Business," is about how to put your computer to work managing your money, handling administrivia, increasing your business, finding customers, collecting money, and getting the information you need.

◅▻ **The Computer User Survival Guide.** Joan Stigliani. Sebastopol, CA: O'Reilly, 1995.

◅▻ **The Office Computing Bible.** Nancy E. Dunn: Englewood Cliffs, NJ: Prentice Hall, 1995.

PC Novice. 120 W. Harvest Dr., Lincoln, NB 68521 (800) 424-7900. This magazine describes itself as providing information about personal computers in plain English. It's basic and nonintimidating.

◅▻ **Working from Home.** Paul and Sarah Edwards. Los Angeles: Tarcher, 1994. Chapter 7, "Outfitting Your Home Office," and Chapter 8, "Equipping and Computerizing the Up-to-Date Home Office," outline how to set up a convenient, functional, and professional office of your own.

◅▻ **Your First Book of Personal Computing.** Joe Kraynak. Indianapolis: Alpha Books, 1995.

III

Becoming the Boss You've Always Wanted to Have

---- ■ ----

Happiness . . . has a direct relationship to the freedom in life to make choices to do the things I want to do.

Ken Kragen

f you've been blessed with having had outstanding coaches, parents, teachers, managers, or mentors, you are indeed lucky. Your job of managing yourself now that you're on your own will be easier. You've undoubtedly incorporated a great deal from them about how to get yourself to do what you need to do. You probably have a sense of what you can put up with from yourself, what you can let yourself get away with, when you need to draw the line, and how you can get yourself to go the extra mile. Whenever you're at a loss as to how to motivate yourself, you can go inward and ask yourself what these people would advise you to do.

If you're like many of us, however, you haven't had the benefit of such expert coaching and direction. Many of our authority figures demanded too much and expected too little. Not knowing what to do, they threatened, ignored, tolerated, abused, belittled, denigrated, and otherwise manipulated us into performances that fell far short of what even we know we were capable of. If that was your experience, when you look inward for assistance in getting yourself to do what you need to do, you risk becoming as ineffectual as your previous role models. You may rebel, and sabotage or otherwise defeat your own efforts.

In this case, what are you to do? How can you find the means by which to consistently draw out the best in yourself? What can you do to inspire performances that will surprise and delight you? To find the answer, we began studying highly effective coaches, teachers, managers, and directors. And we noticed something very important: the best ones don't treat every player or performer they work with in the same way. In fact, the same person can be a screaming terror with one person and a gentle, tender, supportive parent figure with another. Sometimes they show this range of behavior even with the same person, offering a loving hug at one moment and raving angrily at another.

Why such erratic behavior? And is it really erratic? In watching the most effective coaches, teachers, and managers, we've observed that they approach their protégés much as an expert jockey approaches a prized racehorse. The best jockeys learn to ride each horse as if they were playing a fine instrument. They learn to respond to every nuance, every trait, every characteristic of the horse. Sometimes they apply the whip. Sometimes they nudge and talk softly to the horse. Sometimes they dig their heels into the horse's side. Sometimes they shout angrily. Sometimes they almost sing to the horse. And sometimes they do all of the above, but only at the precise moment when it will catapult the horse to the front of the field.

That's how we must learn to manage ourselves. We must become so familiar with ourselves—our whims, our needs, our emotions, our patterns, our preferences, our strengths and weaknesses—that we can literally feed ourselves the exact words, schedule, food, routines, and resources we need to nourish our competence and enable us to operate consistently at our best.

Isn't that what the top sports coaches are able to do for their athletes? Don't they literally prescribe a tailor-made training schedule? Don't they provide a tailor-made diet? Don't they lay out a tailor-made practice routine or workout? Don't they whisper just the right words at just the right moments? Isn't that what the top directors do in their own way for their actors? Isn't that what excellent teachers do for their students? Isn't that what top managers do for their staff? And isn't there a direct relationship between what they put into their protégés and what they are able to get from them?

Like these professionals, you will get out of yourself exactly what you put in. To keep yourself on track, you must be there for yourself. You must be the one who knows how to respond when situations get you down. You must be the one who offers the consolation, guidance, respect, and recognition you need to believe in yourself. You must be the one you can turn to when you are at a loss. You need to have effective solutions and answers for yourself.

That's what this section is about—learning to motivate yourself effectively, helping yourself through the emotional roller coaster being your own boss can be, and being there with the answers to keep yourself going when problems arise.

5

Motivating Yourself to Do
What Needs to Be Done

*Once you get to the pros, coaching is not about telling people
what to do; it's about managing personalities.*

NORMAN VAN LIER
FORMER PLAYER FOR THE CHICAGO BULLS

THERE'S PROBABLY NO greater power than the power to follow through
on what you say you want to do. Whether it's being able to hit a tennis ball
just where you want it to go, deliver a project on time within budget, or get
yourself to stop smoking, being able to count on yourself to deliver what you
want to accomplish is truly a gift. But once you're on your own, it's also an
essential skill.

Yet how often we make promises to ourselves, set goals, make New
Year's resolutions, or swear we'll do something—or never do something
again—only to let ourselves down. According to a *USA Today* report, nine
out of ten Americans make New Year's resolutions, but studies by Alan Mar-
latt from the University of Washington in Seattle show that almost four out
of five people fail to follow through on their resolutions.

When you like what you're doing and you're committed to a clear purpose, of course, following through on what you set out to do is less of a problem. But aren't we usually quite sincere in making New Year's resolutions? So
how do we know we'll be able to do any better on our own? What about the
days when you don't want to do what you know needs to be done? What about
the things you don't like doing . . . the things you want to put off . . . the
things you will get to later? All the best-made goals, schedules, routines, plans,
and to-do lists are useless if you can't get yourself to turn them into action.

This is the same issue every professional athlete or performer must face. In every game, in every match, in every contest, in every show, they must ask, "Will I be able to perform at my best upon demand?" To make sure they can, they have to mobilize themselves every day to train. They have to go through endless repetitions of moves or lines until they can do what it takes under the pressure of a competition or a production. And that's essentially what we have to do to make it on our own. But, of course, athletes and performers have coaches, directors, and managers to help them.

And those coaches strive to understand those they coach so well that they can inspire, motivate, energize, catalyze, outfox, outmaneuver, outwait, out-psych, or in one way or another get their charges to bring forth their best precisely when they need it. And now that you're on your own, that is your job, too. By becoming your own boss, you now must step into that role and serve as your own coach, mentor, and manager.

BECOMING YOUR OWN COACH, MENTOR, AND ADVISER

In other words, you have to get to know yourself very well—so well that you know exactly what will get you going, what will calm you down, and what will help you focus; how to make sure you follow through on what needs to be done when you'd rather not do it, how to keep yourself going when things take longer than you expected, and how to keep yourself going when you feel like quitting or become impatient.

If you begin to think of yourself as your own protégée—and your most important project—you'll be able to notice what you respond to and what you don't. You'll begin to respect your preferences and needs. You'll come to appreciate your natural abilities and limitations and learn to take them into account, instead of fighting yourself or trying to bury the aspects of your personality you don't like.

Four Steps to Becoming an Effective Self-Manager

To become a reliable mentor/coach for yourself you must take four steps:

1. Recognize and make the most of your strengths and weaknesses.
2. Identify the peculiarities of what motivates you.
3. Discover what you need to hear and learn how to say it in such a way that you'll listen to your own advice and counsel.
4. Determine what you can do to assist yourself to function at your best consistently.

In this chapter, we'll discuss each of these steps in detail and provide practical guidelines for managing yourself. But first, review the tips below for how to make sure you can count on yourself to follow through on what you actually want and need to do.

Making Sure You Can Count on Yourself to Do What You Say You'll Do

- **Distinguish between goals and commitments.** A goal, the dictionary tells us, is "the object of some effort." To get more clients is a goal. To have a current up-to-date filing system is a goal. A commitment, however, is "the act of resolving to put forth an effort toward some object." In other words, goals are what you want to accomplish; commitments are what you promise to do to make sure you achieve your goals.

- **To assure that you reach your goals, commit to take only those steps you know you can count on yourself to carry out.** Be sure that whatever you commit to doing is something you actually want to do and that you will do. In other words, don't make commitments to yourself or others that you doubt you will follow through on.

  If you're a person who has a difficult time saying "no," ask yourself, "Is this something I want or am clearly willing to do?" If not, don't commit to doing it. You can do that, after all. What's the worst thing that can happen if you say "no"? Even if you can imagine something awful, how likely is that to happen? Obviously if something negative is likely to happen, then saying "yes" is justified and you'll be motivated to find a way to do it, even if it involves getting help from others.

  Here's an example of what we mean: If your goal is to double the number of clients you serve but you hate making cold calls and have never been able to get yourself to make them, don't resolve to make ten calls a week. Resolve instead to find some other way to get clients. You might commit to joining a networking group, attending a seminar on selling through seminars, or advertising by direct mail with appropriate telephone follow-up.

- **Make bite-sized, realistic goals and commitments.** Dream big, but take one small step at a time. If you dream of becoming a best-selling novelist, for example, you might set a goal of writing and publishing a short story and commit to enrolling in a class on short-story technique.

- **Set completion dates for your commitments and track your progress.** Also, flag a date sometime before the date you've set so that as it approaches you'll be able to revise your commitments accordingly. For example, if you agreed to complete three interviews by the end of the month, cue yourself midmonth. If the interviews are not scheduled yet, take appropriate action.

- **Give yourself some slack, but don't let yourself slack off.** Making a commitment doesn't have to mean becoming enslaved to it. You can always decide en route to go somewhere else, and you can always choose an alternative route for getting there. The only things that really matter are that you do get where you want to go, and that you enjoy the trip along the way.

MAKING THE MOST OF YOUR STRENGTHS AND WEAKNESSES

*Often your strength is measured in how you manage your
weakness.*   PAUL AND SARAH EDWARDS

We each come to self-employment with our own particular combination of experiences, talents, skills, resources, and assets. We also bring along our own personal limitations, concerns, doubts, and inexperience. Like any coach, we've got to work with whatever strengths and weaknesses we bring to the game. To build our success, we've got to make the most of what we've got— good and not so good. Every athlete, every racehorse, every actor and actress, every beauty pageant contestant or political candidate presents this very same challenge to their coaches and mentors.

One gymnast may excel on the balance beam and struggle with her vault, while another is a natural on the vault and wobbly on the beam. One professional singer may sing like a master before a live audience but freeze in studio sessions, while another shies away from live performances but shines in the studio. One political candidate may be dynamic talking to the media and more reserved and distant at one-on-one fund-raising, while another feels stiff and awkward appearing on television but is warm and engaging at in-person fund-raising. A particular individual could be emotionally volatile and stubborn but have amazing stamina and determination, while another may be cooperative and easygoing but tire easily and get sidetracked often.

Whatever the situation, at any given moment in time, the coach or trainer must strive to help those they manage make the most of their strengths and work effectively around their weaknesses. And so it is in managing your own independent career. You need to have a realistic grasp of your strenghts and weaknesses so you can make the most of what you have to work with. Yet it's so easy to take what we do well for granted or even underrate our abilities. And it's equally easy to overlook or avoid thinking about those things we don't do so well. So, thinking about it, when it comes to doing what's required to become successfully self-employed, where do you shine? Where do you stumble? Where are you masterful? Where are you mediocre? What comes natually to you? What is a struggle?

We've developed the following assessment tools to help you take an honest look at these questions. They're based on our work with Bill Charland, author of the book *Career Shifting: Starting Over in a Changing Economy*.

Assessing Your Ability to Perform Essential Self-Employment Functions

Like any self-sustaining economic entity from a Fortune 500 company to a part-time sole proprietor operating from a spare bedroom, in order to survive and thrive on your own, you must carry out six basic functions. Usually one of these activities is your Core Function, what you get paid to do, your raison d'être, so to speak. But to get going and stay afloat, you'll be called upon to carry out all six of these functions adequately and consistently whenever circumstances demand. And while an organization can recruit different individuals who shine at performing these different functions, when you're self-employed, you'll probably have to do them all yourself—at least in the beginning!

If you're like most people, when you set out on your own, you're probably good or even masterful at some of these essential functions, but less good and even poor at others. Some you can do with your eyes closed standing on one foot. Others may leave you cold, feeling inadequate, or wishing you could have a root canal instead. As we describe these six functions and list the type of activities they involve, assess your strenghts and weaknesses, preferences and natural proclivities. As you read through them:

- Identify which of the six functions is the Core Function of your career. Circle that function.
- Under each function, check (√) the activities you do well and those that come easily to you.
- Put an asterisk (*) alongside the activities you don't perform well at, dislike, or find difficult.

1. Creating. In any operation, someone has to create the products and services that will be provided to clients and customers. Of course, some independent careers are creative by nature. A sculptor, screenwriter, or novelist, for example, gets paid to create. It's their core function. But on one's own, not only must the artist do the other five functions, whatever your core function is, you too must be the creator, the visionary who conceives of what you'll be offering and how to make it appealing and valuable to those who need and will pay for it. So, you'll be called upon to perform activities like these:

___ Imagining	___ Designing
___ Innovating	___ Envisioning
___ Performing	___ Perceiving

2. *Problem solving.* In any venture, someone must figure out how to solve the inevitable problems involved in establishing an independent career like getting business, pleasing your clients and customers, and running your office effectively. Some independent careers—such as consultant, private investigator, technical writer, information broker, or software developer—are basically about problem solving. Solving problems is what they get paid to do. It's their core function. But whatever the core function of what you do is, on your own, you, too, will need to engage at times in problem-solving activities such as:

___ Analyzing	___ Diagnosing
___ Observing	___ Investigating
___ Defining	___ Evaluating

3. *Building.* Every independent career requires that someone roll up his or her sleeves and do the hands-on work that gets and keeps things running. Some independent careers like construction, commercial cleaning services, swimming pool maintenance, computer repair services, and hauling services get paid to carry out such tasks. It's their Core Function. But whatever your independent career, from time to time, you, too, will have to engage in such activities as:

___ Assembling	___ Computing
___ Repairing or cleaning	___ Constructing
___ Maintaining	___ Transporting, shipping and packaging

4. *Organizing.* Every operation needs someone to set up procedures, follow through, and carry out the day-to-day administrative tasks of operating as a business. People who have independent careers like professional organizers, indexers, medical claims processors, word-processors, or bookkeepers get paid to carry out such functions. Getting and keeping things organized is their Core Function. But on your own, whatever the core of your work, you, too, need to deal with the data, numbers, files, and other administrative details involved in the financial, clerical, and legal aspects of your work. So, at times, you need to carry out such activities as:

___ Arranging	___ Compiling and tracking
___ Gathering	___ Ordering
___ Recording	___ Filing

5. Leading. In order to survive and thrive, any independent operation needs someone to oversee, coordinate, manage, market, sell, and promote its products or services. In many self-employment careers like event planner, tour guide, public-relations specialist, manufacturer's rep, and seminar leader, such activities are the Core Function. That's what they get paid to do. But all of us who are on our own must carry out these activities at various times in order to run our career as a business. So you'll need to engage in such activities as:

___ Coordinating	___ Selling and promoting
___ Negotiating	___ Managing
___ Marketing	___ Influencing and pursuading

6. Improving. In any operation, someone has to work personally with the customers and clients, listen to their needs, satisfy their complaints, and identify where improvements need to be made. These kinds of interactions lead to the new and improved products and services that keep people coming back to you again and again. People in some professions—like counseling, tutoring, errand services, and massage therapy—get paid to take care of and help people. That's their Core Function. But, again, whatever the primary nature of your work, you, too, must get sufficiently involved with serving your clients and customers to develop enough rapport and trust that they will want to continue doing business with you. So, at times, you'll undoubtedly find yourself doing such things as:

___ Listening	___ Caring
___ Consulting	___ Explaining
___ Teaching	___ Helping

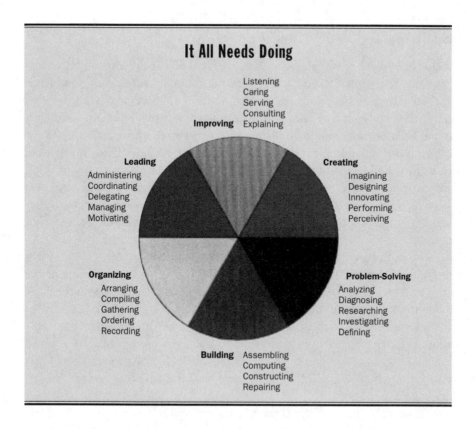

Chances are, as you assess your performance of and preferences for these six essential functions, you're fairly good, if not masterful, at your Core Function. If not, you'll need to sharpen your skills so people will believe in your abilities enough to want to pay you. But sometimes, although we're able to provide this function quite adequately for our clients and customers, we're not so good at doing it for ourselves. We find many people are like the cobbler whose children have no shoes. They neglect doing for themselves what they can do so well for others. A marketing specialist, for example, may have problems getting around to marketing his own services. Or a professional organizer may get behind on doing her own filing.

If that's your situation, in order to survive and thrive, one of your key roles as your own mentor and coach will be to teach yourself how to start doing as good a job for yourself as you do for your clients.

Chances are you also found that you enjoy, or at least like, carrying out the activities associated with your Core Function. If not, we urge you to shift your line of work, because trying to manage yourself when you dislike your work is a difficult task. Why make things hard on yourself?

Building on Your Core Function

As long as you're reasonably good at and like doing your Core Function, it is your greatest strength and can serve as the foundation for your confidence and effectiveness. As your coach and mentor, you'll want to acknowledge, support, nurture, and encourage your proficiency at this function. Lead with it and then begin helping yourself build on this strength to get up to par at carrying out functions you don't like as much or do as well at. In this way, you can steadily expand the base of your competencies. It may mean seeking advice from outside experts and consultants, taking courses and seminars, learning from books, tapes, videos, and CD-ROMs, or, when your budget allows it, hiring other people to help you carry out functions you dislike or do poorly.

Often, however, the budget doesn't allow you to hire others to carry out these functions, and even when it does, you still need to know enough about each of these functions to hire, supervise, and work effectively with the right individuals. So, as your own supervisor and coach, you must help yourself develop some level of competency in each of the six key functional areas. Don't allow yourself to think you're too inadequate, or too superior, to take on learning functions you don't like or don't yet do well. You probably won't get very far on your own if you limit yourself to doing only those things you already do expertly.

What we've noticed is that the *most* successful self-employed individuals rarely start out being fully competent at all six of these key functions. But over the years, they become competent in them one by one. The artist who starts out petrified of selling finds ways to market himself comfortably. The highly technical software-developer-turned-consultant learns to listen to and communicate with customers who don't understand or want to know anything about computers. The psychotherapist who can't balance a checkbook at first learns to develop a client ledger, send out timely billings, and keep careful records to follow up quickly on overdue collections.

As you've undoubtedly already discovered, not only do you usually have to carry out various aspects of these six functions, you must also learn to move quickly and easily from one of these essential, but entirely different, functions to another. Often you must make such shifts again and again throughout the day. One minute you may be deeply involved doing your core work when a glitch develops in your software, an unhappy client calls to complain, a prospective customer returns your call from earlier in the day, or your tax preparer calls urgently requesting that you locate a missing form or receipt.

Like most people, you've probably found that it's easier to shift in and out of some functions than others. Later in this chapter, we'll outline ways to make these shifts more easily, and in chapter 6 we'll talk about ways to quickly and easily make even those shifts that are most difficult ones for you.

As your own boss, it's your job to make sure you feel confident operating within your existing strengths and weaknesses while, at the same time, supporting and encouraging yourself to expand upon them so you'll become more of what you can be. And to do this, you must motivate yourself to do what needs to be done, whether or not you like doing it, and whether or not you can do it as well as you'd like to yet.

IDENTIFYING WHAT MOTIVATES YOU

Know thyself. THE ORACLE AT DELPHI

There is actually a wide variety of ways people motivate themselves. For example, event planner Marsha Hanscom learned quickly that the best way to feel motivated was to set up incentives or prizes for herself. "If I have something special I can work toward, I get a lot more done," she says. She entices herself with promises of rewards for reaching her goals. For instance, she once told herself that if she had a particular exhibit all filled by a certain date, she would send herself to an upcoming national conference. She hit the goal and took the trip!

Diane Vaughn, who has a thriving counseling service, is motivated by the satisfaction she gets from the work she does. All she needs to do is think about how much joy her work brings her and she finds it easy to do whatever is required to make sure she succeeds. Jeffrey Kline, a sales trainer, knows that money is what motivates him. "The more money I can make, the better I produce," he told us. Photographer Ron Allenberg, however, finds that showing everyone what he can do is what keeps him going: "So many people told me that I shouldn't do this—that I'd never make it. Now all I have to do is think about how much I want to prove they're wrong, and I'll do whatever it takes." At times, I, Paul, have motivated myself from an "I'll prove I can do it" position.

Here are some other insights self-employed individuals have had about how to motivate themselves:

> When things look bad, I get discouraged and don't want to do anything much. So I've learned to tell myself the positive side of whatever's happening. I point out why it's not as bad as it looks and how it could even be better than I thought. Then I feel like working all the harder.

When I'm under the pressure of a deadline, I get so much done; but without a deadline, I don't think I'd get anything done at all. It's got to be a real deadline, though. I can't just make something up. So what I do is get myself into situations that involve firm deadlines.

I ask myself what will happen if I don't do this, and if it doesn't look good, then I want to do it.

I think about the kind of person I want to be, and if I'm not living up to who I aspire to be, that's a real motivator. When I am living up to my image of myself, I feel good and I do more of what it takes to do even better.

Facts and figures are what motivate me. I track my progress as if I'm keeping a scorecard. And I watch what my competition is doing. I like to make sure I stay out in front.

Knowing what de-motivates you is equally important. Gil Petersen, a software engineer, discovered, for example: "If I tell myself I have to do something, it's like the kiss of death. I'll do just about anything else. And boy, has that gotten me in trouble. Now if I don't want to do something, I just tell myself I don't have to do it. And usually, once I know I have the choice, I'll go ahead and do it if it really does need to be done."

Kim Freilich dislikes doing billing for her publicity business. "It's so time-consuming," she moans. "But I think of it as dumping the money out of my pockets and counting what will be coming back to me. That gets me through it."

To begin identifying what motivates and de-motivates you, pay attention to what you complain about, what you get excited about, what gets you down, and what picks you up. Then cater to yourself as you would to a prized client. Don't sell yourself short and let yourself get away with less than you know you can do, but make it as easy as possible for yourself to excel. Ask yourself the following questions. Then listen to your responses and observe your behavior to see if it confirms your answers.

There are no wrong answers to these questions. The idea is to learn what you respond to. The two of us work best, for example, when we believe we're doing well. Comparing ourselves negatively with others leads us to start doubting ourselves. We've spoken with people, however, who start slacking off when they think they're doing well. Comparing themselves negatively with others keeps them on their toes. Of course, with some effort you can change such motivation patterns, but when possible, it's easier to simply use the patterns you have to your own advantage.

What Motivates You?

1. What is most important to you about what you're doing? What makes it worthwhile? What makes it a drag?

2. How could you make doing something you need to do worth the effort? What would make you eager to get it done?

3. Which spurs you to do better: compliments and positive feedback about what you've done well—or criticism of your performance and feedback on what you need to improve?

4. Are you more likely to strive to prevent negative things you fear might happen—or to work toward attaining a positive outcome?

5. Do you thrive on competition? Does the opportunity to do better than someone else spur you on—or intimidate you?

6. Are you more interested in improving your own performance—or achieving more than someone else?

7. Do you work better with the pressure of a deadline—or do deadlines make you clutch?

8. Do you work more efficiently when you wait until the last minute to meet your deadlines—or do you like to start early and finish ahead of time?

9. Do you like to begin with the most pleasant tasks—or do you prefer to get the worst over first and save the best for last?

KNOWING WHAT YOU NEED TO HEAR AND SAYING IT IN SUCH A WAY THAT YOU'LL LISTEN

Once we are destined to live out our lives in the prison of our mind, our duty is to furnish it well.

PETER USTINOV

We all have a constant stream of conversation running in our heads. Sometimes this internal chatter is call "inner dialog," or "self-talk." At any given moment this conversation either helps us carry out our intentions or works against us. If you begin to listen to this conversation and observe its effects on you, you will be amazed at how you can not only improve your performance but also greatly increase your enjoyment of whatever you're doing, by simply changing what you're saying to yourself.

Think, for example, of the following alternative sets of inner chatter that might take place if you wake up late one morning.

Scenario 1: "Boy, are you a sleaze. You'll never amount to anything. Didn't I tell you you'd be goofing off the minute no boss was looking over your shoulder? How could you have overslept again? You'll never make it on your own. If the few clients you have ever found out how lazy you are, they'd take their business elsewhere. You might as well forget today anyway. You've already blown it again."

Scenario 2: "Oh, it's late. Did I have anything I had to do this morning? Let's look at the calendar. Oh great! I'm free. Well, I guess I can oversleep once in a while. But it doesn't really matter because, if I need to, I can work some this evening. I'm feeling so rested, though, I'll probably get more work done now anyway. Let's see, what did I want to get done today? I think I'll go on up and start making a few calls."

Inner dialogue or self-talk like this is actually one of the major ways we coach ourselves. Which one do you think will get the best results? You can begin listening to your current chatter to see how well you're coaching yourself. Do you think a good coach would be saying the things you're saying? Even more important, however, notice how you respond to what you're saying. Does it make you feel more confident, more effective, and more eager to do what needs to be done? Or does it work against you? Do you actually perform better based on what you say? Or does it erode your performance?

In addition to such ongoing inner chatter, begin to notice what you say to yourself in response to specific problems or difficulties you encounter. If, for example, your work is harder than you thought it might be, what do you say to yourself about that? If you don't want to do what needs doing, what do you tell yourself? If you make a mistake of some kind, what do you say about it?

The conversations you have with yourself at times like these are the equivalent of the pep talk a coach gives his or her team at halftime. How well do your pep talks work for you? Do they send you back to the game more committed and determined to succeed? Or do they cause you to fall into an emotional sinkhole? Do you go back in with an angry attitude and a chip on your shoulder—or with a greater desire to excel? Do you hit the court running—or do you drop out temporarily?

Being able to give great pep talks to yourself is a valuable skill when you're on your own. In fact, a study of top executives showed that the most effective ones all have aphorisms or favorite sayings that they repeat to themselves now and then—mini-pep talks like "When the going gets tough, the tough get going," "Hang in there, baby; you can make it," "Every day in every way I'm getting better and better," and "Where there's a will, there's a way." Although these examples aren't particularly original, they're popular ones, and they work well for the people who use them.

We suggest that you, too, take a moment when needed to talk with yourself and pretend that you're the coach of your own team—because you are. Think of what you need to hear and tell it to yourself. Find stories that will inspire and encourage you. Look for incidents, quotes, lyrics, or ideas that will help you proceed with confidence and resolve.

What to Do When You Don't Feel Like Doing What Needs to Be Done

What do you do with yourself when you know what you need to do, but you don't want to do it? At one time or another, we've all faced a rapidly approaching deadline only to discover ourselves doing everything under the sun but what we need to do. And as you've probably already found at times like this, begging, pleading, blaming, and shaming do not work, at least not for long. Trying to force yourself to do it doesn't work either. Now that you're on your own, you *know* you can do whatever you want, even if it doesn't seem as though you can. So when you don't feel like doing what needs to be done, you've got to find a way to get yourself to do it willingly.

In other words, you need to find out what would make doing the task at hand sufficiently desirable for you to get actively involved in getting it done. That means you have to believe that it's worthwhile, possible, and intriguing enough to activate your participation. Here are several avenues to consider:

1. Ask yourself what you want to do now. Sometimes you're perfectly willing to carry out a particular task at a later time; you just don't want to do it now.

2. Ask yourself when you would be willing to do it.

3. Ask yourself if you still want it to be done. If not, why not? Does it really need to be done?

4. Ask yourself if you're willing to live with the consequences of not doing it.

5. Ask yourself what you would be willing to do. Sometimes there is part of what needs doing that you are willing to do, and once you get started you may find that's all it takes to get you going.

6. Ask yourself how else it could get done. You may find yourself having plenty of energy and interest, for example, in arranging for someone else to do it.

7. Ask yourself how you will feel once you have done it. Sometimes the prospect of having done it will activate you.

8. Ask yourself why you don't want to do it. Sometimes you can alter aspects of what needs to be done to make it more appealing.

9. Ask yourself what would make you want to do it.

10. Ask yourself how long you would be willing to do it. Sometimes you may be willing to do just a little at a time.

11. Get up and do it. That's how accountant Michael Russo says he handles difficult things he doesn't want to do: "Just do it. Set it up, and put it in motion."

Quick Start Tip: When You Have Trouble Getting Down to Business

Here's a formula for how to get yourself going from psychologist Stanley Coren of the University of British Columbia.

Most Important + Easiest + Quickest = Best Place to Start

Make a list of what you want to accomplish during a particular work period. Identify which steps are the *most important* and which you can do the most *quickly and easily.* Start with the most important steps you can do most quickly and easily.

GETTING IN PEAK CONDITION AND KEEPING YOURSELF THERE

Achieving peak performance begins with the discovery, complete acceptance, and development of skills to exercise consciously the power of volition. Volition is a potential until it is harnessed . . . a potential that you activate . . . through discipline and dedication.

CHARLES GARFIELD
PEAK PERFORMANCE RESEARCHER

We once saw a bumper sticker that read "The more prepared I am, the luckier I get." It reminds us of our favorite definition of luck: Luck is when preparation meets opportunity.

When you watch the winning horse at the Kentucky Derby or the winning car in the Indianapolis 500, it's easy to overlook the preparation that's gone into those seemingly instant victories. Like all successes, the moment of victory arrives in the twinkling of an eye, and we're tempted to chalk it up to luck. Actually, all such triumphs begin with thousands of hours of preparation over weeks, months, and even years before the glorious day—hours devoted to laboriously grooming and training the horse, meticulously building and testing the car.

Successful performers in all fields have groomed and prepared themselves mentally and physically for opportunity. When that magic moment arrives in which they can have it all, they're ready. They're able to remain calm and cool under pressure. They're able to summon the energy they need exactly when they need it and to maintain it for as long as they need to. They can concentrate fully on the moment at hand and not be distracted from what they know must be done. And at the same time, nothing of importance gets past them. Their senses are alert and finely tuned to respond quickly and precisely to the demands of the moment. Operating from this finely tuned state, they appear to be very lucky—just like the highly successful entrepreneurs and propreneurs we've met.

It's easy to think of highly successful entrepreneurs, professionals, and craftspeople as leading charmed lives. When we hear about how Debbie Fields launched Mrs. Fields Cookies, or how Famous Amos rode the chocolate-chip-cookie wave to fame and fortune, or how the names of businessman Harvey MacKay and psychologist Wayne Dyer became household words, it's easy to think "Boy, did they have all the luck!" But we've met and personally interviewed each of these people, and guess what? They weren't any luckier than the average person. They are ordinary men and women, doing extraordinary things.

Yes, they each began with their particular advantages. But so do all of us. They also each had their own handicaps and their own ups and downs. They faced the same things we all face and they were up for it. They were ready to capitalize on the opportunity when luck struck.

What Makes the Magic?

So what is it that enables peak performers to function optimally under pressure, to know what to do and when to do it, to come from behind, to make the difficult look so easy? We wanted to know. We wanted to be able to produce such extraordinary results ourselves. So over the past ten years we talked to more than a thousand highly successful people—from athletes to entertainers, from artists and entrepreneurs to propreneurs—and we've observed two things.

First, of course, they're all competent. A strong degree of competence seems to be a given. But, as peak-performance researcher Charles Garfield found in his studies of the world's greatest athletes, competence, although essential, accounts for only 10 to 40 percent of any performance. What separates the peak performers in all the fields we've investigated from others who were equally competent is that they had conditioned themselves to be able to do the following five things—all at the same time:

1. Remain *relaxed* under pressure.
2. Operate from a *high state of energy.*
3. Stay *focused* intently on their desired outcome.
4. Anticipate a *positive* result.
5. Be fully present in the moment.

If you watch peak performers, you'll see these traits in action. And while they're characteristic of the most successful among us, they can be developed by anyone over time through consistent conditioning, repeated experience, and a commitment to attaining them. All of us can train ourselves to function at this peak-performance state on a regular basis.

As your own coach, mentor, and manager, you're now in a position to condition yourself to perform optimally by cultivating these five traits. When the client calls, when it's time to negotiate the deal you've been waiting for, when you get the big contract—when an opportunity arises—you can be ready to make the most of the moment. Like the athlete, you can be at your peak—energized, focused, calm, cool, and relaxed. Your files and records can be sufficiently in order that you have all the facts, figures, and materials you need at your fingertips when you need them. And when all those things come together just right, it'll look easy.

So how's your luck these days? Are you prepared for success? Are you ready to seize whatever opportunities come your way? The miniquiz that follows can provide a snapshot of where you stand. Take a moment to see how you score. Then we'll discuss what you can do to enable yourself to work even more consistently at your peak.

You can think of the various statements on the quiz as indicators of the extent to which you're in condition, so to speak, to work optimally and thrive on your own. We find the quiz helps to identify the areas in which we need further conditioning, in much the same way as a coach continually assesses the extent to which his protégée is ready for competition and points out which areas need work.

Today, peak-performance training is virtually a science. Top athletic and artistic coaches across the country have a wealth of techniques to draw from to help condition their protégés to perform again and again at their peak. It's not surprising that many of the most successful self-employed professionals

Are You Ready for Success?

Give yourself 2 points for every statement you strongly agree with, 1 point if you agree somewhat, and no points if you disagree.

1. I get out of bed eager to start the day.

2. I know exactly what I intend to accomplish by being my own boss.

3. I am good at the work I do and confident that I can do it well.

4. I spend my day concentrating on the important tasks that will assure that I'll reach my goals.

5. I am relaxed and inwardly calm throughout the day.

6. I have plenty of energy to do what needs to be done.

7. I am not easily distracted. I can concentrate on the tasks at hand.

8. I quickly grasp the situations I encounter and can make decisions rapidly and decisively.

9. I can count on myself to do what needs to be done to achieve my goals.

10. At the end of the day, I still have energy to enjoy my favorite activities.

If you scored 18 or above, you are fit for success. If you scored 10 to 17, you're on the right track but need to step up your training to attain your personal best. If you scored under 10, you're out of shape and need to put yourself on a success regimen at once.

and propreneurs are using some of these same techniques in their work. Here's a five-step program we've developed for conditioning yourself to work at your peak.

A FIVE-STEP REGIMEN FOR PEAK PERFORMANCE

Each time you exercise, you come back stronger. Before long, you flat out get tough, both mentally and physically.
RAFER JOHNSON
OLYMPIC DECATHLON CHAMPION

Preparing yourself to work at your peak is much easier when you're on your own, particularly if you're working from home. On your own at home, you have more flexibility in scheduling your work and greater control over the course of your day, making this basic five-step program much easier to follow.

Step One: Remain Relaxed Under Pressure

If you are relaxing and subconsciously thinking about your coming race, you are going to perform with just about 100 percent efficiency.

MARK SPITZ
OLYMPIC SWIMMING CHAMPION

Do you find that sometimes you're hot and sometimes you're not? We all have times when we drag through the day, times when nothing seems to go right. Obviously, we can't be hot all the time. The trick is to be hot when you need to be.

When you need to be at your best, when you need to perform at your peak, you want to feel relaxed and confident. You want to be calm, alert, and in charge. Unfortunately, it's too often true that the more important the moment, the higher the pressure and the less relaxed and composed we feel. At key moments, instead of enjoying a state of relaxed confidence, you may feel your heart racing and your palms sweating. Your brain may feel as if it's either stuck in slow motion or on fast-forward.

We know about this experience firsthand. It's happened to us all too often. Actually, it's a common experience for most people who are on their own. After all, we are usually doing things that are new to us. You may not even know any other people who have done what you're doing. In chapter 6, we'll go into detail about how to turn this fear and anxiety into confidence. But here are a few quick and easy techniques we and others find useful to get and stay relaxed at any time throughout the day.

1. Learn to notice quickly when your body is beginning to feel tense. Notice where in your body you feel tense, tight, hyper, creepy, queasy, shaky. Then take action to return to a relaxed state immediately, before the tension builds up.

2. Take several long, deep breaths. Slow, deep breathing sends a signal to the brain that all is well; your brain then floods your body with the chemical signals that accompany a relaxed state. So anytime your day gets harried and you start to feel uptight, take a few slow, deep breaths. Count from 1 to 10 as you inhale and from 10 to 1 as you exhale. Take five to ten of these relaxing breaths until your breathing becomes calm and rhythmic.

3. Shake out the tension. Take a moment to shake out the areas of your body that begin to feel tense and tight. Shake out your hands, arms, head, feet, legs, and finally your whole body. Do this until you feel some relief.

4. Take a break in a relaxing locale. Research shows that being in a natural setting can reduce stress. The geologist Dr. Roger Ulrich has found, for example, that even viewing scenes of nature reduced muscle tension, blood pressure, and heart rate in individuals under pressure and helped them recover from stressful events, including surgery, more quickly.

The environmental psychologist Stephen Kaplan found that you can benefit from the stress-reducing advantages of nature simply by spending a few moments looking out the window or walking through a garden. Watching sunrises and sunsets is particularly relaxing. And if you don't mind getting wet, standing in the rain is an unusually renewing experience. So when you feel uptight, go outside. Lie under a tree on the grass. Sit in the breeze on the porch. Walk in the park, or if you have water nearby, stroll by the river, lake, or ocean.

Of course, outdoors is not the only place you can relax. Many people take solace from visiting a museum, art gallery, spa, or public monument. You can even create a special room or area of your home for relaxation. Anthony Lawlor, award-winning architect and author of *The Temple in the House,* writes that setting aside a "sacred" place in your home may be as simple as creating a shelf in the corner of a room—or you may want to consider setting aside a special room for quiet reflection, relaxation, or meditation. You might even want to decorate and design your entire home to have a calming and restorative quality.

5. Take a mental minivacation. If you cannot get away even for a few minutes, close your eyes and imagine that you are in one of your favorite natural environments or some other relaxing place. Perhaps imagine yourself watching the sun set over the ocean, sitting by a bubbling brook in the mountains, or curled up in your favorite nook.

6. Play relaxing background music. Recent research shows that the human brain and body are highly sensitive to sound, and especially to music. Certain types of music have a particular rhythm and cadence that has been found to induce a calm, relaxed state of mind even when played softly in the background. In fact, the musicologist Dr. Stephen Halpern claims that listening to the right music can take you from a highly tense state to one that is relaxed yet alert, in as little as thirty seconds. Robert Ornstein, author of the book *Healthy Pleasures,* calls this phenomenon "musical Valium."

7. Eat right. Good nutrition can help you stay relaxed, too. Judith Wurtman, a researcher at the Massachusetts Institute of Technology, has found that certain foods pick you up or relax you. In her book *Managing Your Mind and Mood through Food,* she recommends that to feel more relaxed, you should eat complex carbohydrates like breads, muffins, pasta, cereals, potatoes, and grains. And Dr. Charles Tkacz of New York's Nassau Mental Health Center stresses the importance of the B vitamins in managing stress, while Dr. Robert

Haskell of San Francisco recommends vitamin C as a stress reducer. Whole grains and leafy green vegetables are high in B vitamins. Foods rich in vitamin C include sweet red and green peppers, brussels sprouts, strawberries, cauliflower, and salmon.

8. Use your natural alarm clock. According to Rob Krakovitz, the author of *High Energy,* the sound of an alarm clock starts your day in distress. It jangles you awake and puts your system into panic. He maintains that when you go to bed early enough, you can program your internal alarm to wake you up without a commotion. Using this natural alarm clock to awaken you works wonders. It helps you ease your way gently, but quickly, into the day.

9. Enjoy a pet break. Stroking and playing with a pet can help reduce stress and even extend life. Petting an animal actually reduces blood pressure, as does watching fish swim around in an aquarium.

10. Take a short nap. Researchers at a large Athens hospital found that people who took at least a thirty-minute nap daily were less likely to suffer from heart disease. This finding correlates with evidence that countries where the afternoon siesta is commonplace have a lower incidence of heart disease. The entertainer George Burns told the *Los Angeles Times* that a daily nap is one of the secrets of his longevity. And Robert Fulghum made the benefits of short naps evident in his popular book *Everything I Need to Know I Learned in Kindergarten.*

11. Meditate daily. If there were one thing you could do that was proven to reduce stress, improve your ability to learn, prevent insomnia, enhance your relationships and job performance, improve your memory, normalize your blood pressure, leave you feeling happier throughout the course of the day, and slow down the aging process, wouldn't you spend twenty minutes a day doing it? It sounds like a prescription for health, wealth, and happiness, doesn't it? And maybe it is.

A large body of scientific research now shows that daily meditation is one of the best, most reliable ways to condition your mind to function in a perpetually calm and relaxed state. Actually, the research is startling. It shows that meditating regularly lowers levels of stress hormones and plasma cortisol, both of which go up with stress, and reduces cardiovascular risk. As a result, it can improve your mood, reduce stress, lower your blood pressure and cholesterol level, improve your sleep, slow the aging process, increase your productivity, and speed up the rate at which you learn. And all it takes is twenty minutes a day!

If you feel meditating is a bit unconventional, consider this: The positive effects on employee productivity and health have been shown to be so dramatic that growing numbers of corporations like Puritan Bennet, a medical equipment manufacturer in Kansas City, Kansas, and R.W. Montegomery, a chemical manufacturer in Detroit, are now encouraging their employees to meditate. Some have seen absenteeism drop 85 percent and productivity rise 120 percent. Others have found that coworkers who meditate are easier to get along with. For more about meditation, refer to the resource list at the end of this chapter.

Step Two: Get Energized! Stay Energized!

> *Create in you an irresistible energy, putting wings on your heart that will allow you to fly beyond all self-imposed limitations.*
>
> GERALD JAMPOLSKY, M.D.

Fatigue is the number-one symptom people complain about to their doctors. Yet the most successful people seem to have boundless energy. They always seem ready to take on any challenge. They jump out of bed raring to go, and they're still going full steam ahead come evening. How do they do it? Here are several ways to get charged up and stay that way.

1. Get plenty of R & R. Sometimes people question why we put so much emphasis on making sure you don't overwork. Perhaps it's because we both tend to be overworkers. But more than that, it's because we know that you can't be at your best when you're tired, worn out, and dragging. It's like overtraining. If you overtrain before a competition or performance, you're burned out when the actual event arrives.

It's an illusion to think you'll get further by overworking. When you're overworked, you don't think at your best, or make the best decisions. Research shows that overworkers actually produce less in more time.

A management consultant we'll call Rita is a good example of what happens when you ignore your need for R & R. She had been out on her own for only a couple of years and was doing quite well. Her strategy had been to assume a leadership role in her professional association and thereby build her reputation as a leader in her field. It was working. She had served as the local chapter president and gone on to a leadership role at the national level. Through the contacts she was making in the organization, she had been able to get several key clients.

When she was offered the chance to head up the association's annual national conference, she jumped at the opportunity, even though she had a major contract under way with pressing deadlines. She believed that doing a good job of producing this conference would be an ideal way to showcase herself and her skills. To meet the schedules for both her contract and the conference, however, she really had to burn the midnight oil.

On the day of the conference, she had done it all. She had completed her project, and the conference was clearly going to be a success. The speakers were excellent. The registration was strong. Now was her time to shine. And, of course, she was introducing the keynote speaker and giving a speech herself on the future of the field. But that morning when she took the podium, she hadn't slept for three days straight. She hadn't had a day off in three months, and the entire week before she'd slept only four to five hours a night.

The strain of such a schedule came crashing down on her at that moment. She stumbled through the introduction of the keynoter. She lost her place repeatedly during her own presentation, and under the pressure of it all her voice cracked nervously throughout. Fortunately, she was able to save face because people respected the fine job she had done. But what should have been a glorious victory for her was instead tinged with embarrassment.

And that was not the end of it. She became ill immediately after the conference and lost a month of work while sick in bed. She also had to go back and tie up loose ends on her project, handling details that hadn't been given sufficient attention. By the end of the year, Rita was burned out on her business. She was wondering if she wanted to continue operating at the level of success she had created for herself.

This may sound like an extreme case, but as your own boss it's your job to make sure that something similar doesn't happen to you, even on a smaller, less visible scale. You are the one who must make sure you pace yourself so you can be at your best when you need to be.

2. *Keep the pressure in bounds.* According to research by Joseph Procaccini of Loyola College in Baltimore, unrealistic expectations are the real culprit in burnout. Burnout occurs when the demands we put on ourselves outweigh our energy supply. On the job, we might blame overly demanding bosses for the burnout we experience. But on your own, it's your own unrealistic demands that slow you down and sabotage your performance.

High expectations are a good way to motivate ourselves to go beyond unnecessary limits. But success requires a delicate balance between the energy we have available and the demands we place on ourselves. When energy and demand are equal, we perform at our peak. If we don't believe fully in our ultimate success, however, we tend to make unreasonable demands on ourselves in order to compensate, and ultimately our performance suffers. On the other hand, when we believe fully in our ultimate success, we instill in ourselves the confidence to work at a sensible pace, and our performance improves.

Poet and publisher Rusty Berkus of Red Rose Press is an excellent example of this point. Rusty's staff members were pushing her to take on major speaking engagements to help sell her books of poetry. She refused to bend to the pressure, however, because she had never spoken before large audiences and public speaking made her anxious. But she did believe in her ability to learn and knew that in order to become an accomplished speaker, she needed to begin with smaller, more informal audiences with whom she could make mistakes and learn without risking her reputation. That is what she did, and now she speaks successfully to increasingly larger audiences. Recently she's even been appearing on radio and television shows, but all because she went at a manageable pace.

3. Know how much sleep you need and make sure you get enough. The National Commission on Sleep Disorders Research reports that most Americans get 20 percent less sleep today than we did 100 years ago. Evidently when there are not enough hours in the day, we take them from the night. But, don't shortchange yourself for more than one or two nights in a row. For some people, eight hours of sleep is a must; for others slightly less or slightly more is required. The goal is to get enough sleep each night that you arise feeling refreshed, but not so much that you feel sluggish. You can find your peak level by noticing how you feel each morning. Schedule your most demanding work for those times of day when you are at your peak. Leave less arduous tasks like sorting mail and filing for low-energy periods.

4. Insist that you take at least one day off a week. You need this break to relax and recharge. Taking off two days a week is even better. If for certain short periods you can't squeeze out a day off every week, insist on at least a day a month.

5. Make sure you are enjoying what you do. There's nothing like loving what you do to boost your energy and keep you going. Usually when you first go out on your own you're excited and turned on by what you're doing, but sometimes after doing it day after day, you don't like it as much as you thought you would. Or after a while, you may feel the need to go on to other things. When this happens, if you force yourself to continue doing what you've been doing, you'll start dreading Mondays again. You'll begin dragging through the day, going through the motions, and slacking off. So watch for signs that your creative energies are waning, and allow yourself to find ways for your business to evolve with you. As actress Sally Field says, "I'd rather act than eat. If you don't feel that way about what you do, then your legs are easily knocked out from under you." Doing your "perfect work" will continually energize and refresh you.

6. Eat high-energy foods. In her book *Managing Your Mind and Mood Through Food,* Judith Wurtman identifies foods her research shows will boost your energy and make you more productive. For high energy, increased mental alertness, and greater motivation, she recommends a diet of protein-rich foods like fish, chicken, and lean beef, low-fat dairy products, dried peas and

How to Have a Good Night's Sleep with Everything Hanging over Your Head

- **Hang your work problems on the coatrack when you leave work.** At the end of the day, as you close the door on work, imagine putting your concerns in a special box or basket where you can pick them up in the morning. Write out a to-do list or an issues-to-address list for yourself so you'll feel confident you won't forget about something important overnight.

- **Chase yourself out of the office at a reasonable hour.** Good bosses make sure their employees go home. Insist that you leave ample time between work and sleep. Allow at least an hour or two to unwind from the workday before trying to sleep. Engage in relaxing, pleasurable activities before retiring.

- **Don't work in bed.** Reserve your bed for sleeping and other pleasurable, relaxing activities.

- **Avoid stimulating food and beverages later in the day.** Caffeine, sweets, and salty and fatty foods keep you wired.

- **Keep your bedroom restful.** Philip Goldberg and Daniel Kaufman, the authors of *Everybody's Guide to Natural Sleep,* recommend keeping the bedroom quiet, dark, and comfortably cool (between sixty-four and sixty-six degrees Fahrenheit).

beans, grains, seeds, and nuts. Also, she suggests that you leave out or minimize energy drainers like alcohol, sugar, salt, coffee, and junk food, which seem to charge you up but actually stress you out. Keep healthy, high-energy snacks on hand like pumpkin seeds, almonds, carrots, hard-boiled eggs, grapes, and whole-grain bread.

7. *Get plenty of exercise.* Do an aerobic exercise (swimming, running, cycling, dancing) at least twenty to thirty minutes every other day. Choose an activity you enjoy. Being on your own, especially if you work at home, allows you more options for fitting exercise into a busy day. Choose whatever times work best for you. You can use your exercise time as a work break or as a way to start or end your day.

8. *Take vacations.* At least once a year, take off a week or more to truly get away from your work and your regular routines and responsibilities. Often self-employed individuals feel that they don't have the time or money for a vacation. In truth, you can't afford not to take time off. An extended break provides fresh energy, new perspectives, and renewed clarity for your business. So price your products and services to allow for a vacation and assess

Instant Energy Builders

When you start to feel tired and burned out, bring yourself back to life in a few seconds with one of these high-energy tips.

- Put on some lively, exhilarating music. Sing along. You can't feel sluggish while singing "Zippa-Dee-Doo Dah," especially if you get up and dance or move around to the music.

- Give yourself a sixty-second round of vigorous applause. Stand up. Take a bow. Whistle and stomp your feet.

- Count from one to ten as loudly as you can.

- Try this high-energy drink from Dr. Rob Krakovitz's book *High Energy*. Mix half a teaspoon of vitamin-C crystals with diluted fruit juice (half juice, half water).

your annual workload to identify slower times of year when taking time away would be least disruptive. There are many ways to keep vacation costs down such as tagging a holiday on to the end of a business trip, using frequent flyer miles, or staying at hostels or college and university student facilities. (See Resources for more information.)

Step Three: Build Your Concentration

> *I always felt that my greatest asset was not my physical ability; it was my mental ability.*
> BRUCE JENNER
> OLYMPIC DECATHLON CHAMPION

Watch the faces of the players during the world basketball championships. Notice the expressions of the Wimbledon finalists. Observe the pitcher who's about to pitch a no-hitter. Take note of the Olympic gold medalist as he or she prepares to dive. What do you see on all these faces? The same thing: concentration—the ability to focus all your energy on accomplishing the task at hand. How do these peak performers develop the ability to focus, to concentrate on their goals no matter what's going on around them? How do they respond readily to any event that's pertinent to the task at hand and ignore all else? Here's what we've observed.

- They know exactly what they want to do and what it takes to do it. They aren't asking themselves, "Do I really want to get that shot in

Creating a Supportive Work Environment

A supportive work environment can help you concentrate and work at your peak. Design and furnish your work space so that it is a place where you like to be. Make sure it nourishes rather than fatigues or distracts you. Now that you're the boss, give yourself the equivalent of the corner office. Make sure it has a window, plants, artwork, music, and other things that sustain you. Consider the following:

- **Lighting.** According to a Harris Poll, lighting is the number-one contributor to productivity. For best results, use natural light when possible, or full-spectrum bulbs. Avoid glare, and light various work tasks appropriately. (For specific lighting information see *Working from Home*, pages 138–41.)

- **Soundproofing.** Columbia University found that, of all environmental factors, unwanted noise has the strongest correlation to job stress. Other studies suggest that people who work in noisy settings are more likely to become discouraged than those working in quieter environments. So find a sound level at which you can remain alert but still be able to concentrate. Mask street and other unpleasant noise with background music or a white-noise generator. Soundproof windows, doors, and noisy equipment. (For more information about soundproofing see *Working from Home*, pages 136–37.)

- **Office furniture.** Poorly designed furniture can cause irritating aches and pains and eat away subtly at your concentration. Furniture should be comfortable and ergonomically designed to avoid muscle strain and fatigue. (For more information on selecting the right office furniture see *Working from Home*, pages 125–36.)

- **Aromatherapy.** Psychologists at the City University of New York have found that odors affect how we feel and how well we think. Peppermint, for example, stimulates productivity. Orange is relaxing; lavender is energizing; spiced apple helps reduce stress. So treat your office to your favorite fresh flowers, potpourris, incense, and oils to help you work more productively.

- **Color.** Dr. Alexander G. Schauss, a clinical psychologist and the director of the American Institute for Biosocial Research, has found that the colors in our environment produce strong psychological and physiological effects. For example, red is energizing; blue is relaxing; yellow stimulates thinking and creativity. When researchers painted classroom walls yellow on three sides and blue in the back, student IQ scores rose an average of 12 points, and teachers felt more relaxed.

- **Fresh Air.** Plants most certainly make excellent decorative items, but NASA research has shown that the right plants can also serve as air purifiers. Placing a spider plant, a peace lily, or golden pothos in your office can literally clear the air, absorbing chemical pollutants like ozone, formaldehyde, and trichloreoethylene generated by your computer, carpet, copy machine, and fax.

now or should I wait until later?" They aren't wondering, "Should I put the ball in this hoop or some other one?" They know what they need to do.

- Their goal—be it getting the ball over the net or making a shot—is the sole focus of their efforts. Have you ever noticed that when being interviewed after a stunning victory, performers often appear to be in a trance of some kind? Their eyes look glazed. Sometimes they don't remember all the events of the game and talk somewhat randomly. They seem disoriented because they are returning from a state of total concentration in which all their attention was on their goal.

- They turn the performance over to the moment. The preparation, practice, study, strategy, and so on are behind them, and they give 100 percent of their energy and attention to what is going on second by second, shot by shot, stroke by stroke. They aren't looking back at what they did the last time. Nor are they looking ahead at what might happen the next time. They're doing what needs to be done right now to achieve their goal.

We can each develop this ability to concentrate totally, but it requires a commitment and a willingness to set up our lives so that we can devote our full attention to the tasks at hand. For example, you can do any or all of the following:

1. Make adequate child-care arrangements so you aren't distracted by family and other parental responsibilities. Some people mistakenly think they can work with children underfoot. Occasionally the nature of your work is such that you can, but often there are aspects of your work that require 100 percent of your attention.

2. Set up time signals so you aren't having to continually watch the clock. You can use a digital watch to alert you when it's time to move on to other activities. You can set a clock radio, program your TV, or use a wake-up service to signal you. Sarah used a cuckoo clock in her therapy office to signal when to begin closing her sessions. This freed her to concentrate totally on her clients without constantly glancing at her watch. The piano instructor Margy Balter sets a timer to let her know when sessions must end.

3. Use an answering machine or answering service so you can be free to work without interruption from constant phone calls. When you need to focus on key tasks, set aside a time of day to return phone calls instead of taking or making them at random.

4. Take definite action. Don't vacillate. Once you get set on a course of action, act. Then evaluate. If you're always doubting and questioning yourself each step of the way, you'll never learn what actually works and what doesn't. Commit to a course of action and observe the results. Research shows that people who overanalyze miss the boat.

5. Get the cooperation of family and friends so they will not be making demands on you during times when you need to be focused on your work.

6. Locate your office or work space away from disruptions and distractions. Attics, garages, back rooms, and rooms off the garage make ideal home offices. Offices at the ends of corridors or set off from customer areas can help you concentrate more effectively.

Step Four: Become an Optimist

> *Nothing splendid has ever been achieved except by those who dared believe that something inside them was superior to circumstance.*
>
> BRUCE BARTON

Worry is one of the biggest drains on our energy. It saps enthusiasm and confidence faster than any other activity. Mark Twain once claimed he had many problems, most of which never happened. And isn't that the truth? Most of the things we worry about never happen, but a nationwide survey found that 42 percent of those interviewed report worrying a lot and spend at least 25 percent of their day worrying.

Alan Loy McGinnis, the author of the book *The Power of Optimism,* defines worry as the misuse of our imagination. Instead of using the imagination to project positive outcomes, the worrier imagines dreaded disasters and defeats. Optimists, on the other hand, use their imagination to rehearse success. And indeed we find that the most successful individuals from all walks of life do this routinely. According to Robert Ornstein and David Sobel, the authors of the book *Healthy Pleasures,* not only do optimists imagine a rosy future, they remember their successes much better than they recall their failures.

They also dwell on the pleasant. They skip over, although they don't ignore, their shortcomings.

In the emerging new sciences of psychoneuroimmunology and psychobiology, this phenomenon is called *positive illusion*. And you see it in world-class competition of all kinds. The world champion goes into competition thinking he or she will succeed. Top ice skaters, skiers, gymnasts, divers, and other performers imagine themselves completing their programs flawlessly. They are all optimists. They *anticipate* success. They don't hope for it; they expect it.

The power of positive illusion occurs in the worlds of commerce, politics, and art as well. Warren Bennis, a professor of business administration at the University of Southern California, has spent a lifetime conducting pioneering research into the nature of leadership: what it is, who has it, and how we can foster it. For his best-selling book *On Becoming a Leader*—a study of the barriers to successful leadership—he interviewed hundreds of leaders from all walks of life such as Apple Computer CEO John Sculley, writer Norman Lear, feminist publisher Gloria Steinem, and Oscar-winning film director Sydney Pollack. In a previous book, *Leaders: The Strategies of Taking Charge,* he pulled together all his research on the process by which people become effective and inspiring leaders. One trait he found all great leaders to possess is what he calls *unwarranted optimism*—the ability to see a positive future even in the face of contradictory evidence.

Research is now confirming that optimists are more successful in all areas of life. Recent studies show that optimists excel in school, have a better love life, make more money, have better health, and may even live longer! Dr. Michael Scheier of Carnegie-Mellon University in Pittsburgh has found that optimists also do better in the face of stress. They take action sooner; break big problems into smaller, more manageable ones; stick to their goals longer; and believe others can help. Optimists also report less fatigue, depression, dizziness, muscle soreness, and coughs than pessimists when facing the same stressful events.

So perhaps it's time to put aside our expectations that we be totally realistic. Having an unrealistically positive view of ourselves seems to be a correlate of greater success. Fortunately, having such a positive outlook can be cultivated and learned. Although the latest research suggests that Pollyanna may have been on to something and rose-colored glasses may not be so bad, it doesn't mean we should look at life through rose-colored blinders. So just what does having a positive outlook mean? Below is a list of traits that Alan Loy McGinnis finds healthy optimists possess. Which ones describe you?

If you tend to be pessimistic by nature, here are a few things you can do to make optimism a regular habit.

Twelve Characteristics of Tough-Minded Optimists

1. Optimists are seldom surprised by trouble.

2. Optimists look for partial solutions.

3. Optimists believe they have control over their future.

4. Optimists allow for regular renewal.

5. Optimists interrupt their negative trains of thought.

6. Optimists heighten their powers of appreciation.

7. Optimists use their imagination to rehearse success.

8. Optimists are cheerful even when they can't be happy.

9. Optimists believe they have an almost unlimited capacity for stretching.

10. Optimists build lots of love into their lives.

11. Optimists like to swap good news.

12. Optimists accept what cannot be changed.

*Reprinted with permission from *The Power of Optimism,* by Alan Loy McGinnis, HarperCollins, 1990.

---

1. Stop hoping and start anticipating. Think for a moment of something that you want very much to come true. Now close your eyes and *hope* for it. Take time to notice what you think about as you experience this feeling of hope. How do you feel? Now open your eyes. Clear your mind. Then close them again. This time *anticipate* what you want to happen. Again take time to notice what you think about and how you feel as you experience anticipation. Then open your eyes and compare the two experiences.

Most people feel much better *anticipating* the results they want. *Hoping* usually involves imagining two outcomes: the one you want and the one you don't. It's usually accompanied by an uneasy sense of yearning. *Anticipation,* on the other hand, usually involves thinking of only one result: the one you want. More often than not it's accompanied by a sense of excited expectation.

2. If you must worry, do it on a schedule. The Pennsylvania State University psychologists Thomas Borkovec and Elwood Robinson suggest that chronic worrywarts contain their worry by setting aside thirty minutes a day in which they can worry. All worry is to be saved for this one period, during which they can worry as much as they please.

3. Associate with optimists. Optimism is contagious, so cultivate positive, upbeat friends and acquaintances. Avoid spending time with naysayers, complainers, and doomsdayers. Join upbeat organizations and groups; avoid downbeat ones.

4. Listen to upbeat songs. Have you ever noticed that popular vocal music generates intense feelings—usually sad, wistful, lustful, or romantic ones? What if you were to put this same emotive power of music to work to generate joyful, optimistic, empowering, stimulating, and exciting feelings? Some songs on the popular market do have this effect. Whitney Houston's "One Moment in Time," Bette Midler's "Wind Beneath My Wings," "Up Where We Belong" from the soundtrack to *An Officer and a Gentlemen,* and "The Rose," by Amanda McBroom, are a few examples. In addition, today there are growing numbers of New Thought vocalists whose albums are devoted to inspiring and empowering their listeners.

Step Five: Be There Now

> *When completely focused on the present, logical and analytical processes are suspended, and as this occurs, the peak performer has the sense that all actions are occurring automatically and effortlessly.*
>
> CHARLES GARFIELD
> PEAK-PERFORMANCE RESEARCHER

Do you ever feel out of it? Have you ever missed an opportunity because you didn't see it coming? If so, chances are you were distracted, lost in thought, living in your own world, listening to yourself talk, planning ahead, reminiscing, or daydreaming when the vital clues of great things passed you by. Doing such things, even frequently, is okay, of course. In fact, daydreams are a great way to relax and get away from it all. But when the situation calls for you to be on your toes, you need to be fully present—in touch with what's going on around you—and able to respond quickly and appropriately.

Have you noticed how the most successful individuals are able to react quickly to the events around them? Nothing seems to get by them. They can respond to any challenge at a moment's notice. They have all their antennae up. Their senses are tuned to hear, see, and sense everything around them. In the field of neurolinguistic programming this state of awareness is referred to as *being in up-time.*

According to the peak-performance researcher Charles Garfield, the key to successfully focusing on the present is learning to be attentive to your senses and to the quality of what you are sensing, rather than to your interpretation

A Five-Minute Warm-up for Peak Performance

Haven't you noticed that professional artists and athletes warm up before they perform? Obviously it helps them perform better. So why don't we warm up to function more effectively? Why do we just assume that somehow we'll automatically be in peak condition to work? Why not spend a few minutes warming up our mind and body, especially at times when we want to be at our best? Here's a five-minute routine we created for getting relaxed, energized, focused, positive, and present.

Minute 1: Relax. Stand up. Shake out your entire body, from head to toe. Close your eyes. Take a deep, relaxing breath. Breathe in slowly to the count of ten and then out to the count of ten. Complete ten such breaths. Ride the wave of your breath for one minute.

Minute 2: Energize. To get your energy moving, start clapping. Keep clapping louder and faster. Then begin stomping while you clap. Stomp and clap faster and faster, louder and louder. If you need to warm up somewhere silently, try the quiet version of this exercise—finger snapping. Snap your fingers quickly with both hands for one minute.

Minute 3: Focus. Now you're relaxed and energized. But you don't want to be a loaded loose cannon. You want to focus your energy toward accomplishing your goals. With your eyes closed, take a minute to visualize your goals and dreams as if they were already happening. Imagine you're living your dream. Go into every detail. Savor the full experience of it for close to a minute. Then focus on what steps you will take today to make those dreams reality.

Minute 4: Anticipate success. With your eyes still closed, prepare for a successful day by taking another minute to review your past successes and the things in your present life that give you great pleasure. Cultivate an attitude of gratitude toward the many things for which you are grateful. Imagine once again the future you anticipate enjoying. Imagine yourself managing whatever problems you encounter. See yourself responding skillfully to any unexpected developments. Feel the excitement as you anticipate achieving your goals.

Minute 5: Get in touch. Before opening your eyes, begin to connect with your environment. Hear and sense what's going on around you. Slowly savor the sounds and sensations. Now open your eyes and take full notice of your environment. Allow your attention to linger over the objects, sights, and sounds about you. See colors. Notice textures. Let the day spring to life. Think of the people you will be contacting. Connect with your memory of them. Imagine yourself making contact with everyone you meet or talk with. Resolve to take the time to look them in the eyes, to reach out a hand to them, to tell them something about yourself and find out about them.

Now feel a wave of calm and boundless energy streaming through your body. Acknowledge that you are alive, and relish the moment. Imagine that energy carrying you like a river effortlessly through the day.

of the meaning. So the first way to begin honing your skills of awareness so you can operate more often in up-time is to become more aware of what you are and are not aware of. Here are a few simple exercises from John Stevens's book *Awareness* that you can use to heighten your sensory awareness.

1. Become an observer of your awareness. Take a moment to observe where you have your attention. Say to yourself, "I am aware of . . ." and finish the sentence with whatever you become aware of at the moment. Do this for a few minutes. You'll notice how quickly your attention moves. As it does, identify whether what you are aware of is:

- An inner sensation: a pain, an itch, a feeling, an emotion, a tightness, a fullness, a hunger, a thirst. Peak performers quickly calibrate feedback from inner sensations.

- An outside stimulus: an object or event you see, touch, taste, smell, or hear. Peak performers block out superfluous stimuli and are hyperalert to relevant ones.

- Mental activity: thoughts, explanations, interpretations, guesses, comparisons, plans, remembered events or activities, anticipation of future activities, daydreams. Mental activity is downtime. It takes you into your head and away from your present experience. Thought stops romance.

2. Focus on each area of awareness. Begin by noticing your inner sensations. Notice how your body feels. Are you relaxed? Where does your body feel tight? How do you feel right now? Mad? Sad? Glad? Scared? Excited? Bored? Agitated? Peaceful? How do your toes feel? Your stomach, shoulders, fingers, elbows, earlobes?

Now shift your attention to your thoughts. What are you thinking about? What do you think of this activity? What do you think about what you're thinking? Maybe you're thinking about what you will have for dinner—or something you forgot to do today.

Now shift your attention to outside sensations. Look around the room. What do you notice? What do you hear? Do you suddenly become aware of sounds you didn't hear before? A clock ticking? The heat or air conditioning running? Is there talking in the background? Can you smell anything? Now move about and touch things around you. Notice the sensations—soft, smooth, hard, sharp, rough, cold, hot. As you do this, notice if you begin evaluating or thinking about these things or if you just let yourself experience them.

Finally, shift your awareness back and forth between inside and outside—between sensations and thoughts, from one sense to another. Which ones do you notice most easily? Focus on those that you are less sensitive to.

Exercises like these and the "Five-Minute Warm-up" on page 176 can help you get out of your mind and into the moment, where you can perform at your best. If you feel self-conscious about doing such exercises, go to a track meet and watch the performers warming up. You'll notice them carrying out similar types of activities. Or visit a theater or dance company and watch how the performers prepare for the curtain to go up. They, too, will be doing exercises like these.

And by the way, you can use any one of the steps in this warm-up as a way to help yourself make the transition quickly—actually in less than one minute—from any of the five basic functions of managing your work.

For example, if you have to break away from working intensely on a problem you're solving for a client to get a file for your accountant (Organizing) or you have to stop to take a call from an unhappy customer (Improving), you can take ten deep breaths to help make the shift from one activity to the other. Or you can take a few seconds to stomp your feet and clap your hands. Or you can visualize closing the door on your problem and see it waiting there ready to take it up again easily when you return. Or you can take moment to connect with your physical environment as you head for the filing cabinet or reach for the phone to take the call. Any one of these simple steps can enable you to shift into the new activity fresh, alert, and ready to function at your best.

Making Success Automatic

You'll find as you begin conditioning yourself using the suggestions in this chapter that you'll be able to access a peak-performance state whenever you need to. When you need to perform optimally, you'll be able to move into this highly productive state. Over time, when the pressure is on, when the stakes are high, you'll automatically relax, feel energized, focus, anticipate doing your best, and remain in the moment. If your heart starts racing or your energy starts lagging, you will automatically say and do the right thing to slow yourself down or charge yourself up.

Conditioning yourself for peak performance is like setting the automatic thermostat on your heating and air-conditioning system, or like setting your car's automatic speed control. When more heat, cool air, or gasoline is needed, the system notifies itself to kick in. Once the optimal level is reached, however, it cuts back. And so it is with learning how to keep yourself in a state at which you can perform optimally.

When we've asked top athletes and entertainers like Olympic gold-medal-winning ice dancers Jayne Torvile and Christopher Dean how they were able to excel under such intense competition, they've frequently told us that the discipline of having performed the same moves, or the same routines, over and over in practice and competition enables them to do it almost automatically. In this same vein, basketball star Isaiah Thomas claimed that when he's at his best, it's as if he isn't even there. He's so in tune with the goal and the present moment that the ball is going into the hoop even before it leaves his hands.

As your own coach and manager, you can train yourself to achieve these superior results as well. It's a matter of making sure you can count on yourself to do what you want to do and what you tell yourself and others that you will do. It's a matter of knowing what motivates you and how to tap that motivation when you need it, and then being in peak mental, physical, and emotional condition.

Taking Care of the Coach

Since as your own coach and mentor you need to be there for yourself with the answers, the direction, the support, the guidance, the reassurance, the appreciation, the expectations, the demands, and the resources, what do you do when you—the coach—become discouraged, baffled, or at a loss? What if you don't have the answers? What if you don't know what to tell yourself? What if you find situations in which you can't manage yourself? What if you fly off the handle? Give bad directions? Make mistakes?

Unlike professional coaches, you can't decide to drop yourself as a client. Although you might like to, you can't take another job with some more talented, compliant, or cooperative protégé. You can't even fire yourself. This job is yours for life—unless, of course, you want to take another salaried position and turn yourself back over to someone else.

So if you get fed up with yourself on occasion, just keep in mind that you're the best you've got. And remember, some people are much harder to supervise and motivate than others. The moment you get out on your own, any authority issues you have are now with yourself. If you tend to rebel or act out when things don't go the way you want, you'll be rebelling and acting out against yourself. If you tend to be recalcitrant, lazy, or stubborn, guess who will have to handle it? You, of course.

Obviously, you can't be perfect either as an employee or as a coach, boss, and mentor. Making it on your own is a learning process. Learning to be your own boss is like learning anything else. You have to get the hang of it. There are many professional organizations and groups you can join that are filled with others who are meeting similar challenges. In fact, when Sarah and several other psychotherapists founded a mental-health institute in Kansas City, we created a group that met every Monday afternoon; its sole purpose was for caregivers to support, nurture, encourage, and sympathize with one another so we would be able to begin the week with renewed confidence and commitment.

Forming such a support group for yourself can be a godsend and is not difficult to do, because many people who are on their own share this need for a sense of mutual team support. Look for noncompetitive individuals who share your level of commitment and who are excited about other people's success. Join with them and you will all benefit.

If you discover that you're really giving yourself a hard time—messing up deals, losing business by abusing drugs, alcohol, money, or sex, or just doing a bad job, get some professional help. You may have observed, as we have, that many of the most successful performers in all fields are using skilled therapists to help them overcome limitations and tap their full potential. Sports teams now even hire team shrinks. This isn't because successful people are sick or have more things wrong with them than anyone else. It's because success demands more of people than mediocrity, and the most successful people and the most successful coaches don't want to see talent and potential bound up in unnecessary limitations. They want to do whatever they can to free themselves of such limitations. They know what miraculous things are possible when ability soars untethered.

And one thing we know for sure: Preparing yourself to work at your peak will be much easier when you're on your own, because you'll have the flexibility and the control to discover what it takes to bring out your abilities and let them soar.

RESOURCES

PEAK PERFORMANCE

*Awareness.** John Stevens. San Francisco: Book People, 1971. A book of exercises designed to increase your awareness of internal and external reality.

Bodyrhythms: Chronobiology and Peak Performances. Lynne Lamburg. New York: Morrow, 1994. This book tells how to organize your waking hours for peak productivity, especially if you can't stay up, or can't stay asleep.

*A classic.

~~~ **Brain Building in Just 12 Weeks.** Marilyn von Savant and Leonore Fleischer. New York: Bantam, 1991. An effective, entertaining program designed to strengthen your intelligence and expand your brain power.

BrainMind Bulletin. Marilyn Ferguson, publisher. P.O. Box 42211, Los Angeles, CA 90042. (800) 553-6463, (213) 223-2500. An eight-page monthly newsletter summarizing the latest psychology, neuroscience, health science, and public policy, brain science, and human potential research.

~~~ **Career Shifting: Starting Over in a Changing Economy.** William Charland. Holbrook, MA: Adams Media Group, 1993.

~~~ **End the Struggle Against Yourself: A Workbook for Developing Deep Confidence and Self-Acceptance.** Stan Taubman. New York: Tarcher/Putman, 1994. Exercises, activities, and personal stories show you how to face self-doubt squarely and learn to integrate and grow from both your limitations and potential.

~~~ **Enter the Zone.** Barry Sears. New York: Regan Books, HarperCollins, 1995. A dietary road map to boost energy and enhance mental productivity and peak performance.

~~~ ***Flow: The Psychology of Optimal Experience.** Mihaly Csikszentmihalyi. New York: HarperCollins, 1990. Identifies the elements involved in working from a state of concentration that's so deep it leads to optimal performance, profound enjoyment, and high levels of energy and endurance Also available as an audiotape program from Nightingale-Conant (800) 525-9000.

The Focused Mindstate. Joel and Michelle Levey. Niles, IL: Nightingale-Conant. (800) 525-9000. These six audiocassettes teach you how to focus your mind and overcome challenges, achieve total concentration, and reach a state of heightened awareness.

The Inner Winner. Dennis Waitly, Ph.D. Niles, IL: Nightingale-Conant. (800) 525-9000. This audiotape album consists of affirmative messages accompanied by musical segments.

Lighten Up! C. W. Metcalf. Niles, IL: Nightingale-Conant. (800) 525-9000. On these four audiotapes C. W. Metcalf teaches you to maximize your

*A classic.

health with humor, exercise your capacity for feeling wonderful, take yourself lightly while taking your job seriously, and even cope with negative stress.

*Managing Your Mind and Mood Through Food.** Judith Wurtman. New York: Harper & Row, 1986. This book outlines how what you eat affects your mood and identifies foods that can help you be more focused and alert.

Mind/Body Medicine Newsletter. (800) 222-4745. A quarterly newsletter by David Sobel, M.D., and Robert Ornstein, Ph.D., covering the latest facts, tips, and information on topics related to maintaining a healthy lifestyle.

Mind Mapping. Michael J. Gelb. Niles, IL: Nightingale-Conant. (800) 525-9000. These four audiocassettes teach you to think faster and more creatively, get more done in less time, and involve both sides of your brain for quicker, more efficient problem solving.

Mind Tools. This well-laid-out problem-solvingWeb site includes articles and shareware covering various issues of memory, stress management, and goal setting. **http://www.demon.co.uk/mindtool**

*Never Be Tired Again.** David C. Gardner and Grace Joely Beatty. New York: Harper & Row, 1988. A nutrition, fitness, and lifestyle program that can triple your energy level in seven days.

The Seven Spiritual Laws of Success: A Practical Guide to the Fulfillment of Your Dreams. Deepak Chopra, M.D. San Rafael, CA: New World Library, 1994. A long-running *New York Times* best-selling business book, this minibook is filled with timeless wisdom that shatters the myths that success has to come from overworking and driving yourself.

*Silent Pulse.** George Leonard. New York: Dutton, 1978. Sets forth the fascinating thesis that each of us has at the heart of our existence a silent pulse that can literally be in synchronization with the universe around us. It's beautifully written and puts a new perspective on how we relate to ourselves and the world.

*A classic.

Motivating Yourself

⌁ **Chicken Soup for the Soul, A Second Helping of Chicken Soup,** and **A Third Helping of Chicken Soup.** Jack Canfield and Mark Victor Hanson. These best-selling books contain a collection of stories that will warm your heart and inspire you to action. (800) 443-2314. Eight audiocassettes are available through Nightingale-Conant (800) 525-9000.

⌁ **End the Struggle Against Yourself: A Workbook for Developing Deep Confidence and Self-Acceptance.** Stan Taubman. New York: Tarcher/Putman, 1994. Exercises, activities, and personal stories show you how to face self-doubt squarely and learn to integrate and grow from both your limitations and potential.

⌁ **Getting It Done: The Transforming Power of Self-Discipline.** Andrew J. Dubrin. Princeton, NJ: Petterson's/PaceSetter Books, 1995. An eight-step model for how to kick past procrastination, concentrate, become your own leader, and transform negative energy into positive results.

⌁ **How to Stay Up No Matter What Goes Down.** Sarah Edwards. Here's How (Box 5190, Santa Monica, CA 90409). Thirty three-minute motivational pep rallies for renewing your resolve, determination, enthusiasm, and confidence.

⌁ **The One-Minute Manager.** Kenneth Blanchard and Spencer Johnson. New York: Berkley, 1986. The most basic of guides for how to be an effective boss. If you apply its simple principles to managing yourself, you'll love your new boss.

⌁ **What to Say When You Talk to Yourself** and **The Self-Talk Solution.** Shad Helmstetter. New York: Pocket, 1987. A comprehensive program for re-placing this negative chatter with positive self-talk. (Many tape albums on the same subject.)

Staying Relaxed and Energized

⌁ **Beating Job Burnout: How to Transform Work Pressure into Produc-tivity.** Dr. Beverly Potter. Berkeley, CA: Ronin Publishing, Inc., 1994. Al-though written with the salaried person in mind, most of the ideas for becoming cooler, calmer and more confident apply when you're your own boss as well.

Boundless Energy. Deepak Chopra, M.D. New York: Harmony Books, 1995. Chopra shares his secrets to understanding how to banish fatigue by better meeting one's biological needs.

Budget Lodging Guide. Campus Travel Service. Fullerton, CA: B&J Publications, 1995. A comprehensive source of information on economical campus accommodations for summertime vacation travelers.

Chronic Fatigue. Deepak Chopra, M.D. Niles, IL: Nightingale-Conant. (800) 525-9000. On these four audiocassettes Dr. Chopra teaches you to eat energizing foods, counteract stress, identify your mind/body patterns, use the circadian rhythm for maximum energy, and balance the five senses as a major source of vital energy to conquer chronic fatigue.

Finding Your Perfect Work: The New Career Guide to Making a Living, Creating a Life. Paul and Sarah Edwards. New York: Tarcher/Putnam, 1996. Career guide for how to blend personal goals and dreams with practical realities of earning a meaningful and prosperous livelihood working on your own.

Healthy Pleasures. Robert Ornstein and David Sobel. New York: Addison-Wesley, 1990. A fascinating book about how the simple pleasures of life are actually good for your health. It documents the latest laboratory research with practical suggestions about how to live a life you enjoy.

The How-to-Be Book. Thomas Thiss. Minneapolis: Deaconess Press, 1995. A fable with exercises. This book provides a clever, simple, and practical way to reduce and eliminate stress.

Insomnia. Deepak Chopra, M.D. Niles, IL: Nightingale-Conant. (800) 525-9000. Dr. Chopra provides proven techniques to help you eliminate the underlying causes of insomnia—and create a balanced mind and body.

In Your Mind's Eye. Eli Bay. Niles, IL: Nightingale-Conant. (800) 525-9000. On these audiotapes Eli Bay guides you to a deeply meditative state where you'll feel calmer and more energized for peak mental and physical performance.

On Campus USA and Canada—Budget Accommodations for Tourists, Students, and Groups. Glenshaw, PA: Key Guides. One-hundred-and-four-page book listing campuses providing low-cost summer vacation accommodations in North America.

The Pleasure Principle. Paul Pearsall, Ph.D. Niles, IL: Nightingale-Conant. (800) 525-9000. Dr. Pearsall presents cutting-edge medical research revealing how to add happy, healthy, productive years to your life. A major breakthrough in preventive medicine, *The Pleasure Principle* teaches a form of wellness that treats every aspect equally—your mind, body, spirit, and lifestyle.

The Relaxation and Stress-Reduction Workbook. Martha Davis. New York: Fine Communications, 1995. Clear and simple techniques for reducing tension, clearing your mind, and coping with stress. Includes examples, checklists, exercises, and specific assignments.

Relaxercise. Sensory Motor Learning Systems. Niles, IL: Nightingale-Conant. (800) 525-9000. In this soothing program, eleven simple exercises are taught to help relieve chronic aches, enhance sports performance, and promote faster recovery from muscular injury or strain. Six audiocassettes.

Sleepnet. A hub of information that will link you to many other sleep-related Web sites, it's informative, cheery, easy to browse, and well designed. **http://www.sleepnet. com**

Stress Space on the Web. This Internet site discusses stress-related issues and provides ample links to other stress-related sites. **http://www.foobar. co.uk/users/umba/stress**

OPTIMISIM

Learned Optimisim. Martin Seligman. New York: Pocket, 1990. A well-documented book and free of psycho-babble. Seligman argues optimisim and pessimism are learned styles; therefore, pessimism can be unlearned.

On Becoming a Leader. Warren Bennis. New York: Addison-Wesley, 1989. Using interviews with leaders from all walks of life—from Norman Lear to Gloria Steinem—Bennis identifies the basic ingredients of leadership.

The Power of Optimism. Alan Loy McGinnis. New York: Harper-Collins, 1994. McGinnis has created an action plan to bring out the best in yourself, take charge of your life, and keep your enthusiasm high based on what he has found to be the characteristics of tough-minded optimists. Also available as an audiotape program through Career Tracks.

MEDITATION

Beyond the Relaxation Response. Herbert Benson. New York: Berkley, 1984. Benson combines relaxation response with a faith in a healing power inside or outside one's self.

The 5-Minute Hour Stress Relief System. Frank Jordan. PSI-Tronics Visions, Inc., 1995. P.O. Box 5552, Boise, ID (800) 581-3782. CD-ROM or video that leads you through three five-minute meditations that leave you feeling like you had an hour-long nap.

*How to Meditate: A Guide to Self-Discovery. Lawrence LeShan. New York: Bantam, 1984. A history and guide to meditation.

The Inner Art of Meditation. Jack Kornfield. Niles, IL: Nightingale-Conant. (800) 525-9000. Ideal for anyone seeking serenity, *The Inner Art of Meditation* provides a path for creating a Zenlike simplicity and balance in all aspects of your life. Six audiocassettes.

Insight Meditation: The Practice of Freedom. Joseph Goldstein. Boston: Shambala, 1993. Short essays answering questions most commonly asked regarding insight meditation. Goldstein's writings are especially helpful to the confused beginning meditator.

Meditation Internet News Group. Discusses issues related to meditation. **news:alt.meditation**

Mindfulness Meditation. Jon Kabat-Zinn. Niles, IL: NightingaleConant. (800) 525-9000. In this audiotape, Jon Kabat-Zinn guides you in the practice of cultivating mindfulness—nonjudgmental, moment-to-moment awareness. Discover the strength of your life path.

A Path with Heart. Jack Kornfield. New York: Bantam, 1993. A psychologist and teacher in the Teravada Buddhist Vipassana tradition, known as "insight meditation," provides basic instructions for a meditation practice.

Peace Is Every Step. Thich Nhat Hanh. New York: Bantam, 1991. Thich Nhat Hanh, a Vietnamese Zen master, teaches breathing meditation and mindfulness and deals with transforming anger and other unpleasant emotions.

---

*A classic.

The Relaxation Response. Dr. Herbert Benson. New York: Berkley, 1984. Sets forth a simple meditative technique for handling stress, anxiety, and fatigue and explains physiologically why relaxation affects us so positively.

TM: Transcendental Meditation. Robert Roth. New York: Donald I. Fine, 1987. Comprehensive summaries of many research studies on the effects of meditation on performance, health, self-esteem, learning ability, and productivity.

CREATING A SUPPORTIVE WORK ENVIRONMENT

The Aspiration Series. Inspire yourself moment by moment with one of these breathtaking wall posters that combine startlingly original four-color photography with powerful, inspiring messages on subjects like reaching for the sky, facing your fear, goals, vision, risk, and perseverance. Available framed or unframed. Or counter negative attitudes with "can-do" wall or desk posters, mugs, or calendars. To order or request a free catalog contact, The Executive Gallery (800) 848-2618.

Bassett Aromatherapy. Provides diffusers and essential oils to relax and boost productivity with aromatherapy. Or for more information about aromatherapy in the office see Bassett's Web Page. **http://www.eskimo. com/-joanne** or call for a free catalog (206) 451-0845.

House As a Mirror of Self: Exploring the Deeper Meaning of Home. Clare Cooper Marcus. Berkeley, CA: Conari Press, 1995. Based on twenty-five years of research, this book is an opportunity to explore how your home expresses who you are.

Nature's Air Filter. Developed by a NASA researcher, this small fan-powered filter boosts a house plant's natural ability to clean the air in your office of indoor toxins and pollutants like radon benzyne and formaldehyde. It cleans the air of a 240-square-foot room twice each hour. Hall Environmental Group, Inc., Winterpark, FL (800) 285-5723.

The Temple in the House. Anthony Lawlor. New York: Tarcher/Putnam, 1994. A thought-provoking exploration of how one can integrate quiet, inspirational spaces into common, everyday places, this book opens possibilities for how to incorporate such restorative spaces into an office, home, or home office. It's illustrated with 175 black-and-white photos and line drawings.

 Working from Home. Paul and Sarah Edwards. Los Angeles: Tarcher/ Putnam, 1994. In Chapter 6, "Finding the Right Office Space," and Chapter 7, "Outfitting Your Home Office with Furnishings and Supplies," we have practical ideas for how to set up a supportive, productive personal work environment.

Music

 Earthtunes. These tapes and CDs feature nonsynthesized, non-looped sounds of nature by nature recording artist Jonathon Storm, including recordings of streams, rivers, forests, glaciers, and other wilderness locations. Excellent for relaxing or refreshing your energy and as background for masking unwanted sounds or working productively. To order or for a free catalog write Earthtunes, 6190 Beaver Valley Road, Port Ludlow, WA 98365, or call (360) 732-4811.

 Healing Music. Jim Oliver, Deuter, Jeffrey Thompson, and Boris Mourashkin. Roslyn, NY: Ellipses Arts, 1995. Four-CD set using sound to heal the mind/body and to heighten awareness. (800) 788-6670

 Magic of Healing Music. Bruce and Brian Becvar, in collaboration with Deepak Chopra, M.D. San Rafael, CA: Shining Star Productions, 1995. Using the principles of Ayurvedic medicine as a foundation, this three-CD series provides intuitive, inspired, contemporary melodies using the Western tonal scale. (800) 727-6568

 Relax with the Classics. A collection of Baroque masterpieces scientifically selected for relaxation, each piece has been sequenced so you can work your way into a more-relaxed state for optimal concentration and learning. Mindware. To order or for a free catalog, write the Lind Institute, P.O. Box 14487, San Francisco, CA 94114, or call (415) 864-3396.

 Soundwave AudioActive Cassettes. This series of tapes and CDs by the pioneering musical artist Steven Halpern, Ph.D., author of the book *Sound Health,* are scientifically composed to enhance productivity, creativity, relaxation, and alertness. We regularly work with Halpern's productivity CD playing in the background. Inner Peace Music, P.O. Box 2644, San Anselmo, CA 94979-2644. Write or call (415) 485-0511 for information and a free catalog.

6

Riding the Emotional
Roller Coaster

I learned to master the trembling of my limbs, to control my heartbeat and my breathing, to wipe away the sweat that burned my eyes. . . . I was intoxicated by the satisfaction of having overcome my fear of the unknown.

DOUCHAN GERSI, EXPLORER

BEING ON YOUR OWN is an emotional experience. Usually it's quite literally an emotional roller coaster, with moments of soaring exhilaration, intense apprehension, overwhelming opportunities, paralyzing fear and doubt, gut-wrenching disappointments, and unbelievable elation—punctuated by periodic moments of deep satisfaction, unbearable impatience, momentary rejection, alternately devastating and delightful surprises, fleeting frustrations, intriguing curiosity, and a growing sense of confidence and self-assurance. In other words, on your own you know you're alive!

Being on your own is such an emotional experience because you're usually living every day on the edge of your greatest fears and joys. Much more is at stake. Your ego, your self-confidence, even your very survival may seem to hang in the balance from day to day, at least at first. Any day can bring a big break. One phone call can make your week, your month, or even your year. Or the same call can be a cancellation, a rejection, or a bad turn of luck that crushes budding hopes.

And there's so much more to prove. There are the people who believe in you, the people you don't want to let down, the people who said you couldn't do it, the people who discouraged you from trying whom you're determined to show you can do it. And then, of course, there's yourself, the part of you that believes you can do great things and the part of you that doubts; the part that's confident and the part that's concerned.

Also, in a salaried position, with the boss, coworkers, and subordinates around to impress and keep up a stiff upper lip for, it's easier to keep emotions in check. But on your own, often there's no one to keep up an image for and so your true feelings are more free to come out, and they often do, sometimes to your surprise.

But, of course, business books don't talk about the emotional aspects of being your own boss. Somehow being emotional—especially overreacting or feeling not in control of your emotions—is an embarrassing, almost taboo, subject. To reveal that you're having unfamiliar and unexpected emotions is like admitting to some flaw in your personality. Certainly politicians like U.S. Representative Pat Schroeder and former U.S. Senator Edmund Muskie learned how we in this country construe emotional expression to be a sign of weakness. Both were criticized and denigrated for allowing their emotions to break through in tears during a speech.

Actually, having strong emotional reactions is a natural and normal aspect of being human, especially at times when you move out of what motivational speaker and author Jim Newman refers to as your *comfort zone*—the familar experiences, events, and environments in which you feel at ease and in control. So is it any wonder we have strong emotional reactions to becoming our own boss? Being on our own takes almost all of us right out of our comfort zone and into highly unfamiliar, unpredictable, and capricious circumstances.

Having strong emotional reactions, however, is not the problem. In fact, it can be an asset. Recent psychological studies show that organizations that employ personnel with narrow, limited emotional responses are devoid of creativity and therefore stagnate. A recent study done at Bell Laboratories found that the most valued and productive workers were not necessarily those with the highest IQs or academic achievements. The standouts excelled in what Daniel Goleman has called "emotional intelligence," the ability to read's one's own feelings, to control one's impulses, calm oneself down, and maintain resolve and hope in the face of setbacks. In his book *Emotional Intelligence,* Goleman asserts that IQ contributes only 20 percent to the factors that determine success in life.

Yet most of us get very little preparation for dealing effectively with our emotions. The most common solution for dealing with emotions in a business setting is to avoid having them. It's almost as if we're expected to hang our emotions on the coatrack on the way into work.

In fact, with a few exceptions, like rooting for our favorite sports team or cutting up on New Year's Eve or at a our high school reunion, we're expected to keep our emotional experiences within the narrow range of what's con-

Components of Your Emotional IQ*

Knowing your own feelings: Are you aware of feelings such as anger, disappointment, anxiety, and joy?

Using your feelings in making good decisions: Do you trust your feelings to help guide your choices?

Managing your feelings to keep distress from impairing your ability to think: Can you proceed despite fears, doubts, and concerns?

Motivating yourself despite persistent setbacks: Can you resist letting mistakes or disappointments keep you from proceeding?

Staying hopeful and delaying gratification: Can you wait to allow yourself time to achieve your goals?

Empathizing with others and developing rapport: Can you sense or imagine how others are feeling without they're telling you?

Cooperating with others: Can you work toward win/win solutions?

Handling feelings in relationships: Can you listen to others' needs and take their advice when appropriate?

*From *Emotional Intelligence, Why It Can Matter More than IQ,* by Daniel Goleman.

sidered to be acceptable and manageable. We're encouraged to experience intense emotions vicariously through movies, sports, television, or books. People who express their emotions outside these acceptable bounds are often referred to as hysterical. As a result, we have virtually no experience handling unfamiliar and unpredictable levels of intense emotions in a work context.

So what are you to do when suddenly you feel panicked about pressing deadlines and having more work than you think you can handle? How should you react to feeling hopeless after being turned away repeatedly by possible customers? What can you do when you're furious about an unexpected and seemingly unfair cancellation? How do you deal with the hostility you feel about having to ask again and again for a client to send you a check?

The assumption is that somehow we're supposed to handle all these situations in a calm, cool, and collected manner. But being on one's own has upped the ante, raised the stakes, and demands that we access a wider variety of emotional responses than we're used to. Now as the boss you've got to know what to do with a wide range of your moods, reactions, overreactions, escalations, dispositions, and morale. And that's what this chapter is about—handling the rich array of emotional reactions you experience. In this chapter you'll gain a new perspective on your emotions, from which you can view them as powerful assets that can guide you to precisely that right response to any emotionally charged situation.

A New Perspective on What to Do with Your Feelings

> *At the very instant that you think, "I'm happy," a chemical messenger translates your emotions, which have no solid existence whatever in the material world, into a bit of matter so perfectly attuned to your desire that literally every cell in your body learns of your happiness and joins in.*
> DEEPAK CHOPRA, M.D.

What a sense of relief we felt when we first learned about the new perspective on feelings that we're about to describe. This new perspective comes from Leslie Cameron-Bandler's book *The Emotional Hostage,* cowritten with Michael Lebeau, and we recommend it to anyone who wants to become the master of his or her fate. Cameron-Bandler is one of the pioneers of neurolinguistic programming—the study of internal reality. Using her discoveries, along with other findings from the new field of psychoneuroimmunology and the work of acting coach Gene Bua, we've found that you can greet your emotions, no matter what they are, as trusted friends and valued resources. Using the concepts we describe here, you need never again feel at the mercy of your emotions. Instead you can call upon them to enrich and enhance the quality of your life.

Emotions As Valued Messengers

We now believe that all emotions, those that have been thought of as negative as well as those considered to be positive, are designed to serve as physiological road signs that point us toward appropriate action. Once we can learn to read the language of our emotions, we no longer need to get waylaid in negative emotional pit stops for hours, days, or even a lifetime. Instead, we can use emotions as way stations where we can stop to ask directions and get fueled up for the journey ahead.

Instead of thinking of negative feelings as impediments to getting where you want to go and therefore as something to be avoided at all costs, you can view them as biochemical messengers bearing valuable directions that tell you what you need to do next to get to where you want to go and provide you with the fuel to get there. Understanding the role of emotions in this new way is enormously helpful to those who are self-employed and routinely find themselves outside their comfort zone, faced with a broader, richer, more intense range of emotions that are hard to hide, avoid, bury, or ignore.

Let us take a few minutes to tell you what we've learned about emotions and how they can become valuable tools for becoming successful on your own.

Physiologists now recognize that our emotions flow naturally and powerfully from our perceptions, traveling through our nervous system and our bloodstream, simultaneously flooding every cell of our bodies with their messages. You've probably heard of the classic fight/flight reaction. The fight/flight reaction was first identified near the turn of the century by Dr. Walter Cannon of the Harvard Medical School. Cannon discovered that when the brain registers a threat of some kind, it floods the body with chemicals that prepare us to stand and fight or turn and run. Our blood pressure increases, our heart rate goes up, our rate of breathing accelerates, and more blood flows to our arms and legs. Every cell becomes charged with energy and prepares us for action.

Over the years, scientists have suggested that the fight/flight mechanism is actually an anachronism, a vestige of an era long past when humans lived in the wild and needed to flee from or fight off the dangers they encountered. The interpretation has been that this mechanism is no longer suitable to our modern world, because fighting and running are rarely appropriate responses to the daily threats we encounter. Therefore, the theory went, we try to avoid or repress this fight/flight reaction, and that takes a heavy toll on our bodies.

We learn to exercise "self-control." How many times did you hear that in school. But as we try to stop or repress this reaction, we interrupt the flow of energy the body has been generating for us. And holding back and storing up this energy takes a lot of effort. Over time, it causes stress and we end up feeling chronically fatigued and worn out. In fact, now research shows that ultimately such stored-up emotional energy can even lead to chronic stress, high blood pressure, hypertension, and disease.

But what, then, are we to do with all the emotional energy our bodies keep manufacturing? If we can't run or fight, if we can't repress or avoid, is our only hope, as some might suggest, to evolve into a more functional being someday, like Spock from *Star Trek*—someone who doesn't have these bothersome responses? We believe that would be a grave loss and that, in fact, it's not our human physiology that's outdated; it's our understanding and use of it that need updating.

Instead of calling this innate physiological reaction the *fight/flight* response, we should think of it as a *ready state*. In this ready state, empowering energy surges through our bodies. But we need not limit the use of this energy to running away or clubbing someone just because these would be our most primitive prewired responses. We can use the same energy to think on our feet, to take immediate action, and carry out any number of other productive activities.

As twentieth-century human beings, we have access to a wide variety of emotional and behavioral reactions. Centuries of social and psychological evolution have provided us with a greatly expanded repertoire of responses that go far beyond simply fighting or fleeing. If you think back to the last time you experienced a fight/flight response, do you remember how energized you felt, how alert, and excited? It's almost like an electrical charge. Can there be any more empowering state of being? In some ways, doesn't it resemble the peak-performance state we discussed in chapter 5? It's like Luke Skywalker's light sword in *Star Wars*—a force so powerful we have to learn how to wield it. And that is, in fact, exactly what today's top performers in all fields are learning to do. They are learning to direct and command that energy, speeding it up or slowing it down, according to their needs.

To take this interpretation a step farther, what if this ready state is not just the way our body responds to fear or threat? What if every emotion we experience produces its own unique and equally precise ready state, which brings us an ample supply of the exact type of energy we need to respond appropriately? The latest research in psychoneuroimmunology indicates that this is, in fact, the case. Research now shows that, whatever emotions we experience, our entire body prepares us appropriately for the circumstances at hand.

When you feel angry or sad or happy or scared, your entire physiology reflects these emotions. All the cells in your body are angry, sad, happy, or scared. How could a mechanism as sophisticated and efficient as this have become outdated? Certainly the human body would not be prewired so exquisitely to carry out such an intricate and precise process if this process were not designed to serve us.

From psychoneuroimmunology we learn that there's nothing inherently harmful in our emotions themselves. Any harm comes about because instead of making productive use of our emotions, we allow them to rage through us like a forest fire or repress them until they burn us out. In reality, our emotions are as natural—and as vital—as breathing, digesting, eating, or sleeping. Instead of trying to hide them, deny them, ignore them, and avoid them, we can learn to consciously utilize them just as man has learned to use fire to light the darkness and to fuel the engines of industry.

Each emotion is like a biochemical gift that comes with instructions and a full set of batteries. In other words, there are two components to each emotion—one mental and one physical. The mental component is the message or signal that tells you what you need to do, and the physical component is the energy or fuel that activates whatever behavior is called for.

So, on the one hand, if we ignore the message, we simply flail about in the energy—ranting and raving or wallowing and sinking—until it passes through us. On the other hand, if we try to stop the physical energy from surging through and carrying us into action, we become immobilized. So, our task is to listen to the messages our emotions bring us and to use the energy they generate to initiate behaviors that will produce desirable results for us.

Let's use the feeling of *disappointment* as an example. Disappointment flows from the sweet memory of a desired experience that is now lost. Think about a time when you were disappointed. What had you lost? And what feeling came over you when you realized it was gone? Usually disappointment engenders a sinking, empty feeling that, if we allow ourselves to experience it fully, eventually carries us to a feeling of *acceptance* of that which can never be. In other words, disappointment puts us in the ready state for letting go, so we can move on and fill ourselves again with what can be.

In fact, the word *emotion* derives its meaning from the Old French verb *esmovoir,* meaning "to set in motion," "to move the feelings." Emotions are feelings in motion. And they do move. Once you experience them, they flow on. Their energy carries you somewhere else, and you can guide that journey. For example, as we just said, *disappointment* moves to *acceptance* and acceptance opens you to the possibility of entertaining new desires.

In fact, the quickest way to stop feeling some way you'd rather not feel is to go *through* the emotion. If you allow yourself to experience the feeling, it will take you somewhere else. The way we get stuck in our feelings is by trying to stop them and not experience the accompanying emotion. So to tap into the powerful tools our emotions bring, we must do two things: first, we must check the truth of the message; and second, make use of the energy the message brings to respond appropriately.

Checking the Truth of the Message an Emotion Brings

Remember, our emotions arise from our perceptions. So, if we falsely perceive something, we will experience the feeling and put ourselves into a ready state for a situation that doesn't exist. For example, if we falsely perceive that something is lost to us forever when in fact it is not, we end up accepting the loss of something that is actually still possible and available to us. We give up on what we could still achieve.

Here's an example from our own lives. We had an opportunity for our local radio show to be picked up by a national network. We were excited. That excitement generated plenty of energy to make all the necessary arrangements to get the first show on the air with just a few days' notice. We'd aired two successful shows. Then we were notified that our role on another station precluded us from continuing on that network. Our hearts sank. We were disappointed.

But if disappointment serves to prepare us for loss, what had we lost? Only that one opportunity. We did have to accept that. But we didn't need to accept defeat in placing our show. There were still many other opportunities, and once we realized that, our disappointment shifted quickly to *hope* and then to *frustration*. And that was great!

Surprisingly, frustration is a very functional emotion. It makes you feel uncomfortable, as if you had just sat down on a hot plate or something had sat down on you, trapping and constraining you. It brings a rush of energy for breaking through whatever roadblocks you've encountered. Frustration says, "Something is in the way of what I want. Here's the energy to do something about it!"

It took a full year before we found the right station. But over that year, our quest was fueled by our impatience and kept alive by our hope, and an ongoing feeling of frustration. All that emotion was useful. Thank heavens for our impatience and our hope and our frustration. Where would we be today without them?

We probably wouldn't have found another network for our show had we allowed ourselves to mistakenly accept defeat, because *acceptance* is like a low-power vacuum cleaner that sucks away your energy. It prepares you to withdraw, to let go, to give up. Had we accepted defeat we wouldn't have had the necessary energy to keep sending out proposals and relentlessly talking up what we wanted.

As you can see, recognizing the message each emotion brings can guide you to take the appropriate action and assist you in using the energy it brings appropriately. Knowing, for example, that disappointment is designed to help you let go means that whenever you begin to feel disappointed, you can check the message to be sure that in reality what you desire is lost. If it is, you can use that sinking feeling to let go of what can no longer be.

But, if what you seek is only delayed until some unknown time in the future, you need not give it up (although you certainly can if you choose). Instead, you will move on to other emotions, like *frustration* and *determination* that are associated with not yet having something you still believe is possible. And you can use the energy from those emotions to help you get there.

So to make the best use of your feelings, start by listening to their message and check your perceptions to be sure the message matches your actual situation.

Making Use of the Energy Each Emotion Brings

The energy each emotion brings has its own unique qualities—a rhythm, tempo, intensity, and a scope of its own. Some emotions slow you down; others charge you up. Some take you into the future; others propel you into the past. Some engage you; others detach you. And you can use whatever energy an emotion brings to move yourself to virtually any other state you wish.

But particular types of emotional energy move more easily along certain paths. Think, for example, of how easily you can move from feeling *happy* to feeling *hopeful,* and from feeling *hopeful* to feeling *enthusiastic*—or how easily you can move from feeling *disappointed* to feeling *hopeless.* Undoubtedly you've moved through these emotional chains yourself at times.

But now think of how difficult it is to move from feeling *disappointed* to feeling *happy.* How many times have you told yourself or others to cheer up when you, or they, were feeling too *disappointed* to do that. Or how often have you wanted to feel *confident* but instead, despite your best efforts, you felt *anxious?*

Fortunately, even in cases like these you don't need to wait for outside circumstances to move you from one mood to another. Remember, emotion is about movement, the movement of feeling. A feeling will carry you along on its appropriate course. You don't need to fight it, nor do you need to simply go passively along for the ride. If you know the route, you can use the energy of that emotion to propel yourself to wherever it is you want to go.

Actually, there are many routes you can take to get from one emotion to another. You have undoubtedly already learned ways to move in and out of certain emotional states. But there may be some emotional states you tend to get stuck in and have a hard time moving on from. We all do at times. For these times we've developed the Emotional Road Map that follows. Using concepts we've just discussed, you can use this road map to deal with most common feelings self-employed people tell us they have the hardest time handling.

The Emotional Road Map points out the valuable signals each of these emotions brings and suggests ways to allow the energy of each emotion to take you to the appropriate action to achieve your goals. Use it any time you're feeling stuck in an unpleasant, or unproductive, emotion and can't seem to get where you want to go. If you would like, take a moment to review The Emotional Road Map now. Or, if you prefer, you can refer to the road map later when you need it and skip on now to page 229, where we'll talk about what to do when you don't like the way you feel.

■ THE EMOTIONAL ROAD MAP ■

Most people don't know it's possible to enjoy . . . all their emotions. The key lies . . . in the emotions themselves. Each emotion is a slightly different riddle that has embedded within it the clues you need to benefit from it.

THE EMOTIONAL HOSTAGE

The road map that follows provides a step-by-step guide for identifying the useful messages and valuable energy each of the so-called negative emotions brings. The guide suggests how you can use that energy to respond productively and move on. While these are certainly not the only productive ways to respond to these emotions, we have found the road map to be useful for ourselves and others we've shared it with.

At no point are we trying to say that you should or shouldn't feel any particular way. There is no particular way you should or shouldn't feel, but denying your feelings can be very costly when you're in business for yourself. In reality, you can feel any way you want to for as long as you want to. But you don't need to be enslaved by your feelings or trapped by them until your external circumstances change. Our goal is simply to assist you in understanding what you are doing and in getting the energy of that emotion moving in a direction you desire.

Like any road map, this one can be dull reading unless you've got somewhere you want to go, so we suggest that in using this map you turn directly to the emotions you're personally grappling with.

■ FROM ANGRY TO SATISFIED ■

Anger is a signal that you perceive some harm or threat to your well-being. It signals that you need to take action to stop or prevent what's happening. If damage has already been done, it says that you need to take action to right the damage or prevent it from occurring again. Anger can also be a signal that you think some important standard or value has been violated or that some wrong has been done to you.

Anger is an intense, fast-moving emotion. What a rush of energy it brings you—plenty to make sure you safeguard yourself from any further insult! The value of all this energy is lost, however, if you just flail around in it, yelling and carrying on ineffectually. Haven't you heard people shouting pointlessly at store clerks? Perhaps you've done it yourself. Most of us have at one time or another. Whether you feel like yelling at yourself or someone else, anger is meant to be put to use. It shouldn't be buried or endlessly thrashed around in.

It's meant to produce results. The message anger brings is "Back off! Shape up! See to it you don't do that again!"

If you ever doubt the power of this emotion consider this: Denying anger doesn't neutralize it. Research shows that chronic unresolved anger, whether turned inward or expressed ineffectively, can lead to high cholesterol levels and self-destructive health habits like smoking and overeating that can lead to heart attacks and other disease. So, the key is learning how to use the potent energy that anger brings us to resolve transgressions and prevent them from happening again.

Anger is never a comfortable energy to experience. It's not supposed to be. Making someone feel sorry or miserable is rarely sufficient to address the problem effectively, however, especially in a business situation, where you may need to do business with the individual again or where your reputation is affected. To be effective you need to use your anger in a way that assures you that people know what you expect of them and that they can't cross the limits you've set to protect your well-being and values. Here's one road map for getting results when you feel angry.

> **Anger→ Gratitude→ Outcome→Curiosity→Reassurance→Satisfaction**

- **Direct the energy you're feeling** into verifying for yourself that indeed there is some actual or potential wrong or harm to your well-being. Just getting angry because life isn't going the way you want it to is a real waste of time and energy.

  If there's no harm done, ask yourself if you would rather be right or get on with your life. This one question will save you a lot of unnecessary trouble. If there is an actual wrong, harm, or potential harm to you, be grateful that you've seen this danger signal so that you can act now to protect yourself.

- **Shift your energy to what you want to accomplish with your anger.** Define the outcome you desire from your anger. Do you want people to stop doing something? Do you want them to rectify something? Do you want to be sure they never do something again? Just what action do you want them to take? Generally, having them admit that they're wrong or getting an apology will not accomplish what you need. You need a commitment from them to stop or not to repeat the action, to cover your costs, make corrections or repair damage, and so forth.

- **Generate possible actions you can take.** Think about what you can do to elicit a commitment to stop, prevent, or rectify any harm to you. Select the one you believe will be most effective.

THE EEMOTIONAL ROAD MAP

- **Prepare yourself to take action with confidence.** This is an important step because often there is a sense of helplessness involved in anger. If you have difficulty dealing with anger, recall times in the past when you have stopped or prevented yourself from being harmed or wronged, and feel reassured that you can do that again. Acknowledge that it's okay to express your anger and that you can effectively protect yourself with it. Now imagine yourself taking the action you've identified until you feel satisfied that you've found a solution to the situation and are confident you can carry it out.
- **Find effective anger role models.** If you grew up in a dysfunctional family where expressing anger was dangerous or where you never saw anyone express anger productively, you need to find some anger role models. That is, you need to see someone safely and effectively expressing anger. Look for such people among highly successful individuals who are well respected and admired by people who work with them repeatedly, by choice. We also recommend observing highly effective animal trainers. You will see how such trainers command respect and get results from their animals with appropriate anger and how they also convey their affection and respect for the animals even while they're angry at them.

The acting coach and director Gene Bua is one of the most effective people we've met at expressing his anger. When Gene's angry about something, you know it. And it's unpleasant. It's always caused by your failure to do something you're fully aware he expects of you and that you have agreed to do. But once he's expressed his anger, it's gone. It's been effective and it's over. There's not a trace left. His energy flows right on to the next issues at hand.

For example, all his students sign a contract before their first class spelling out the payment policy. And when people don't pay their tuition on time, Gene gets angry. He says something like this in a loud, angry voice: "I expect you to give me your checks at the beginning of the first class of the month! I do my part in this agreement. I'm here every week. I teach the class. And I should not have to chase you down to get paid!" And then that's that. But his message is delivered so powerfully that any late checks are on his chair within minutes.

Breaking an Anger Habit

As the Greek Stoic philosopher Epictetus said, "If you do not wish to be prone to anger, do not feed the habit." Often people with high standards and high expectations spend a lot of time being angry that life is not as it should be. They are constantly comparing the way things are with the way they think they ought to be and then feeling angry about the disparity. This, of course, is their right, but often such anger habits greatly diminish the quality of their lives and the lives of those around them.

To break this anger habit, you can shift your attention from making negative comparisons to finding similarities between how things should be and how they actually are and feeling grateful about these. You can ask yourself what difference it really makes that something isn't just as you think it should be. Often we think that things have to go a certain way if we are to obtain our goals. Actually there are many routes to the same goal, and amazingly, there is no necessity that they go any one particular way.

Sometimes highly perfectionist people are afraid they can't handle things unless everything goes according to their plans. In such cases, building self-confidence by remembering times when you handled emergencies and unexpected events well can assist you in developing tolerance for the unexpected and enable you to respond more easily to whatever happens.

Escaping Perfectionism

Psychologist Joseph Weintraub of Babson College in Wellesley, Massachusetts, is a scholar of perfectionism. He says if you work for someone who's a perfectionist, "there are no coping mechanisms other than to quit." Obviously Weintraub wasn't thinking about the plight of the self-employed individual who works for a perfectionist. When you're your own perfectionist boss, you can't quit on yourself. Instead you need to realize that research shows employees who work for perfectionist bosses a) usually have bad morale, b) get sick more often than others and c) are driven to put performance first, so their interpersonal relationships with customers and others suffer.

So, if you want to be a healthy, motivated self-employed worker others enjoy doing business with, you'll have to give up your perfectionistic habits. Here are some guidelines you can use:

1. You don't have to give up your high standards. They are your target, not an imperative. You can do a good job, and ultimately a better job, by not trying to be perfect all the time.

2. Practice becoming more *patient*. There is time to do a good job, even if it doesn't feel as though there is.

3. Set clear, reasonable goals. As a perfectionist, you will probably need to get outside feedback from colleagues to learn what is "reasonable."

4. Realize there are things in life you have no control over and therefore cannot be responsible for. So, when something you cannot control arises, relax and respond productively to the new reality at hand.

5. Set clear work hours. Don't allow yourself to work past sixty hours a week. Research shows that productivity declines after sixty hours per week. Overworking becomes counterproductive.

As the noted family therapist Virginia Satir reminds us, "Life is not the way it's supposed to be. It's the way it is. The way you cope with it is what makes the difference."

■ FROM DEPRESSED TO ENCOURAGED ■

Depression literally slows you down and is the most draining of emotions. When you feel depressed, the past, present, and future all look bad. Your entire body goes into a withdrawal-ready state. Temporary depression is an appropriate part of the grieving process and can be expected at a time of major loss. It helps you to retreat so you can heal from your loss. Under such circumstances, it's important to allow yourself to retreat and not try to force yourself into feeling good.

Depression at times other than a loss, however, is a strong signal that you need to change your life in some significant way. It means your life is not providing you with sufficient gratification for you to want to continue it as it is. It tells you that you are pulling away, and the sooner you take action to create better circumstances for yourself, the easier it will be for your depression to move on. (*Note:* We are not speaking here of clinical depression, which requires medical and/or psychotherapeutic treatment. If depression continues uninterrupted over several weeks, you should seek professional help.)

Because depression is such a low-energy emotion, the first step in pulling yourself out of it is to generate enough energy to begin taking some action. Here's what we recommend.

Depression → Encouragement

- **Identify something that is better now than it once was.** It can be anything, even a very small thing, like how now you don't have to take your children to day care, or how you can sleep as late as you want. No matter how bad things look, Sarah always reminds herself of the stomachaches she used to have every day from the stress of her salaried job. Now she hasn't had a stomachache in years. Paul always remembers how much he used to dislike practicing law; now he enjoys what he does.

- **Project what is better now into the future.** Imagine a future that continues to reflect the improvement you've noticed—a future, for example, of spending time with your children at home, of mornings getting up feeling rested because you can sleep as late as you want, of no more stomachaches, and of work you enjoy.

- **Identify something else that is better now and then repeat the above process.** Do this over and over until you have built a future that dispels the depression and creates a growing sense of encouragement. This shift will probably not be immediate. But keep using this process. Cameron-Bandler describes it as being like lifting a heavy object from the ocean floor; you have to keep pumping more and more bubbles of air into it to get it to rise.

Beware! Depression Is Contagious

A landmark study at the University of Texas at Galveston has discovered that depression is contagious. In other words if you spend a lot of time around someone who's feeling depressed, don't be surprised if you, too, start feeling depressed. And vice versa. If you're feeling depressed, don't be surprised if those around you start feeling depressed. This was especially true for individuals in the study who depend on others to bolster their self-esteem, soothe, or calm them. So self-confidence and personal satisfaction seem to fortify us against depression, but even confident, successful individuals were subject to "catching" depression if they lived with someone who was depressed. The remedy:

1. Spend time around upbeat, enthusiastic, positive people.

2. Let family, friends, and colleagues know when they are bumming you out.

3. Reduce the time you spend with people who continually drag you down.

4. Make sure you are refreshed and relaxed when supporting someone who's depressed.

5. When you need support and recognition, turn only to upbeat individuals who have a track record of being supportive.

■ FROM DISAPPOINTMENT TO HOPE ■

Being on your own is filled with disappointments, small and large. Knowing how to manage feelings of disappointment is virtually a self-employment survival skill. And actually, as we mentioned previously, it can be a valuable sign that can help direct you toward getting more of what you want.

Disappointment is a signal that you need to decide whether to carry on striving toward something or let it go. It's how you feel when you're expecting something you want and don't get it. It helps you recognize when something is over or isn't going to happen and signals that you need to reevaluate and renew your resolve to take action toward whatever else you want. It's a passive, low-energy emotion that's an ideal ready state for helping you let go of something that is not possible. Here's what you can do when disappointment strikes.

> **Disappointment → Possibility Test → (Letting Go) → Acceptance →**
> **Hope → Frustration → Patience → Determination → Anticipation**

- **Ask yourself if having what you want is still possible through your own efforts.** Give your desire Cameron-Bandler and Lebeau's Possibility Test, which follows.

- **Accept what cannot be.** If what you want is no longer a possibility, it's time to let go and accept that the situation is out of your hands.

The Possibility Test: How to Know What's Possible

Before giving up hope, before succumbing to disappointment, ask yourself the following questions.

- Is there still something I can do to make this happen?
- Can I think of a time I or anyone else has ever done this?
- Can I imagine circumstances under which I could do it?

If the answer to any of these questions is yes, your dream is still possible. Now you must decide if you still want to pursue it. If you do, go for it. If not, let it go and move on.

- **Allow your energy to move on.** Once you let go and accept the impossibility of what you wanted, you'll find that your energy will start to shift as you begin moving toward feeling *hopeful* that the situation will change at some time in the future. You'll begin feeling a desire to pursue other, more feasible goals.

On the other hand, if the possibility test indicates that what you want is still possible, disappointment is not the most productive feeling, because it prepares you for giving up. However, once you recognize that what you want is still possible, your emotions will begin to shift. You may begin to feel hopeful and desirous. And you may start to feel frustrated that you haven't yet attained your goal. Frustration will provide you with the energy to continue toward the outcome you desire. When you feel frustrated:

1. Remind yourself what a useful and energizing, albeit uncomfortable, emotion frustration can be.

2. Take a deep breath and focus on the fact that what you want is still possible.

3. Recall times in the past when it didn't look as if you could do, be, or have what you wanted, but through your continued efforts you ultimately did get what you wanted. This will help you move into an I-can mindset.

4. Resolve to be patient while renewing your determination to achieve your goal. Avoid the temptation to obsess about what's wrong. Focus on what you want and on action you can take to get it.

As you continue imagining the desired outcome you are now determined to attain, you may begin to feel a renewed sense of enthusiasm and excitement, start to anticipate the outcome you're striving for, and begin looking forward to enjoying it.

■ From Discouraged to Feeling Encouraged ■

Discouragement is a feeling that arises when you take on what for you is a highly challenging goal and your progress is slow or nonexistent. Some fields, such as many of the arts (acting, dance, comedy, creative writing, screenwriting, and so on), are by nature discouraging because the odds of success are so low. Unless you are unusually well prepared,lucky, and well connected, you will need fierce dtermination and dogged persistence to succeed. Those who get easily discouraged may give up before they have the chance to make it.

To feel *encouraged,* we need to perceive increments of progress toward our goals. If we shoot so high or undertake something so difficult that we repeatedly fall short of our goal and can sense no progress toward it, we begin feeling discouraged. In fact, research shows most people begin to feel discouraged if they fail to achieve a goal 75 percent of the time. So feeling discouraged is a sign that we need to aim at a target that we can actually hit and feel that we're making some headway toward our eventual goal. As your own boss it's your job to provide yourself with this sense of progress. The best coaches and teachers don't make demands beyond the reach of their protégés; they help them keep stretching by setting attainable goals and then continually extending them.

In other words, if you're getting nowhere trying to obtain a place on the podium at your national convention or are falling far short of your goal to earn $10,000 a month, focus instead on something you can reasonably expect to accomplish and that would be a step toward your ultimate goal. You might aim to speak to a regional program or to do $5,000 of business a month. As you attain these goals, you will feel increasingly encouraged and can then set your goals higher and higher as you progress.

Here's one road map for shifting from feeling discouraged to encouraged.

> **Discouraged → Pride → Curiosity → Anticipation → Encouraged**

- **Compare where you are now with where you were at some time in the past** and note the progress you've made. When the road to success becomes long and weary, it's easy to miss the progress you are making. Focus on this progress, no matter how small, until you get some sense of accomplishment.

- **Compliment yourself on your accomplishments,** and allow yourself to feel proud of the movement you've made.

- **Become curious about what you know you can do next** that will take you one step further.

- **Imagine other times in your life** when you ultimately achieved your goals by taking one step at a time.

- **Imagine yourself carrying out the next step successfully** until you begin anticipating further progress and feel encouraged about reaching your ultimate goals.

■ FROM FEELING LIKE A FAILURE TO ■ FEELING LIKE A SUCCESS

Feeling like a failure often follows having made a mistake or not having accomplished a goal. It is not a signal to quit or give up, although this is a common misconception about this emotion. Rather, it's a signal that you need to do things differently in the future.

The feeling of failure is actually one of the most basic of human survival tools. Without it, we could not master anything. No one ever learns to do something perfectly on the first try. As James Joyce observed, "Mistakes are the portals of discovery."

Does the baby who falls give up trying to walk? Does the child who fails to tie his shoe give up forever on tying shoes? No. In fact, think of how quickly and eagerly the young child pushes you aside to try again. On its own, the feeling of failure tends to flow naturally into wanting to try again. The desired outcome fuels this drive to do it until you succeed. The brain is busily calibrating, assimilating, and making thousands of necessary adjustments so you can do it better the next time. So what happens as we grow up? Somehow the natural urge to go forward toward completion that comes from the feeling of failure gets sidetracked.

At some point in our lives or in a particular area of our lives, we decide that we are no longer learners, that we ought to have mastered certain things and should have nothing else to learn. And we decide that if we don't do these things correctly, we have failed. Failure becomes a finality instead of an intermediary step to success. Or after having experienced multiple failures, we come to equate failure with ruin and feel hopeless and defeated—giving up instead of feeling eager and determined to continue on.

Therefore, building a history of success for yourself is very helpful for being able to remain resilient in the face of failure. The parent who takes a child to the swimming pool, for example, and throws that child in the water before teaching him or her to swim is creating a dramatic and memorable failure for the child, even if he or she makes it to the side without drowning. But don't we do that to ourselves sometimes? Don't we throw ourselves into situations without the experience or preparation we need to assure our success? We can create ample opportunities for success by making sure we are prepared and by agreeing to do things we know we can accomplish. Then occasional failures are just a misstep from which we can quickly recover and carry on.

One of the benefits of being self-employed is that "failing" never needs to lead to being reassigned or fired. As the boss, you can always allow yourself a chance to learn from trying again.

So whenever you feel like a failure, what you want to do is recapture the natural feeling of forward movement that failure can bring with it instead of spiraling downward into defeat and despair. To this end, we suggest taking the following steps when you've made a mistake or failed to accomplish a goal.

Failure → Pride → Satisfaction → Reassurance → Successful

- **Feel pleased with yourself** for having had the courage, fortitude, and confidence to have taken action in the first place. People who wait until they're perfect before they act wait forever. Only those who try will ever succeed.

- **Forgive yourself** for having caused any negative consequences from your mistakes (to yourself or others). Correct any problems or damage as best you can.

- **Reassure yourself that mistakes and failures are a learning opportunity,** and take *pride* in learning from your experience. Identify what did and didn't work and what you want and will do differently. Sometimes you may know precisely what went wrong; in which case, resolve to try as best you can.

- Feel the satisfaction of having acquired new insights and abilities from your experience, and feel reassured that with these learning experiences under your belt you will perform more successfully in the future. Imagine yourself doing so, and instill in yourself a feeling of success.

■ FROM FEAR OR ANXIETY TO ANTICIPATION ■

Confidence is the antidote to fear.
ALEXANDER ROMAN, SPORTS PSYCHOLOGIST

All the people we've met experience some fear and anxiety when they move out of their comfort zone into the unknown—especially when, as is the case with being on your own, the stakes are high. You can bet that all your heroes have been fearful and anxious at one time or another. Reportedly Johnny Carson was nervous every night before his performance on the *Tonight* show! If he remained ill at ease during all those years, surely you can understand your feeling nervous about your major undertakings. So give yourself a break: don't panic or get down on yourself if you are feeling anxious or fearful as you leave behind the once-presumed security of the paycheck.

Fear and anxiety are normal reactions to a totally unfamiliar future. These feelings are a signal that you can foresee a path ahead of you that might hold dangers for which you are not prepared. These emotions are a signal to you that you need to begin preparing to cope with or avoid possible upcoming negative consequences. So trying to ignore fear and anxiety is foolhardy. Thank goodness those reactions are there to alert you now so that you can take whatever actions are necessary to make sure things go well in the future.

As is true of all emotions, fear and anxiety have several characteristics that can help you work with them. Fear is an intense, active, fast-paced emotion that arises from thinking about the future. Actually, it provides you with an incredible amount of highly charged energy, although you may feel the impulse to use it to either freeze or run.

But you can calm your fears by shifting your attention from the uncertainty of your future to the reality of your present. You can also reduce your fear to a more manageable level by simultaneously taking several deep, relaxing breaths while you concentrate on your present situation. Here's a step-by-step process you can use to walk yourself through a fear attack.

> **Fear or Anxiety → Safety → Curiosity → Feeling**
> **Capable → Self-Confidence → Anticipation**

- **Bring your attention into the present.** Fear signals a possible future danger; so when you start to feel anxious, immediately shift your attention away from the dreaded future to the present and concentrate on the here and now. You can take action only in the present anyway, so it's a good place to be when you feel apprehensive.

- **Notice that you are safe for the moment.** For example, if you are feeling anxious about an upcoming speech, stop thinking for the time being about your upcoming moments at the podium and recognize where you are right now and that you are just fine.

- **Focus on what you can do now** to protect yourself from negative future possibilities. Once you begin feeling safe in the moment, click into your curiosity and ask yourself what you can do at this point to safeguard yourself against the future you fear. What could you do to prepare for the imagined future situation? What are you afraid will happen? How could you prevent that? Become intrigued and fascinated with answering these questions. Begin breaking down what you can do into small, specific steps. For example, if you're going to be speaking before a group of potential clients, how can you make sure you are sufficiently well prepared that you will succeed? If you're anxious about having enough business next month, what steps can you take now to bring in business? If you are afraid you won't meet an important deadline, what steps can you take now to avoid the problem?

- **Recall times in the past when you have taken the needed steps** to meet a future challenge. Do this until you begin to feel capable. Other than for the purpose of identifying what you can do to prepare now, avoid repeatedly recalling times when you were not prepared.

- **Imagine yourself preparing to meet this challenge or threat,** mentally rehearsing the steps you will take to prepare until you feel *confident* in your ability to avoid what you fear and to achieve a positive future.

- **Begin anticipating the experience of success** you've been rehearsing. As you *anticipate* meeting the challenge, you may well begin to *look forward* to doing so.

Now let's take a few minutes to talk about using this process to respond to a few of the most common fears and anxieties we face on our own.

Mastering Performance Anxiety: Performing Under Pressure

George finally had the opportunity to give his first sales presentation to a Fortune 500 company. He was a manufacturer's rep, and he'd been working for months to get this appointment. Now he had it! But the minute he put it on the calendar, he was gripped by paralyzing anxiety. He kept imagining that all the figures would get turned around in his head. He saw himself standing before these important people and losing his place, not being able to find the papers he needed, and so on. He became so anxious that he had to lie down on the floor to try to recover his balance.

He called us for advice. "I'm immobilized," he reported. "What should I do?" "Look around the room," we suggested. "Is there anything frightening there?" Of course there wasn't, and soon he was feeling much better. At the moment, he was perfectly safe. From the safety of his office, we suggested that he ask himself what the worst thing that could happen at the upcoming meeting would be. The worst thing he could imagine was that he'd make a fool of himself and wouldn't get the account. "So," we asked, "could you live through that?" And of course he said he could. "But" we asked him, "how likely is that to actually happen?" It wasn't very likely. Although he had missed making sales, he'd never actually made a fool of himself during a sales presentation.

By now he was actually laughing, and we asked him to begin thinking of ways in which he could prepare himself for success. At this point he began planning how he could prepare and organize his presentation so that the numbers he needed would be at his fingertips.

Mastery is the cure for performance anxiety. Once you know that you can handle anything that might come along, the anxiety of doing it will go away. There's nothing like experience to take the pressure off. So, if performance anxiety hits, begin by identifying what you know you can do. Then challenge yourself to go one step beyond that. In George's case, he was taking a bigger step than he was actually prepared for. He was going from working with small accounts to a Fortune 500 account all in one leap. So we suggested that, before giving the sales presentation, he prepare further by extending his track record as follows:

1. Build a history of success. Do what you do until you know you can do it well consistently. Begin with volunteer work or small projects until you have a string of positive memories of successfully doing whatever is involved. When interviewed on A&E, the lyricist and songwriter Stephen Sondheim told about how, when wanted to do his own Broadway musical, his mentor told him to go through the following steps:

- Begin by producing an existing successful musical.
- Then take a successful play you like and musicalize it.
- Next take a flawed play and musicalize it.
- Then take a work that was not written as a play and musicalize that.
- After this, you'll be ready to create and produce your own original musical.

Carefully building such a sequential track record of success is invaluable. It predisposes you to success each step of the way while you're accumulating the experience to perform at an even higher level.

If you can't actually go through multiple performances, however, you can mentally rehearse your performance repeatedly. Peak-performance researcher Charles Garfield found that mental rehearsal is one of the key strategies that world-class athletes use to achieve peak performances. And George actually had a number of successful sales presentations from the past that he could mentally review. As Eleanor Roosevelt said, "I believe anyone can conquer fear by doing the things he fears to do, provided he keeps doing them until he gets a record of successful experiences behind him."

2. Get the bugs out of whatever you need to do well in a series of dry runs where mistakes don't matter. Would an Olympic athlete go into competition with a new routine he or she had never performed well in practice? Would a concert pianist go onstage to play a piece he or she had never rehearsed? Confidence goes up and nervousness comes down with each successful experience you have. George, for example, arranged to do a dry run of his presentation before several colleagues from a field similar to that of his prospective client. It went well, and this rehearsal uncovered several areas where he wanted to gather more information. Obtaining the additional data provided him with a still-bigger boost in confidence.

3. Mentally replay the string of positive memories you have built before of times when you needed to perform at your best. When doubts creep in, remind yourself that you have done what you will be doing before and therefore you can do it again. Give yourself the evidence of this by mentally reviewing your past successes.

4. Convince yourself you'll do a good job. If you're convinced you'll do a good job, you'll feel confident and your anxiety will disappear. Think of several things you know you can do well. Perhaps you're a good driver or a good tennis player. Now ask yourself how you know that you'll do a good job with these tasks and how many times it took you to demonstrate this to yourself before you were convinced. What can you do now to convince yourself that you'll do a good job at this task? Take the necessary steps to convince yourself, because once you are convinced, everyone else is more likely to be, too. If you believe, so will others.

5. Remember, fear, anxiety, and excitement feel very similar. All three of these emotions provide a high state of energy. And remember, a high state of energy is one of the cornerstones of a peak performance. So turn your anxiety into excitement. Instead of using the impulse you feel to run away, use it to run headlong toward what you want. Let the energy you feel flowing through you go into your performance. It's okay to feel so much energy. Don't sit on it or try to contain it. Use it, and it will empower you.

Overcoming the Fear of Failure

No one wants to fail. But fear of failure is never an excuse not to proceed. No one succeeds without the risk of failure. So don't let yourself off the hook just because you fear failure. Use your fear instead to help ensure your success by alerting you to possible pitfalls and directing you to take whatever steps you can take to avoid them.

When Lionel left his job in mortgage banking to do investment counseling, he had a wife and two children to support. The children were still so young that neither he nor his wife wanted thought she should take a job. So he very much wanted his new business to work.

The truth of the matter was that Lionel had been asked to leave his job, and he was fully aware that he had engineered his dismissal. He just didn't feel he was cut out to work for someone else. This was his big chance. But he was terrified of failing. He just didn't know it. He was so afraid to look at the possibility of failure that he almost defeated himself: "I was so afraid of failing that I didn't want to see even the most obvious potential problems. I couldn't face them. I took any work that came along, even if I didn't like it and had to charge much less than I knew I was worth. I pretended that everything was fine. But it wasn't. My wife saw problems coming, but when she would point them out I thought she wasn't being supportive of my business. I was angry and resentful, and most of all, I was envious of people I knew who were doing better than I."

Fortunately, Lionel wanted to succeed so much that he was finally willing to admit his fear of failure. Admitting his fear was the turning point. Then he could begin to look at what he feared and take steps to make sure he could handle those situations effectively. He sought the advice of colleagues and attended several marketing seminars. In the process, he realized that he had to take a stand on the type of work he was willing to do and the fees he needed to charge. He also got a lot of encouragement. "If I had just paid attention to the way I was feeling in the beginning, it would have saved me and my family a lot of agony. But the important thing is that I did it. I am my own boss and I have been for five years!"

Russell Seeley served as CEO for a major corporation before leaving to form his own consulting firm, which works with other manufacturing companies. Seeley attributes his success to the fact that he never ignores possible problems. "You've got to be willing to look the problems square in the face," he told us. And, as with Lionel, that's what a fear of failing can help you do. It can get you to look at the problems, and once you've taken steps to prevent them as best you can, your chances of success will go up.

Also, keep in mind that people are often more interested in what you do when things don't go well than in how you respond when everything is going smoothly. So handling a particular failure or problem well, should one occur—rebounding and going on—can be very impressive. It can actually strengthen your reputation and improve your skill and knowledge.

Conquering the Fear of Success

Fear is a signal that you perceive danger ahead. While there's no inherent danger in success, if you are fearful of it, that's a sign you are perceiving it to hold some danger for you. So let your fear lead you to the thought or stimulus that's convinced you success is dangerous in some way. This thought will most likely be linked to some early experience or decision in your life, and therefore if you have difficulty identifying what you fear about success, psychotherapy can often be quite useful in helping you identify the source of your fear.

Once you know what you fear, either you will recognize it as harmless and your fear will diminish, or you can use your creativity to protect yourself from whatever potential harm there may be. For example, when a woman we'll call Meredith went out on her own to publish a magazine, she was gripped with fear every time things started going too well. As Sarah talked with her, Meredith remembered that when she was growing up, her father died of a sudden heart attack the night he received an award for his many business and civic contributions. In her young mind, she had linked his death with success. In fact, she remembered some relative shaking her and saying "He worked himself into the grave."

As she recalled these events, the line "I don't want to be successful like Daddy" ran through Meredith's head. Once she realized this, she could reassure herself with plenty of external evidence that many successful people live long lives. And she could, of course, see to it that she did not work herself into ill health.

Mike's situation was different. He was living near poverty when he came to talk with Sarah. He restored antique automobiles, but he had set up his business so he couldn't possibly succeed. When Sarah suggested changes that could make the business profitable, Mike became very apprehensive. As they talked, he remembered how his father had failed at his one attempt to start a business. After that time his father had never been quite the same. "The light had gone out in his eyes," Mike recalled. Suddenly Mike realized he feared that his own success would be a painful, ongoing reminder to his father of that past failure. "It would be like opening an old wound, and just seeing me would be like rubbing salt in the wound," Mike said.

How clever Mike had been to set up his business so he could do it without really succeeding at it! By doing it that way, in Mike's mind, he could ensure that his father would feel sorry for him instead of being threatened by him. Of course, before Mike talked this out, he had no idea he was sabotaging his success. He decided to speak with his father and discovered that he wanted his son to succeed, so much so that he volunteered to help him out in the shop.

Getting Past the Fear of Rejection

Whether it's being turned down for a loan by one bank after another, losing out on one proposal after another, being passed over for a much desired contract, or having another manuscript rejected by a publisher, making it on your own usually means coming face-to-face with rejection. No one likes it, but everyone has to deal with it. And it's rarely easy at first. Rejection is an evil-eyed dragon that stalks us all until we cool its flaming tongue and remove its razor-sharp fangs. Here's our list of potions for taming this demon. Each is a question you can ask yourself when the pain of rejection begins nipping at your heels. They've become standard tools of our trade, as valuable to us as our personal computer.

1. *Do you still want to do the work you're doing?* When faced with repeated rejection, you're often tempted to say something like "Hey, I don't need this!" or "Who needs to put up with this?" And of course you're absolutely right. As your own boss you don't have to put up with anything, unless you want to. You have choices. You didn't have to start this business. You don't have to keep it going. You're free to quit anytime you want. Is that what you want? Or do you want to proceed?

2. *How much do you want this?* Okay, so if you still want to do it, how much do you want to do it? Do you want it enough to put up with whatever it takes for as long as it takes? We've found that the more rejection a particular venture involves, the more you need to want to do it. So to test your resolve, use a scale from one to ten, with one meaning you don't want it at all and ten meaning you want it more than anything in the world. We've found that if you don't score at least an eight or above, chances are you don't want it enough to stick with it through the long-term rejection many solo ventures require, and you owe it to yourself to do something that means more to you.

3. *Are you taking this too personally?* Like artists, it's easy for propreneurs to overidentify with their work. This is particularly true in a service business like consulting or in creative fields like writing. There's a tendency to think that the bank or the customer is rejecting you and judging you personally as inadequate. In actuality, most business rejections have less to do with you than with the circumstances. Or, as Laura Huxley put it so nicely in the title of her book, *You Are Not the Target.* If you can remain sufficiently detached

and realize you are not the target—that this isn't even about you—you're more likely to ascertain what the actual circumstances are and know what steps to take next.

Banks, for example, have different guidelines. Contractors have different selection criteria. If you find out which of their needs your proposal didn't meet, you can make the necessary modifications or approach other sources whose criteria you could meet.

4. Are you being realistic? Selling yourself, your product, or your service is often a numbers game. What looks like rejection may simply be a matter of statistics. For example, novices at selling are often surprised to learn that there is a sales/rejection ratio for most businesses. For example, it will take a certain number of calls to get an appointment and a certain number of appointments to get a sale. Only experience will determine what your ratio is. So if you need to make twenty calls to get one appointment and five appointments to get a sale, you need not consider the first nineteen calls to be rejections. They're simply par for the course, and each one takes you closer to your goal.

5. Is that no really a "no"? Before letting the claws of rejection impale you, always consider that a no is not necessarily a "no." While we were growing up, most of our parents told us, "When I say no I mean no. And I don't want to hear another word out of you." So most of us learn to take "no" seriously. But in a grown-up world, "no" isn't necessarily so.

Do you know that some businesspeople routinely say no at first simply to determine if the person is serious enough to pursue the issue? And you would be amazed at how many people change their mind after talking with you for a while. Times change. Circumstances change. We've come to hear "no" as meaning "not now."

We learned this lesson the hard way. When first beginning to sell radio advertising for our Los Angeles show, we were taking no to mean "no," only to discover that companies that said no to us were advertising on other shows shortly thereafter. We were actually making sales for representatives of the other shows, who walked through the door we'd left open by not going right back in again. Since that time we've made many sales that begin as one or even several "no's."

6. Who's the best judge? Is your product a good one? Is your service valuable? You know the answers to those questions, if you stop to think about it. To feel rejected is to let someone else provide those answers. When based on reactions from your market you can see room for improvement, welcome the feedback and make the needed changes to make your product as good as you know it truly is meant to be. Then go back. If possible, thank those who offered the suggestions and show them what you've got.

7. *What can you celebrate right now?* It can be hard to keep moving ahead when you encounter one rejection after another. There's no reward for your efforts. So we've learned to celebrate every milestone along the way to our goals. Success is a process. If you wait to congratulate yourself until the end, there'll be nothing left to celebrate. So celebrate the calls you make . . . the opportunities you get . . . the progress you make . . .

8. *Who thinks you're great?* One of the antidotes for the fear of rejection is a little support from your friends. When you're feeling your worst, ask yourself, "Who thinks I'm great? Who always believes in me?" And get together with them fast. We have a support system of people now who believe in us and our work. When setbacks or rejections occur, we get together with the folks who think we can't possibly lose. This loosely knit group of friends acts as an informal mutual-admiration society; we get each other through the tough times.

When you get thank-you letters or notes of appreciation from friends or customers, save them. Put them in a "stroke file." At times when you're getting a lot of no's, get out those notes and remind yourself there are people who value and appreciate your work so much they were moved to be sure you knew about it.

9. *Can you take matters into your own hands?* Nothing can finish off a venture more effectively than having to wait endlessly for someone else's okay to get under way. Entertainers and writers usually face this type of chronic rejection. They can't get a part until they're in the union, and they can't get in the union until they get a part. The successful ones don't wait for someone to discover them. They find some way to perform. They may, for instance, volunteer to appear in trade films or organize their own theater group. Remember, success is always attracted to a moving target. So if you're not getting the break you want, rather than feeling rejected, take charge. Don't let your success rest in the hands of someone else. Don't wait for another no. If the bank won't give you the loan you need to expand, raise your own funds. That's what the singer and songwriter Amanda McBroom, who wrote the popular theme song for the movie *The Rose,* did in order to cut her first album. If you can't seem to get a bid, volunteer to do a project for someone who could influence your future customers.

A researcher, for example, with a new computerized scanning system for the health field found that prospective clients remained skeptical despite his best efforts to sell his service. Rather than feeling rejected, he started demonstrating the system free of charge to key professionals. Within six months his practice was thriving.

■ FROM GUILT TO SELF-CONFIDENCE ■

Guilt is a much maligned emotion because it can spiral downward to feelings of worthlessness, hopelessness, and despair. Actually, however, guilt can be a very valuable emotion. It is a signal that you have violated one of your own personal standards. It informs you that you have let yourself down, that you have not lived up to what you expect of yourself, and it provides you with the opportunity to take steps to ensure that you won't violate that standard again.

In fact, a Case Western Reserve University study by psychologist Roy F. Baumeister found that, while people will often try to rationalize their guilt away, attending to it can be good for both you and the others involved. It is a feeling that arises when you feel *empathy* for someone you're concerned you wronged or when you're *anxious* about losing a relationship you value or being rejected by or excluded by others because of your behavior. The discomfort of feeling guilty serves to motivate us to correct or make up for our behavior.

So, if you are sufficiently tolerant of imperfection, as any good boss would be, you need not feel worthless when you admit to not having lived up to something you expect of yourself. You can break the downward spiral and look forward instead to doing better in the future.

Of course, the feeling of guilt is also complicated by the fact that sometimes it arises when we're trying to live up to someone else's standards or expectations instead of our own. For example, a woman might feel guilty about working late because her parents told her her family should always come first. Here's one road map for dealing with guilt.

Guilt → Curiosity → Reassurance → Self-Confidence

- **Ask yourself if you have, in fact, violated your own standards** or whether you are feeling guilty because you haven't done what someone else thought you should do.

- **If you are feeling guilty because you are trying to meet someone else's expectations** and have failed, identify what your own standards are in this situation and act accordingly. If you haven't actually violated your own standards, you will probably no longer feel guilty and, if necessary, can clarify with others what they can and cannot expect from you.

- **If you have violated your own standards and expectations, begin, with a sense of curiosity, to evaluate whether this is a standard that you still want to maintain.** If it is, with respect and appreciation acknowledge that you want to make sure you will not violate this standard again.

- **Recall times in the past when you successfully lived up to your stan-dards** even though it was difficult, and feel reassured about your ability to live up to your personal standards now.

- **Imagine yourself taking the necessary steps** in the future to live up to these standards in the most difficult situations, and feel pleased and confident about your ability to do so.

Confidence Builders

Here are a few things to do when you need to boost your self-confidence:

- Adjust your posture to one that is confident.

- Remember a time when you felt and acted confident.

- Talk to yourself, telling yourself that you're great, reminding yourself of things that you appreciate about yourself.

- See yourself doing something amazing, such as climbing a mountain or flying a plane.

- Identify something within the situation that you are already confident about.

- Feel your own backbone, and imagine it to be a steel rod.

- Identify a clear outcome for yourself in the situation.

- Play a particularly affecting piece of music in your head, one that makes you feel confident.

- Think of people who make you feel confident and imagine them small and sitting on your shoulder, talking into your ear.

Reprinted from *The Emotional Hostage*, by Leslie Cameron-Bandler and Michael Lebeau. Future Pace, 1986.

■ FROM HOPELESS TO DETERMINED OR ACCEPTING ■

Hope springs eternal in the human breast.

ALEXANDER POPE

Emotions often occur on a continuum from small to large, from weak and mild to strong and intense. Disappointment, for example, is mild in comparison with hopelessness. Yet hopelessness is milder than depression. These three emotions are similar in that they all involve proceeding into a future without something you desire. They are all low-energy emotions that prepare you for letting go.

Hopelessness is more final than disappointment, however, and not as bleak as depression. It's the appropriate emotion to feel when you've done everything you can do and it isn't enough. It occurs when you cannot envision a future that includes something you've wanted and prepares you for giving up any expectation of attaining it in the future.

Therefore, the first thing you need to do when you feel hopeless is to ask yourself if, in fact, there is nothing else you can do. Is there any possibility that you can still do something? If there is, imagine the future you want and allow yourself to feel the frustration of not yet having accomplished it. Feel challenged and determined to discover what remains to be done and to do it.

Hopelessness → Frustration → Feeling challenged → Determination

---

If you have done all there is to do, however, it's time to heed your feeling of hopelessness and let go. You can help yourself let go of something that has been important to you by doing the following.

- **Recall times in your life when you have let go of desired outcomes** and were freed to go on to other things that were satisfying.

- **Feel reassured by these memories** and accept what cannot be attained.

- **Imagine yourself in the future walking away from this goal and moving on with confidence** toward other things that you can accomplish. In this case your road map will look like this:

Hopelessness → Reassurance → Acceptance → Confidence

When Susan and Peter left the public-relations firm they were working at when they met and married, they were excited about their plans for launching a nationwide seminar program that would help couples rebuild shaky relationships. They prepared brochures, took out ads in the paper, created lots of media exposure for their inaugural seminar, and held a small but successful first seminar.

Unfortunately, the expenses of holding the seminar exceeded the money they brought in. There was no money left for promoting a second one. Still hopeful, however, they used telemarketing—working the phones themselves until they finally filled another seminar. It, too, was a success for those who attended, but again expenses exceeded income.

After several months, Susan and Peter were exhausted and on the point of bankruptcy. As weeks passed, their dream of a national seminar looked increasingly hopeless. They had done everything they could think of. And although it was painful, they decided to let go of that dream before it did them

i. Once they accepted that their future would not include national couples' seminars, they were free to begin thinking of what else they could do. Since they were both highly skilled public-relations specialists, they decided they would open their own PR firm, doing publicity for seminar leaders.

By shifting their focus to the history of success they'd had in PR, they began envisioning a new future, one in which they were running a successful firm and were able to proceed toward that goal with confidence. Their subsequent success in PR provided them with the funds to conduct, through their church, free seminars for dysfunctional families. Susan now says, "This work is actually much more gratifying than the original seminars we'd planned. When everything seemed so hopeless, it was actually just a sign that we needed to proceed in a different direction."

From Inadequacy to Self-Confidence

Many high achievers make a habit of comparing themselves with very successful people because they aspire to such levels of achievement. Too often, however, in making these comparisons they focus on the ways in which they fall short. As a result they end up with a chronic feeling of inadequacy, and of course, people don't perform at their best when they're feeling inadequate.

Feeling inadequate is usually the result of comparing what you can do or have done with what someone else can do, has done, or thinks you should do. It's a passive emotion that tends to stop you in your tracks. It prepares you to withdraw from the action before you get in over your head and allows you time to regroup and get better prepared.

This ready state can be valuable if you are truly not prepared to accomplish something you're about to undertake. We know of several cases where it has alerted people to turn down a contract or project they were truly not equipped to take on. A computer consultant we'll call Phil is a good example of someone who did not heed such a warning signal. Phil came to us after a disastrous failure. He had been approached to lead a large nationwide training program that would introduce a complicated software package to several thousand employees. He did not know much about the package, and he didn't like what he did know. But he really liked the prospect of six months of steady work at a good fee. The fee was so good, in fact, that he could live off the income from it for an entire year. He couldn't resist taking the project.

As soon as he signed the contract, however, what had begun as a vague feeling of apprehension swelled, and he began feeling very inadequate. He felt he would need weeks to learn the program adequately, and he had only days. He should have heeded the signal then and there and done what he could to salvage what was looking like an impossible situation. Unfortunately, he didn't. The first session went so poorly that he was fired immediately.

In any situation where you begin to feel inadequate, the first thing you need to do is restore your sense of adequacy so that you can make the necessary decisions to proceed successfully.

Inadequacy → Feeling Capable → Self-Confidence

- **Remind yourself of your own capabilities,** accomplishments, and past demonstrations of competence. Focus your attention on what you know you can do and have done well. Review your strengths in detail.

- **Continue reviewing your strengths and assets** until you begin to feel adequate to do those things you know you can do well.

- **Act from your own sense of competence.** Once you are feeling adequate again, you will have access to just what you can and cannot contribute to the situation at hand and you can proceed accordingly with confidence.

In Phil's situation, there were many alternatives he could have dealt with quite adequately. He could have asked for additional time. He could have offered to do portions of the training and provided someone else to handle other aspects of it. Or he could have told the company honestly that this program was not his strength and referred them to someone else. In the process he could have highlighted his own unique areas of expertise so the company could call upon him in the future if it needs assistance with other programs. Experience shows that turning away work you cannot do adequately commands respect and builds your reputation as someone who can be trusted.

Breaking an Inadequacy Habit

Of course, turning down work that you can actually do because you suffer from a chronic sense of inadequacy is another matter. For example, we once worked with a nutritionist who had a modest private practice. Joanna was frustrated with her income, but she was convinced she couldn't raise her fees. Also, she felt that many of the patients who came to her needed to be referred to a well-known nutritionist with whom she had studied.

When we asked her why she couldn't raise her fees and why so many patients needed to be referred out, her reasons were as follows: she didn't have a doctorate; she had never written a book; she had never done a research study; and she didn't have an ongoing research study to put her clients in. She planned to do all these things eventually but felt she had to build up her income first. Clearly she didn't feel adequate at this point.

In reality, Joanna was perfectly capable of handling 98 percent of the people who came to her and could command more than double her current fee. But she was living in the shadow of her mentor, to whom she was constantly comparing herself. This mentor was thirty-five years her senior and had an outstanding international reputation. He had written many books, lectured at many schools, and even received professional awards for his pioneering research. Obviously Joanna, only five years out of graduate school, didn't stack up well in her comparisons.

In this case, instead of serving as a valuable signal, her feelings of inadequacy had become needless and habitual and were diverting Joanna from moving ahead with her success. This is one reason swimmers and runners are often trained not to look backward or sideways to see how they're doing. They are taught to put all their attention and energy into getting across the finish line as quickly as they possibly can.

If, like Joanna, you have a habit of comparing yourself negatively to people whose success or skills you admire, here's what we suggest.

1. Make sure those you use as role models are people you want to be like. If you tend to aspire to be like someone other people think you should be like, you are doomed to feel inadequate. An intellectual sister who is always comparing her success to that of her athletic brother, for example, is setting herself up to feel inadequate no matter how well she performs in academia. The brother has a completely different set of skills and abilities from hers, and she has no desire to acquire them. You'll never feel adequate if you're comparing yourself to someone whom you don't want to be like. Look around for people to admire who are sufficiently like you that you would want to be like them.

2. Compare yourself positively. Instead of noticing the ways in which you don't measure up to those you admire, notice the ways in which you are similar. Even if you find this hard to do at first, search until you find the similarities. You will. We truly admire only people who reflect an image of what we already know is the best in ourselves. So we have to train our eyes to see what's similar.

3. Use their achievements to set goals for yourself. If you would like to do what those you admire are doing and have done, whenever you see or hear them doing those things say to yourself, "That's for me!" "That's what I'm going to do!" "That's how I'm going to be!"

4. Imagine yourself doing those things that you admire. In Joanna's situation, for example, she would imagine herself working successfully with new, challenging clients, raising her fee and having people gladly pay it, writing a book, speaking internationally, or doing her own research project.

5. *Resolve to learn how to do the things you aspire to do.* Take action to master skills and carry out those tasks that will lead to building your mastery.

6. *Try on your role models for size.* As you watch them at work, imagine yourself inside their skin, doing what they're doing. How does it feel to be them? Then imagine how you would do it. How would you integrate your own skills, values, and personality? In your mind, experience yourself on that podium or behind that desk.

7. *Act as if.* In the course of your day, act as if you've already achieved the stature of your role models. Notice how this colors the way you walk, talk, and perform.

■ **FROM FEELING IRRESPONSIBLE** ■
TO ASSUMING RESPONSIBILITY

Irresponsibility is one of those feelings that our society holds in contempt. Sometimes if we don't live up to our own demands, we begin accusing ourselves of being irresponsible, which leads to our feeling guilt, shame, anger, or resentment. Actually, feeling irresponsible is a signal that one of the following is true:

- You don't believe anything needs to be done.
- You don't think it's yours to do.
- You don't believe you are capable of doing it.

Once you determine that something needs doing and that there's no one better qualified to do it than you, the feeling that you can't do it will usually shift and you will probably begin feeling responsible and start considering how to go about it. So when you start feeling irresponsible, give the situation Cameron-Bandler's and Lebeau's Responsibility Test that follows.

If you agree that something does need to be done and you are the person to do it, but you feel you can't do what needs to be done, you'll probably start feeling inadequate. In that case you will want to develop the confidence you need to proceed. So refer to the road map for changing inadequacy into confidence.

"I kept feeling like I should do my own taxes," Maxine, who works as a paralegal, complained. After all, she knew tax law, and her taxes did need to be done. She'd already asked for one extension. Why wasn't she doing them? She felt irresponsible and guilty. It wasn't until her boyfriend pointed out to her that she was actually one of the most responsible people in the world that she realized she needed an expert to handle the tax aspects of several invest-ments she'd made. She truly wasn't the best-qualified person to complete her taxes that year. Had she given herself the responsibility test as soon as she be-gan feeling irresponsible, she would have saved herself a lot of time and dis-comfort.

The Responsibility Test: Knowing What You're Responsible For

- Does anything actually need to be done?
- Are you the most qualified person to do it?
- Are you able to do it?

■ FROM LETHARGIC TO MOTIVATED ■

Lethargy is an emotion you may feel when faced with tasks you know should be done but you don't want to do them and, therefore, you lack the necessary will or motivation to carry them out. It's a passive, slow, low-energy feeling that signals disinterest or lack of involvement in what you feel needs to be done. It's a signal that you don't find the tasks at hand desirable and want to withdraw from them.

Instead of passively hoping that your mood will change or resentfully do-ing what you don't want to do, you can heed the signal your lethargy is send-ing and begin asking yourself some questions designed to make the tasks at hand more desirable so you'll want to become actively involved. Here's a way to use that energy to get going again.

Lethargy → Curiosity → Motivation → Determination → Ambition

- **Ask yourself if this work is worth doing.** Is the outcome worth the effort? If the tasks at hand aren't worthwhile, why are you expecting yourself to do them? Why not let yourself off the hook? You'll be amazed at how quickly your energy and your emotions will shift when you do.

- **If the tasks are worthwhile, ask what aspects of them you have at least some mild interest in.** Begin asking yourself questions about what's involved, questions that have some importance to you.

- As you are asking these questions, pick up your tempo somewhat. (Playing some moderately paced music in the background while you work may help.)

- You'll probably begin to feel curious about your answers.

- Shift the feeling of wanting to know the answers to feeling that you **must know the answers,** and you will begin to feel motivated and determined to find them.

- **Finally, think** about how finding what interests you about these tasks will help you achieve your goals and you will undoubtedly begin feeling ambitious—and assuming you've had enough sleep and R & R, you'll start feeling motivated to begin doing the worthwhile things at hand.

■ FROM FEELING OVERWHELMED TO FEELING CAPABLE ■

Feeling overwhelmed is a signal that you are trying to take care of too many tasks all at once without setting priorities. When you are feeling overwhelmed you are probably aware of many tasks you must do immediately. Doing many things simultaneously is, of course, impossible, but your mind and body are probably racing from one thing to another, trying to do them all, like a whirlwind of energy not knowing where to land.

As time passes and the pressure builds, feeling overwhelmed can spiral downward into feeling immobilized and hopeless. But to focus and utilize this maelstrom of energy that being overwhelmed provides before it spirals downward you can do the following when you first start to feel overwhelmed.

> **Feeling Overwhelmed → Focused → Motivated → Capable**

- Slow your tempo at once by taking a deep breath.

- **Remind yourself you have all the time in the world.** (Refer to chapter 3 if you have trouble believing this.)

- **Begin breaking down the overwhelming situation into the various tasks involved and start setting priorities**—what needs doing first, second, and so on.

- Focus only on the one task that must be done first.

- Switch your thinking from **I must do this** to **I can do this.**

By this time you'll probably feel motivated to begin the first task and capable of moving on to the next one once that's completed. At times, as your

Handy Guide to the Emotional Road Map

All emotions, no matter how unpleasant, are valuable signals designed to point you in the direction you need to go and supply you with the precise energy best suited to responding appropriately. Use this summary as a reference for how to put unpleasant emotions to work in your best interest.

Feeling	Message	Direction
Anger	You face some harm or threat; take action to stop or prevent it.	Gratitude Curiosity Reassurance Satisfaction
Depression	Focus on improvements.	Encouragement
Disappointment	Carry on or let go.	Possibility check Hopefulness
Discouragement	Set shorter-range goals.	Pride Curiosity Anticipation Encouragement
Failure	Learn, go on.	Test Pride Satisfaction Reassurance Success
Fear Anxiety	You face a future that holds danger you are not prepared for; prepare to cope or avoid negative consequences.	Safety Curiosity Feeling capable Self-Confidence Anticipation

Feeling	Message	Direction
Guilt	You have violated a personal standard; take steps to assure you won't do so again.	Curiosity Reassurance Self-Confidence
Hopelessness	It's time to let go.	Possibility check Determination Acceptance
Inadequacy	You're comparing yourself in an unfavorable way; consider your assets.	Feeling capable Self-Confidence
Irresponsibility	You aren't convinced; evaluate the situation	Assuming responsibility
Lethargy	You're faced with tasks you know you should do but don't want to; get involved.	Curiosity Motivation Determination Ambition
Feeling Overwhelmed	Too many large tasks at once; break the situation into smaller tasks and prioritize.	Focused Motivated Capable
Feeling Stuck	You're out of options; step away and find new ones.	Appreciation Curiosity Reassurance Self-Confidence Progress

sense of control returns, you may also realize that you need to reschedule, refer, or engage others to help you carry out your commitments or desires.

■ FROM FEELING STUCK TO MAKING PROGRESS ■

Feeling *stuck* is a signal that you need to step away from whatever approach you're using and find another option. Feeling stuck is a way of telling yourself that you've got to do something differently. It's a passive but high-energy emotion. Therefore, taking any action will usually help get you moving again. Here's what you can do when you feel stuck.

> **Feeling Stuck → Appreciative → Curious → Reassured → Confident**

- **Appreciate all the bound-up energy you're feeling,** and begin using some of it to feel curious about various alternative actions you could take.
- **Recall times in your life** when you were able to come up with new options that worked out well for you. Do this until you feel reassured about coming up with options for this situation.
- **Imagine yourself** generating new options for this situation until you feel confident about finding a new direction.
- **Generate at least ten options,** no matter how outrageous they might seem, that would represent progress toward your goal.
- **Select and take some action now** on the one you like most.

Diane had been trying to get a computer for over six months. First a friend was going to get one for her through his job. But after several months of delay, he told her the discount policy his office had offered was no longer in effect and he couldn't get it after all. Then her boyfriend told her he knew someone who thought he could pick up a surplus computer for her. Several months later, still no computer.

"I feel stuck," she told a friend. "I just don't seem to be able to get a computer even though I know it would really help my business. I just don't have the money to pay full price for one." Her friend's response was enlightening. She said, "Thank goodness you're getting fed up with your situation, Diane. You've got to try some other approach. What if you were going to be shot at dusk unless you had a computer? What would you do?" Immediately Diane knew what she'd needed to do. She sold her camera and her exercise bike, realizing she never used them anyway. And while she didn't get it all done before dusk, within the month she did have her computer!

When You Don't Like the Way You Feel

As you can see from the Emotional Road Map, each emotion brings us a particular energy with its own unique qualities. As with other forms of energy, we can harness the various energies our emotions bring us and use them to carry us from one place to another. As you come to understand the qualities unique to each emotion, you can use them like a throttle to help you shift from one feeling to another along the Emotional Road Map. Here are a variety of ways you can use the particular qualities inherent in emotions to make the emotional roller coaster of being your own boss a more enjoyable ride.

Charging Up or Calming Down

Sometimes you undoubtedly need to boost your energy so you can keep on going strong. But at other times, you probably find yourself wanting to relax and calm down. Fortunately, emotions have varying degrees of energy. Some pick us up and speed up our psychological and physical systems. Others relax and slow us down. So you can use your emotions to better manage your energy level. For example, if your want to feel more energized, you might arouse your *enthusiasm* by thinking about the many wonderful and exciting possibilities that could await you. Playing background music with a quick tempo or calling up a high-energy, enthusiastic, fast-talking friend can also pick up your mood.

On the other hand, if you want to calm down or relax, you can slow your emotional pace by thinking about areas of your life with which you are *content*. Or you can think of and allow yourself to experience things in your life that you find *satisfying*. You can also breathe more slowly and deeply, play background music with a slow and gentle tempo, or call up a friend who is usually calm and relaxed.

Slow-paced emotions	Fast-paced emotions
lethargy, boredom, apathy, discouragement, patience, calm, acceptance, satisfaction, dread, caution, and contentment	anxiety, excitement, impatience, enthusiasm, frustration, panic, restlessness, exhilaration, anger

Taking Initiative or Letting Go

You undoubtedly have times when you know you need to jump in and take more of the initiative. But, then, at other times, you realize you have to let go, shift gears, and get on in a new direction, either temporarily as when you have to break from a work project to take a customer call or over the long run when economic conditions require you to redirect what you're doing. Your emotions can help you make these shifts because emotions also require varying degrees of engagement: Some are passive—they have no forward movement; they disconnect from your energy. Others are active—they have direction; they move you forward and carry your energy toward an outcome.

Feeling *hopeless, bored,* or *apathetic* are passive emotional responses. So are feeling *satisfied, calm, depressed,* or *resigned.* They can help you let go and become detached from a situation. Feeling *friendly* or *ambitious,* however, are active responses, as are feeling *determined, frustrated, curious, agitated,* or *disgusted.* These feelings can help you become more involved and invested in what you're doing. So when you want to show more initiative, cultivate active emotions. Activate your *curiosity,* or *interest,* for example. If you're feeling *bored,* you can become involved by focusing attention on what *pleases* you. If you are feeling apathetic, you can become *dissatisfied* or *irritated* about the absence of something engaging and you'll start feeling motivated to find something you care about doing.

On the other hand, let's say you need a break or need to get some perspective on your situation. You can distance yourself from your circumstances by engaging more passive emotions. You might focus, for example, on what you find *satisfying* or what you feel *grateful* about.

PASSIVE EMOTIONS	ACTIVE EMOTIONS
hopelessness, apathy, satisfaction, calm, boredom, depression, resignation, pleasure, and self-pity	friendliness, ambition, determination, frustration, curiosity, fear, disgust, and agitation

Getting in a Better Mood

As we all know, it's difficult to shift directly from one intense feeling to another entirely opposite one. That's why telling yourself to cheer up—or worse yet, having someone else tell you to cheer up—rarely works. But one of the easiest ways to actually change your mood is to vary the intensity of what you're feeling. Many emotions are simply more or less intense variations along a continuum of the same mood. Here are several examples:

Disappointment → Sadness → Despair → Grief are on the same continuum, with disappointment being less intense and grief being more intense.

Satisfaction → Happiness → Joy → Ecstacy are on a similar continuum. So are feeling **Concerned → Upset → Anxious → Panicked** and **Curious → Interested → Aroused → Obsessed.**

So, to change your mood more easily, you can shift to the less intense end of the continuum of emotions you'd like to be feeling. For example, while it's difficult to go directly from feeling *despairing* to feeling *joyful,* it's much easier to move from *despair* to a mild level of *satisfaction* if you allow yourself to take a long, soothing bubble bath or get out and shoot some hoops. So, if you want to feel *happy,* but you're feeling *blue,* you might begin by doing something that you derive a sense of *satisfaction* from. Or, if you want to become more *interested* in something you've been putting off because it feels so *dreadfully dull,* you might change your mood by becoming *curious* about how you'd get it done or about what it could mean for your success.

Quickly Improving the Way You Feel About Any Situation

You probably experience times when you've got to feel better about your situation right away. Maybe you're on the spot and have to perform at your best under pressure. Or maybe you get a phone call from an important client right in the midst of a major computer crisis, and you've got to shift quickly into a congenial, friendly conversation. In situations like these, here's one of the easiest ways to change how you feel fast. Shift your time frame. Emotions usually arise in relation to the particular time period you're operating from. *Regret* and *nostalgia,* for example, are rooted in recalling the past. Other feelings like *curiosity* and *boredom* relate to being in the here and now. Still other emotions, like *anxiety, hope, dread,* and *ambition* relate to imagining or thinking about the future. Some feelings arise from comparing various aspects of the past, present, or future. Here are more examples:

PAST ORIENTED	PRESENT ORIENTED	FUTURE ORIENTED
remorse, regret, nostalgia, guilt, disappointment, reassurance	acceptance, contentment, curiosity, boredom, lonely, overwhelmed, patience	anticipation, anxiety, ambition, dread, concern, hope, hopeless, impatience

So, if you're feeling *panicked* about a current crisis, to feel more *confident* and in charge shift your perspective to the *pride* you felt after handling the last crisis you overcame. Or, if you feel *disappointed,* you can shift from thinking about what has been to what could be. If you are feeling *bored* or *lethargic,* you can imagine what you would be doing in a more exciting future, which may give you the energy to start doing some of those things in the present. If you are feeling *anxious* or *afraid,* you can feel better fast by shifting your attention from thinking about the possible future you're dreading to the present siutation or even a more secure time in your past.

Keeping Everything in Perspective

On your own, there are undoubtely times when you feel *overwhelmed* and other times when you feel *grouchy* and *irritated*. These emotions, like many, illustrate how directly the way you feel has to do with how much of any particular situation you choose to pay attention to at any one time. For example, feeling *overwhelmed, inadequate, discouraged,* or *in awe* is usually the result of paying attention to extensive amounts of your entire situation. These are feelings most people have when they start to think about everything they have to do for all their clients over the next six months . . . or when we think about all the many, many things we'll have to do to accomplish a big lifelong dream . . . or when we start to think about everything we have to do this month in our work, our personal life, and our family life?

On the other hand, feeling *fascinated, irritated, grumpy,* or *disagreeable* usually arises from paying attention to minute details, like entering data into a computer or sorting beads by color and size. So one way to keep things in better perspective and dramatically alter the way you feel is either to broaden or narrow the range of what you pay attention to.

For example, any time you start to feel overwhelmed or discouraged, one way to quickly shift your feelings is to break whatever you're dealing with down into small tasks. Shift from thinking about *everything* that needs to be done to the *one thing* you could do now. Or, if you're feeling *irritated* and *disagreeable,* one way to shift your feelings fast is to change your focus to the bigger picture. How significant, for example, is this issue that's bothering you to your overall life? Or what happens if you think about this issue from a historical perspective—or if you put it in a global perspective? How important will it be years from now?

After learning about this aspect of his emotions, an event planner told us, "I realize I spend my most unpleasant days vacillating between feeling irritable about having to handle so many little pesky details to feeling overwhelmed by the magnitude of all the things I have to do to pull an entire event together on schedule. Now I realize that once I've planned a project, I can find a middle ground and relax while I work by limiting my thinking to only the goals and progress I've set for this particular day."

Staying Motivated and On Track

Another way to change how you're feeling is to start, or stop, making comparisons. Many, many emotions arise from various mental comparisons you're making between how what you have matches, or doesn't match, what you want . . . or how well you're doing matches, or doesn't match, how well you or others think you should be doing . . . or, how things were, could be, should be versus how they are.

When reality matches your desires, you may feel *contented, agreeable, satisfied,* or *pleased.* But when there's a mismatch between reality and what you want, you might feel frustrated, disappointed, envious or inadequate.

REALITY MATCH	REALITY MISMATCH
agreeable	frustrated
fulfilled	disappointed
satisfied	guilty
content	humorous
grateful	envious
pleased	inadequate
proud	impatient
confident	discouraged

One of the most common ways we see self-employed people making themselves miserable is by comparing the way things are with the way they think they should be or wish they were. Some of the most miserable people we know are people who have very high standards and expectations that both they, and life, continually fail to live up to.

Maria, for example, wanted to become a successful, highly paid public speaker. So, she worked hard to qualify to join the National Speakers' Association. After joining, however, her confidence plummeted, because she compared herself with the speakers she heard make presentations at the local and national meetings. And she compared their fees. She was just getting $500 a speech whereas many of the better-known speakers she admired were getting $5,000, $10,000 and up. They got standing ovations; she simply got polite rounds of applause. They got a rush of heartfelt personal letters praising their presentions and telling about profound changes their speeches had catalyzed; she got adequate evaulations summarized on standard form-letter thank-you notes. She felt *inadequate* and *discouraged.*

On the other hand, perceiving a mismatch between what you have and what you want can fire your ambition and spur you to work harder with greater *resolve* and *determination* until you achieve what you want. In fact, that's why and how people who have high standards and expectations are so often driven to achieve them. Many of today's most successful public speakers started in just this way. Listening to the best motivational speakers in the world *inspired* Mark Victor Hanson to rise above the *despair* of a devasting bankruptcy. He became *determined* to become such a speaker himself and worked relentlessly to achieve that goal. He has since gone on not only to become one of the nation's leading motivational speakers but also to cowrite the runaway best-selling books *Chicken Soup for the Soul* and *A Second Helping of Chicken Soup*.

So, as you can see, you can use the feelings generated from making mental comparisons either to motivate, or de-motivate yourself. Fortunately, you can have high standards and high expectations for success and still enjoy yourself in the process. Here's how:

1. Combine your efforts to *achieve* with *tolerance, gratitude, anticipation,* and *patience.*

2. Use the gap between what you have and what you want to spur your *determination, ambition,* and *dedication.*

3. Focus on the progress you're making toward your goals by comparing where you started from and where you are now and feel a sense of *achievement, appreciation, satisfaction,* and *accomplishment* as you go along.

In fact, you can feel more successful anytime you want without abandoning your ultimate goal. Simply switch your attention to the things you're doing that *are* working and think about what's happening that *does* match the way you believe things should be. This will lead you to feelings of *satisfaction, accomplishment, pride, gratitude,* and *fulfillment.*

At any moment, of course, there are things that match and things that don't. So you always have a choice of which to focus on. So, if you want to motivate yourself to work harder, focus on how you want things to be. If you want to relax and refresh yourself, focus on what you've already accomplished.

We've found that the key to enjoying your work is being able to switch back and forth between motivating yourself to work for future goals and feeling proud, pleased, and grateful about what you've accomplished so far. In fact, feeling successful seems to be a matter of striking a balance between *desire* and *contentment.*

As accountant Michael Russo told us, "You are always breaking through your comfort zone. There's a piece of you that wants to stop and just digest what you've accomplished, which is fine. But you can't stay there too long. You have to keep jumping and taking those risks. And the more you take the jump, the easier it gets, and eventually you realize you can handle anything that comes along."

Persevering with Confidence

One way to help yourself to continue making those jumps is to consider whether you think about what you're doing as possible, or necessary. Your emotions will probably vary considerably depending on which perspective you take. For example, how do you feel when you believe you *have* to do something, *must* do something, *need* to do something, or *should* do something? In other words, when something seems as if it is a *necessity,* how do you feel? Check the following choices:

If I think I *have* to do something, I feel:

- Resistant or determined?
- Guilty or tenacious?
- Desperate or driven?
- Pressured or challenged?
- Overwhelmed or motivated?
- Obligated, regretful, or pleased?

There are no right or wrong answers. And your answers may vary depending on what the task or activity is. But, as you can see, turning a task into a *necessity,* by signing a contract or setting a deadline, versus making it *optional* by leaving it open as to when or if you will do it, can dramatically alter the way you feel about it. The key is knowing which works best for you in various situations. So notice, for example, how you feel when you tell yourself that you *must* do something as opposed to when you tell yourself you *can* do it. What happens to your emotions when it becomes a choice instead of a requirement? In other words, do you respond better to *possibilities* or *necessities*?

Many people respond best to possibility thinking. Possibility thinking is often called having a *can-do attitude.* Feelings often associated with a *can-do attitude* include *optimism, caution, curiosity, disappointment, confidence,* and *hope.* But now notice how much different you feel if you think something is *impossible* as opposed to *possible.* What happens when someone tells you you can't do something or you shift your focus from what you can or could do to what you can't do?

Some people are challenged by doing the impossible, but most people are more likely to feel *helpless, despairing, disappointed, discouraged,* or *inadequate.*

In fact, most of us can produce a dramatic shift in the way we feel by simply changing our thoughts from "I *can't* do that" to thinking "*How* could I do that?" This one simple shift can be a quick way to move from feeling pessimistic to feeling optimistic, from feeling discouraged to feeling encouraged, from feeling disappointed to feeling curious, or from feeling hopeless to feeling motivated.

How desirable something is to you or how willing you are do it also affects how you feel. When you want something, for example, you might tend to feel *motivated, patient,* or *impatient, ambitious* or *determined.* If you don't want to do something, you might feel *resistant, lethargic,* or *stubborn.* So giving yourself a choice, or making things more desirable, interesting, and intriguing, can help you shift the way you feel about what you're doing.

Shifting Concentration from One Work Activity to Another More Easily

Just as it's more difficult to shift from one intense state of feeling to an opposite, equally intense one, so it's also more challenging to move from certain types of work activities to certain other quite different ones. As we discussed in chapter 5, when you're on your own, you've got to perform all the functions an entire larger organization has various personnel to carry out. So, one moment you may be *creating* a marketing brochure, only to realize if you want to complete the project today, you must stop what you're doing and get *organized* so all the materials and supplies you need will be delivered before five o'clock. Or you may be working intensely at *solving a problem* for a client when a prospective client you've been trying to reach for days finally returns your calls and you must put on your sales hat and *lead* them to make a positive decision.

While such demands are a regular part of the workday for most of us who are self-employed, it's easy to experience such inconveniences as interruptions. And it can be a challenge to get in the right frame of mind to handle one such demand after another. But, fortunately, you can use the information you've just learned about emotions to shift more easily from one activity to another.

Viewed in the context of what we've been discussing, it's no wonder shifting from one function to another can be so difficult at times. Each type of activity you engage in requires its own focus, it's own time frame, and it's own feeling state.

- Creating, for example, asks that you have a wide focus, one that's open to many possibilities. Being creative, whether it involves writing ad copy, selecting a name for your business, or designing the packaging for your product, asks that you step out of the present limitations and imagine what could be in the future. And it requires you to become *curious* about various possibilities for the future.

- Problem solving, on the other hand, requires you to narrow your focus to the issues at hand, deal with the present realities, and propel yourself with the feelings of *frustration* and *impatience* that come with knowing there's a mismatch between what you want and what you have right now.

- Building activities like assembling, computing, and fixing things also require you to narrow your focus to the task at hand; and they involve staying in the present moment to complete the tasks at hand while *anticipating* the end results from achieving your goal.

- Organizing tasks, be they ordering supplies, filing paperwork, tracking expenses, or paying bills, also call upon you to narrow your focus to the task at hand; but, in addition, they usually require that you shift your time frame to work in accord with the plans and procedures you've established in the past. Generally, they involve working from a feeling of *discontent* until you have things running the way you understand they should be.

- Leading activities like selling, promoting, managing, negotiating, persuading, or coordinating require you to open your focus so you can attend to a wide range of activities simultaneously and compare what's happening now with your future goals and plans. These activities are generally propelled by feelings of *ambition* or a desire to *achieve* what you image is possible.

- Improving activities like listening, consulting, explaining, serving, and helping require you to narrow your focus of attention to whomever you're working with and shift your attention to the present moment so you can relate fully to their needs. Such activities call for you to operate from a feeling of *caring* and *concern*.

Whenever you're called upon to do something that requires a quite different focus, time frame, and feeling from the ones you've been working in, shifting gears is more difficult. Shifting from doing something like *creating*, for example, which requires a wide-open, future orientation to doing something like *organizing*, which requires a narrow, past orientation, can produce stress. So when you're eagerly working on *creating* a new seminar, it's no wonder you feel *irritated* and *bothered* at having to stop to perform an *organizing* activity like tracking down a missing file or move into an *improving* activity like taking a call from a confused client. Or when you're *leading* a rapt audience with a dynamic sales presentation, it's no wonder you break your stride if you must suddenly switch gears to fix the overhead projector. In each of these cases, you're literally being required to alter your state of being.

But here are several things you can do to respond more easily to the demands of having to wear multiple hats throughout the day.

1. Acknowledge that you are being required to change your state of being. Productivity is the result of working in a mental and emotional state that's ideally matched to the tasks at hand. So, if you're working productively in one state of mind and suddenly you're called upon to reorient yourself to operate in another entirely different state, it's natural that your initial reaction is to feel somewhat *confused, disoriented, irritated,* or even *angry.* This reaction is only temporary, however, so use it as a reminder, or trigger, that you're being called upon to switch your mental and emotional state. It provides you with the chance to decide how you want to best handle the situation.

2. Cluster similar functional tasks throughout the day to buffer your productivity. To the extent possible, put similar work functions together so you can reduce the amount of bouncing you have to do from one mental and emotional state to another. Do *organizing* tasks like filing and bill paying together, for example. Or do *improving* tasks like taking calls and meeting with clients in similar time periods.

3. Schedule work clusters throughout the day for the greatest productivity. To further enhance your productivity and peace of mind, set up your daily schedule so that work clusters are clearly defined. For example, potter Vivian Carmire works in her studio in the mornings. During this time, she doesn't take phone calls or see clients. This is her *creative* time. It's also the time when she fires and cleans her ovens (*building* tasks). In the afternoon she makes

Doorways for Shifting from One Function to Another

Function	Tasks Like	Focus	Time Frame	Feeling
Creating	Imagining Designing Innovating Envisioning Performing Perceiving	Wide	Future	Curiosity Perplexity
Problem Solving	Analyzing Diagnosing Observing Investigating Defining Evaluating	Narrow	Present to Future	Frustration Curiosity Determination
Building	Assembling Computing Repairing Cleaning Maintaining Transporting Packaging	Narrow	Present	Anticipation Determination

herself available to her customers (*improving* tasks). She takes calls, meets customers, and makes deliveries. Around 4:00 P.M. each day, after her daughter comes home from school, she sets aside half an hour for administrative details, like processing the mail, filing, and so forth (*organizing* tasks). On weekends, she does marketing and sales activities by exhibiting at shows, openings, and fairs (*leading tasks*).

4. Routinize tasks that are most difficult or unpleasant to you. Usually the most difficult shifts to make are those that are most different from the work state you enjoy most and do most naturally. For example, Tom Burkinsky is a marketing consultant. He loves to work with people, helping them solve problems and collaborating with them on creating marketing compaigns. So he rarely has a problem switching among various tasks related to leading, improving, creating, and problem solving. Frequently, though, he puts off keeping up with administrative details but feels *irritated* that they don't get done. Ultimately Tom plans to hire someone else to take over these *building* and *organizing* tasks; however, for now, while he's getting his business under way, he's

Function	Tasks Like	Focus	Time Frame	Feeling
Organizing	Arranging Compiling Tracking Gathering Ordering Recording Filing	Narrow	Present to Past	Discontent Desire for Order
Leading	Coordinating Selling Promoting Negotiating Managing Influencing Persuading	Wide	Future	Ambition Desire to Accomplish
Improving	Listening Caring Consulting Explaining Teaching Helping	Narrow	Present	Caring Concern

established a routine to help himself make the shift to the functions he tends to put off or get most irritated by. Every day when he gets back to his home office, he puts his favorite music on the stereo and, while he's unwinding from the day, he handles administrative details until his wife gets home with the kids.

5. Give yourself permission to define when you will and won't shift from one activity to another. Just because something arises for you to respond to doesn't mean you have to drop everything and shift out of your productive work state into some other one. If you're in the middle of grappling with a complex project (*problem solving* and *creating*), you don't have to take an incoming call (*improving* or *leading*). You can let your answering machine or voice mail pick up the call. By listening to the incoming call in the background, you can even screen your calls, if you wish, so you can decide if you want to interrupt a productive work cycle or not in order to take a particular call.

Allow yourself the flexibility you need to define for family, friends, clients, and customers how and when you can best serve and meet their needs. Don't be embarrassed to do this. Work with those involved to find a schedule that meets each of your needs and stick to it. When someone wants you to drop everything, unless it's an emergency of some kind, remind them that you've established your schedule so you can do the best possible job for them. Then, let them know exactly when and how you will respond to their needs.

6. When you want or need to shift your work state, clear the existing state first so you can switch with less difficulty to whatever work state is called for. In other words, don't try to do one function from the state of mind that's best suited for another. In chapter 5, we described a Five-Step Regimen for Peak Performance. Any one of the activities described in that regimen can be used to help you clear one state of mind so you can shift your focus, time frame, and emotions to another.

Let's say, for example, you suddenly get a long-awaited call that could lead to a project or order you've been working hard to get. Of course, you want to be at your most creative and articulate, but you're lost in the deep space of juggling a million details for an event you're managing. To help make the shift from a narrow, present-oriented state to a creative, outgoing, future-oriented state of mind, you could tell the caller you're delighted to hear from her and ask if she would hold for a moment while you get her file. Then on the way to the filing cabinet, you can physically shake out your entire body, take ten deep breaths, and even let out a whoop. Chances are, by the time you get back to the phone, your mind will be clear and you will be ready to communicate at your best.

7. Consciously use focus, time frame, and emotion to make the shifts you desire. Now that you know that mental and emotional states are associated with different time frames, tempos, focus, and intensity, use the information you've learned in this chapter to consciously shift from one to another. Think of each of these characteristics as a doorway to and from the state of mind you desire. Here's a summary of doorways we've found to be useful in getting from one state to another.

DESIGNER EMOTIONS: PRESELECTING YOUR FEELINGS

These are just a few examples of how we can purposely shift our emotions to ones that will be most useful to us. The more you know about your own preferences, the easier it is to focus on the experiences around you in a way that will be manageable and productive for you. All your assumptions, expectations, and definitions affect the way you experience everything you encounter. In fact, the *premise* from which you approach a situation can not only change your feelings about it, but can actually determine the outcome as well.

As we said earlier, emotions flow from perceptions, and if you have perceived a situation inaccurately, you will be emotionally charged and ready to respond at a situation other than the one at hand. This effect is somewhat like showing up to a party in the wrong clothes. Actually, it's easy to misperceive a situation because our perceptions are colored by the premise from which we approach a situation. For example, let's imagine that you are calling a client to collect an overdue bill. Here are three possible premises you could be holding in your mind as you place the call:

Premise 1: "No one ever pays me on time. This guy is just trying to bilk me out of my money. I'll probably never get this check, unless I take him to court. People want to get away with as much as they can."

Premise 2: "I bet Harold is having a hard time with his business right now because of the recession. I'm sure he's feeling bad about being so far behind on his account. I wonder what kind of arrangements we could make to help him out."

Premise 3: "I wonder why I haven't gotten this check. I think I'll call and find out. There are many possibilities."

How would you be feeling as Harold answers the phone if you are operating from these premises?

- From Premise 1, you might be feeling angry.
- From Premise 2, you might be feeling compassionate.
- From Premise 3, you'd probably be feeling curious.

What do you imagine you'd say during your conversation with Harold operating from these different premises? How do you think Harold would respond to you? Do you think the outcome of the conversations would be different? Chances are they would be very different.

By paying attention to and even predetermining your premise at any given moment, you can totally alter your emotional reality, your behavior, and your results.

In other words, we can create our own emotions. This does not mean we're suggesting that you be dishonest or deny your real feelings. We have just said that all feelings bring a valuable message and are worth attending to and utilizing. What we are saying is that you will experience different emotions depending on how you are perceiving your circumstances at any moment, and that the emotions that flow from those perceptions will cause you to act differently and therefore produce different results for you.

So if you are going into an important meeting or placing an important phone call, why not check your premise first? Exactly what is the situation? How do you want to approach it? What aspects of reality will assist you in approaching it in the way you desire? For example, here are two very different scenarios that derive from actual situations.

Terry and Carolyn are accountants. Both have been on their own for less than six months. They belong to the same professional association. In fact, they've met each other. Sarah talked with them separately one evening at the same meeting.

Earlier in the week, Terry was meeting with the chief financial officer of a moderate-sized company. If she could get their business, it would be her largest account to date and it would cover her operating expenses for the first year. As she was driving to the meeting, these thoughts were racing through her mind:

"These big firms are a man's world. It's so hard for a woman to be taken seriously in this field. They always treat me like I'm a little crumb on their table. I'm sure they're locked into using a large company. I sure hope I can crack through their armor."

As you can imagine, by the time Terry got to the meeting she was filled with anxiety and an underlying hostility.

Carolyn also had an important meeting that week with a prestigious potential client. On the way there, her mind was racing with excitement:

"This is the chance I've been waiting for. Everything I've done in the past five years has prepared me for this meeting. I know the industry figures. I know their position in the marketplace. There is so much I can do for them!"

Again, as you can imagine, Carolyn almost danced her way into the lobby. You can also probably imagine the conversation these two women had at the end of the week when they ran into each other at an association meeting. Do they live on the same planet? How could a nearly identical situation be such a struggle for one person and such an opportunity for another? Obviously, their premises are showing.

Checking Your Premise

Of course, it's always easier to see someone else's premise at work than to recognize your own. But, if you're repeatedly getting results you don't want, or if you frequently feel emotions you'd rather not be feeling, check your premise. If you usually feel scared or apprehensive when you make a sales call, check your premise. What are you saying to yourself about sales calls? If you routinely get angry when bills arrive, check your premise. What are you saying to yourself about bills? If you feel tired every time you look at the piles that need filing, check your premise. What are you saying about filing? Here are several possible premises and various feelings they're likely to elicit.

ALTERNATIVE PREMISES FOR SALES CALLS	POSSIBLE EMOTIONS
I've never been able to sell.	inadequacy
I love showing my portfolio to people.	excitement
I know I can help these people.	confidence
People hate to part with their money.	anger

ALTERNATIVE PREMISES FOR BILLS	POSSIBLE EMOTIONS
These bills will put me in my grave.	fear
Boy, have I invested a lot this month!	pride
Everyone always wants theirs.	anger
Let's get these paid.	determination

ALTERNATIVE PREMISES FOR FILING	POSSIBLE EMOTIONS
I shouldn't have to do this grunt work!	resentment
I can't wait to get this put away.	motivation
I'm so tired. I can't look at this mess.	overwhelmed
I wonder how I should organize all this stuff	curiosity

Listen carefully to what you say about yourself, your customers, the economy, your field. And recognize that the premise you take into everything you do will determine the way you feel about it, how you approach it, and, to a large extent, the results you will get.

How Misperceptions Can Trip You Up

The premise we start any activity from is based upon our perceptions of the situation at hand and our collective memory of all situations we perceive as similar. But as you can see, a premise built upon misperceptions can trip you up. Here are four ways we commonly come to a misperception and how to avoid them.

1. **Overgeneralization.** Because something or someone has been one way in the past, we may assume that it will be that way now. We may generalize that what happened in one situation will happen in this one.

   To avoid overgeneralizing, ask yourself how this situation is the same and how it is different from previous situations. How have you changed? How has the situation changed? How might others involved have changed?

2. **Projection.** Because you feel or think a certain way, you may assume that others in the situation think and feel that way, too. If you are aware, for example, that you left material out of a presentation and are therefore critical of yourself, you may project that others in the room are also critical, when in fact, they have no knowledge of what you've left out and are not feeling critical at all. Or sometimes because something has been one way in the past, we project that it will be that way again.

   To avoid projecting, look for concrete signs of conclusions you reach—i.e., someone's scowl or cross tone of voice—and check out to verify that you're reading the signs correctly—i.e., ask "Do you disagree? Are you disappointed?"

3. **Distortion.** If we have incomplete information, we tend to fill in the missing pieces and imagine what seems to be the likely scenario. Sometimes these assumptions distort the actual situation.

   To avoid distortions, try imagining a variety of possibilities and test these assumptions by seeking additional information.

4. **Discounting.** Sometimes we ignore key information about a situation because we don't want to face it, find it irrelevant or improbable, or don't think it's important. So, we just fail to notice it—or if we do notice it, we decide it's insignificant.

   To avoid discounting, think about the situations you approach from various perspectives: your own, that of the others involved, the history behind the situation, and the future implications of the situation. This will help you account for all the important variables so you can operate from a realistic, but confident, premise.

Adjusting Your Premise

When you hear a negative, self-defeating premise running around in your head, consider whether you can find any evidence that would support your adjusting your premise to a more positive, self-affirming one.

For example, if you hear yourself saying "No one can make money in this economy!" ask yourself if that's actually true. Aren't some people making money? Great fortunes were made even during the Great Depresson. So, who is making money? Is anyone in your field doing well in this economy? If some people are, perhaps you could, too. What could you do so you, too, can produce more income? After finding the needed evidence, you might adjust your premise regarding the economy to "Some people are making money. Why not me?"

If you're a woman and you hear yourself saying, as Terry was, "This is a man's world," you might ask yourself if there aren't some women who have done well in the world. Do you know of any successfully self-employed women in your field? If they're doing well, perhaps you can, too. If there aren't any people like yourself who are doing well, then ask yourself if you know of other people who have done things that had never been done before. If they could do what they did, couldn't you do this? And you might adjust your premise to "The world is opening to me, too."

At the very least, you can always adjust your premise to a neutral position in which anything is possible. Sarah created one of her favorite premises based on one she learned from the acting coach Gene Bua. When she is about to go into an important situation, she runs through this routine: "First I remind myself of who I am and what I do. I say to myself: 'I am a woman. I'm a writer, speaker, and media personality.' Then I remind myself of who I'm meeting with, saying 'He is a man. He has his own business. He needs to let

---

A Premise for All Occasions

1. Remind yourself of who you are. "I am a woman/man."

2. Remind yourself of what you do. "I am a . . ."

3. Remind yourself of who it is you're meeting with—"a man or woman who does what?"

4. Remind yourself of the situation. "Our reason for being here is to . . ."

5. Remind yourself of life's infinite possibilities. "And anything can happen."

others know about his business.' Then I remind myself of our situation: 'We are meeting to discuss how I can help him promote his business.' Then I close the premise by reminding myself, 'And anything can happen!'"

As you come to appreciate and consciously use your emotions to help accomplish your goals, you'll find that the roller coaster of events even the most difficult day brings can be stimulating and challenging instead of debilitating and stressful. You'll also be better prepared to figure out what you can best do about whatever comes your way. You'll be able to stay up, no matter what goes down and you may even discover you can actually enjoy the roller-coaster ride of being your own boss.

RESOURCES

Avocado. This interesting Web site on dealing with mood disorders includes most frequently asked questions about depression. **http://avocado.pc. helsini.fi/-janne/mood**

*Don't Tell Me It's Impossible Until After I've Already Done It.** Pam Lantos. New York: Morrow, 1986. An inspiring and motivational story of how changing your outlook can dramatically change your results and other techniques for doing the seemingly impossible.

*The Emotional Hostage: Reclaiming Your Emotional Life.** Leslie Cameron-Bandler and Michael Lebeau. Moab, UT: Real People Press, 1986. In our view, one of the most important books ever written because it gives you the tools and understanding to create a world of full emotional choice.

Emotional Intelligence. Daniel Goleman. New York: Bantam, 1995. Emotional intelligence includes self-awareness and impulse control, persistence, zeal and self-motivation, empathy and social deftness. Goleman shows how emotional intelligence can be nurtured and strengthened in all of us.

The Feeling Good Handbook. David Burns. New York: Plume, 1990. An invaluable guide to dealing with fears, anxieties, panic attacks, procrastination, and communication problems.

*Life Without Fear: Anxiety and Its Cure.** Joseph Wolpe, M.D., and David Wolpe. Oakland, CA: New Harbinger Publishing, 1988. Learn how to

*A classic.

systematically desensitize yourself to anxiety-provoking people, places, objects, and situations.

Love Is Letting Go of Fear. Gerald Jampolsky, M.D. Berkeley, CA: Celestial Arts, 1979. A classic book about choosing peace of mind every day and every minute.

Managing Your Anxiety: Regaining Control When You Feel Stress, Helpless and Alone. Christopher J. McCollough and Robert Woods Mann. New York: Tarcher/Putnam, 1995. A practical self-help program that helps you not just cope with near-immobilizing anxiety, but overcome it.

Release Your Brakes. Jim Newman. PACE Organization (Box 1378, Studio City, CA 91614), 1988. Newman, who originated the concept of the comfort zone, sets forth how we use our emotions to put on the brakes and prevent ourselves from achieving our fullest potential. He then introduces his method for taking off the brakes and testing our limits.

When Anger Hurts: Quieting the Storm Within. Matthew McKay, Ph.D., Peter D. Rogers, Ph. D., and Judith McKay, R.N. Oakland, CA: New Harbinger, 1989. A step-by-step guide to changing habitual, anger-generating thoughts while developing healthier, more effective ways of getting your needs met.

Your Perfect Right. Robert Alberti and Michael Emmons. San Luis Obispo, CA: Impact, 1990. The assertiveness bible; helps the nonassertive speak up and the aggressive tone down.

*A classic.

7

Staying Up No Matter
What Goes Down

If you continue toward your goal, it will happen but not necessarily on your time schedule.

KEN BLANCHARD, AUTHOR

NOW THAT YOU'RE THE BOSS, not only do you have to keep yourself motivated and on track; you've also got to be the one with the answers and the solutions. There's no one to refer things up to or delegate down to. You're the one who must evaluate your progress and assess your performance. You have to help yourself understand and respond to your circumstances no matter what they may be, on a day-by-day, minute-by-minute basis. In other words, you have to be the supervisor—the one who oversees and directs, the one with super-vision. You have to be what we call a contextual coach; in fact, it's now one of your most important roles.

Creating a contact for success. Here's an example of the vital role contextual coaching can play. In the 1980s Olympic gold-medal gymnast Tim Dagget broke his leg, less than a year before the qualifying tournament for the games in Seoul. Tim's coach helped him put this major setback into perspective so that he could decide whether to try to compete, or not.

With guidance from his doctors, family, and coach Tim decided he would try to prepare for the competition. Here's how he says he was able to frame the task ahead of him at the time: "There are a multitude of things I can do to qualify for the Olympic Games while I'm recovering. There are also things I have no control over at all . . . and if I dwell on those points or worry about them, then I'm taking away from the time I could be spending on the things that can get me to the Olympics. Everybody in the world isn't going to be an Olympic champion. Maybe my leg won't recover in time for Seoul, but the feelings and memories I'll have from just trying will be good enough for me."

As you can imagine, this premise enabled him to work effectively toward his goal and to come out a winner whether he ultimately qualified or not. We hope you'll never be faced with a challenge as severe as Tim's, but you need to be able to put whatever challenges you do encounter into a *context* that will help you respond to them effectively.

For example, if you don't have as much business as you need, how should you interpret this? If suppliers and potential customers are not taking you seriously, what meaning do you make of this? You can interpret these circumstances many different ways. You can take them to mean you're not suited to be on your own, or that you need to do something differently. How you respond will depend on the context you advise yourself to place these developments in.

That's what this chapter is about: providing a context for what to do when you don't know what to do, a context for knowing how you're doing and what you need to do next. We'll also provide a context for how to approach three of the most common problems most self-employed individuals face at one time or another:

- Getting the world to take you seriously
- Not having enough money coming in
- Feeling as though you want to quit

EIGHT THINGS TO DO WHEN YOU DON'T KNOW WHAT TO DO

If you knew you couldn't fail, your spirit would always be looking for success—and would find it.
ARNOLD AND BARRY FOX, AUTHORS

Being self-employed presents numerous situations you don't immediately know what to do about. And when these situations arise, of course, you can't go to your supervisor. So what are you to do?

If you have a network of professional advisers (a lawyer, accountant, computer consultant, and so on), you can turn to them for help in their areas of expertise. But unless you have an unlimited budget and they have unlimited patience, you can't turn to them for advice on the majority of the decisions you need to make. For example, should you take on a particular client?

Can you get a particular project done according to the proposed schedule? Can you bring it in within the quoted price? What should you do about an overdue bill? Are you going to use the same print shop you used last time even though you weren't totally satisfied with them, or should you take the time and the risk to find a new one? Do you use a consultant thousands of miles away whom you know to be good, or, to keep costs down, do you use someone local whose reputation you're not sure of?

The decisions we face when we're on our own are endless and relentless. And we have to resolve most of them by ourselves. Here are several guidelines we've found useful for those moments when you don't know what to do.

1. *It's okay not to know.* Who doesn't have a memory of being called on in class as a child and not knowing the answer? Now, years later, when we encounter something we don't know, we may still get that sinking feeling because we believe that somehow we're always supposed to have the right answer on the tip of our tongue. Well, of course, we don't—and we don't have to. The first step to discovering anything is admitting that you don't know but would like to.

2. *Assume something effective can be done.* No matter what situation you're presented with, if you start from the premise that *problems are solvable,* you'll get much further. You may not know what to do at a particular moment about a specific situation, but you will be able to find out what to do. You have a world of information at your beck and call. In other words, wherever there's a will there's a way, especially today. This is the Information Age, after all. And if you can't find what you need, an information broker can find answers to the most arcane problems, often for only a few hundred dollars.

3. *Your gut will guide you.* Sometimes you want something so badly, or you're so afraid of losing out on something that looks good, that you make a snap decision even though the little voice in your head or the twinge in your stomach is whispering, "Don't do this!" At other times that little voice is saying, "Go for it!" but your mind is hung up on insignificant details. You probably can remember countless times when you wished you'd heeded that little voice.

Ellen worked as a systems analyst but had been wanting to start a gift-basket service for years. Finally she decided to start the business on the side. She sold a few baskets here and there, but she wanted to sell enough so she could leave her job and devote all her time to her business. Then she met Suzanne. Suzanne had her own travel agency and told Ellen she wanted to order one hundred baskets for a cruise that would set sail in two months.

This could be Ellen's big break! She was excited. But a little voice in her head kept telling her not to incur any costs on this project without money up front to cover her out-of-pocket expenses. Although Suzanne had promised that having these baskets was essential to the trip, she claimed that her cash flow wouldn't allow her to pay for them until after the tour was launched. In her excitement, Ellen decided to go ahead and make up the baskets. She spent many hours and, of course, incurred the full cost of all the materials. So you can imagine her horror when she called to arrange for delivery of the baskets only to have the office manager tell her that the tour had been canceled.

Suzanne took the position that since she hadn't used the baskets, she didn't owe anything for them. In fact, in the crush of her many other projects, Suzanne had conveniently forgotten about Ellen's baskets. Now a lawsuit is pending. Ellen may still get her money, but she's lost valuable time and gone to needless expense. She told us, "I knew I shouldn't have done that. Suzanne even told me about disputes she was having with other vendors. I knew I could have a problem. I just didn't want to pass up the opportunity."

The point, of course, is to trust your *gut*—that inner sense of knowing that the psychiatrist Eric Berne called "the little professor." And even then you will make mistakes from time to time, but at least they won't be ones you knew better than to make in the first place. And you'll get some vital gut training. As Nolan Bushnell, the founder of Atari and Chuck E. Cheese Pizza Time Theater, has said, "If you're not failing occasionally, then you're not reaching out as far as you can." Or as the creativity consultant Roger von Oech reminds us, "Errors are stepping-stones to new ideas." One way to do it right is to do it wrong but not for long.

4. Focus your attention away from the problem.

When a problem develops, instead of focusing on the problem, focus on your desired outcome. Focusing on the complexities of the problem takes your attention and energy away from what you want to accomplish. It traps you in the details of the problem itself. For example, if you see a friend fall into an open manhole, you won't be of much help if you jump into the hole with him, will you? Well, that's exactly what happens when you get ensnared in the complexities of some problem you face. Focus instead on what you want to accomplish, and you'll know better what needs to be done.

Let's say you notice that your revenues are falling. Instead of focusing on this problem, you'll get better results by focusing on what you can do to increase your income. If a client is slow in paying, instead of focusing on your cash-flow problems, focus on how to motivate the client to send you the check quickly. Once you focus on your ideal outcome, you can work backward to figure out how to get there from where you are.

5. Generate multiple possibilities. Once you have a clear idea of where you want to go, start generating as many possibilities as you can for getting from here to there. Postpone evaluating these ideas at first. Just let your mind come up with as many options as you can. Sometimes the more bizarre an idea is, the better. Try using the tips below for generating a variety of workable possibilities. They are distilled from *Whack on the Side of the Head,* by the creativity consultant Robert von Oech.

6. Grapple and let go. After you've grappled with your situation for a while, put it aside. Just let it go. Do other things you need to do. Let your subcon-

Thirteen Wacky Ways to Generate Workable Possibilities

1. Pretend you know what to do. Maybe you do.

2. Think of impractical ideas. They may lead you to practical ones.

3. Come up with illogical ideas. They may lead you to logical ones.

4. Come up with wrong answers; they may lead you to the right ones. In fact, come up with the stupid, foolish, and absurd answers. They may lead to smart, feasible ones.

5. Turn the situation into a metaphor: What if it were a contest? An elevator? A cowboy movie? A vacation?

6. Propose solutions that break the normal rules. As von Oech says, "You can't solve today's problems with yesterday's solutions."

7. Play "What if?" Pretend you're a wizard. What if things could be any way you can imagine? How would the situation you're facing get handled then?

8. When you find the right answer, look for a second one. It may be better than the first.

9. Imagine doing what needs to be done backward. This perspective may give you insight into how to move forward.

10. Consider how someone in another profession or field would approach this. What would an architect do in this situation? An actress? A farmer?

11. Pose the questions you're asking differently. What if the problem isn't what you think it is? As Emerson said, "Every wall is a door."

12. How would your idols handle this situation?

13. Turn what you're doing into a game. Play with it.

scious mind work on it while you sleep or go to the movies. Often the decision, solution, or answer you've been looking for will come to you spontaneously in the midst of something else you're doing. You can get some of your most productive ideas and solutions this way.

7. Talk it out. Sometimes you can struggle with something mentally and get nowhere, but in talking the situation through with someone else you may find that the answers emerge almost magically. The person you're talking with may offer a new perspective or see a nuance you've overlooked because you're so close to the situation.

This person doesn't even need to be an expert on the subject at hand. We're not talking here about getting someone's advice, although that is always an option as well. And certainly if you do that, you should seek the opinion of an expert. What we are talking about here is the value of articulating your situation to see if someone else can understand and relate back to you what he or she hears you saying. Having someone feed back what you're saying is like holding up a mirror in which you see your thought processes. From this new vantage point, you can gain a better perspective on what you need to do.

8. If all else fails, act. As a rule, it's better to do something than nothing. So if you need to act and still don't know what to do, try something. Test out some approach in a small way if possible, and assess your results. If that doesn't work, the results may suggest to you what to do next.

Questions That Help Solve Problems

When you don't know what you need to do, ask yourself these questions, or have a friend or colleague ask them of you.

1. How do you want this to come out?

2. What's important to you about this?

3. How will you know if you've found the answer?

4. When have you handled something like this successfully in the past?

5. What's an example of one possible way you could handle this?

6. How could you do that?

7. How do you know that?

8. What stops you from . . . ?

9. What would happen if you did (or didn't) do that?

Making Sure You're Taken Seriously

To earn your own respect is to have the greatest respect of all.
PAUL AND SARAH EDWARDS

The most common complaint we hear from people who work from home on their own is that they aren't being taken seriously by clients, customers, family, or other business contacts. And this is not surprising because there is still some institutional prejudice against being self-employed, especially if you're working from home. For example:

- Trade suppliers sometimes won't extend credit or give priority to small businesses.
- Large companies may put a freelancer or independent contractor at the bottom of their list of who gets paid.
- Unscrupulous individuals may even figure they can break contracts with self-employed individuals they don't think will have the funds to sue them.
- Sometimes potential customers assume home-based, freelance, or single-person businesses are less substantial and reliable and require them to be twice as good as a larger business would need to be.
- Many banks categorically refuse MasterCard and Visa merchant accounts to home-based businesses.
- Many temporary employment agencies won't send personnel to a home office.

As the ranks of thriving, successful independent workers continue to grow, however, these institutional barriers are coming down fast. In the meantime, we each have to find ways to make sure that those we deal with do take us seriously. So, over the years, we've been curious as to how the most successful self-employed individuals go about assuring that they are taken seriously.

Surprisingly, many of the most successful self-employed individuals we spoke with reported that they never have problems with being taken seriously. In fact, although it is one of the most common concerns self-employed people have, it was actually a concern for only one out of five of those we spoke with. Here are some comments that suggest why they are not having this problem.

The publicist Kim Freilich told us, "I've always been taken seriously by business contacts because I have a very expensive brochure and the reaction

I get is that no one spends that kind of money on a brochure who isn't serious."

The private-practice consultant Gene Call reported, "I never have had a problem being taken seriously. I have never thought of working from home on my own as a negative. I keep a clear separation between home and office. I've always made housekeeping a priority, so everything is neat and clean. Between 9:00 and 5:00 my home looks like an office. I always go out for breakfast, for example, so there will be no cooking odors or anything like that. I dress for business and return to the office after breakfast."

Wellness researcher Dean Allen said, "People take me seriously because I'm an expert. I think of myself as a recognized professional. In fact, I think I'm one hundred years ahead of my time—and I project that. I won't let anyone treat me any other way."

The accountant Michael Russo has found, "To be treated with credibility, you have to be projecting credibility. You have to project that you're in it all the way."

The career consultant Naomi Stephan told us, "If I approach what I do seriously and I take myself seriously, then they have to take me seriously, too. One bank told me I couldn't get MasterCard and Visa because I didn't have a bona fide office. So I changed banks." Not only did she get a MasterCard and Visa merchant account at her new bank, she also got a $10,000 secured loan to purchase her office equipment.

The bookkeeper Chellie Campbell has had a different experience: "The big firms automatically think I'm the secretary, but I let it roll off my back. I make a joke out of it." They're surprised to discover she runs a five-person office and earns $36,000 a month.

The professional organizer Dee Behrman remembers that when she first went out on her own, she didn't have the confidence she needed to be taken seriously: "I felt like I was on shaky ground, and that affected my credibility. After building up my confidence, I've had no problem being taken seriously."

As you can see, there's one theme that runs through all these comments: *If you take yourself seriously, you will be taken seriously.* But just what does that mean? It sounds so simple. Yet there's a lot that goes into simply believing in yourself. Here's an example of how it can be both complex and simple.

When Sarah was practicing psychotherapy, one of her clients was a young woman who had a long history of personal problems. Through their work together, the young woman began to feel better and better about herself, and as she felt better about herself, she felt better about her life and did better in her life. She felt so good, in fact, that she soon met and fell in love with a man from her church. This young man also had a history of many problems, both in school and on the jobs he'd tried to hold. But he, too, was feeling better about himself and was changing his life—especially now that he was in love.

As the months passed, this couple grew healthier and healthier, and happier and happier. Within the year they decided to marry. Their families and friends in the church were very happy for them. But before they could marry, they had to attend a prenuptial interview with the priest. They were both nervous about this meeting, and when the day arrived they were devastated by the priest's probing questions. He wanted to know if they thought they were now actually mature enough to marry, or whether they would fall back into their past problems. He wanted to know if they were certain they would be able to handle the many responsibilities of marriage, which he enumerated.

Under interrogation, the couple's confidence collapsed. They became uncertain. She became tearful and inarticulate; he got angry and loud. The priest took this as an indication that perhaps they were not as prepared for marriage as they thought and invited them to think about their decision further.

Sarah's client called for an emergency session and arrived in tears. Clearly the couple had gone into the interview seeking reassurance from the priest—validation that they were, in fact, becoming the people they so desperately wanted to be. The priest, on the other hand, was wanting them to reassure him of their progress. He was pulling for them, hoping to see this progress confirmed by their answers to his questions. The interview was actually their chance to shine, but they had taken it instead as evidence of his doubting their abilities.

As the young woman came to realize this misunderstanding, her confidence returned. She left the session excited and clear about what she needed to do. She explained the situation to her fiancé, and they returned to talk to the priest with renewed confidence, eager to show him how happy and successful their lives actually were. As you can imagine, the priest was elated and their wedding was a marvelous celebration, not just of their marriage but of their victory over their pasts.

Of course, while most people going out on their own do so with a good and sometimes sterling past, we have nonetheless often thought how similar the plight of this couple was to that of a self-employed person who wants to be taken seriously. Underneath it all, the banks, the potential customers, the suppliers, and the many other people we have to deal with are usually actually pulling for us. They're predisposed to want us to be someone they can do business with. It's to their advantage. But they have to see this first. Others have let them down, and they don't want it to happen again. So, they need us to demonstrate that they can trust us, invest in us, and count on us to deliver for them.

As someone who's newly venturing into the unknown and potentially treacherous territory of self-employment, you're probably eager for any sign of support from those you could work with to validate that, indeed, you can and will succeed. The last thing you need is to be required to prove yourself worthy to every supplier, lender, and customer. Yet, until you're established, that's exactly what you must do. The prize is there for the taking. But you must believe in your own competence and find ways to demonstrate your reliability, dependability, and credibility to others.

In many ways, being taken seriously is like a *rite of passage*. The tradition of going through a rite of passage traces back to the most ancient and primitive of cultures. Throughout time, people have had to stand the test. Granted, sometimes the test may not be a fair one. It may even be an irrelevant one. But one way or another, if you want in you've got to pass the test. You've got to have one of the magic passwords.

Think about it. Chances are, you routinely require such proof yourself from those you do business with. What criteria do you use to screen people before you hire or are willing to buy from them? If you read about a seminar on a topic of interest to you, for example, what do you want to know about the instructor or the company before you pay several hundred dollars to attend? If you need to hire a consultant, or you're selecting a doctor, a mechanic, or a hair stylist, what criteria do you use? A reference from a friend? The size of their office? The location? Their written materials? Their academic background? Their list of past clients? Whatever you use to check them out, those are the magic passwords they must have to get your business.

DRAWING FROM FOUR AVAILABLE SOURCES OF POWER

Fortunately, there is a variety of magic passwords and many different routes to being taken seriously. As we discussed in chapter 2, psychiatrist and author Eric Berne identified four sources of power, any one or any combination of which can bestow on you ample credibility to be taken seriously. Understanding these four sources of power is very useful in explaining why some people have such an easy time establishing themselves while others struggle to be taken seriously.

The best password to anywhere, of course, is to have power from all four of these sources. President Franklin D. Roosevelt is an example of someone who had them all. But very few of us are so well endowed. The more of them you do have, however, the easier it will be for you to be taken seriously. Fortunately, most people can build enough of at least one to be able to succeed on their own.

As you read about these sources of power, you may find yourself feeling angry or resentful or even discouraged. They can serve as the root of prejudice and discrimination. They are undoubtedly the reason for your having missed out on some past opportunities that went to others who you felt were no more qualified or even less qualified than you. But we would invite you to look at these sources of power with new eyes. You'll find you have strengths in some areas and not in others. Think about where your greatest strengths lie and how you can use those to build your sense of authority and stature.

Position Power: Using Your Title

Position power is authority and respect that you command because of the position you hold. The president of the United States, of course, is the ultimate example of position power in this country. Chief executive officer, chief financial officer, foreman, executive secretary, office manager—titles like these bring with them position power. In fact, any position of authority, however small, imbues the person who holds it with a level of authority commensurate with their title.

As self-employed individuals, most of us have very little position power. This is especially true if you are changing fields. It can be particularly frustrating and even surprising for those who are accustomed to the ease with which their previous position opened doors and produced results for them. To suddenly discover that you must build a new reputation before you can command the degree of authority you're used to can be disconcerting. But it can be done. You have other sources of power available to you, and even though you are on your own, there are ways to create the illusion of position power as well.

For example, you can refer to yourself on your card, letterhead, and stationery as president or founder of your own company. "John J. Callahan, President, Corporate Design Services," commands more authority than "John Callahan, Freelance Designer." Or if you want to imply that you're part of an organization, you might give yourself the title "Executive Vice President." There are actually many ways the business name you choose can build your credibility and help you be taken more seriously. For information, see chapter 4 of our book *Getting Business to Come to You,* which we wrote with the marketing consultant Laura Douglas.

You can also capture a bit of the glow from any past position power you may have held by highlighting your previous position on promotional materials or in introducing yourself to others. This is of value, of course, only when your past position has some direct relevance to what you're doing now. For example, when Tom Drucker went out on his own as a management consultant, he always mentioned his prior position as an executive with the Xerox Corporation. And it did, in fact, confer upon him more authority than the average novice management consultant would otherwise command.

To enjoy the benefits of position power, some self-employed individuals have also taken part-time teaching positions at a college or university. These positions enable them to say something like "I am a professional potter. I teach pottery at the art institute." Others have become active in professional or trade associations and have gotten elected to positions of authority within those organizations as a way of building their stature. Some individuals have even founded a trade or professional association as a way to enhance their position power. Still other self-employed individuals have arranged to take positions as regular radio or television commentators or magazine columnists. And, of course, writing a published book in one's field is a proven way to boost credibility.

Historical Power: Using Your Past

Historical power is authority based upon your lineage or your family name. If you're the son or daughter of a respected prominent family or you're carrying on a long-established family business or profession, you automatically inherit the benefits of historical power. Of course, most people going out on their own do not have such an asset. And this is one reason some people buy a business, a practice, or a franchise from someone else who does have some degree of historical power. This is also why you will see slogans like "In Business for 35 Years" on promotional materials.

Sometimes you can gain some degree of historical power by having studied, apprenticed, or worked with a historically prominent individual in your particular field. Therapists, for example, who have studied personally with the founder of a particular psychotherapeutic modality often include this fact in their biographical and promotional materials, and when introducing themselves and what they do. A neurolinguistic programmer, a hypnotherapist, or a family systems counselor, for example, might all highlight the fact that they have studied with the famed medical hynotherapist Milton Erickson. A photographer we met made a practice of pointing out that she had studied with Ansel Adams and had been one of his protégés. Our colleague Dr. Jessica Schairer was a protégée of John Crystal, the famed vocational counselor whom Richard Bolles credits as the source of many of the ideas in his popular book *What Color Is Your Parachute?* This reference has helped Schairer establish herself as a specialist in the psychological aspects of pursing a self-employment career.

Of course, getting references from long-standing leaders in your field is another way of mustering a degree of historical power you could not command on your own.

Cultural Power: Using Your Credentials

Cultural power arises from the values of the culture within which you work. The academic degrees you hold, the schools you attended, the past experiences you've had, the clients you've served, the money you have, the car you drive, the way you dress—these are all what we refer to broadly as your credentials, and they are all sources of cultural power. Each field and each community will have its set of expected credentials.

A diploma from the Harvard Business School, for example, has traditionally been a passport for being taken seriously in the business world, but it won't help as much if you're trying to break into a career on the stage or as an organic gardener. The formal academic or professional background that will provide you with cultural power varies widely from field to field.

In some fields, having a certain degree, certification, or other credential is a mandatory ticket without which you simply cannot succeed—particularly on your own, where you are operating without supervision. Other fields are more open, and often people will forgo the time and expense of obtaining particular formal credentials. In fact, in some circles, it's a negative to have an academic background, so some Ph.D.'s find it helpful to leave that credential off their promotional materials. You will find, however, that being taken seriously will be much easier if you do invest in obtaining the expected ticket for entrance into a field, whatever that may be.

In an effort to enjoy the benefits a credential conveys without investing the time and money involved in obtaining further academic credentials, some self-employed individuals will earn a credential through their professional or trade association or an independent licensing body of some kind. The National Speakers' Association, for example, has a certification process for its members. Insurance professionals, management consultants, and financial planners can obtain certification through their professional associations, too. Such credentials matter most to the members themselves, but with referrals accounting for a major percentage of how much business one has, such respect can mean a lot.

Some colleges and universities offer certificate programs in fields like public relations, script writing, and so on. These are not full degree programs, but they do provide a credential upon completion. And often the greatest value in completing such programs is the important contacts you make in the process.

In addition to these more formal credentials, every field also has a set of informal credentials, which we call the ideal image. Successful people in any field look a certain way, act a certain way, drive certain types of cars, have certain beliefs, skills, and attitudes, and so forth. The better you fit that ideal image, the easier it will be for you to be accepted and respected in that field. Certainly dressing for success in your field is a simple and relatively inexpensive ticket that will help you get in the door. It's one that anyone can acquire, even on a limited budget. All you need to do is to take note of the most successful people in your field and follow suit, adapting their choices to your own style and preferences. Your goal here is to get past the doorman, so to speak, not to become a carbon copy of someone else. And even if those at the top of your field have clothes, materials, and equipment you can't afford, you can usually acquire the needed "look" without necessarily paying an exorbitant price.

Some people rebel at the idea of dressing for success or otherwise putting on the trimmings of success. And, of course, as your own boss you are free to dress and conduct yourself however you please. Just be aware, that how you dress and act can make the job of being taken seriously a lot easier or a lot harder.

Kathryn and Mark gave communications training courses for educators until government cutbacks dried up funds for teacher education. They quickly decided they would shift to offering their courses for corporate managers. But they were unable to even get in the doors of the personnel directors who could hire them. They recognized that they had little corporate experience, so they conducted a number of complimentary programs for executives from various companies to build a track record with corporate managers. Their evaluations from these programs were good, and they received some glowing references. They thought they had solved the problem of being taken seriously.

And yes, they were able to get appointments with several personnel directors. But still none hired them. "They still don't seem to be taking us seriously," Kathryn told us. Having done a lot of corporate training ourselves, we could see the problem. Kathryn and Mark did not convey the image of corporate trainers. They dressed too casually, Mark in a sport coat and open collar, Kathryn in slacks and flats. Corporate culture, at that time, called for both men and women to wear suits, with ties for men and high heels and hose for women. We shared our observations with Mark and Kathryn. They were amazed after making these simple changes at the altered reactions they got. Suddenly they were being taken seriously.

Ironically James Wade had the opposite experience. His background as a marketing expert had been with the banking industry where more formal attire was expected. When he opened his own PR firm, however, he had the opportunity to do business with several new multimedia start-up companies. He found it difficult to establish rapport and be taken seriously when he showed up in suit and tie to meet with the young execs who were wearing sweaters and slacks. He came off as stodgy and outdated instead of creative and on the cutting edge. He told us, "I was amazed at how much better my appointments went when I shifted my wardrobe to what is called 'business casual.'"

In addition to image, another form of credentials involved in cultural power includes being able to talk the talk and walk the walk. Every field has a vocabulary and a set of concepts and issues that its members are expected to use and understand. Using the right vocabulary, so to speak, says you're one of the club. In any field there is a certain way things are done and other agreed-upon ways that things are not done. These informal and often unstated rules may or may not actually be important to doing a good job, but they are the passwords. The best way to make sure you can talk the talk and walk the walk is by participating in the professional and trade associations or organizations of both your field and the fields of your customers and clients.

An aspiring professional speaker we'll call Joyce told us of an unfortunate example of how this aspect of cultural power works. Joyce wanted to speak to corporate management groups that hire outside speakers. So she paid to be featured in a showcase where corporate meeting planners came to see prospective speakers. Joyce gave an excellent presentation, and many meeting planners rushed up to find out how they could book her. One meeting planner asked her what she charged and she freely volunteered that she had spoken for many different fees, so it all depended on what was needed.

Obviously Joyce had committed an unspoken no-no, because within minutes the many meeting planners who were clustered around her began drifting away, and she got no bookings from the showcase. She had no idea what she had done, but in talking with other speakers she discovered that the unwritten rule among these meeting planners was that professional speakers don't discuss fees in public and most certainly don't indicate they have flexible fees.

Joyce paid a very high price to find out the rules. From that point on, however, when she prepares to market to a new clientele she does her homework first so she can talk the basics of their talk and walk the path they walk without stepping on any unexpected land mines.

Personal Power: Using Your Charisma

Personal power is the authority you command by the force of your own personality, will, intention, and results. Here is where everyone can excel. This is the one most valuable source of authority you can have. It's why we can say with confidence that if you take yourself seriously, others will, too—at least over time. This power may be called charisma, and while that word is usually reserved only for those special individuals who can move crowds of thousands with simply a look or a word, we believe all people have the capacity for a charisma that comes from developing their own personal effectiveness to the fullest. All of us have our own unique personal qualities that can imbue us with influence and authority.

If we do not use or develop these qualities, of course, no one will perceive them. You may have had the experience of meeting people who made no particular impression on you whatsoever. They may have seemed like wallflowers receding into the woodwork. But when you met them again, perhaps years later, you were amazed at their transformation into impressive, unforgettable individuals. Whereas they once passed unnoticed in any crowd, now heads turn when they entered a room. Whereas once their voices were lost in normal conversation, now everyone listened to them with rapt attention. Whereas you once would have forgotten their names if you ever heard them in the first place, now their names remain emblazoned in your mind.

Such individuals are outstanding examples of the magnetism of personal power. And we can all command this power. We all have the ability to be stunning, awesome, arresting, prominent, sensational, noteworthy, and significant. We all have the capacity to inspire trust, confidence, dependability, legitimacy, authority, and credibility. But we must each develop these capacities in ourselves. The more competent, capable, and effective you become, the more you will reflect these qualities in everything you do—the way you talk, the way you walk, the way you dress, the way you conduct yourself. You won't need to affect credibility; you will simply project it.

We've always been intrigued how often when asked if success has changed them, highly successful individuals will quickly say, "Oh, no. I'm just the same. Success hasn't changed me." Chances are they are not the same. Success has probably changed them considerably, in that they're probably much more of all they can be. You can't achieve success and maintain it for very long without becoming more of what you're capable of being.

Success demands more of you. To achieve success you have to bring out your best qualities. You have to overcome your worst qualities. You have to become a more effective, more capable, more caring, and more productive person.

But here's the best news. Your own personal power is the most valuable of the four sources of power. The other three can only get you in the door. Personal power, however, enables you to produce the results you need to make sure you can come back again and again. The offspring of successful entertainers and politicians are often asked if their family name helped or hindered them in following in their parents' footsteps. Usually they will say that yes, the name did help them, but only to gain access, only to get in the door. Once they got the audition or got into the office, they had to produce results or they didn't get to come back.

Personal power is what enables you to produce results. Nothing produces success like results. If you produce results for people, you will be taken seriously. You will get repeat business. You will get referrals. The better the results, the more seriously you will be taken, and the more your personal power will grow. Then you'll find people actually going out of their way to support you.

Developing personal power, however, is a process. When I, Sarah, opened my private practice as a psychotherapist, I had very little personal power. I had been accustomed to having the power of the United States government behind me when I spoke, and believe me, people listen to someone who holds the power to give or withdraw federal grant funds. But having left that power behind, how was I to get people to listen?

Without my title, I discovered people didn't even remember my name an hour after they met me. Usually they didn't recognize me the next time they saw me. Ideas I raised and comments I made during conversations were often attributed to someone else. Sometimes people had to ask me to speak up so they could hear me. I felt my lack of personal power dramatically. I felt as if I had become an invisible woman.

But I began working with people who already knew and trusted me. I attended personal-growth classes, took lessons in projecting my voice, read books on self-esteem, took acting and improvisation classes, hired an image consultant, and forced myself to give speeches and seminars until I felt at ease speaking from a podium and could capture and hold people's attention.

As time passed I could literally feel my self-confidence growing. People I counseled were improving from our sessions. My personal power was building. I started to feel, look, and act like someone I would admire. Once I began to feel like the person I'd always wanted to be, people started remembering my name, recognizing me, and even seeking me out because others had told them about me. I began enjoying the strength and assurance that personal power imparts. And I can tell you with all confidence that if I can develop personal power, anyone can do it.

To boost your personal power, identify and maximize your talents, your strengths, the things you do well. Use them, develop them, refine them, and improve them. Begin working with people or companies that already know you and do take you seriously. Establish a history of results. This is exactly how Michael Cahlin built Cahlin Williams Communications. When Michael began his public-relations and marketing company, he worked with smaller companies that the larger agencies wouldn't take. Often he wasn't their first choice. He charged a lower fee with certain specified goals and an up-front retainer. The balance was due upon satisfaction after a trial period. He says, "After they saw the results, they were willing to pay the money. Now after seven years I'm getting bigger clients and I'm beginning to be their first choice." He has a thirty-to-forty-page capability statement now. It's his track record, and when people see it they take him seriously.

You Don't Have to Fake It to Make It

So you see, to be taken seriously you don't need to put on a facade and hype yourself like a carnival pitchman. Quite the contrary. If you approach the hurdles people seem to put in your way to being taken seriously as part of the race, getting over them simply becomes a matter of taking them in stride.

Hurdlers expect the track to be strewn with hurdles, and they know that how they get over them is what will enable them to win. So if you think of being on your own as like running hurdles, you won't be surprised by the barriers you encounter. They're not obstacles; they're there to test and hone your skills. They make you a more accomplished runner, so to speak.

From this perspective, we no longer need to resent the demands suppliers, customers, and other institutions place on us. We no longer need to rebel against them or be intimidated by them. We can think of them as rites of passage, not as personal indictments of our abilities. They become a chance to show off, an invitation to dance. And they enable us to become much more effective, confident, productive, and capable.

That's what J. B. Morningstar found in starting her own line of healthy chocolates. She told us, "We think we have to do a little dance and that if they don't like it, we have to keep trying harder until we get the dance right. We think we have to try to be someone we're not. But that's not it. It's about finding the best in yourself and showing that you can do what needs to be done in the language your marketplace understands."

In other words, it's not a matter of having to choose between doing it your way or doing it their way. You don't have to try to give people what you think they want. You can give them more than they've dared to dream. The screenwriter Quinn Redecker, who wrote the Academy Award–nominated screenplay for *The Deer Hunter,* put it this way: "You have to do what you care about passionately and make them like it. You have to show them something, something they like. Take them someplace they've never been. Show them something they've never seen."

It's been said that there are two sets of rules: the rules for people who want to get in and the rules for people who are in. And it's certainly true that everyone gives you greater latitude once they trust you and believe in you based on a track record of success. But truthfully, people are willing to make exceptions, give a chance to the novice, consider the unusual, the new, the different, the untested—if you can make doing this so appealing and desirable that they can't resist it. And that's what personal power is all about. It's about developing and showing off your magnificence and excellence as only you can. And when you do that, not only will people take you seriously, they'll do so eagerly.

Five Attitudes That Get in the Way of Being Taken Seriously

There's one thing that will sabotage all your other efforts to be taken seriously, and that's having an MBA—a *Marginal Business Attitude.* Whether you're a freelancer, consultant, an independent contractor, an artist, a performer, or a craftsperson, if you're self-employed, you are in business. And if you don't have an SBA—a *Serious Business Attitude*—ultimately no power base or amount of image building will convince your public that you're for real.

A Marginal Business Attitude will show through in your business dealings like a potbelly in a bathing suit. And just as when your fly is open or your slip is showing, chances are no one will point it out to you. Instead of wondering why everyone's looking at you so funnily, however, you'll be wondering why no one is taking you seriously. This means you've got to be the one who makes sure your attitude is on straight. Here are five common signs of a Marginal Business Attitude and how to avoid them.

1. *I'll work when and if.* One of the benefits of being your own boss is the flexibility to do the kind of work you want when and if you choose. But erratic hours coupled with excuses and exceptions sends a message that you're not serious about your work. Someone with a Serious Business Attitude puts business first during business hours.

Here's an example of what we mean. An event planner had been trying to get a contract with a certain corporation for many months. Finally they called her on the spur of the moment and asked if she would do a special event the following week. She told them she'd love to, but that she had houseguests that week and asked that they call her another time. To this day, she continues to complain that she isn't taken seriously. To be taken seriously, you have to be there and deliver when you have the opportunity.

2. *I don't have the money for that.* Often self-employed individuals bemoan the fact that they don't have enough money to do what they know they need to do to be successful. If you really believe in yourself and take your business seriously, however, you will have the confidence to use credit and profits to buy what you need to be taken seriously. Serious business owners realize that money begets money. The money you spend on your business allows your business to grow. Money reproduces itself. You invest money to make money. You will have the confidence to use credit and profits to buy what you need to be taken seriously.

A home-based seminar leader, for example, aspires to big-time fees of $5,000 a day. His courses are excellent, so he could command such fees. But although he knows he needs a laser printer to create topnotch handouts, he hasn't purchased one. Although he knows he needs exposure, he doesn't advertise in the trade journals, nor does he have a newsletter to keep in touch with previous and prospective clients. He wants to do all these things, but he believes he can't afford to and continues to complain that he doesn't get the respect or command the fees he deserves.

In fact, with a laser-quality printer, he could design his own ad for the trade journal and create the marketing newsletter he wants to send out. And, at his fee, he would be able to cover the cost of the printer with less than half of the income he receives from the first client these marketing efforts bring. So, to be taken seriously, you have to throw what money you have in the direction you want to go. Your success will follow.

3. *I can't charge that much.* One of the most common mistakes propreneurs make is to underprice their services. It's almost as though they have an inferiority complex because they're small or work from home.

Here's a good example of how this works. A home-based newsletter publisher was just barely keeping his doors open when he finally hired a business consultant to help diagnose the problem. The consultant's advice was to triple the price of the publication. The owner reacted angrily: "Gee, I can't do that! People won't buy it at this price!" "That's right," the consultant replied. "A newsletter as cheap as yours can't be that good." The publisher tripled the price and tripled his subscriptions in three months.

To be taken seriously, your price must convey value. Serious business owners charge what they need to charge in order to succeed. They make sure their price covers the income they want to make plus all their costs of doing business. Then they offer their product or service to people who need it and have the resources to pay for it. And they make what they offer so appealing that those who need it will willingly pay that price.

4. *Being on your own is so tough.* We've noticed that serious business owners love the challenge of being on their own and realize that ups and downs are part of the process. They take the fluctuations in stride and talk about what they're doing rather than what's being done to them. They have a "lucky me," not a "poor me," attitude.

Marginal business operators, however, always have a ready complaint, a catastrophe, or a slight to report. They give their power away by complaining. When we complain we assume that someone else can solve the problem, that someone else holds the power to make things better. But you have the power. So seize it. When times get tough, focus on your purpose and your goals, and get on with what you're doing. Complaining isn't going to change things anyway. When you hear yourself complaining, take some action right then and there to do something about whatever's bothering you.

It doesn't matter what field you're in: success flocks toward success and runs from failure. So you have to expect and project success.

5. I do a lot of different things. Those with a Marginal Business Attitude tend to dabble in multiple things at the same time on the grounds that if one thing doesn't work out maybe something else will. They try to be all things to all people in hopes of being something to someone.

We know an aspiring propreneur who falls into this category. Every time we talk with her she has some new direction for her business. First she was a freelance foreign-rights distributor for publishers. Then she was creating greeting cards. Next she was starting a national association. As she speaks of these new directions, she also complains bitterly about how people never take her seriously.

To be taken seriously, you need to decide what you want to do most and give 100 percent of what you've got to that for as long as you've got. That type of commitment says that you have a Serious Business Attitude. Is it any wonder that ads reading "In Business for 25 Years" are taken seriously?

We have many other examples of how a Marginal Business Attitude can work against people who are trying to make it on their own: the young mother who lost a project when she didn't meet her promised delivery date because her daughter developed a cold; the typesetter whose printing contractor always lets him down so he gets behind on his jobs; the electrician who can't afford an answering machine so his teenage son forgets to tell him about calls from prospective customers; the musician whose music gets little radio play because he charges for his demo tapes to cover the cost of their production.

If you want to be taken seriously, you have to take yourself and your business seriously enough to do what you know you need to do to succeed. And when you do, everyone else will, too. In fact, they'll start making exceptions for you. It's true that there are two sets of rules: rules for those who want in and rules for those who have demonstrated they can play by the rules.

In *Working from Home* we identify a dozen money-saving ways you can give yourself a Fortune 500 image—simple things like using a federal ID number instead of your Social Security number on business-related forms, using software so you can pay your bills by printing out customized checks instead of writing them out in longhand, using VIP call forwarding to your cellular phone so you won't miss key calls. Attending to little details like these helps to convey that you are serious about yourself and that you mean business.

What to Do When You Don't Have Enough Money

*We were born to be rich or inevitably to grow rich through
the use of our faculties.*

RALPH WALDO EMERSON

USA Today reports that worrying about having too little income to pay the
bills effects 55 percent of all households. But shrinking the month to match
the money is particularly challenging to those of us who are self-employed.
Those who have been on their own for any time at all will tell you that cash
flow is the lifeblood of surviving and thriving on your own. It takes the place
of your paycheck, and without a reasonably steady flow of cash, both you
and your goals and dreams will go hungry.

Often when a business is slow in taking off or hits a stall, people will ask
us, in desperation, "Where can I get some outside money?" In most cases,
however, this is the wrong question. Banks and investors are rarely interested
in loaning money to self-employed individuals—especially when those individuals are struggling to stay afloat. Outside money from loans and investors
can be a way to finance expansion of an ongoing single-person business (see
Credit Sources in chapter 2), but they are not a reliable route for getting the
operating expenses you need to get a business going or keep it afloat.

Ninety-nine percent of the time when you become self-employed there's no
need to locate outside money for operating expenses. You're not Donald
Trump. You don't have a big payroll. Chances are you don't have significant
overhead, especially if you're working from home. You need to make enough
money to support your business and yourself. And if you are providing the right
product or service, your clients and customers can provide you with that support. Ultimately your customers are your only source of funding. Even if you
are able to get a loan, it's your customers who will enable you to pay it back.

If you discover there's not enough money coming in, don't start from the
premise that you must find some outside money. And don't take it as a sign
that you need to fold up shop and take another job. Start from the premise
that there's a way for you to get enough customers to pay you sufficiently to
support yourself. In other words, when you experience a cash crunch, don't
ask how you're going to find someone to loan you some money. Ask instead
how you can get the money you need from increasing your service to more
clients or customers, or doing more business with existing customers.

Like it or not, when you're self-employed, money is a barometer of how
well you're doing. And we can be thankful that it is. The constant feedback a
bank balance provides means that you can't fool yourself into complacency
for very long. Jerry Gillies, the author of the best-selling book *Money-Love,*
puts it this way: "Money is a vehicle to take you to your desires. It's an ex-

tension of your personality. So-called money problems are not problems at all, but results that are dissatisfying. If you get results that don't satisfy you, it is because you are doing something to achieve those results. Many people want to solve their money problems without changing what they are doing to achieve those results. You have to change what you are doing if you want to change the results [you're getting]."

So if you don't like the state of your cash flow, look at what you are doing that's resulting in less income than you want and identify what you can do differently to produce better results.

The Only Three Reasons for Not Having Enough Money

It's easy to come up with a myriad of reasons for not having enough cash on hand: your marketing let you down, people don't appreciate the value of your service, the competition is undercutting your price, your overhead is too high, the market is sluggish, and on and on. Most of the endless list of reasons we give ourselves for not making as much money as we would like, however, are simply excuses. When it comes right down to it, unless you are wantonly overspending, there are only three reasons for not having enough money:

1. *You don't have enough business.* This is the most common reason for not having enough money. If you were operating at your peak capacity and your time was filled with paying clients and customers, chances are you would have enough money.

2. *You're not collecting the money you're due.* This is the classic cash-flow problem many small businesses face. It happens when you're actually making enough money from the work you're doing but you're not getting paid soon enough to have the money on hand when you need it.

3. *You aren't charging enough.* If you have plenty of clients to fill your time and you're collecting everything you're owed and you still don't have enough money, you are not charging enough or you're not packaging your products or services in a way that allows you to charge what you need.

There are many ways to change what you're doing that will produce better results in each of these areas.

Diagnosing What You Need to Do to Get More Business

All the people we interviewed for this book told us that at one time or another they didn't have enough business. Although the solution to not having enough business is really a simple one—get more business—the question becomes why you don't have enough business and what you can do about it. Here are several questions you can ask yourself to determine what you need to do:

1. *Is there actually a need for what you're offering?* If there seems to be little interest in what you're providing, see if anyone else is making money with this product or service. If no one is, it could be a sign that you need to change the nature of your product or service to something for which there is more of a demand. This was the problem for Rosalind, a family counselor. She wanted to teach parents how to convey values to their children, but parents weren't interested in her classes. She did discover, however, that many parents wanted to learn how to teach their children to deal with sex, drugs, and potential child abusers. So she restructured her programs to meet that need, and her classes began to fill. And by the way . . . she's still teaching values. They're just in a new package.

How can you determine whether there's an ample demand for what you offer? And if not, how can you repackage or redefine what you do to meet a more pressing need.

2. *Are there too many other people offering what you do?* Frank wanted to teach presentation skills to corporate managers. At first he thought his proposals weren't up to snuff. But by talking with some of the personnel buying these programs, he learned that in his community there were at least five trainers for every company needing these programs. As a result of this glut, very few of these trainers were earning a full-time living from presentation-skills training.

Given this reality, Frank had several choices. He could travel to other communities to offer training. He could come up with a strategy to beat out the competition. He could develop training programs on other subjects to supplement his income from presentation-skills training. Or he could offer presentation skills to some market other than corporate America. He decided to do the last and began offering presentation-skills training for professional fund-raisers. Although he could not charge as much per day, he got more work.

How could you carve out such a niche for yourself?

3. *Are the people who need you aware of what you offer?* If other people are succeeding at what you're doing and there's plenty of demand for it, this may be a sign that not enough people know about you. And that means you need to step up your marketing efforts. If people who need your product or service don't know what you have available, how can they do business with you?

For example, in health-conscious Los Angeles there are plenty of people who would love J. B. Morningstar's healthy chocolates, but they were a brand-new product. People didn't know about them yet. In order to get enough business, J. B. had to create a high profile for her delicious and healthy candy. The more she did this, the more customers she had. How can you make sure more people know about you?

4. Is your offer desirable? People may need what you have to offer and they may know about it, but if they find your product or service too expensive or not in a form they can use, they will do without it or go elsewhere to buy it. You may remember that when Jean and Shaun started a referral service, they set their business up so that in order for them to make enough money, vendors had to pay a listing fee, and people who were interested in a referral had to pay a small fee, too. Vendors were willing and eager to pay for their listing, but individuals were not willing to pay for the referrals. In other words, their offer was desirable to the vendors but not to the customers. Other referral services that have upped their listing fee and given away the referrals have flourished. How could you make your offer more appealing to a larger number of people?

5. Are you doing a good job? If you get business, but your clients or customers don't come back and don't send anyone else your way, it's an indication that you need to do a better job of what you're doing or you need to find a different set of customers who will be happy with what you're providing. You can use the criteria on the next page to honestly and objectively assess your performance.

Lifesaving Measures to Turn Around Tough Times

The key to dealing with tough times is to keep your energy and your efforts up. Slow times need not be fatal or even inevitable unless you succumb to them. When business slows down and money starts to get tight, it's not time to cut back on your sales, PR, marketing, and promotional efforts, although this may be what you're tempted to do. Slow times are a signal to move into high gear, to approach your situation as a challenge and call forth your greatest creativity and ingenuity.

There is always some way to approach a slowdown that will get you through it victoriously. We know propreneurs who have even had to declare bankruptcy; after regrouping and starting again, they still came out on top. In fact, in many such cases the bankruptcy was a turning point leading to their ultimate success. From prayer to promotion, the propreneurs we've interviewed all have their favorite strategies for turning slow times around. Here are several secrets from the source.

Kim Freilich, publicist: "Before my baby was born, I was turning business away. I didn't want to take on too much. But I hadn't done enough planning ahead, and after the baby was born I found myself without enough

How to Know If You're Doing a Good Job

On your own, no one else is there to give you a monthly or quarterly performance evaluation, so how do you know if you're doing a good job? Here are some useful criteria you can use. The more of these you get, the better job you're doing.

- **Compliments, appreciation, and gratitude.** The comments of customers and clients are an important indication of how well you're doing. If they go out of their way to tell you how much your product or service has meant to them, you know you're doing well. If you get frequent complaints, however, you need to take the time to figure out why and make needed changes.

- **Repeat business.** When clients and customers come back again and again, obviously what you're doing is working for them. If they go elsewhere, you should look at what your competition is doing that you're not. If some people come back and others don't, take a look at how you're meeting the needs of some and not of others. You may be able to make a shift in how you serve those you're losing so that you can get them to come back, too.

- **Referrals.** When colleagues, clients, or customers send other people to you, consider it to be an outstanding performance evaluation. It says, "We think you're great." If they don't, it could be a sign that you need to improve. It could also be a sign that they're not aware that you would appreciate referrals, or that they don't know how to go about referring others to you.

- **Meeting internal standards.** We all have our own internal criteria as to what constitutes a good job. Honestly evaluating yourself regularly against your own greatest expectations is one way to keep track of how well you're doing. If you find yourself skimping and slacking off, don't berate yourself; just do whatever you need to do in order to improve.

- **How you feel while working.** If you're eager to get to work, enjoy yourself while you're working, and feel pleased with your output, it's usually a sign that you're doing a good job.

- **Progress toward your goals.** If you can see steady progress toward your goals, you're on track even though it may be taking a little longer than you expected.

business. I made a vow I would never again turn down business unless I didn't want to do the work. I took the Scarlet O'Hara pledge: 'I will never go hungry again.' Now I will farm work out before I'll turn it away."

Gene Call, private practice consultant: "I view slow times as a chance to be creative. I have to plan for times of the year when business is slow. I offer discounts on seminars at the end of the year. I get out and talk to people. I create a new seminar I think my clients want. If they're not buying, I view that as meaning I haven't found the right vocabulary to motivate them. I view everything I do as practice. I'm always looking for ways to make it better."

Michael Cahlin, marketing specialist: "When business is slow, I remind myself that not all the rewards I get are in how much money I make. Anytime I'm not having to work for someone else, things are pretty good. When times are slow, I target a market I think will take off and start going to trade shows and making cold calls. I will cold-call anyone. I find that nine out of ten people don't like their current agency."

And that's exactly what personal power is all about. It's about developing and showing off your excellence as only you can. And when you do that, not only will people take you seriously, they'll do so eagerly.

Cindy Butler, a professional shopper: "I cut back staff and work longer hours. At times I've had to take on other kinds of work and limit expenses until companies are contracting out again."

Chris Shalby, a public-relations specialist: "I had to get past the if-we-can-just-get-through-the-next-month mentality and start thinking of having a regular flow of income. I don't wait for my clients to ask for me to do other work. I propose things I think need to be done. They usually take me up on my proposals."

Ellie Kahn, a corporate biographer: "I have to push myself to make calls and make contacts to increase my visibility. My business comes mostly from word-of-mouth, so I have to use every occasion in my life to connect. I also use publicity. I've had to shift my marketing to reach organizations who could pay my fees, and not focus on people who think what I do is a great idea but can't afford to pay for it."

Dean Allen, a wellness researcher: "The best way to make sure I have plenty of business is to do such a great job that people can't resist coming back and referring to me. Also it's a matter of having the right contacts. I go to the people who could refer to me and demonstrate what I can do. I've spent eight hours just showing someone with influence what I do. When things were slow I'd talk about new things I was working on."

Michael Russo, an accountant: "Because my business is cyclical, I don't expect every month to be high. I know where I stand in relation to last year at the same time. You anticipate the slower times so they're not a shock. And I'm always out there hustling. The bottom line is that you have to keep

Avoiding Slow Times

The best way to deal with slow times is to take steps to prevent your business from slowing down in the first place. Here are several ways to protect yourself from that sink-or-swim feeling of suddenly discovering you don't have enough business.

1. When you're first starting out, line up several clients before you leave the security of your job.

2. Don't rely on one client as the primary source of your business. Even if you have to subcontract business out, build a base of several reliable clients.

3. If you must work with only one client at a time, make sure to set aside several hours each week to market for future business no matter how busy you are in serving that one client.

4. To avoid sudden dips in business, keep your advertising, networking, and other marketing efforts under way during even your busy times. If you wait until business is slow to get more business, you could find yourself without business for months, until your renewed marketing efforts can draw a response.

knocking on doors. You have to make people know you exist. There are people who need you as much as you need them."

Dee Berhman, a professional organizer: "It's a myth that there's never enough business. No matter how much you earn it's always perceptual. I've learned to shift my thinking to believing that I always have what I need."

Sherrie Connelly, a management consultant: "Success comes from responding to possibilities and creating from possibilities. When times are slow, I look for the prime possibilities."

Five Ways to Get Business Fast

The lead time for getting business in the door can be considerable—from as short as several weeks up to several years, depending on the type of business you do. Lead time can be especially long if you're working with large companies that must go through layers of decision making. But if you need business fast and don't have time to wait for the normal marketing process, here are five stopgap measures for getting instant business on an emergency basis. Just be sure you keep up your ongoing marketing efforts, however, so you won't have future emergencies.

1. Get on the phone.   The quickest, surest way to drum up business is to get on the phone and call prospective customers or clients. Begin with your past-client list. Satisfied customers are your quickest and surest source of instant business. Then call contacts who have expressed interest in the past. Use the Yellow Pages or an industry directory, or one of the directories available on-line or on CD-ROMs to find a list of names of other people who might need what you have to offer. Although we know most people hate cold-calling, it does work. And once you get started, it's not nearly as hard as you might think.

Set a goal to make a specific number of calls every day. Just go down the list one by one. Reward yourself for the number of calls you make, not just the number of sales. It may take a lot of calls to get a sale, so the more you make the better. To make this process easier, use any of the following ideas as conversational entrances and as added incentive for immediate action.

If you hate calling by phone, get on-line and start promoting yourself among the many forums, news groups and BBSs your clients and customers participate in.

2. Make a special offer prospective clients can't refuse.   Virtually anything can serve as an opportunity to offer a special promotion. You can have a spring special, a New Year's discount, a free initial consultation, and so on. If, for example, you have a word-processing service you might offer every fourth page free or you might do a complimentary cover-page layout for reports of six or more pages. If you have a bookkeeping service, you might give away one month of service with each yearlong contract signed before a certain date.

A newsletter publisher used a similar promotion when one of his long-running weekly advertising accounts suddenly decided to take a three-month vacation. He called companies that had been hemming and hawing about advertising and told them a special one-time one-month opportunity had come along and he wanted to offer it to them first. He had three one-month specials sold in just two days.

3. Offer a pricing incentive.   Some money beats no money. So offer a special price that's so tempting prospective customers simply can't say no. This can be one of the quickest routes to new business. For example, when Ben Rolada started a community magazine in the suburbs where he lives, he used a special pricing strategy. He needed revenue to cover the production costs of his first issue. So he offered his inaugural advertisers a chance to advertise at half the going rate. And he gave top service for that price: he prepared the ads for no additional fee; and he offered to write a feature article sometime during the year about their product or service. This approach enabled Ben to break even immediately.

His first issue was a success. And since he let the advertisers know how special and unusual this one-time offer was, they were willing to renew at the regular rate. And, of course, having so many satisfied advertisers made getting new ones easier.

4. Subcontract or do overload work. Your competitors can be a good source of quick business. Some professionals get 25 percent or more of their new business from competitors. So scout around and find out who's busy; call to find out if they need backup or if they've had to turn away any projects.

One instructional designer was able to get business quickly in this way when the project she'd been working on was suddenly canceled due to a hostile corporate takeover. She called other instructional designers she knew and told them her plight. Sure enough, one designer had just turned down a job that he didn't have time to do and she got the work.

5. Volunteer. There's nothing worse for morale than having no work at all to do. Therefore, doing some work beats doing nothing. And any work tends to beget more work. Often what begins as a volunteer effort ultimately becomes paid work. Many volunteers are able to turn their experiences into future paying contracts or orders. At the very least, volunteer efforts can be a source of experience and references that you can leverage into getting additional business elsewhere.

What to Say to Others When Things Aren't Going Well

It's a proverbial dilemma we all face when business is slow. You're out talking with colleagues, customers, or prospective clients and they ask, as they always do, "How's business?" What do you say? Do you lie and say, "It's great"? Or do you dare tell them just how bad things are? We've found that people have varied and strong feelings about this situation. Some people are adamant that, when asked, business is always good and sometimes it's very good. Other people are equally adamant that honesty is always the best policy. Still others say that the health report you give on your business should depend on whom you're talking with.

Those who always say business is great believe that you have to put forth a positive, upbeat image no matter how bad things are. Some people feel this is true only when it comes to clients or prospective clients. They don't want to cast any doubt about their future reliability. As one person told us, "I would never let a client know my business is down. Who wants to do business with someone who may not be in business soon? Besides, if you're not busy, people may think you're not very good at what you do. It's like going into an empty restaurant. You say to yourself, 'If the food's so good here,

Who to Pay When There's Not Enough to Go Around

1. When you are temporarily short of funds, pay the following bills first:

   - Expenses related to your bringing in more business—for example, advertising

   - Suppliers whose services you depend on in order to continue offering your product or service—materials, electricity, and telephone service

   - Bills that will pay for themselves—for example, a printing bill for a newsletter that will generate business

   - Bills from people who are giving you referrals

   - Bills from people who have gone out of their way to help you thrive

   - Legally required payments like sales tax, licenses and other taxes

2. Arrange to make partial payments when necessary.

3. Pay the minimum on credit-card charges.

4. Defer optional expenses—things you can do without or do yourself, like magazine subscriptions, airline clubs, memberships, housecleaning.

why isn't anyone here? So keeping up the front of being busy is important to me."

Those who believe honesty is the best policy, however, usually claim that customers and clients know when you're putting them on, so saying things are great when they're not throws even more doubt on your credibility.

Actually, many of the people we talk with are conflicted about what to say when business is bad. "I think I should say that things are fine, but I don't," one person said, "I tell the truth and worry about whether it will affect my reputation." Another person finds that "I never know what to say, so whatever I say sounds pretty bad."

After listening to all aspects of this dilemma, we believe both sides are right. You need to be—and can be—honest and upbeat at the same time. Here are some truthful, upbeat answers people have used when asked the question, "How's business?" that not only inspire confidence but also may help you get business when you need it most.

Tell those who ask:

"It's getting better."

"It's about to take a definite upswing."

"It's taken a little downward dip, but we're about to start a promotion."

"We're creating more."

"How'd you like to help us create some more?"

"We're expecting a really good season."

"It's been a little soft up until now, but let me tell you about this new thing we're doing."

"Let me tell you about what I'm doing with one of my clients."

"We're about to do something that's going to take us through the roof."

"Business is as it needs to be. Right now it's slow, and that gives me time to develop new material."

"I'm busy, but I can still take on more business."

"I can't complain."

"We're plugging along."

Collecting What You're Due

Many people who go out on their own have a casual attitude about collecting fees—at first. The prevailing paycheck mentality leads us to assume that people will pay their bills when they recieve them or certainly within thirty days. Sometimes it's a big surprise when the money you've earned doesn't come in automatically. Far too many self-employed individuals end the year with thousands of dollars of unpaid invoices.

Fortunately, this isn't necessary. But you do have to put your foot down when it comes to getting the money you're due. If you do the following three things, you should not have a collection problem:

- Accept only clients who can pay. We don't believe you're doing anyone a favor by allowing clients or customers to build up a debt they can't pay. If people cannot pay your fee, we suggest referring them to a service or product they can afford.
- Get clear payment agreements and make very few exceptions.
- Follow up immediately on any late payment.

If you find these policies to be too hard-nosed for you, we suggest that you set up a sliding fee scale of some type for people who can't afford your standard fee. Decide how many such customers you are willing to serve, and charge them only what they can pay. Be aware, however, that if you take on too many reduced-fee clients you'll develop a reputation for bargain rates.

Here are some additional guidelines for making sure you get paid with as little effort as possible.

1. Establish a payment policy and make it clear before you begin any work.
Design a policy that best suits your needs. If you are to meet with someone
and there is to be a charge for the appointment, make sure he or she understands the costs ahead of time.

2. Get a signed contract. Before starting any job, get a signed agreement as
to what you will do, what the fee will be (sometimes this will need to be an
estimate), and when payment will be due. This agreement can take the form
of an order form, a letter of agreement, a contract, or a purchase order. For
additional information on negotiating such contracts see *Getting Business to
Come to You,* which we wrote with the marketing consultant Laura Douglas.

3. Get money up front whenever possible. Payment up front in full is prefer-
able but is not always possible. At least get partial payment up front for projects that will involve your efforts over a period of time. Make sure your
up-front payment covers all out-of-pocket expenses. Professional speakers,
for example, often require half their fee in advance in order to hold dates for
their clients. Kim Freilich gets 50 percent up front for publicity tours she
books for publishers. Michael Cahlin requires a monthly retainer that's applied to his fee. He tells his clients, "I'm a small business. I can't wait for a
thirty-to-sixty-day billing period. But I don't take a lot of other clients. You
are always a top priority for me. And I work with you personally. You won't
ever be working with some underling."

4. Collect payment in full upon delivery. Whenever possible require that
your fee be paid in full at the time you deliver the service. Professional speakers, for example, usually require that the balance of their fee be paid on-site
the day of the speech. Word-processing services usually require payment on
delivery of the work. Psychotherapists and other health professionals usually
request payment at the close of each session.

5. If you must extend credit, check it out and tie it down. We advise extending credit only when absolutely necessary and then only with companies
that have an excellent credit rating. Credit is a privilege. Large companies are
sometimes the worst in abusing this privilege and will occasionally delay payment for three to six months. As a single-person business, you often cannot
afford such a delay. So be sure to get written contracts, with payment dates
clearly spelled out. Act immediately when a payment is late. Call the person
with whom you have the contract. If you do work on credit with a company
that has a bad credit history or appears to be having financial problems, acknowledge that you are not doing business; you are gambling.

6. If they don't pay, don't work. If some clients are behind in their payments, do not continue working. Stop working when they stop paying. If you

do otherwise you are saying it's okay not to pay and you're setting yourself up for continued collection problems.

7. Establish a cancellation fee. When establishing your costs, get a clear agreement about your cancellation policy. Cancellation fees should cover any costs you've incurred and lost-opportunity costs.

8. Take legal action if necessary. Most states have some provision for adjudicating small claims. Usually the cost is small. Do not hesitate to take unpaid bills to court. Propreneurs have told us how surprised they were to discover how easy it was for them to recover money that was clearly due them and what a positive effect it had on their self-esteem.

9. Take 100 percent responsibility. Making sure you get your money is completely up to you. If you are not getting the money you're due, don't complain. Don't feel sorry for yourself. It means you took a risk. You worked without money up front. You extended credit. Look at the situation and acknowledge that you allowed it to happen, then see to it that it doesn't happen again. People respect people who respect themselves.

Can You Raise Your Prices or Fees?

If you are working full-time at capacity and collecting the money you're due, feeling as if you are still not making enough money can be one of the most frustrating aspects of being on your own. It can eat away at your morale, create friction with family members, and generally erode your quality of life to the point where you may yearn for a return to the paycheck. But we find that the clearer you are about your financial expectations, the more likely you are to create self-employment opportunities that will actually meet them.

Obviously you need to cover your costs of doing business and keep your business running. Therefore, you need to itemize all your costs including your overhead, and make sure that your fees cover these costs with enough left over *to support yourself at a level that makes it sufficiently worthwhile for you to continue working on your own.* This is simple enough, but it's at this point that many people run into difficulty. What is the level that will make it worthwhile for you to work for yourself? How much is enough? When you can set your income goals anywhere you want, where do you set them? What can you expect? What should you expect? How do you make sure you don't get discouraged by setting unrealistic goals and yet still not settle for less than you have to?

In order to define precisely what you need and want to earn at any given time without limiting yourself, we suggest identifying three specific income goals as follows.

When It's Time to Raise Your Fees

We all would enjoy bringing in additional income without having to work any harder. But most of us hate to raise our prices. We worry that higher fees will turn off new customers. We fear existing clients or customers will cut back on what they buy from us, or worse yet, take their business elsewhere. But actually, many people are surprised to discover that their business increases when they raise their rates. Should you be charging more? Look for these signs that it's time to raise your fees:

1. **Have your business and living expenses increased?** As the cost of living and doing business goes up, your fees need to go up too. So run a report on your business expenses over the past two years to see if and where they have increased. Compare the relationship of your personal income to your business expenses. Unless you raise your fees, a consistent increase in business expenses means a corresponding decrease in your personal income. Your fee increase needs to cover your increased costs plus allow some room for expenses to continue growing. They probably will and you won't want to raise your prices again soon.

2. **Are your fees lagging behind those of others in your field?** If so, it could be time to give yourself a raise. Self-employed and home-based businesses chronically undercharge. Don't fall into this trap. Do you know what others in your field are charging? If not, find out. What's the going rate these days? Sometimes trade and professional associations publish nationwide fee surveys. How do your fees compare? You may discover you're operating at an outdated rate. And actually, customers shy away from products and services they perceive are too cheap,

3. **Do clients agree all too readily to your price?** If you never get a shred of price resistance, it's probably time to raise your prices. To test the waters, notice how your clients respond when you quote your fees. Watch their reactions carefully. Do they comment with a degree of amazement,

1. How much money do you need to make in order to survive? This is the figure you must bring in to keep a roof over your head, clothes on your back, and food on the table. This is an amount below which you cannot go. If the business is promising in the long run, you may be willing to subsist at this level for some period of time as long as you can see how building your experience and clientele will ultimately enable you to earn more. But if your business cannot provide you with this figure, you must make some fundamental changes now in the way you are operating.

It's very sad when people have struggled to make it on their own, gone into

"That's reasonable." Do they snap up your offer a bit too eagerly? Such reactions are a clear indication that you could increase your fees without much resistance.

4. **Have your reputation, service, and expertise grown?** When you're new and less experienced, it makes sense to charge a somewhat lower fee. But as your experience and expertise grow, you can do a better job more quickly. Your time literally becomes worth more. And as your stature and reputation grow, so should your prices. And, as you become better known and more accomplished, new customers will more readily accept higher fees. Most ongoing customers actually expect periodic price increases. Having proven yourself to be a reliable and valued service over the years, you should be able to raise your prices commensurably.

5. **Have you added new technology or other new advances to the way you work?** If so, the value of what you offer has increased. You can command a higher fee for better, faster, or higher-caliber results. Take an inventory. What equipment, training, and other improvements have you added over the past two years to what you do or how you do it?

6. **Is the economy picking up?** Have you been riding out an economic downturn? In tough economic times, prices in an industry often remain static until things pick up. During stagnant times, no one thinks much of raising prices. But as the economy picks up, pent-up demand makes raising prices easier.

The more these signs apply to you, the more likely it's time to raise your fees. They are evidence that you owe it to yourself to raise your rates. Doing so need not be a traumatic event, however. Here are several specific strategies for raising your fees with as little resistance as possible.

debt to keep themselves afloat, and then, psychologically exhausted from not having known what they were in for, had to give up before their venture could become viable. Therefore you need to know exactly what your subsistence level is and have some idea about how long you are willing to live at this level.

This survival figure, and the others that follow, are all completely subjective. Here are three hypothetical examples based on composites of actual individuals. Cheryl, a single mother who transcribes court reporters' notes, believes she can live on no less than $25,000 a year and says she would live at this level indefinitely if it meant she would never again have to work for someone else. Mark, an actor, can squeeze by on $15,000 a year as long as he sees himself making some progress in his career. Kyle, a management consultant, with a family of four, isn't willing to live on less than $45,000 a year, and he doesn't want to live at that level for any more than three years at the longest.

2. How much do you need to feel satisfied? This is the figure your business must be able to produce at some point in the foreseeable future. When you are busy full-time, working at capacity, the fees you charge will eventually need to be able to bring in this figure or beyond; otherwise you will start to feel resentful and bitter about your work.

How to Let Your Clients Know about Price Increases

So, you realize it's time to raise your prices, but you're concerned. You envision horrified clients scurrying away like rats deserting a sinking ship. Fortunately, you can raise your prices without scaring clients away. Here are seven strategies to ease your way into a higher, more profitable fee:

1. **Establish Preemptive Raises.** Build a standard annual cost-of-doing-business fee increase into your written contracts. This is the easiest way to raise prices. Increases will never be a surprise. You won't have to deal with the discomfort of announcing an increase to unsuspecting clients. As long as it's not a substantial annual increase, you probably won't get much resistance. When January first of each year comes around, for example, you can simply start billing at the new rate. A standard annual increase might be 5 percent.

2. **Raise Prices for New Clients Only.** To avoid displeasing a dependable clientele, you can raise fees for new clients only. Valued repeat customers are so desirable, you may want to reward them for their loyalty by keeping them at their originally quoted fee. Of course, as years go by, the time will come when you must raise your fees even for your oldest and dearest clients.

3. **Break the News Gradually.** To reduce the shock of a fee or price increase, announce it in advance. Send a letter, post a notice on your premises, or include it on invoices. Specify when you will be raising your fees and what the new fees will be. January or July first are common times for fee increases. But you can do it at any time. Make the announcement as far in advance as possible. Allow at least thirty days' notice, so regular clients can adjust their budgets to accommodate your new fees.

4. **Provide a Grace Period.** Another way to accommodate existing clients when raising your fees is to delay their fee increases. Tell existing cus-

For Cheryl this amount is $35,000, about $5,000 more than she was earning as a legal secretary before going out on her own transcribing court reporters' notes. Mark is more concerned about acting than he is about earning money; but he's married and he and his wife want to have a child. His wife works, too, however, so if he can ultimately earn at least $30,000 a year, he'll feel satisfied. Kyle won't be satisfied with anything less than $75,000 a year. And he thinks that by working full-time himself he could easily attain that in his consulting firm.

3. How much would you really like to make? Your business must be able to at least hold the potential of hitting this figure or you are likely to feel that you've created your own dead-end job. Each year the Roper organization

tomers that you have raised your prices but that because they're such valued clients, you will not be raising their fees until some specified time in the future. Some people carry their existing clients at the old rate for one year. Then, at the time of their next fee increase, they raise them to the level of the previous increase. Or, alternatively, you might give existing clients a one-time exception at their old rate.

5. **Run a Last-Minute Special Offer.** Make a special offer of some kind featuring "last time at these prices." Not only does this approach prepare clients for a fee increase, it can bring you a rush of repeat or new business. And they all will know that when they call later, your rates will have gone up.

6. **Pretest an Increase.** To be on the safe side, before raising rates for existing clients, you can test the waters with new clients. If they don't balk at your new fees, you'll know you're on more solid ground to raise prices for existing clients too. This is particularly true if you know your new fees are within the range of what others are charging. Your satisfied customers would have little to gain by risking the uncertainties of working with someone else for just about the same price.

7. **Make Special Exceptions.** You can always weigh the value of a profitable long-term client's business against your need for greater income. One long-term high-volume client may be a mainstay for your business. Their business may justify continuing to carry them at your existing rates while raising everyone else's. Meanwhile, build up a full clientele at your new rate. But when you are comfortably established and have ample new business coming in steadily at your new rate, don't hesitate to raise your fees even for a client you've been carrying for several years at the old rate. At this stage, losing a client who won't pay your new fee will make time for you to serve new ones who will.

does a poll of how much money Americans believe they need to fulfill their dreams. The figure keeps going up. In 1994, the median figure mentioned was $102,000 a year.

If Cheryl has dreams that she believes will require $102,000, she is in the wrong business. In fact, if she is hoping to make more than about $40,000, she will probably become disappointed with her business, because that's near the top of what someone can make working full-time transcribing court reporters' notes. Mark, of course, could make a fortune if he hit it big as an actor, so there's no intrinsic limit on his future. Kyle has expectations of earning over $150,000 a year, so he will have to add two associates in order to achieve his ultimate goals.

Having these three figures clearly in mind should help clarify what you need to charge and whether you need to raise your fees. Now let's talk about if, when, and how you can actually raise your fees. The amount of money you can charge as a propreneur is determined by three variables.

- Your self-esteem. You have to be able to state your fees or prices with sufficient confidence and comfort to inspire acceptance of them.

- Your reputation, credentials, and results. Your customers or clients must perceive you as being sufficiently skilled and capable to warrant the fee you're asking.

- The marketplace. Your fees or prices must be within a range that keeps you competitive with others. Retailers and service providers alike have learned that if people can go elsewhere and get comparable results for much less money, they will.

In other words, there are limits to what you can charge at any given time for any given service or product, and you have to determine what those limits are in your field and in your community. First you must determine if there is the potential in your field to charge what you need to charge. If not, you must begin by planning how you can refocus or completely change your business so that you can at least potentially earn what you consider to be enough money.

If, for example, Cheryl eventually hopes to earn $50,000 a year, she must make other plans. Given that there are so many hours in the day and she can work only so fast even at her best, Cheryl will probably not be able to earn $50,000 a year at the prevailing rates for her chosen occupation. If she doesn't want to leave the field, however, she might meet her income goals by hiring others to work for her. Or to bring in additional income she might teach workshops on how to do what she does.

Once you determine that you can at least potentially charge what you need to, you must determine if you now have sufficient stature to command that fee or price. For example, people expect to pay more for treatment by a psychiatrist than by a psychologist. Therefore, as a newly graduated psychologist, you will want to find out the going rate newly graduated psychiatrists are charging. You will also want to find out what the established and well-respected psychologists in your community are charging. You can then set your fees in relation to those at the level that your skill, credentials, and self-confidence justify.

Often self-confidence is the key. Many people fear raising their prices only to discover when they finally work up the nerve to do so that no one complains and sometimes their business actually improves. For example, Gail Bretz of Florissant, Michigan, had been operating her secretarial service, GLB Services and Topnotch Resumes, for two years before she decided it was time to raise her prices. Then not only did she raise them once, she raised them twice! After reading conversations about pricing on the *Working from Home Forum* on CompuServe, she concluded "My skills are worth the money and I don't want to deal with any clients who think otherwise. If you charge bargain hunter prices, you may have plenty of work, but you will also have plenty of trouble with those clients. I just don't think they're worth it. I prefer clients who know that I am worth every penny they pay me." And, by the way, not one client has commented on Bretz's new prices, even though they are now significantly higher!

If, however, you find that you can't initially command the fees you want, you can immediately outline for yourself a course of action for establishing the reputation, results, and self-confidence you'll need to raise your fees to the level you desire. In the chapter on pricing in *Working from Home,* we outline a variety of strategies and guidelines for setting your best possible price.

Do You Have to Cut Your Costs and Living Expenses?

You'll notice that in our discussions about what to do when you're not making enough money, we haven't talked about cutting back your expenses. The reason for this is that we believe in starting from the premise that you deserve to earn the amount of money you aspire to earn—that is, enough for you to feel satisfied, well rewarded, and comfortable. As the bookkeeper Chellie Campbell says to her clients, "Don't ask 'How can I cut back to live within my means?' Ask 'How can I create the means to live as I desire?'"

That's what Liz Danzinger did. Danzinger was working at a full-time job as an editor when she had her first child. She soon realized that she didn't like leaving her new baby all day long for work. But she also wasn't willing to give up the two-career lifestyle, so she decided she needed to create a job for herself working from home that would replace the salary she'd been making while allowing her to work half the time. She knew that meant finding another line of work. After careful exploration, she opened Work Talk, doing technical writing for companies. Now ten years and three additional children later, she still works twenty hours a week and is making more than she would have been making had she stayed in her job.

Of course, once you determine how to create the means you desire, you sometimes must begin doing so within the means you have. But then, you're only living at this lower financial level temporarily. You're cutting back not because you don't have what you want but because you want to do those things that you need to do to create what you want. For most people, these are two very different experiences.

For example, when John and Margaret started their balloon business they knew they couldn't immediately achieve the level of income they'd been earning as managers for a local retail chain. But they had developed a business plan that would put them at double their previous income within five years. Margaret recalls, "We felt like newlyweds again, starting out our lives together eating macaroni and cheese. It was fun even though we had some really tight months. We could enjoy those times because we knew where we were headed. We knew what we were working for. We didn't feel sorry for ourselves. We felt proud about having the courage to do this. It's taking longer than we'd projected, but we can see our progress and we know we'll get there. We even eat out once a week now!"

Here are several tips for setting financial priorities so you feel like the money you have is working to produce what you want from life.

1. *Track where your money is going.* Often people have no idea just where their money goes. Running expense reports with money management software is a simple way to make it abundantly clear where your money is going. Once you see where it's going, you can evaluate if the way you're spending is getting you what you want from life. After running a report on her business account, for example, Pauline Grossman realized that she was spending hundreds of dollars a year on printing and copying bills, most of which she could eliminate by purchasing her own copier and laser printer. After running a report on her personal account, she was horrified to see how much of her income was spent on cigarettes. When she thought about what she'd rather be using that money for, she was finally able to quit smoking, something she'd been wanting to do for years.

2. *Cut unimportant costs to free up funds for what you really want.* With the money Pauline saved on copies and printing, she was able to set aside funds to attend a national conference she had been wanting to attend. With the money she'd been spending on cigarettes, she was able to set aside funds for her family's first real vacation. They went to Hawaii.

3. Sell "stuff" you don't want; invest in what you do. We talked in chapter 3, "Having the Time of Your Life," about applying the 80/20 rule to your life. You can do the same thing with money. By having a garage or yard sale, for example, you can recoup funds for the new things you want. In our case, selling off a camera we rarely used financed our first computer. Selling an exercise machine neither of us ever used paid for a new living-room wall unit to house our radio broadcast equipment.

4. Decide what's most important to you and put your money there. That's what Elaine St. James did. She and her husband took a look at their lives and decided to reprioritize the way they were spending their money so they could get more enjoyment from life. They decided, for example to:

- Make the things in their lives like their cars, home, diets, and finances small enough, few enough, and simple enough that they could easily take care of these things themselves instead of paying other people to do it for them.
- Buy in bulk.
- Resign from organizations that were unrewarding and unproductive.
- Drop subscriptions to magazines they didn't actually read.
- Get rid of all but one credit card.
- Drop call waiting.
- Get a secondhand car.
- Buy clothes that don't need dry cleaning.
- Replace their DayRunner with a simple calendar.

Making these and other simple decisions so greatly improved the quality of their life that St. James decided to write a book about their experience called *Simplify Your Life*. In this book she shares "100 Ways to Slow Down and Enjoy the Things that Really Matter." Of course, the fact that these things simplified St. James's life doesn't mean they would yours. Many of the decisions the St. Jameses made would just complicate ours. For example:

- Buying in bulk would be a hassle for us. We'd rather pay more and leave our time free to do other things we enjoy.
- Using only one credit card would create unpleasant tax-time hassles for us when we had to sort and separate business from personal expenses item by item. The small added cost of having two cards (actually we have three, one for travel expenses) is well worth it for us.

- We'd love to drop call waiting, but the resulting game of "telephone tag" would complicate our day and week and we might even lose money from missed business opportunities.

- We would prefer, if at all possible, to buy new cars. We don't enjoy inheriting other people's problems.

- Clothes that don't need dry cleaning need washing, drying, pressing, folding, so for us that idea gets a big "Ugh!"

- Using a simple calendar would be a double "Ugh" for us. Our time management system clears our minds to focus on one thing at a time without time-consuming and costly oversights that slip our minds.

What's important is not what works best for St. James or for us. It's what works best for you. Often such decisions will be a time-versus-money trade-off. How do you want to spend your time so you can create the money you need to spend your time the way you want to? Clearly what may be important in one person's life is unimportant in another's. We must each decide what will make our lives most enjoyable and put our money, and our time, there.

Defining Your Financial Priorities

Too often financial priorities get defined as a list of things we want to buy: a new car, a new house, a new computer, a laser disk, new tires for the car, paying off the bills, putting a new roof on the house, replacing the water heater, etc. This "purchase list" approach to financial priorities can result in a life filled with things but scarce on whatever truly matters most to you. A study by Merck Family Fund recently verified the old maxim that money doesn't buy happiness. The survey found that 28 percent of the 800 adults polled said they had voluntarily made changes in their lives that resulted in less income but "a more balanced life." Seventy-one percent said they have more "things" than their parents, but only 49 percent described themselves as "happier." And 66 percent wanted to spend more time with family and friends.

So, to set your priorities, instead of thinking about "things" you want, think about the "life" you want. What is most important in your life right now? As you answer this question, summarize your conclusions with three words that represent the three most important things. For example:

- Family, Success, Relaxation
- Security, Health, Finding a Mate
- People, Service, Peace
- Wealth, Happiness, Travel
- Love, Simplicity, Fun
- Freedom, Creativity, Education

Think of your independent career as the lifeboat that will carry and support you in living such life goals. To stay afloat and live the life you desire, you need to operate and maintain your career as a business and keep it running at peak performance. So, make your professional financial decisions based on what will best enable your business to thrive in accordance with your top three life goals.

If you live with others, share your priorities with them, invite them to define what they want most from life, and support one another in achieving these goals. Allocate available household funds accordingly. Doing this will help keep money and money matters in their proper perspective, as a resource to support you in the life you want to lead.

Generally, we find that if you make sure you have plenty of business, collect what you're due, and charge what you're worth, you'll probably be able to create the security and prosperity you're seeking. These steps will help you avoid slow periods, but if they come along, you'll know how to handle them confidently and take action to turn them around fast.

What to Do When You Feel Like Quitting

Feeling, from time to time, that you want to quit working for yourself is as normal as feeling that you want to quit your job. And who hasn't felt like that at one time or another? In fact, we found that most of the self-employed individuals we spoke with in writing this book had entertained the idea of quitting or doing something else at least once. Even though you may not actually quit, we find that allowing yourself the option of quitting is very important for working successfully on your own.

Without the option to entertain the idea of quitting, you become enslaved to your own so-called freedom. Research studies of individuals who work from home clearly show that those who work from home because they choose to are much happier and more satisfied than those who work from home because their circumstances have led them to believe they have no other option. We're convinced the same is true of working for yourself.

So whenever you feel like quitting, we suggest responding the same way a manager would upon hearing that a valued employee is considering looking elsewhere for employment. Take your desire to leave seriously. Look into the source of your dissatisfaction and do what you need to do in your own best interest. For example:

1. Do you feel like quitting because you need a break? Often people feel like giving up when they're tired out, burned out, or bummed out. If this is your situation, give yourself a break. Get some sleep. Take a long weekend. Go on vacation. Do whatever you need to do to get refreshed and rested. Then you can reevaluate whether you still want to quit.

2. Do you want to quit because you don't like what you have to do in order to succeed? Since there is almost always more than one way to do something, if you hate the way you're doing it now, explore other ways you could do what needs to be done or consider how to refocus your work so that you will like it better. Jeannette loved making gift baskets, for example, but she hated selling them. She was about to give up when she called in to talk with us on our radio show.

We asked her this question: If you could run your gift-basket business exactly the way you would want to, how would you run it? She said, "Oh, I'd have someone else sell the baskets, and I would make them." So we suggested that she do just that. At first she wasn't sure this was possible, so we asked her to imagine how she would do it if it were possible. Immediately she said she would find a partner, and so that's what she did.

3. Do you want to quit because succeeding as your own boss is not what you thought it would be? Sometimes being out on your own allows you to discover just how much you enjoy working for and being part of an organization. And if that's the way you feel, that's okay. You know what you need to do. Being your own boss is often an ideal way to position yourself for a permanent job offer. It provides you with more status and makes you more desirable. So parlay your situation into a job you will enjoy more. Deciding you want to take a job again is not a sign of failure; it's simply a sign that you've realized what you really want to do.

4. Do you want to quit because it's time to expand or move on to something else? Sometimes if you've been doing the same thing for several years you can get burned out even though you're doing well enough at it. The dissatisfaction you feel may be a sign that you've settled into your comfort zone and are no longer growing. Why not diversify, try out a new sideline, expand, or take on a whole new direction for your business?

5. Do you want to quit because you don't feel that you're succeeding? If making it on your own has been too hard for too long, it's easy to feel like throwing in the towel. When that's the way you feel, it's time to take an objective look at what you're doing. You don't have to keep going. How much do you want this? How long are you willing to continue? Consider the following insights into why making it on your own is sometimes so difficult and why it can take so long. Then follow your heart.

Does It Have to Take So Long and Be So Hard?

Most of us go out on our own with visions of sugarplums dancing in our heads. We may fear failing, but we don't expect to fail. We expect success to be right around the corner. And society encourages our optimism. Movies and television feed our expectations. In one movie Diane Keaton plays a divorced woman with low self-esteem who decides to start her own business and becomes an overnight millionaire—in less than thirty minutes of screen time. A television series features a young mother who decides to write a children's book and, after minor setbacks, gets it published within the thirteen-week season. Magazines and newspapers feature inspiring stories of immigrants and high-school dropouts who have built successful businesses overnight.

We love these stories, and thank goodness for them. They tantalize us and make us think we can do it, too. They give us the courage to rise above our doubts and limitations and go for our dreams. They help us believe that dreams come true. Sometimes, however, it doesn't go the way it does in the movies, television, books, or magazines. Sometimes success is not around the corner or even around the block. Sometimes it takes what feels like a long, lonely lifetime. And it's at those times that we most need to understand why it's taking so long, why it seems so hard for us while it seems so easy for others.

The two of us know a great deal about times like those. In 1980, we had a dream that involved writing best-selling books, speaking, and doing seminars around the world, appearing on radio and television, writing magazine columns and articles, and much more—all to tell people about the joys of going out on their own and working from home. In our mind's eye, we saw crowds of men and women packing into our seminars, lines of people forming to get our books. We saw their faces excited and eager to learn about the positive changes they could make in their lives.

That was the dream. It burned in our very souls. It lit those early days with intoxicating determination. The reality, however, tested us to our very core. It took us five years just to get our first book published. No one showed up for our first publicly advertised workshop—no one. There were many long, dark years and hours of despair and dejection. But seven years later, the dream began coming true. Now we're living the lives we imagined in 1980. In the midst of the worst of those years, however, we learned several important things that helped us understand why pursuing our dreams was more difficult than we had expected, and that helped us to continue with renewed resolve.

Success Has a Schedule of Its Own

We've learned that in making it on one's own, each person is truly traveling his or her own path to success, and each journey takes as long as it takes. For some it's short and fast; for others it's long and tedious. The rate of success, however, has nothing to do with the ultimate outcome—unless, of course, you quit before you finish. Here are four common patterns of success rates.

1. The fast start. Tova Borgnine enjoyed instant success. Forget that Tova is married to a famous and wealthy movie star. She had found a rejuvenating facial mask and, on a whim, decided to take out an ad to sell it. The orders flooded in. She was overwhelmed with the response. It came before she'd even made a full commitment to her business idea. From that one ad has grown a multimillion-dollar business, Tova Beauty Products.

Sandy Gooch also had a fast start. She opened one of the first truly natural health-food stores in Los Angeles. She had to cancel the ads she placed in the local paper even before they all ran: there were more people coming to her store than her employees could handle.

Such fast starts are like fairy tales that come true for real-life Cinderellas. Peggy Glenn was making more money from her typing service within her first six weeks than she'd been making on her job. Ann McIndoo made over one-hundred-thousand dollars within a year of opening her computer-training service. Michael Russo brought in 240 percent more business during the first year of his accounting practice than his initial projections. In 1988, thirty-one-year-old Lisa Lamee was laid off from her thirty-thousand-dollar-a-year job as an import buyer. Instead of finding another job she decided to turn her love for cooking into Le Saucier, a mail-order and retail business that distributes over five hundred exotic sauces. She installed a toll-free number and was almost immediately drowning in orders.

We know of many such instant success stories. They're a real inspiration. Of course it's what we all want. But know this:

You don't need instant success to succeed!

While it's tempting to drop what you're doing and take off on a wild search for instant success, that is a mistake. Most successfully self-employed individuals did not have a fast start. And fast starts pose their own challenges. For example, when a woman we'll call Jill started her business, offering human-potential seminars, she had such an immediate rush of business that she was overwhelmed: "I didn't feel I deserved it. I don't know why people flocked to me in such numbers. Frankly, I couldn't handle it because I really didn't know what I was doing. The business took over my life." Finally she moved to another city and started over again. This time, since no one knew her there, she was able to start more slowly.

2. The slow-and-steady route. Many very successful businesses start out more like marathons than sprints. They build momentum over a period of time instead of igniting on the spur of the moment. In fact, this is a more commonplace experience than the instant success. Most propreneurs gradually build their businesses week by week, month by month, and year by year. As one caterer told us, "On New Year's Eve I realized I'd made it. I'd been on my own for five years! It sort of sneaks up on you." As long as you can see the gradual progress you're making, this pattern can actually be more comfortable than, and certainly as rewarding as, a fast start.

3. The roller-coaster ride. Some people discover that making it on their own is a series of peaks and valleys, feasts and famines. Michael Cahlin, for example, finds that "one month you may bring in seven thousand dollars, the next month seventeen thousand dollars." While you're riding high in a business like this, it's tempting to think the highs will last forever—and, of course, there's no reason not to enjoy them while they do. It's useful, however, to plan ahead financially for the valleys. And when they hit, it's important to realize that they don't mean that you're going under. In businesses like these, the valleys don't last forever, either. You can use these downtimes to gear up and build for the next climb.

4. The endurance trials. As was the case with us, some success comes after years of perseverance and determination. When this is your situation, it's particularly important that you be highly motivated. If you don't have a lot of desire to do what you've set out to do, you'll have a hard time remaining positive and continuing on doggedly. Three years passed, for example, before wellness researcher Dean Allen broke even. But now he has all the business he can handle; he doesn't even have to market. He says, "Even when I was starving to death I never seriously thought of quitting, even though I was pressured by girlfriends to get a job. I felt like if I gave up I would die. Doing something else would be the kiss of death."

In addition to being highly motivated, it's also important to keep your eye on your ultimate goal and not get bogged down in your current reality. Look, instead, at the progress you have made and keep taking steps forward to where you want to be. It's especially important not to compare yourself with others, especially fast starters. That's just too demoralizing.

Two Factors That Determine Your Success Rate

Achieving success out on your own is a process much like growing up. As you think back to when you were twelve or thirteen years old, you'll undoubtedly remember that some kids matured much more quickly than others. Girls fill out their sweaters at different rates. Boys' voices deepen at different times. If you've had children of your own, you'll undoubtedly remember that they all walked and talked on their own schedules. Each did ultimately walk and talk, however, just as each of us did ultimately mature. Our unique genetic composition and social environment combine to determine the rate at which we achieve various developmental milestones.

So it is with being on your own. Instead of your genetic heritage and social milieu determining your rate of success, however, two other primary factors combine to influence when and how you will succeed: the receptivity of the marketplace and the resources you bring with you when you start out on your own. Just as child-development experts agree that it's unwise for parents or teachers to try to force a child to develop more quickly, it's equally unwise for us to try to force ourselves to develop our businesses faster than our circumstances will support. But just as there are things parents can do to nurture a child's development, there are also steps we can take to work within the circumstances of the marketplace and our resources to nurture our journey to success and make it as quick and easy as possible.

Is Your Market More or Less Receptive?

Your market is the body of existing or potential buyers who need or want your product or service. Most propreneurs don't think a lot about the market before going out on their own. They start out with either an existing skill, an idea, or a desire they want to pursue. This is one of the characteristics that sets propreneurs apart from classic entrepreneurs, who are more likely to tailor what they set out to do to market trends and patterns of what, when, and how people are spending their money.

If you think about the fast-start success stories we described, they were all examples of individuals who were in the right place at the right time. The market was ripe for their products. People who tried to do what they did before or after them most likely met with different responses. For example, in any particular venture or type of work you undertake, you may find yourself in one of the following situations.

1. Ahead of the market. This was our situation. We were seven years ahead of the market. In this case you have to have patience, and do a lot of educating and hand-holding to help people get on board. Your growth will be slower and perhaps even an endurance trial while the market catches on. When it does, however, you may become the leaders in your field and even be in a position to be acquired.

CASE IN POINT: When Sue Rugge started Information on Demand, one of the first information-brokering companies in the country, few people knew what information brokering was. She had to literally define that business, educating people about her service and showing them how it would benefit them. It took her eight years, but ultimately she thrived, and as the market caught up with her she sold her company for a substantial profit.

2. *Right on the market.* In this case, your business will take off like a rocket. There will be lots of immediate demand for what you do. As our fast-start examples illustrated so well, all the business you need will be there for the taking. You can count on other people jumping on the bandwagon, however, and you will have to stay alert to keep up with your competition.

CASE IN POINT: Sometimes people hit on a hot idea. Twenty-four-year-old Keri VanderSchuits certainly did. She loved to dance to live rock music, and to create firm and attractive support she would sew appliqués on her bras. Every time she wore one of these bustiers, other young women would go wild asking where they could get one, so she decided to invest $500 dollars in creating a line of ten bustiers. She put them in a shopping bag and went from boutique to boutique. Putting another $500 dollars into her business, she hired help, and her fledgling business has grown into a $200,000-a-year proposition. Soon lots of others were selling bustiers too, but she kept hers unique and they continued to be popular.

3. *In a growing market.* In this case, you can actually see that a particular business is already in demand and taking off, so you can join in to share in the profits by starting such a business yourself.

CASE IN POINT: Forty-one-year-old Robert Dobnick was working in showroom design when he saw that showroom construction was booming. There was clearly a demand for specialists in this field, so he became one. He started Robert F. Dobnick Design Consultants two years ago. He designs and plans wholesale showrooms and earns $150,000 a year.

4. *In a stable or declining market.* In this case you will have a lot of competition right from the start from others who have already captured most of the business. Therefore, unless you can find a special untapped niche, you will have a battle on your hands. To break into this type of market, you will need to be better or cheaper in order to take over business from others.

CASE IN POINT: Ann MacIndoo was one of the first to begin computer training in law offices, and her business took off like a flash. She was making over $250,000 a year within only a few years. By the time Jerry Conklin graduated from college, however, many businesses were already computerized. The demand for computer training was far less than when Ann began. And companies like Ann's had a corner on the existing markets. But Jerry wanted to do computer training and he was good at it. Therefore he had to find a specialized niche that had not yet been tapped. He chose publishing, because publishers were slower to adopt new technology and his family had connections in that industry.

5. *Dealing with a fad.* In this case your venture may take off like a sky-rocket and then peak fast. So you will have to use some of your profit and resources to expand quickly into other ventures before your original idea fizzles out.

CASE IN POINT: When women's clothing began to feature shoulder pads, a Midwest-based woman saw the opportunity to start a mail-order business selling shoulder pad inserts in various sizes and shapes. The business took off fast because the demand was high and she was one of the only sources. But soon fashions changed. In order for this business to continue, the owner had to look for new products. She chose headbands, which were just coming into fashion as shoulder pads were about to fade.

6. *Joining an evergreen.* Certain types of work are always in demand and may well always be: accounting, bookkeeping, and secretarial services of various kinds are a few examples. In this case, with the right credentials and connections, you will usually be able to break into such a business at a steady but perhaps gradual pace. Or if you want to speed up the process, you can specialize in an untapped market, offer a new approach, or apply a new technology to existing markets.

CASE IN POINT: There were many dentists in practice in Pasadena, California, when Craig Scheele graduated from dental school. He wanted to build his business as quickly as possible, however, so he decided that he would specialize in the patients other dentists hated to see. He focused on difficult patients: people with heart conditions and dental phobias and hospitalized individuals. Needless to say, his business grew quickly. Fortunately these people had friends and relatives, and ultimately he had a well-rounded general practice.

7. *Without an existing market.* Sometimes your idea or skill has no existing market, in which case you have to create one. You have to convince people that they want or need what you have to offer. And once you do, you will have created a new industry, a new field, in which you will be the leader. As with being ahead of the market, this is usually a long, involved process, but once you begin doing well you will be joined by others. You may also be in a good position to be acquired.

CASE IN POINT: Boyd and Felice Willat were the first people to create a personal time-management system, the DayRunner, a system for managing your life. No one had ever heard of such a concept before. Reps didn't know where to place it; stores didn't know where to display it. Boyd and Felice built a market for the DayRunner, however. They convinced the reps of its viability and showed the stores how to merchandise it. They built a multimillion-dollar industry, which now includes many competitors.

Evaluating the market conditions for your business can help you understand what you're up against and give you insights into why you're encountering whatever challenges you are. It is senseless, for example, to attempt to understand your rate of progress by comparing it with that of someone who is dealing with an entirely different market. Propreneurs often do this, however. But, to take one of the above examples, why should Jerry measure his progress in offering computer training by comparing it with Ann's? Such comparisons would be useless. The businesses were started under two completely different market conditions.

Sometimes, in looking realistically at market conditions you will decide that you want to rethink the type of product or service you offer simply because you have taken on more of a challenge than your available time, money, or energy can sustain. Many librarians, for example, wanted to do what Sue Rugge did with Information on Demand, but very few were willing to go knocking on doors the way Sue did. She had to go door-to-door calling on potential customers and educating them as to the value of information research. To this day Sue says, "If I hadn't been laid off, I am not sure I would have had the guts to quit and start my own business. Doing the work was the easy part. It was selling a service no one knew about that was hard."

Now many information researchers work freelance for companies like Sue's. Others waited until the pioneering tasks of educating the market were well under way and started out on their own once their services were beginning to be more in demand.

Barbara Cooper is a marvelous songwriter and singer. Her style, although New Age, is reminiscent of the big-band era. Her albums are all done with a full orchestra. This sound is not the norm in New Age music. The big-band sound peaked in the forties and is just now starting to return to popularity. But over the years Barbara has been determined to find a niche for her music. It has been an uphill battle, but it's starting to pay off with the renewed popularity of Tony Bennett and Frank Sinatra.

Like Barbara, you have a choice about what type of work you want to do and how you choose to focus on it. Some people have taken on more difficult tasks than others. But too often our choices as propreneurs are made unknowingly. Evaluating your market can assist you in knowing just what you're up against and what you'll need to do in order to survive and thrive. With this knowledge you can decide what you're willing to commit to and how to proceed accordingly.

Are You More or Less Ready?

Just as we don't all start out in the same market conditions, we also don't start out with the same degree of personal and professional readiness. The resources each of us brings to self-employment vary greatly and affect how quickly and easily we will succeed. Here are six resources that can help you survive and thrive on your own. The more of these you have, the easier it will be. The fewer you begin with, the longer it will take you to acquire them or to succeed without them.

1. *Your experience level.* The level of experience you have in what you do and in managing yourself as a business will determine how long your learning curve will be. If you have been doing what you do for many years, know your field well, and have experience in marketing and managing yourself, your learning curve will be much shorter than that of someone who is relatively new to his or her field who has little marketing or self-management experience.

Mike Greer, for example, had worked for several firms as an instructional designer over several years. He had become very good at his work and knew the ins and outs of bidding, pricing, billing, negotiating, and delivering his product. Melissa was also a good designer, but she was new to the field and had always worked under another designer. Whereas Mike's business was profitable from day one when he went out on his own, Melissa barely survived the first year. By the third year, however, she was doing fine.

2. *Your contacts.* Who you know and their willingness to serve as clients, gatekeepers, referral sources, or mentors can greatly enhance the ease with which you move into self-employment. The more contacts you have, the less time it will take you to get established.

Kim Freilich and Chris Shalby both had major clients already signed up before they started their PR firms. Kim had been working as a publicist for a midsize publisher and had valuable contacts already in place. Chris also had a host of valuable contacts from his having done PR in-house for a large organization. Libby Goldstein, however, had just moved to Baltimore and didn't know a soul when she started her PR firm. As you can imagine, getting started for Libby took more time and a lot more effort than it did for Kim and Chris.

3. *How much money you have to capitalize yourself.* While having lots of money isn't necessary, it can certainly help get things moving more quickly. If you don't have experience, you can buy it. You can hire a marketing consultant, a PR firm, or an ad agency. You can attend top-notch courses and classes. If you don't have contacts, you can buy advertising to get the expo-

sure you need. Or you can buy access to contacts through club and organizational memberships, donations, and fund-raising activities.

When Naomi Stephan left her position as a university professor to become a career consultant, she took a six-month leave of absence and worked for a Yellow Pages company to learn about advertising, sales, and direct mail. She used savings, a loan from her parents, and a ten-thousand-dollar bank loan to purchase her office equipment. This capital provided her with the cushion she needed to be debt free and supporting herself in her brand-new career within eighteen months.

Marie Wallermeyer, however, had been working as an employment counselor when she was laid off. She had to bootstrap her career-consulting business. She had to live off of, and finance her business with, the fees her first clients brought in. Things were very tight. She had to take a part-time job for three years, but ultimately she made it, too. It just took longer.

4. *Your credentials.* As we discussed earlier in this chapter, credentials open doors and smooth the way. You don't always need them, but having them makes your job easier.

As a psychiatrist Tom went directly from his psych residency into private practice. With his credentials, he was able to quickly get referrals from several agencies and from the hospital with which he was affiliated. Terry, on the other hand, had no counseling, ministerial, or psychotherapy credentials, so when she started offering personal-growth classes, she had to build her enrollment strictly with her personal power. It was a slow process. Recently divorced, she also had very few funds. In fact, at first she had to hold her classes in a library and split the fees with the library while she lived with friends. Then for five years she held her classes in the living room of her one-bedroom apartment. Now, however, she has a thriving practice. Her classes are all booked up. Her calendar is full of private appointments, and she has recently built a new home and studio for her work that she and her new husband have jointly financed.

5. *Your results.* The more dramatic your results, the quicker and easier you will be able to become established.

When Cyril came to the United States from Australia, he had $250 in his pocket. He didn't know a soul in this country. He'd been a typesetter, and typesetting jobs were few and far between. But he loved people. He saw an ad for a multilevel marketing company and started selling its health products. He loved the products and found he could sell them to anyone. Soon he began teaching others to sell them. The people he trained were so excited about what they learned from him that, before he knew it, he was teaching sales skills for other companies. Within a year he was doing sales-training programs for major corporations. All this was based on the results he was able to produce.

Jeffrey also became a sales trainer. He'd been selling on commission for a manufacturing company. His own sales record was marginal, but he thought it was the product, not his skills, that were holding him back. He discovered how much money sales trainers can make and decided he could do that. People who came to his classes, however, complained that they hadn't gotten much. Some even asked for their money back. But Jeffrey kept at it. The promise of future fees motivated him to stay with it. As his skills improved, so did his results, both in the field and in the classroom. Ten years later he was making the fees he had initially aspired to.

6. *Time.* As you can see from the above examples, even if you don't have any of the other resources, you can still make it. Lots of people do. But you will need time—and patience and determination—to complete your learning curve. As actress Sally Field says, "Miles in the saddle is a great thing."

We hope that after reviewing the preceding discussion of personal resources and market issues, you are feeling pleased with your own progress in view of your particular circumstances. Certainly that is our goal in having described them. You undoubtedly have certain assets that are enabling you to succeed, and which you can capitalize on even further. You also undoubtedly have some limitations that are making your progress slower or harder than you might like, and which you must work around and compensate for in some way.

STAYING THE COURSE

As your own coach and mentor, you will need to play up your assets, acknowledge yourself for possessing them, and take pride in having acquired and used them. It's important not to take them for granted. There are people who must struggle desperately for the very things that come so naturally to you. So point out these strengths to yourself frequently, especially when you are feeling discouraged or doubtful.

Make sure to lead with your strengths, whatever they might be, and encourage yourself to continue empowering yourself by fully developing your talents and resources. This is exactly what every good coach and mentor does, no matter what the field. Every top athlete and every top performer in every field has certain strengths and weaknesses. The coach's job is to bring out the strengths and shore up and overcome the weaknesses. If you are struggling to find how to best match your strengths to the needs and circumstances of the marketplace, our book *Finding Your Perfect Work* can guide you in pinpointing the best possible match that will increase the odds of your succeeding as quickly and easily as possible.

Taking a Personal Inventory

You are the best you've got. But you're enough, and you can be even more. Give yourself time to develop the resources you need, even if you must redirect your efforts or even start over. As long as you are still breathing, there is no end to your capacity to grow and develop. Every day you can be more, do more, and have more of what life has to offer.

RESOURCES

WHEN YOU DON'T KNOW WHAT TO DO

The Artist's Way, A Spiritual Path to Higher Creativity. Julie Cameron. New York: Tarcher/Putnam. 1992. This book is actually a twelve-week course for how to tap into your creativity. It's an excellent resource for anyone who suffers from blocks, from writer's blocks to simply not being able to get yourself to work productively.

Idea Fisher. Irvine, CA: IdeaFisher Systems, Inc. (800) 289-4332. This unique software program is a tool for enhancing both creativity and productivity. It enables you to brainstorm solutions and quickly come up with creative ideas and solutions. It stimulates your thinking by prompting you with problem-solving questions. Add-on programs are available for strategic planning speeches and presentations, and breaking writer's blocks.

Intuition. How to Use Your Gut Instinct for Greater Personal Power. Dr. Marcia Emery. Niles, IL: Nightingale-Conant. (800) 525-9000. This six-cassette audio program and guidebook teaches you how to use your intuition to generate powerful ideas, solve tough problems, and make better decisions.

The Intuitive Edge: Understanding Intuition and Applying It to Everyday Life. Philip Goldberg. New York: Tarcher/Putnam, 1995. This book teaches not only what intuition is but also how to recognize and cultivate it.

*A Kick in the Seat of the Pants: Using Your Explorer, Artist, Judge and Warrior to Be More Creative. Roger von Oech. New York: HarperCollins,

*A classic.

1986. Enables you to move through the four stages of coming up with and implementing good ideas and solutions without getting stuck anywhere along the way.

⌒ *Whack on the Side of the Head: How to Unlock Your Mind for Innovation.** Roger von Oech. New York: Warner, 1993. A classic guide to creative thinking, this book opens the locks that prevent you from being innovative and through stories, mental exercises, and case histories shows you how to think on your feet or your seat when you need to most.

BEING TAKEN SERIOUSLY

⌒ **Don't Slurp Your Soup: A Basic Guide to Business Etiquette.** Betty Craig. New Brighton, NM: Brighton Publications, Inc., 1991. A guide for navigating social business situations with aplomb. While at times directed to salaried situations, much of what this book offers is equally relevant to self-employment issues from making introductions to business meals, tipping, sending gifts, eating out, travel, and international and sports etiquette.

⌒ **Fabled Service, Ordinary Acts, Extraordinary Outcomes.** Betsy Sanders. San Diego: Pfeiffer & Company, 1995. A former vice president of Nordstrom shows how companies have become reknown by serving their customers. Although based on the experiences of larger companies, most of the principles are an excellent guide for how to produce results for those you serve and actually illustrate, although unintentionally, why self-employed individuals can do well shoulder to shoulder with larger companies.

⌒ **Multi-Cultural Manners.** Norine Dresser. New York: Wiley, 1996. Each culture has its own behaviorial expectations, social rules, faux pas, and taboos. In today's increasingly global and multicultural world, if we want to be taken seriously, we should be sensitive to and aware of these expectations. Dresser's book explains how to do that.

⌒ **On the Wings of Self-Esteem.** Dr. Louise Hart. Berkeley, CA: Celestial Arts, 1994. Using personal power requires a good amount of self-esteem, but through life's ups and downs many of us have lost our belief in ourselves. This book can help you to restore your confidence by explaining how self-esteem gets eroded and through a series of exercises directing you toward claiming the positive aspects of yourself and your life.

*A classic.

Money Matters

⌇ The Business Bible: Ten Commandments for Creating an Ethical Workplace. Rabbi Wayne Dosick. New York: HarperCollins, 1993. Illustrated with stories, vignettes, and legends, this book provides evidence that you don't have to compromise your ethical beliefs in order to earn a good living.

⌇ Collection Strategies. Micky Kinder. Career Tracks. (800) 334-1018. A four-cassette audiotape and/or two-volume videotape on using the mail, phone, and outside agencies to retrieve money you're owed without alienating your customers.

⌇ Creating Affluence: Wealth Consciousness in the Field of All Possibilities. Deepak Chopra, M.D. San Rafael, CA: New World Library, 1993. Chopra believes that affluence is our natural state, and in this book he takes you through a series of simple steps and everday actions for changing the way you think about wealth so you can create affluence in your own life.

⌇ Desktop Credit Manager. Dana Point, CA: Lord Publishing. (800) 525-5673. This software and workbook provides techniques, agreements, and form letters to help you reduce bad debt, get paid faster by slow payers, and deal with collection problems.

⌇ Earn What You Deserve: How to Stop Underearning and Start Thriving. Jerold Mundis. New York: Bantam, 1995. An excellent step-by-step guide for those who are always running short of money or worried they will be, to turn money from a source of anxiety to a permanently abundant element of your life.

⌇ Estimating & Invoicing. Dana Point, CA: Lord Publishing. (800) 525-5673. With this software program you can create professional estimates and invoices on your letterhead. It enables you to total up invoices, protect against underbilling or overbilling, and speed your collections.

⌇ Getting Business to Come to You. Paul and Sarah Edwards and Laura Clampitt Douglas. Los Angeles: Tarcher, 1991. Identifies the marketing methods of the most successful home-based businesses. See especially Chapters 4 and 5.

⌇ *Money Is My Friend. Phil Laut. New York: Ballantine, 1989. Provides methods for eliminating financial fears and making money a fun, fascinating and creative enterprise.

*A classic.

 *Money-Love: How to Get the Money You Deserve for Whatever You Want. Jerry Gillies. New York: Warner, 1978. Teaches you how to rethink self-defeating attitudes about money. It shatters myths our culture and families teach us about money and provides a new outlook on property and how to achieve it permanently.

 *Self-Esteem. Matthew McKay and Patrick Fanning. Oakland, CA: New Harbinger, 1987. Without a good dose of self-esteem you may find it difficult to charge the fees you need and can command. This classic book provides techniques for assessing, improving, and maintaining your self-esteem.

 Simplify Your Life: 100 Ways to Slow Down and Enjoy the Things that Really Matter. Elaine St. James. New York: Hyperion, 1994. This book, also mentioned in chapter 3, can help you set your financial priorities straight so that you're earning to live and not living to earn. While your priorities and conclusions may be different from St. James's, her take on simplifying your life can help you clarify what matters most to you..

 Working from Home. Paul and Sarah Edwards. Los Angeles: Tarcher, 1994. Chapter 14, "Managing Money: Financing and Cash Flow Management," provides information on how to finance a self-employment career, collect the money you're due and maximize your cash on hand. Chapter 22, "Pricing: Determining What to Charge," outlines the pros and cons of various pricing strategies and provides formulas for deciding how much to charge when you're on your own.

---

*A classic.

8

Overcoming Obstacles

The world breaks everyone, then some become strong at the broken places.   ERNEST HEMINGWAY

THERE ARE TWO TYPES of obstacles along the road to self-employment: hurdles and hazards. The hurdles are par for the course. They're the things we will probably all encounter at one time or another if we want to be self-employed. Hazards, on the other hand, are not par for the course. They're un-expected and hopefully you'll never have to face one, let alone more than one. But unfortunately, you may. Knowing the difference between hurdles and hazards, however, can help you overcome them more easily.

TAKING HURDLES IN STRIDE

If you find a path with no obstacles, it probably doesn't lead anywhere.
                                                              UNKNOWN

As we mentioned earlier, a hurdler isn't distressed to encounter a track that's laid out with hurdles. He or she doesn't curse the fact that they're there, or that there are so so many. Hurdles are expected on the track, and the hurdler has trained to leap them. In fact, the way a hurdler takes the hurdles in stride is what determines the outcome of the race. And so it is with the hurdles of self-employment. We must take whatever hurdles we encounter in stride.

The difference between the hurdles we face when going out on our own and those on the track, however, is that while the hurdler knows and expects the track to be lined with hurdles, and even knows where and when to expect them, when we go out on our own, most of us don't know what hurdles to expect. We may fear that we'll encounter some, but we don't know what they'll be or when they'll occur. So we're not trained for them. And that's how they trip us up. So, to take hurdles in stride, we need to know when and where to expect them. Unfortunately, no one talks much about many of the run-of-the-mill hurdles you can expect to encounter when you're on your own. That's why we wrote this book. We wrote it to alert you to hurdles most people experience but few people discuss and to provide you with specific strategies for taking them in stride. Here's a list of this kind of to-be-expected, but "unmentionable" hurdles you've been reading about throughout this book:

- Living with the ambiguity of not having a paycheck
- Having to experiment to get results instead of following set rules or procedures
- Adopting new ways to think about money
- Having to enhance your own personal power to replace the authority that came with whatever position you held on a job
- Getting yourself to do things you know you need to do when you don't want to
- Having the responsibility for doing everything yourself
- Running out of time to do all the things it seems you need to do
- Handling the minutiae of administering your work as a business
- Dealing with the range of unusually strong emotions that arise from being self-employed
- Facing situations when you don't know what to do
- Not always being taken seriously
- Not having enough cash on hand to pay the bills that are due
- Needing more business but not liking or knowing how to market yourself
- Facing slow times
- Being told "no" when you're hungry for a "yes"
- Having to prove yourself to others when your abilities should be obvious
- Losing business to someone else
- Having to raise your prices when you can't afford to lose clients
- Waiting for success that's coming more slowly than you expected
- Not getting paid on time after finishing a job well done

- Needing to develop new skills like marketing, negotiating, money management, collection and new office technology you find intimidating

Then, of course, there are the two most common hurdles of all: Murphy's Law and O'Toole's Corollary. Murphy's Law tells us that if something can go wrong it will. And O'Toole's Corollary asserts that Murphy was an optimist. Of course, everyone who's trying to achieve any goal may encounter these two hurdles. We all need to be prepared for them. But, on a job, the role of the organization you work for is to take care of as many of the day-to-day Murphy's and O'Toole's hurdles as possible, so you're free to handle the particular hurdles you've been hired to navigate.

For example, when Clyde Gleason was downsized out of his managerial position, he felt well prepared for the hurdles of managing his own consulting business. After all, he'd run an entire region for a multinational company. He was used to dealing with hurdles. That was his job. What took him by surprise were the many invisible hurdles the company had been shielding him from. When his hard disk crashed, for example, he was distraught. Where was the in-house computer technician who would have been in his office within minutes? Where was the backup computer, so he could get on with working with his new clients? He found himself uncharacteristically yelling at his computer.

As a first-rate accountant, Georgia Kirkland had spent five days a week for ten years handling financial hurdles for her clients. She was confident she could do the same for herself. What she hadn't anticipated was how much of a hurdle marketing to get new business would be for her. She borrowed heavily from her fiancé, who was equally confident of her abilities. Shortly after their honeymoon, they were verging on bankruptcy. It was some time before Kirkland got up to speed at leaping over the marketing hurdle.

Here's the best formula we've found for taking such hurdles in stride. It's based on our own experience and the way we've observed others handling these unwelcome, but often unavoidable, hurdles.

1. Accept hurdles as par for the course. Although a hurdle you didn't expect may seem like a hazard to you, chances are it isn't, especially if you recognize it quickly and do some immediate problem-solving. Most likely it only seems as if you've stepped on a land mine because being on your own is still somewhat new. After several years on his own, for example, Gleason can laugh about his screaming fit. "I've faced just about every possible situation now," he told us. "A $10,000 check bounced that was going to cover my out-of-pocket expenses, a client canceled a project midstream after an in-house staff change, an airline ticket didn't arrive by Express Mail so I missed an important meeting. I couldn't even list all the things that have happened, but now I

Making Sure Hurdles Don't Trip You Up*

Too often we trip over hurdles because we simply don't see them, even if they're in plain view before us. Here are the four reasons this happens and how you can make sure you see the hurdles that lie ahead before you run into them:

1. **Don't discount the existence of a problem.** Sometimes we don't see a hurdle coming up because we discount that it could be a problem. For example, take the case of people who do business from their back pocket and have no idea how much money is owed to them or how much they owe others . . . until they're faced with bankruptcy. They don't recognize they have a problem until it's too late. Then they say, "I don't know what happened. It just hit me out of nowhere!" To avoid this type of collision, keep your eyes and ears open to situations you need to attend to and take action on. Ask yourself, "What could happen if . . . ?"

2. **Don't discount the significance of a problem.** Sometimes we see a problem, but we don't think it's important enough to do anything about. In this situation, for example, people might recognize that they're getting behind on paying their bills or that collections are slow, but they don't consider that to be important. They might say, "I'll get around to it later" or "It's no big deal." To avoid collisions like these, don't overlook the importance of possible early warning signals. Check out the smallest glimmer of trouble, so you can take action early to prevent problems from developing.

3. **Don't discount that something can be done about the problem.** Sometimes we admit there's a problem and we know it's an important problem, but we deny that anything can be done about it. For example, lots of people say "Everyone has financial problems these days. The economy is bad. There's not much anyone can do about it until things pick up." To avoid this type of collision, whenever you encounter a problem, remind yourself: "Problems are solvable."

4. **Don't discount your own ability to do something about a problem.** For example, some people admit there's a problem. They admit it's important and that perhaps someone could find a solution. But they don't believe they can solve it. To avoid collisions like these, whenever you encounter a problem, remind yourself: "Problems are solvable, and *I* am capable of finding a solution" . . . even if it doesn't seem so at the time.

*This material is based upon the work of Jackie Lee Schiff and her colleagues who wrote the book *The Cathexis Reader*, published by HarperCollins.

don't think there's much left that could stop me in my tracks. I've learned not to let these things get to me."

In other words, the surest way to avoid stumbling over a hurdle is to see it coming and take action to avoid hitting it.

2. Let go, to get on. When you've hit an unexpected hurdle, don't fight it. It doesn't help. It's happened. Maybe it shouldn't have. Maybe you could have avoided it, maybe not. Whether you like it or not, it's blocking your way right now and you have to get through it, around it, under it, or over it. So get to it. If you need to inform others of a delay or difficulty, do so immediately and let them know how you will handle any part of the situation that affects them. Then set about addressing the reality of the moment. You need not explain or complain. Veteran stage actor Allan Rosenberg put it this way after losing long-sought-after roles on two television series, "I wasn't so devastated. Actors aren't supposed to be employed for more than three years."

3. Become a problem solver. For some people problem solving is a way of life, a way of being. Natural-born problem solvers take hurdles in stride more easily. In fact, sometimes they actually find life more exciting and interesting when there are a few unexpected hurdles to spice up the course. If a software program won't install correctly or the file for tomorrow's presentation is erased, natural-born problem solvers quickly and willingly drop whatever they're doing and leap to the challenge of searching for solutions. They begin experimenting with alternative ways to install the program. They stay up all night, if necessary, to re-create the presentation.

Those of us who aren't problem solvers by nature, however, don't like problems. We want and expect everything to run smoothly, and when it doesn't our nature is to vacillate between being furious or feeling panicked. But on your own, since there's usually no one there to solve your problems for you, you can use natural-born problem solvers as a model and teach yourself to be a problem solver when you need to be.

You can become a formidable problem solver, even if it will never be your favorite thing to do. You'll discover there is a definite sense of satisfaction from making possible something that seems impossible at first. Marketing consultant Robbie Bogue would agree. When he opened his marketing consulting firm, he expected that the many contacts he'd made over the years as a respected marketing professional would help him land business on his own. He was on a first-name basis with many CEOs. But, surprise! His corporate contacts abandoned him. They didn't take his venture into self-employment seriously. From their perspective, he was just biding time between jobs.

"Being downsized in the eighties was like being divorced in the fifties," Bogue says, but he solved the problem. He incorporated his business, Marketing Excellence, and completed requirements to become a Certified Management Consultant. These two credentials were proof enough to his corporate contacts that Bogue wasn't going back to a corporate job and, at last, his phone started ringing.

Are You a Natural-Born Problem Solver?

How many of the following statements describe you? The more that do, the more naturally you'll gravitate toward a problem-solving approach to hurdles:

1. I feel best about myself when I'm figuring out what needs to be done.
2. I grow more confident when I analyze and investigate something I don't understand.
3. Complexities intrigue me.
4. I'm nearly always eager to jump in to solve a problem when I see one.
5. I feel at ease working alone for long hours figuring out something I don't understand.
6. I like finding the answers to things I don't know.
7. Time flies by when I'm lost in the details of a complex problem.
8. I'm most alert and energized when faced with a seemingly impossible situation.
9. The more complex the problem, the more interesting it is to me.
10. I'm certain most problems are solvable.

4. Become a creative thinker. When you've tripped over a hurdle and you're lying flat on your face, there may not seem to be many options. But once you stand up and look at your situation from a more commanding position, it's surprising how many options you have. In other words, we have to look at a problem from outside the box it's put us in. People who are natural-born creators find doing this comes easily to them. Creative thinkers automatically see novel and unusual ways over, under, around, and through hurdles. Here are several examples.

Twenty-three-year-old Doug Triola wanted to produce and direct a screenplay he'd written about acquaintance rape called *A Reason to Believe.* While he had a master's degree in fine arts and some experience working as an assistant program coordinator for a few studio films, he didn't have the nearly $200,000 he'd need to produce what he'd written even as a low-budget film. But Triola was a creative thinker. He cast unknown actors, shot scenes on university campuses, used his contacts from the film projects he'd worked on to get discounts on film, costumes, equipment, and so forth, and he enlisted his mother, a caterer, to feed the cast and crew. Still he had only a third of the budget he needed.

Becoming a Problem Solver

If you're not a natural-born problem solver, that's okay. Many of us aren't. But when the situation demands that you be, here's what you can do to become a problem solver:

1. Start by becoming intrigued with finding a solution. Say to yourself, "There must be a solution to this. I wonder what it could be?"

2. Pretend you have all the time you need. Since nothing can happen until you get through, around, over, or under the hurdle, whatever time you have is best spent doing so. And whatever time you have is still whatever time you have, but put it to the best possible use at once by working to solve the problem.

3. Try out various possible solutions. Say to yourself, "I wonder what would happen if I did this? Or this? Or this?"

4. Stop saying "I don't know what to do." This only confirms and feeds your doubts. Say instead, "I wonder what else I could do?"

5. When you can't think of anything to do, take a break and something will probably occur to you.

6. Talk the problem through with someone else, not so they can solve it for you, but so you can clarify and listen to your own thinking and gain a fresh perspective.

7. Read about what others have done. Magazines, newsletters, books, and on-line databases are filled with stories and advice about how other people have overcome particular hurdles. On-line searches are especially helpful because you can search by using key words like "collections," "loan default," and "contract negotiation," etc.

8. Turn into a bulldog. When a bulldog gets hold of something it wants, it never lets go. Let your frustration drive you to your own version of such dogged determination.

9. When you hit a dead end, call in an expert. That is one way to solve the problem.

10. Make a habit of basking in feeling the satisfaction from whatever solutions you find.

So he had a creative idea. He got local television news stations to cover the making of *A Reason to Believe* and then sent those news clips out to potential investors. His creative idea worked. He raised just enough money to complete a twenty-eight-day shoot. But then came the next hurdle: he didn't have enough money to edit the film. Time for another creative idea. With a $1,000 loan from a filmmaker he knew, he was able to get a 35-millimeter rough cut and a high-quality videocassette of the film. With this in hand, he took on a new identity and became his own booking agent. He contacted colleges across the country and sold himself and his partner as lecturers with a new film on acquaintance rape. Over the next month, he traveled across the country, speaking and showing his film in lecture halls and gyms on thirty college campuses. No one ever knew the film was only a rough cut. He raised over $60,000 to finish the movie.

Richard Pierce also needed an innovative approach to keep his fledgling software company afloat. Pierce had been successfully self-employed selling sophisticated software packages. So when he decided to go into the software business developing the integrated business management software package *Business Plus,* he started out with a cash reserve. But development time

Are You a Natural-Born Creative Thinker?

How many of these statements describe you? The more that do, the more naturally you'll gravitate toward using creative thinking to take hurdles in stride:

1. I think of myself as imaginative, creative and innovative.

2. I often think of things no one else has thought about before.

3. I feel best about myself when I'm doing something that's hasn't been done before.

4. I grow more confident when I see my own ideas and concepts taking form.

5. I am at ease trying to do things no one else has done.

6. I enjoy exploring new possibilities and creating new realities.

7. Time flies when I'm fantasizing, imagining, and exploring things that could happen or might be.

8. I don't mind working long hours at something other people think is impossible or a little wacky.

9. I feel most alert and energized when a new idea pops into my mind, and the more unusual the better.

10. I often see things differently than other people.

dragged on, costs mounted, and his savings dwindled. The newly married Pierce was putting in eight-hour days as a water bed salesman before diving into ten-hour programming marathons. Nonetheless, he got several months behind on his mortgage payments. Then one day, his five-week-old baby needed diapers and he didn't have the money to get them! At this point, he was desperate, so desperate that he came up with a creative approach to raising money fast.

He got on the phone and started calling his potential customers. Six months later he'd raised $1 million without selling one share of stock in his company. How? Essentially, he offered his investors a royalty. He told them that once the software came out, for each $100,000 they invested, he would pay $1 per package on the first million programs sold. And sell they did. CA$HGRAF *Business Plus* and CA$HGRAF *Home Office Plus* sold at the rate of nearly $40 million dollars in 1995.

5. Be audacious. Timidity will never get you over a hurdle. You've got to take a leap, even if it's a leap of faith. You've got to risk that you'll break your stride, kick the hurdle, knock it over, or even fall down. We're not talking about throwing all caution to the wind and risking your life, limb, and future happiness, although frankly some people do. We're far more cautious than that. But that doesn't stop us from having *chutzpah*. *Chutzpah* is a Yiddish word, which like *audacious*, means bold, daring, fearless, without restriction to previous ideas, unrestrained, and uninhibited.

Certainly it was audacious of Doug Triola to invite the local news station to cover the making of his movie. After all, a less audacious individual might have thought, Who am I to get news coverage? Who would want to cover a news story about a low-budget movie by some unknown man with an unknown cast? And certainly it took chutzpah for him to call college campuses and book himself and his roughly cut film for a lecture tour. Can't you just hear the naysayers who would have told him, "You can't do that!"

But that's what people might have said to Deborah Martin, too. Deborah and her husband, Tom, started a home business imprinting towels with company or team logos. They hadn't been in business long when they got a call for a $70,000 order from Apple computer. Well, as a start-up company, they didn't have enough credit at any textile mill to fill that large an order. That was a hurdle. But Martin didn't let it slow her down. She thought, "What do I have to lose?" She called the company back and boldly announced that their policy required all new customers to make a 50 percent up-front deposit on an order of that size! She actually asked this large, national computer company to send her a check for $35,000!

She didn't actually think they'd go for it. But, they did! They told her that wouldn't be a problem. So she got bolder yet and asked that the money

Becoming a Creative Thinker

If none of the above describe you, don't despair. You may always feel you prefer to rely upon conventional, proven approaches you know will work. You may continue to pride yourself on seeing things as others do. You may always prefer to avoid experimenting with seemingly impossible, "weird" ideas. And when you need clever ad copy written, a creative logo designed, an imaginative Web page developed, or a clever business strategy, you may always prefer hiring an outside creative expert. But that doesn't mean you can't think creatively when the situation demands it. You can. You can use naturally creative thinkers as your model and teach yourself to do the following when the situation demands creative thinking:

1. Imagine you could do, be, or have whatever you want from the situation at hand. Ask yourself, "What would be the most desired outcome of this situation?"

2. Tune in to your emotional reaction to this possibility. Strong emotion (remember, it's energy in motion) will help spur your creativity. Ask, for example, what you find exciting about the possibilities. Excitement provides wonderful creative energy. Frustration and determination can work as well, however.

be wired directly to their bank—which they did. To this day, Martin still doesn't believe they did it, but her chutzpah brought them the first of many big orders and paved the way for what has grown into a million-dollar home business. So she says, "Never be afraid to ask for what you need. All they can say is no."

Robert Wallace agrees. He had to use both chutzpah and some creative problem-solving to jump over a pretty big hurdle while launching his business, Arizona Sun, a line of sunscreens and skin-care products. First of all, it took chutzpah just to think that he and his wife, Ellen, could start a sideline business in a field like skin care where the major players are all big, established companies with megabucks to develop, produce, and market their products. But Wallace had a unique product made from plants and cacti that was perfectly suited to a nearby clientele of Arizona resorts filled with sun-soaked, skin-thirsty patrons. And sure enough, one big opportunity came along that showed just how promising his business could be, but it presented a string of hurdles that required a really audacious move.

Wallace got an order his employees thought was impossible to fill. The customer wanted 500,000 bottles of his hand-labeled product delivered within just a few weeks. Deciding to take the order was itself a bold move for

3. Use the energy your emotion brings to begin imagining various possibilities. Let your mind provide a range of ways to obtain your desired outcome . . . everything from the ridiculous and outrageous to the tried and true.

4. Don't push or force yourself. Just allow possibilities to come to mind. If none do, don't be alarmed. Tell yourself, "I'll think of something . . . if not now, later." And pretend you can. Ask yourself, "If I could think of an idea, what would it be?"

5. Temporarily turn off all limiters. Avoid words like *can't, unable, should,* and *shouldn't.* You may quickly think of many reasons why whatever possibilities come to your mind won't work, but set these doubts aside. Say to yourself, "So what?" Think instead, "What if they could?"

6. Identify the possibilities that would be most ideal and most appealing. Don't be tempted to return to what would be most practical and possible. Start thinking about what specific steps you could take to set the most appealing ideas into motion. Continue to draw from the way you feel about these possibilities to keep you going. Let your emotions fuel your action.

several reasons. First, hurdle #1: Filling the order would cost $498,000 and he couldn't borrow any money. Hurdle #2: He would have to move very quickly because if he didn't make the deadline, he would owe the $498,000 and still have to pay for all the ingredients, packaging, and other costs of trying to fill the order. Then, hurdle #3: He didn't know how he would get the labels on the bottles in time because he couldn't afford to buy a machine that would put them on. All 500,000 labels would have to be put on by hand.

Using chutzpah, Wallace first convinced the manufacturer to get their trucks ready to ship. Then he convinced the label company to stop their presses and make up and ship 500,000 labels. Finally, he convinced the bottle cap supplier to drop what they were doing and send out 500,000 caps. And he did all this with no credit!

Then, using some creative problem solving, he came up with an idea for getting the labels on the bottles in eight hours. There was a large church near his home that he figured had a youth group. So he called the church and made them an offer. If they would have two hundred teenagers in their social hall on Saturday, he would supply pizzas, a disc jockey, and a check at the end of the day for $1,000. The church thought this was a blessing! It would take them years worth of car washes to bring in that much money. So it was a deal. The kids finished putting on the labels by 5:00 that Saturday. The truck drove the bottles to the manufacturer, and the entire order was shipped within two weeks. Wallace got his $498,000, paid everyone the money they were due, and that order launched his home-based company.

So, truly, when it comes to getting over, around, under, and up from hitting hurdles, where there's a will, there's a way. You don't have to let the hurdles self-employment sets in your way, trip you up—at least not for long. You can take them in stride by accepting them as par for the course, letting go so you can get on, and becoming an audacious problem-solver and creative thinker.

SURVIVING HAZARDS

Misfortune is great, but human beings are even greater than misfortune.

RABINDRANATH TAGORE
NOBEL PRIZE–WINNING POET

While hurdles, even unanticipated ones, are a normal, routine part of being on your own, hazards are not. They're by nature devastating. No one really plans for them . . . although we may pray for protection from them and even take preventive steps to avoid them, like buying disaster or business-interuption insurance. But, still, they do happen.

A natural disaster could strike your home office. Information broker Sue Rugge lost her home, her home office, and $48,000 of receivables in an Oakland wildfire. Ron Williams's carpentry business which he had started right out of high school, was washed away when torrential rains burst a Fort Dodge, Iowa, levee. The flood wiped out everything and, like Rugge, Williams had no insurance to cover the loss.

One year right after Christmas, John Hart's family gift basket business they'd been building for eighteen years went up in flames. Two million baskets turned to ashes in moments.

Neal Coonerty's bookstore in Santa Cruz, California, was demolished in an earthquake.

Your major client may suddenly cancel, leaving you with less income than your monthly mortgage. That's what happened to Chellie Campbell's thriving bookkeeping service.

Economic, legislative, or technological changes can suddenly make what you do obsolete. The recession wiped out Arielle Ford's thriving public-relations business. The Tax Reform Act of 1986 eliminated the need for the specialized type of tax accounting Payne Harrison provided, drying up all demand for his business. The oil embargo sent Mark Victor Hanson's prefab housing business down the tubes overnight.

Linda Erlich's husband had a heart attack, which threw their business into bankruptcy. Ann Kingsley's partner, who handled the financial side of the business, left their growing cookie business. And Kingsley ended up $100,000 in debt. The office manager poet Rusty Berkus hired when she moved her publishing company, Red Rose Press, out of her home, quickly ran through Berkus's entire line of credit, leaving her without funds to reprint her books. Nora Mulholland's office manager erased all her company's computer records. Sandye Linnetz's husband helped her run the financial aspects of her balloon business. When her marriage broke up, so did her business, and when she took over the books, despite ample sales, she discovered her company was failing.

While running two successful businesses at the age of twenty-four, Tricia Holderman developed a life-threatening illness that left her temporarily without the use of her hands and feet. Before she recovered, she had acquired two million dollars in medical bills. Bette Claire Moffat found her home-based publishing company going under while she struggled to both run her business and care for her terminally ill mother. Martha Sahn's teenage son suffered an incapacitating injury just as she began her business as a manufacturer's rep selling custom accessories.

After buying what he thought was a successful newsletter business so he and his family could move to their dream home in a beautiful, remote area of Idaho, Gary Dunn discovered the newsletter had no subscribers left. The publisher had supposedly refunded money to past subscribers, but angry subscribers were calling to demand the money they claimed never to have received. And after finally making a long-awaited move to his dream home in the Pacific Northwest, Bill Seavy found the move left his relocation business financially strapped.

Just after Connie Connors expanded her New York public-relations company out of her home, a burglar broke in and stole all her equipment! The expansion and the theft left her with no money just as her clientele took a sudden unexpected dip.

Hopefully none of these things will ever happen to you. But perhaps they have already or could someday. While such disasters can happen to anyone, when you're self-employed, you're particularly vulnerable to them. And you know it. There's no sick leave, no worker's compensation insurance, often no disability, and usually when you take off, there's no one to carry on until you come back. Often clients can't wait or let things slide a bit, the way an employer will for a valued worker. Often they need to go elsewhere if you're not available. But we want you to know you can survive such hazards. Each of the individuals we've mentioned, and so many others we've met, have faced such hazards, and they have survived. And, should you need to, you can too.

The experiences of survivors like these provide us with a wealth of inspiration as well as valuable insights and specific guidelines for how to respond to what might initially seem to be a devastating, if not fatal, setback. Every year for ten years, *Success* magazine has done a feature on comeback stories. In fact, that's how we met some of the people mentioned above. *Home Office Computing* also does such features. In reading these articles and talking with these and the many other survivors we've met, we're always struck with how similarly these survivors cope with adversity.

Survivors use the same strategies we just outlined for taking hurdles in stride. They accept the existing reality. They let go to get on. They become creative problem solvers and act audaciously. But they also demonstrate another characteristic which Al Siebert, an ex-paratrooper and Ph.D. psychologist, calls the Survivor Personality.

The Survivor Personality

Al Siebert, the author of *The Survivor Personality,* has found that survivors gain strength from adversity. They thrive under pressure, develop an inner resilience, and convert misfortune into good luck. But Siebert says, "It isn't what a person is like" that makes a survivor. "It is how a person interacts with situations that determines survival." He's discovered that a survivor personality can be learned, but it can't be taught. A survivor personality emerges from struggling with great challenges. The survivor can be described as having developed the following traits:

1. **Curiosity:** an eagerness to know and learn and understand

2. **Flexibility:** the capacity to bend without breaking

3. **A Need to Have Things Work Well:** a compelling desire for things to flow harmoniously; an intolerance for dysfunction

4. **Empathy:** a capacity to identify with and experience the feelings, thoughts, and attitudes of others

5. **Resourcefulness:** an ability to respond creatively and imaginatively

6. **Resilience:** the power to return to center; the strength to spring back readily after being bent down

---

Becoming a Survivor

> *The moon in the water broken and broken again . . . still it is there.*
> CHOHSU, HAIKU POET

We all know qualities like these could help us survive the hazards life brings, but what we don't always know is how to access these qualities when we need them. Is being a survivor an innate ability that comes naturally to all or just some of us? Are the survivors we read about extraordinary in some way? Are some of us born to survive while the rest of us are doomed to go under when the going gets tough? That's what we wanted to know. So, over the past fifteen years, we've been conducting many hundreds of interviews and reviewing countless stories of people who have made it on their own despite the hazards life has thrown at them, and we've discovered that as Bruce Laingen has said, "We're like tea bags. We don't know our strength until we get into hot water."

We may or may not think we would be able to overcome certain disasters, but when they occur, we often surprise ourselves. Sometimes we're disappointed in ourselves and wish we could somehow be more valiant and courageous. Other times we amaze ourselves, rising to the challenge with a confidence we never knew we possessed. Whatever your reaction, understanding the process involved in recovering from a disaster can help you better navigate its demands and tap into the survivor characteristics we all have. Here's the process we've observed most people go through to survive, and even thrive, after disaster strikes.

1. Experiencing the devastating reaction. Max Carey knew his business was in trouble. The gas company had cut off the service to his home. The bank had repossessed his wife's car. But the final straw came when, while dining out, he discovered his American Express card had been canceled. Carey had been successful all his life. Suddenly he was broke. He was failing. It was an unfamiliar experience. On the way home that night, he pulled the car into a nearby parking lot and cried.

Chellie Campbell purchased the bookkeeping service she had been working for in the booming eighties. The business had been doubling every year, so as the new owner she was riding high for ten months. Then suddenly her largest client, whose account represented 75 percent of her business, announced they would no longer be doing business with her. They gave only two weeks' notice. The impact was devastating. Campbell remembers, "I considered my options: murder, suicide, or bankruptcy. None was attractive."

Although Campbell can now make this statement jokingly, at the time it was no joke. Thoughts of suicide, from fleeting to serious, are not uncommon. Although there may be an initial stage of shock and denial, sooner or later the moment comes when the reality of a disaster hits, and hits hard. Often our reactions are extreme, frightening and unsettling in and of themselves. Tricia Holderman actually tried unsuccessfully to pull out the cord on her life-support system when doctors told her they didn't know what more they could do for her.

One man locked himself in his apartment for two weeks, pulled the curtains, and stayed in bed in the dark. Another woman literally tried to run away from her problems. She put on her running shoes every morning and ran six, nine, twelve miles. By late afternoon, she was out the door running again. Others try to drown their pain by turning to drink and drugs. One woman gained fifty pounds while she tried unsuccessfully to avoid bankruptcy when a client reneged on paying her for a major event she'd spent three months producing.

"I had one really bad night," an artist remembers. Her partner—the one with the sales experience—left her sitting with $20,000 worth of materials that had to be paid for in fifteen days. "I'd never sold anything in my life. I felt betrayed. I cursed. I screamed. I ranted and raved. I cried hysterically." Of course, no one, other than she, knew about her reaction. Like so many of us, she thought it was a sign of weakness. It's not. It was her reaction to the devastation that had befallen her. We each react in our own way to disaster, from tears to tantrums, blaming to withdrawing, and often our natural reactions can feel as extreme as the disasters themselves.

It's important not to take such early reactions as signs of weakness. In fact, they are signs that we have recognized the severity of our situation. They're evidence that you're in a wrestling match with demons, both the ones within you and the ones life has presented to you. And experiencing and facing the devastation seems to be a first and necessary step to recovering from it. In the midst of struggling with the pain, the despair, the anger, be it momentary or prolonged, there comes a clarifying moment that puts things in perspective and unlocks our resources to carry on.

2. *Reaching a clarifying decision.* When Tricia Holderman discovered she was too weak to pull out her life-support system, she took it as a sign that she needed to dig in and fight to survive. And she did. *She made a decision to live.* Moving in with her parents, she began a long road to recovery. Twenty-nine operations later, she was slowly rebuilding her janitorial company which specializes in cleaning services for doctors and dentists.

Experiencing the depths of a disaster seems to lead to life-shaping decisions like Tricia's. Such decisions become a turning point that enables us to move on. For Chellie Campbell the conclusion she reached was a simple one, but it carried her through many difficult months. "I told myself I had built this business up once. *I can do it again.*" And as you will see in a moment, she did. After breaking down in tears that night in his car, Max Carey faced the fact that *he hadn't given his business everything he could.* The next morning he was a different man. He mounted a heroic effort that took his marketing business from the brink of failure back onto the road to success.

When Neal Coonerty's Santa Cruz bookstore was destroyed in an earthquake, he became physically ill looking over the damage. He saw no way he could start over. Then, amidst the rubble, he saw a rocking horse that had been in the children's section of the store. In that moment he realized *the store was an important and intimate part of people's lives* and of the community. He decided he would open another store. He started in a tent!

When Ron Williams's Iowa carpentry business was wiped out by the flood, friends came to his factory to help salvage what was left. But he sent them away. It seemed pointless. After viewing the devastation, he didn't care anymore. He decided to let it go. Then over the weekend, it occurred to him he had no place to go to work on Monday morning. That spurred his decision to start again. He persuaded his local banker to loan him $50,000, sold his damaged property, put his home up for sale, and three months later he was working again at full capacity.

For Sandye Linnetz, it took a second disaster to clarify the first. After she discovered that her ex-husband had left the business buried in debts, she awoke one morning to find herself and her children near death from carbon-monoxide poisoning. The next morning while recovering in the hospital, her father called to inform her that she'd been summoned to appear in court the next day for involuntary bankruptcy. But she was so happy that she and her children were alive, that *everything else fell into perspective.* Suddenly she could see her financial situation as a challenge, not a disaster. She turned into a virtual selling machine, calling hundreds of friends and contacts until the business came bounding back in full force.

When the Oakland wildfire wiped out Sue Rugge's home and office, there was no housing available in the area. She lived in six places in four months. Struggling to keep her business afloat as she moved from one friend's home to another, she forwarded customer calls to a colleague in Colorado. Her assistant who lived two blocks from her had lost her home in the fire, too. Between them they didn't even have her clients' telephone numbers. Once Rugge realized she wouldn't collect even half of her receivables, she asked herself, "How many times do I have to start over?" And she decided *she didn't want to continue with her business.* Instead, since she still had customers calling, she sold her ringing phone to another broker who needed business and decided to open a new business, Informational Professionals Institute, offering continuing-education seminars for other independent information professionals and their staffs.

Arielle Ford also reached a decision that took her life in a new direction. After losing 75 percent of her business to the recession, she closed her Beverly Hills office and moved to LaJolla. "The gift of the recession," she says, "was that I got to redesign my career. I had been making so much money in the eighties, *I didn't take time to think if I liked what I was doing.* The money was too good to give up. I always had to know what was going to happen next, but I learned to let go of the outcome." She began each day with a prayer: "Dear God, I surrender this day to you. What would you have me do?" Now, she says, "I'm really living out my dream. I work only on projects that are good for the planet." This decision has paid off personally and financially. She does publicity for authors. "I'm crazy about my clients," she says and when we talked with her, her clients had four books on the best-seller list!

As you can see from these remarkable experiences, struggling with the sheer weight of a disaster brings startling moments of clarity. Often these moments reveal a simple, but profound, truth, an instant of realization in which we can make a decision to accept responsibility for what will come next for us. This clarity unleashes previously untapped, ignored, buried, or temporarily abandoned inner strengths that allow us to see new possibilities and spring into action with new, and sometimes surprising and amazing, resolve.

3. Connecting with an untapped inner strength. Most of the individuals we've told you about reached a point where they felt they could not go on, and then they did. Not only did they go on, they did so with an inner resolve and strength that surpassed what they would have perceived possible. Sandye Linnetz became a virtual selling machine. Max Carey found he could give more to his business than he had been. Sue Rugge found a buyer for a decimated business! Neal Coonerty got a loan for a bookstore in a tent! Tricia Holderman came back to life when there seemed to be no life left to live.

When facialist Lori Tabak developed a repetitive stress injury, doctors kept prescribing more and more medication for her. Each week she became weaker. Each week she was able to see fewer clients. Eventually she could see only one client a day. Her boyfriend, medical personnel, and other friends began talking to her and treating her like an invalid. Her savings had dwindled to nearly nothing. Then, she put her foot down. "I decided I wasn't willing to live this way. I was not this disease." She began cutting back her medication. She broke up with her boyfriend. She found the inner strength to take her life back. Each day she grew stronger, gradually adding clients and eventually getting out again to market herself. Today both she and her business are healthy.

With $20,000 dollars of debt hanging over her head and the realization that without her sales partner the dream to sell her own creations was about to flounder instead of take off, the artist who'd never sold anything in her life discovered she could sell. "Something came over me. I felt driven. I called everyone I knew, everyone I could think of," she remembers. "It wasn't that I was no longer afraid of selling. My voice was shaking. My knees were weak after every call. I still don't know why people didn't hang up when they heard my quavering voice. But they didn't. Some actually asked me to speak up. Somehow I sold the whole order, got money up front, and I paid the bill."

Then came the real surprise! "I ordered more. That shocked me as much as anything. Once I'd survived the first crisis, I could have put it behind me, looked for another sales partner, or just dropped the whole idea. But I didn't. I ordered more materials and put myself right back under the gun again. How could I have done that? There I was back on the phone, doing it again and again, until it was just part of being a successful business."

As you can see, from a place of newfound strength and resolve, creative and innovative ideas and solutions come to mind that enable us to kick into action.

4. Kicking a supreme effort into action. When disaster strikes, it's not useful to ask, "Why me?" Of course, after you've survived a hazard of some kind it never hurts to look for any lessons you can learn from hindsight, but when you're in the midst of it, action, not analysis or recriminations, is what will keep you going and get you back on track again. And fortunately, if you avoid analyzing the why's and wherefore's and let go of the recriminations, the renewed strength that comes from getting clear about who you are, what you want, and where you're going helps propel you into taking the action you need.

Like others we've mentioned, when Gary Dunn discovered the newsletter he'd purchased, *The Caretaker Gazette,* had no subscribers, no advertisers, and no job opportunities to list, which is the main reason people would subscribe to it, he kicked into a supreme effort that kept his dream of a new lifesyle in a new community alive. Not only did he have to essentially rebuild the newsletter from scratch, he also had to assuage angry ex-subscribers who were demanding their money back. And he had to act fast.

First he conducted a telephone survey of previous subscribers to determine their likes and dislikes. He discovered that the biggest complaint was that the previous publisher had taken the newsletter off track, covering information that could be found elsewhere. With that feedback, he sent a direct-mail solicitation to the old subscribers to entice them to resubscribe and let them know that the new publisher was putting the newsletter back on track. About 40 percent of the old subscribers renewed, and that was enough to get him going. Then through selective advertising and publicity, the subscriber base began growing. To boost revenues Dunn also added sales of related publications and books. He started renting his mailing list and began carrying classified and display ads. Dunn says, "Bringing this back has been a tremendously rewarding experience."

Bill Seavy had to act fast, too. The costs of undertaking a long-awaited move to the Pacific Northwest had strained the reserve of already limited capital he needed to keep his urban-to-rural relation service, The Greener Pastures Institute, operating smoothly. So he launched an all-out effort to get cash flowing:

- He introduced a new book, *Returning to Small Town America,* with Dearborn Financial Publishers.

- He contracted with the Denver Buffalo Club to send 125,000 postcards advertising his "Country Club" package to a carefully culled list of Western enthusiasts. The package included the Greener Pastures newsletter, Seavy's new book, and a small-town critique. This Western card deck was the first of its kind.

- He got publicity for the Greener Pastures program in several national magazines and newspapers like *USA Today* and *America West Airlines Magazine.*

- He set up a Home Page on the World Wide Web.

He then sent a letter to a selected list of possible investors which outlined the above initiatives and others. The letter opened with the following message: "Dear Potential Investor: This is an opportunity for a shrewd investor which may not exist in a month or two because, by then, we won't need the funds." The letter went on to solicit $2,000 investments on which Seavy would pay 15 percent interest with a payback of equity within two years.

When Linda Erlich's husband had a near-fatal heart attack, the lawyers declared their business situation hopeless and told them to throw in the towel on their mailing service. But Erlich was determined to prove the lawyers wrong. She talked their employees into pay cuts or freezes, scraped together everything she owned, and launched a yearlong advertising blitz in the local paper and the Yellow Pages. She joined every possible local business and civic group and started networking nonstop. These efforts brought the company back from bankruptcy to even greater success.

When Chellie Campbell decided she would rebuild her bookkeeping business, there were many significant things she had to do and she, too, had to do them fast. As you recall, her biggest client was leaving with only two weeks' notice. First she had to dramatically cut expenses or go into bankruptcy. So she let all her staff go, except one half-time employee. She went to her landlord and told the truth. Given the options, the landlord tore up the lease and wrote a new one for less space and about one sixth what she'd been paying. She went to the bank and renegotiated the payments on a note. Then she contacted all her creditors and negotiated payment schedules until her expenses matched her income. She had to borrow additional money. And most of all, she started marketing like a fiend. Every morning Campbell would look at the paperwork on her desk and ask, "Which of these things will make me money now. What can I do that someone is going to pay for today?" It took six months of nonstop effort, but she got her business back on track.

Clearly rallying a supreme effort can produce a supreme result.

5. Rallying resources and support. To rally such supreme efforts, survivors draw upon whatever resources and support they have. If you recall, Dunn turned to ex-subscribers. Linnetz sold everything she had. Erlich's daughter dropped out of college to help her out. Sue Rugge's friends took her in while she had no place to live; a colleague agreed to take her business calls; colleagues from a professional association sent her gifts, a CD player, and a collection of her favorite music and personally recorded tapes. Others turned to friends as well. In fact, again and again, we see how survivors call upon others to help them rally their efforts.

When Ann King faced a cash-flow crisis after her financial partner left her alone to manage Blooming Cookies, Flowers and Baskets, she begged a long-time friend Ashley Ghegan, to quit her job and help develop and implement a survival plan. They became partners in what has grown to be a nationwide company. When an arsonist torched their facilities, they didn't miss a beat. They temporarily began making their cookies with another baker. In fact, that crisis became an unexpected publicity opportunity. Since the fire got a lot of television coverage, many sympathetic viewers became new customers.

Poet Rusty Berkus turned to her friends and loyal customers when her office manager depleted her line of credit. One book was out of print. Her newest one was ready for its first printing. Orders were backing up. So, Berkus sent fund-raising letters to friends and readers. She offered a special prepublication edition of the new book to those who would make a special contribution for an early order.

"I got so much love and support," Berkus says. "People really wanted to get behind me and my project." Old boyfriends provided money. Her children, who she didn't think had any extra money, contributed funds. "People who loved my work and were inspired by it sent money, even though they got no tax deduction."

Like Rusty, many survivors turn to their existing customers for help. Isidoros Garifalakis did. After undergoing quadruple bypass surgery, he had hired a comptroller to run his welding business. Then one day, bank officials showed up at his door, took over his business, and threatened to close him down. It seems his account had been seriously overdrawn. To keep his business afloat, after firing the comptroller, Garifalakis turned everything he owned over to the bank . . . his home, his savings, the money for his children's education. Then he went to his satisfied customers. Several lent him money. Others sent business his way. In thirty days he'd gotten $80,000 in advances from old customers. He was on his way to rebuilding what has become a new multimillion-dollar business.

Chellie Campbell had some unexpected help. She had the good fortune to be selected to be in the Small Business Administration's Women's Network (WNET). Through this program she was assigned a mentor. Her mentor was a highly successful businesswoman, Patti DeDominic. DeDominic, who later became the local and then national president of the National Association of Women Business Owners (NAWBO), provided Chellie with both specific direction and emotional support throughout her crisis. "She gave me good advice" Campbell says, "and I followed it." Following in her mentor's footsteps, Chellie has mentored many other women business owners herself and has served as president of the Los Angeles chapter of NAWBO.

Many survivors turn to professionals for help. Facialist Lori Tabak enrolled in an intensive growth seminar to help restore her mental and emotional strength while recovering from repetitive stress syndrome. After the Oakland fire, a psychotherapist offered Sue Rugge six weeks of psychotherapy free of charge. Sue continued seeing the therapist until she and her husband had moved into their rebuilt home. After the oil embargo snuffed out his prefabricated housing business, Mark Victor Hanson, who has since been a frequent guest on our radio show, listened to motivational audiotapes for many hours a day. Using the inspiration from these tapes, Hanson came back strong, becoming a top motivational speaker. You may know him as the co-author of the best-selling books *Chicken Soup for the Soul, A Second Helping of Chicken Soup,* and *A Third Helping of Chicken Soup.*

When Marty Babusa's new business came to a surprising stall after a glowing start, he voraciously read business books and magazines and paid for the advice of a marketing consultant. In March of 1991, Babusa, an avid fisherman who lives in the country-music capital of Branson, Missouri, caught a twenty-three-pound, four-ounce brown trout, smashing the previous national trout-fishing record by over six pounds. His catch brought him much nationwide publicity. With legendary trout fishing waters only three and half miles from his home, Babusa decided to open a fishing guide service for the five million visitors who come to Branson every year. He called his business Trophy Trout Fishing.

But as the momentum of his initial accomplishment waned so did his business. By following the marketing consultant's advice, however, Babusa has been dramatically stepping up the visibility, and with it the success, of his business. He installed a toll-free 800 line in his home office. He offers a faxback service of a new brochure to callers anywhere in the country. And he undertook a targeted advertising campaign. One result has been a new joint venture. A Branson-based audiovisual company contacted Babusa with an offer to coproduce Branson's first trout-fishing video called *Trophy Trout Fishing with Marty Babusa.*

Connie Connors also brought management consultants on board when the recession struck her marketing company right after she moved out of her home office. "It took a lot of soul-searching," she remembers. "I had no money, no employees, and no clients. I had to ask myself, 'What do I want to do in life?' and I realized I wasn't happy with the company I had created." That's when she brought in a husband-and-wife management-consulting team. They were willing to work with her on a contingency arrangement. Connors also set up an advisory board and got support from a financial investor who became her partner.

Partnering, both formal and informal, is often part of a successful survival strategy. As you recall, Bill Seavy rebooted his relocation service after a costly move by teaming up with The Denver Buffalo Club, a popular Denver restaurant, to do a promotional campaign. Nora Mulholland found vendors can be good partners, too, when her company, Office Furniture Brokers, got hit with a triple whammy, all within six months. First, she lost a key support person, then replacement personnel erased the $12,000 inventory database she'd invested in, and finally Mulholland discovered the same person neglected to tell her about $45,000 of consignment bills. "I was surprised," she told us, "how agreeable vendors were when I went to them for help. They can be your most important partners when you're in trouble." You'll find more information about a wide range of creative partnering options in the book we wrote with Rick Benzel called *Teaming Up*.

STARTING AGAIN WITH CONFIDENCE

In the midst of winter, I find myself invincible.
SOEN NAKAGAWA

As you can see, even after the most disastrous of falls, it's possible to start again. But as Robert Nelms, speaker and consultant on *What You Can Learn from Things That Go Wrong*, says, "Failure puts you in direct contact with ultimate truth. It's as close to the key to infinite wisdom as anything on earth." So, if along the way to your goals, you've found yourself waylaid by too many hurdles and hazards and it's clear the road you're on isn't taking you where you want to go, use the following thoughts to help you get back up and start again.

1. Remember, you're on your own, but you're not alone. Like the many people we've mentioned in this chapter, most successful individuals have turned down one or more dead-end streets on their journey to success. It's disappointing, yes, but you've undoubtedly learned a lot along the way that has better prepared you for the next phase of your journey. So, your chances for a future more to your liking have already gone up immensely.

2. Don't give up on living a glorious dream. As you can see from the experience of others, there are many roads to the same destination. So, don't settle for less than something marvelous for your life. With the knowledge you now have, you may want to reshape and redefine your dream; you may even want to replace it, but don't settle for less. Continue dreaming great dreams.

3. Wipe your slate clean.   You can start afresh from this day forward. You can dump the old baggage and throw out or wash the dirty laundry from previously unsatisfying efforts to be on your own. Each day is brand-new. Anytime you are reminded of a previous situation that didn't go well for you, remember that this is a totally new situation. You never stand in the same river twice.

4. Use what you've learned.   While you still may not have it all figured out, proceed confidently with what you now know and pay attention to the results you get from everything you do. Your results from day to day will point you toward what you need to do to get where you want to go.

Margot Fraser had a long, wintry road to travel in bringing Birkenstock shoes to America, but come summer, she said, "We don't know who we are until it's called for." And it's true. So, surprise yourself. As certified management consultant James Sirkin discovered in the process of becoming successfully self-employed, when you're on your own, you always have a choice about how you define your success. "When things don't work out," Sirkin told us, "you can tell your spouse you've failed and you're going out of business, or you can go tell your spouse you're starting a new business." He chose to do the latter.

RESOURCES

CREATIVE THINKING AND PROBLEM SOLVING

⬧ **Breaking Through: Creative Problem-Solving.** Thomas Logsdon. New York: Addison-Wesley, 1993. Behind-the-scenes stories of people whose simple, creative solutions have changed whole industries, from the Wright brothers to the creation of the electric toothbrush, and how you can apply their creativity to your problems.

⬧ **The IdeaFisher.** Marsh Fisher. Princeton, NJ: Peterson's/Pacesetter Books, 1995. You learn how to work with your mind—how to use its innate ability to store, remember, and recombine information to meet all types of challenges.

▢ **Idea Fisher.** Irvine, CA: Idea Fisher Systems, Inc. (714) 474-8111. This unique software program by Fisher Ideas Systems, Inc., is a tool for enhancing both creativity and productivity. It enables you to brainstorm solutions and quickly come up with creative ideas and solutions. It stimulates your thinking by prompting you with problem solving questions. Add-on programs are available for strategic planning, speeches, presentations, and breaking writer's blocks.

🖎 **Thinkertoys: A Handbook for Business Creativity in the 90's.** Michael Michalko. Berkeley, CA: Ten Speed Press, 1991. Hundreds of tricks, tips, and tales to stimulate startlingly creative thinking for new business ideas, new products, and marketing techniques for brainstorming and overcoming mental blocks to creativity.

INSPIRATION, MOTIVATION, AND SUPPORT

▦ **Health, Mental Health, and Addictions.** This America Online site provides information on addictions like smoking and other chemical dependencies. You can access to Medline, get lists of other related Internet sites, and search this site by specific illness or problem and get specific information on the topic.

🖎 **Hunter in a Business World.** Thomas C. Hartmann. Penn Valley, CA: Underwood Miller, 1994. This intriguing book is for those who are easily bored and hate details but want to run their own show. Many entrepreneurs feel they are "different" from everyone else and have had many hard knocks trying to fit into the traditional worlds of school and work. In this book, Hartmann, who's had this experience himself, explains why and how he's learned to to tap into the entrepreneur's innate advantages.

🖎 **In the Spirit of Business.** Robert Roskind. Berkeley, CA: Celestial Arts, 1992. Based on the principles from *Course in Miracles,* this book provides insights into making the best of the worst situations, dissolving fear, building a new relationship with money, earning a living ethically, and finding the gift in failure.

🖎 **Lighten Up: Survival Skills for People Under Pressure.** C. W. Metcalf and Roma Felible. Reading, MA: Addison-Wesley, 1992. How, when life doesn't want to cooperate, you can be more relaxed and resilient, productive and creative by bringing a sense of humor to the "serious" world of work.

🖎 **Man with No Name.** Wally Amos. Santa Rosa, CA: Aslan Publishing, 1994. A true comeback story. The inspiring saga of "Famous Amos's" descent from his cookie company into destitution and despair to his rebound from circumstances that would have driven most people under.

Moving Mountains: The Art of Letting Others See Things Your Way. Henry M. Boettinger. New York: Collier Books, 1989. A classic book on how to organize your thoughts, ideas, opinions, and arguments so that people will listen.

Risk-Taking for Personal Growth: A Step-by-Step Workbook. Joseph Ilardo, Ph.D. Oakland, CA: New Harbinger Publishers, 1992. Ilardo, a therapist and teacher of interpersonal communication and group dynamics, shows you how you can learn to take risks. By taking risks you can determine the kinds of risks you need to take, conquer fears, and commit with confidence to needed action to dispel your self-doubt.

Storms of Perfection. Andy Andrews. Charlotte, NC: Internet Services, 1992. Fifty plus celebrities, sports figures, and other highly successful individuals like Joan Rivers, Alexander Godunov, Sally Jesse Raphael, and Kenny Rogers relate their worst rejections and biggest setbacks and how, in their own words, they overcame them.

The Survivor Personality. Al Siebert. Portland, OR: Practical Psychology Press, 1994. How life's best survivors gain strength from adversity, thrive under pressure, survive change, develop resiliency, and convert misfortune into good luck.

*A classic.

Closing

Enjoying Your Success

Success is really a dreamlike experience.
BRUCE JOEL RUBIN
SCREENWRITER, DIRECTOR,
AND PRODUCER

CONGRATULATIONS! Wherever you are on your journey to success, you're doing it! You're living the dream of seven out of ten Americans. You are on your own, or about to be. You are your own boss. You are a success! Have you noticed yet?

Some highly successful people we've met tell us, "Oh, I'm not a success yet! I'm not going to be successful until . . ." For them success is reserved for the things they haven't yet attained. Actually, success is a process. There is no finish line; there are only milestones. As you achieve one set of goals, you set new ones in an ever-unfolding journey.

From our perspective, if you're on your own, or taking the necessary steps to be, you are already successful, right here, right now. You have had the courage, ingenuity, and confidence to do what you've done to get as far as you have at this moment. And that makes you a success.

Take, for example, the story of scriptwriter David Mickey Evans. Evans's script *Radio Days* was sold to Columbia Pictures for a record $1.2 million. Evans disagrees, however, with references to his so-called overnight success. He points out that *Radio Days* was his twenty-second screenplay. He had been writing scripts for low-budget horror and Western films to pay his way through college. The most he had ever made from any of these scripts was $3,500, so he had to work as a bartender, security guard, and phone installer to stay in school.

When he graduated from college, he owed $50,000 in student loans and had nowhere to live. For three years he lived at his brother's home, isolated in a small room with a bed and a computer. He was lonely and discouraged. At one point he needed money so badly that he called the navy recruiting office to find out about officer training. When he signed the Columbia deal, he had $4 in the bank.

So when did David become a success? Was it when he signed that $1.2-million deal? We don't think so. We think David became successful the moment he began steadfastly pursuing his desire to write screenplays. He was a success at each step in his struggle to stay afloat throughout those many years. Yet how easy it is to overlook all the success along the way and focus on some specific desirable outcome.

THE FIVE STAGES OF SUCCESS

Actually, the process of being on your own involves at least five major stages, and each is a victory in itself. Getting through these stages can seem frustrating and discouraging if you concentrate strictly on getting to the end. But if you can acknowledge and enjoy each stage en route, the journey can be as rewarding as arriving at your ultimate destination. Where are you along this success continuum?

Stage One: Exploration

The journey to anywhere usually begins with deciding where you want to go. And in making it on your own, this means exploring what you want to do. Many propreneurs feel as though they're responding to some type of calling, which makes this stage a short and easy one. These fortunate individuals seem to have been born knowing what they wanted to do with their lives. Like the world-famous ballerina Suzanne Farrell and the choreographer George Balanchine, they don't feel they've chosen to pursue their work as much as that it has chosen them. Farrell told the *Los Angeles Times,* "[Balanchine] was meant to do ballets. I was meant to dance. Call it Providence. We had no say in the matter."

Others of us, however, find the exploration stage to be much longer and more difficult. Many aspiring propreneurs are fraught at first with a lack of clarity about what type of work they want to do and how to proceed on their own. This was a particularly difficult problem for me, Paul. I had been raised from the time I was four years old to believe that I would become a lawyer. And I did. But once I began practicing law, I found it was not how I had wanted to spend my days. I was not enjoying the career my mother had chosen for me. One day I was eating lunch with a wealthy and respected attorney who asked me how I liked practicing law. I guess my response was less than convincing; the attorney picked up that I wasn't really satisfied. He proceeded to tell me that he, too, would rather be doing something other than practicing law and that if he had it to do over again he would pursue something else.

This candid revelation stuck in my mind. I was haunted by the possibility of being in the same situation as this lawyer after a lifetime career: successful perhaps in the eyes of the world, but a captive of an erroneous decision made long ago. Within the year I decided to leave my profession. Having no idea what I wanted to be now that I was really on my own, I spent several years searching for a new direction for my career.

So who's successful? The prominent, affluent man who works for a lifetime wishing he was doing something else, or the young man who drops out of a promising career to struggle with what he really wants to do? It's all in the way you choose to look at it.

I found that like other aspects of success, the process of determining what you want to do can't be hurried or forced, whether you like it or not. If you allow yourself the time to explore and discover, to mentally try on and investigate the many possibilities open to you, ultimately you will identify what you want to do. And when you do, you'll know it. You'll find yourself feeling committed to a specific line of work.

Your success begins the moment you begin the process of exploration, however. Even if you must explore for some time, even if you are trying out one thing after another and seemingly getting nowhere, even then, and throughout the entire exploration process, you should consider yourself successful because you've had the courage to set forth on a journey to find yourself. We wrote *Finding Your Perfect Work* to help people move more smoothly and confidently through this stage.

Stage Two: Preparation

Once you know where you're headed, the next stage involves preparing to undertake the journey. Many people attempt to bypass this stage. They jump right into doing what they want to do, with little forethought or preparation. Of course, as your own boss, you can proceed any way you choose. Research shows, however, that individuals who take six to nine months to prepare themselves for self-employment make it more frequently than those who jump in unprepared.

The preparation one needs to do, of course, varies from person to person. For some, it's a matter of learning—reading about their field or taking marketing courses. For others, it's a matter of money—saving enough to have a financial cushion before leaving the paycheck behind, or cleaning up past debts and establishing credit. For still others, it's a matter of lining up initial business or setting up a team of professionals to support their ventures.

Usually people who don't take steps to prepare for going out on their own end up taking the needed steps later. Fortunately, it's never too late to undertake whatever preparation you need, even if you have to start over again after an initial attempt. And even when you must start over, you should consider yourself a success because you are continuing to move toward your goals. On your own, success lies in running the race, not in finishing first or even in finishing the first time.

Stage Three: Start-up

Actually, starting out on your own is probably the most exciting and energizing of the stages. You not only have formed your dream and committed yourself to it, you also have taken action and turned it into reality. It can be exhilarating. But this can also be the most frightening stage, because you are leaving behind the world as you know it in exchange for a future you can only imagine.

Although you may feel like a greenhorn and may be living on a shoestring until things get going, many people are looking at you right now and seeing someone who is doing what he or she wants to do. Your tomorrow holds unlimited potential. Any day could bring you your break—not by happenstance, but as a result of your own efforts of today and yesterday.

Stage Four: Survival and Growth

Unless you are fortunate enough to have a fast start, this stage of success is probably the most challenging. It's the time during which you discover all the things you didn't expect, all the things you didn't know about and therefore couldn't prepare for. During this stage it's easy to get so fixated on all the things that aren't working yet that you forget to notice that you are making it.

Everything may not be going exactly the way you want it to, but since completing this stage may take you weeks or even years, it's important to keep in mind that you're doing it! And as long as you keep on doing it, ultimately you'll get where you want to go.

Stage Five: Bull's-Eye

When you finally attain your full dream, when you are actually living life the way you want to, what a moment! Celebrate and enjoy. Of course, sometimes the reality of your dream is as full of surprises and challenges as the journey you took to get there. You may be astonished by what you encounter once you achieve your goals. And you may quickly dream new dreams. But before traveling on, let yourself enjoy what you've worked for. Don't let anything interfere with the pleasure of what you've achieved.

SUCCESS IS SUPPOSED TO FEEL GOOD

May you have all the success you can enjoy.
SARAH AND PAUL EDWARDS

Despite all the changes and surprises that it brings, success is supposed to feel good. It's what you've worked for. Yet few of us are particularly well prepared for success. As the actor Charlie Sheen pointed out in a television interview, we learn as children how to work hard toward some future possibility of success and we even learn how to deal with failure, but we're rarely taught much about how to live with success.

In actuality, the price of success must be paid in full in advance, so whatever success you've achieved, you've already paid the price. So now is the time to enjoy the prize. You should do whatever you need to do to make sure that you can enjoy what you've worked for. Here are some ideas for overcoming five of the most common problems people have that prevent them from fully enjoying their success.

Keep Success Manageable

A Pamela Lawson wrote to the *Los Angeles Times* about how surprisingly unsettling success can sometimes be. She suggested, and we would agree, it should come with a warning label that reads "May cause drowsiness at peak dosage. May diminish your gift or passion for an extended period of time, but will regain full capacity as dosage is regulated. Do not take any other drugs while taking this medication. A temporary change in character may occur while taking this medication, and judgment may be impaired. If symptoms persist, consult your physician, nutritionist, or spiritual adviser. Do not commit suicide while taking this product."

Obviously Lawson speaks poignantly from experience. Sometimes the whirl of success becomes not only exhilarating and rewarding but overwhelming and distressing. This is especially true the faster it comes and the more it soars beyond your original expectations. So understanding and preparing for what success will mean can help keep it in perspective.

Success, of any degree, acts as a magnet. It attracts more of everything your way—more money, more business, more phone calls, more mail, more bills, and more opportunities. So whether success turns out to be all it's cracked up to be will depend in large part upon how ready and willing you are to handle the abundance it brings. When you have very little coming into your life, orchestrating it is relatively easy. The more that comes to you without any effort on your part, however, the more important it becomes to let in only those aspects you want so success won't litter your life. Never think that you must accept everything success brings simply because it has come to you.

As we mentioned in chapter 2, in order to seize the reins of their success, many propreneurs consciously decide to limit or even cut back their businesses. They choose not to expand. They choose not to complicate their lives. This is one example of how you can shape your success into a way of life that makes having achieved it worthwhile.

You also can elect to take on only those clients, customers, projects, and jobs that you enjoy. You can refer others elsewhere. You may be able to raise your prices as a way of keeping your business manageable. And you most certainly can use the resources success is bringing you to make sure you don't become enslaved by your success. As you grow, for example, you can hire administrative personnel and outside services. You can purchase and use technology that was once beyond your budget to help keep your day, your desk, and your disposition clear for what's most important to you.

Know Your Success Is Here to Stay

Nothing can ruin the satisfaction of success more quickly than an ever-present lingering fear that it will all disappear tomorrow. Sometimes people subconsciously imagine that if they notice and enjoy their success it will somehow magically go away. Some people even seem to believe that if they're sufficiently miserable or drive themselves relentlessly they can ward off future misfortune.

In actuality, you've created whatever success you've achieved from the events and circumstances around you. As the bookkeeper Chellie Campbell says, "You've made it up." Every day brings a completely new set of ingredients for you to create more with, so you might as well approach each day from the premise that you can do it again. You might as well expect your success to continue. We've found that the more you enjoy success, the more it enjoys you and the more it just keeps hanging around.

That does not mean, of course, that you can take your achievements for granted and assume that, having achieved what you have, you're all done. We're never done! Every day is a new chance to play. And if you drop out of the game, of course you can't win. But playing doesn't have to be a grind or even difficult. You can play on your own terms. That's what it means to be your own boss. So, success doesn't mean you can't take a rest or relax. In fact, the most successful people we know are the most relaxed. They take more vacations and have more fun than anyone else we know. That's because the more momentum you build up for your business, the easier it is to keep going and the less energy it takes to create more.

Adjust Your Relationships to Your Success

Certainly success brings changes in the way people relate to you. In some ways, these changes make your life simpler. Your calls may be taken more eagerly. Doors may open more readily. But, in other ways, your life becomes more complex. You may experience an influx of people who see you as their opportunity. You may find yourself besieged by salespeople and other solicitors. Friends and family may become jealous of you or make new demands on you. And you may find yourself the target of people who are not pleased with your success. But you need not let these changes stand in the way of enjoying your new life.

While there may be those who are jealous or resentful of your success, there are as many others who genuinely enjoy associating with successful people. So spend your time with people you enjoy who enjoy you. Cultivate a habit of generosity. As Phil Laut, the author of *Money Is My Friend,* reminds us, the more willing you are to prosper others, the more willing others are to prosper you. So, enjoy giving freely of your time, your knowledge, your money, and your energy to the individuals, projects, and causes you admire and want to support.

Feel Worthy

Sometimes people feel undeserving of all the bounty success brings. This is especially true when the degree of success you've achieved seems disproportionate to the amount of effort you've put out. And if you've achieved success far beyond that of others around you, you may even feel somewhat embarrassed or guilty about succeeding on your own.

In some ways our culture reinforces a sense of ambivalence about success. Even though this is the land of free enterprise, where the entrepreneurial spirit abounds, there is also an underlying implication at times that people who do well are somehow doing so at the expense of others.

But you deserve whatever rewards you can create for yourself from your honest labor. So it's important to be on peaceful terms with your good fortune. We've found that one of the best cures for feeling unworthy is gratitude. Simply allowing yourself to feel grateful for what you've been able to accomplish may allow you to accept and enjoy your success more fully.

We realize some people have a problem with the idea of gratitude. In the process of growing up, many parents and teachers were a bit too eager to remind us that instead of wanting something more or being disappointed about something we don't have, we should feel grateful for what we do have. That's not what we're talking about here. From our perspective you always have a right to want more, and have more and be more if you wish. The desire for more from life is what keeps us alive and growing.

We believe it's equally important, however, to let yourself enjoy what you have, to allow yourself to fully savor the feeling of satisfaction that comes from having accomplished something you've wanted. So while you undoubtedly have even greater things to do, go ahead and let yourself revel a bit in the pleasures of what you have already created.

Acknowledge Yourself

And while you're at it, acknowledge yourself for what you've accomplished. You probably deserve a medal of honor for getting where you are today, but there are few outstanding-service awards for self-employed individuals. So we suggest that you give yourself one. Find some way to demonstrate to yourself just how much you value your perseverance, your dedication, and your willingness to sacrifice for your goals.

Jean Zalinsky bought herself a gold ring the day she reached her financial goal. Three years later Jean says, "I love this ring because to me it represents the commitment I made to myself. Every time I look at it I feel a sense of self-satisfaction that makes everything I've gone through to get where I am worthwhile."

Like Jean, the successfully self-employed people we've interviewed have told us that no matter how difficult their journey was, they would do it all again in a minute. In fact, the more challenging it was, the sweeter the joy of accomplishment, not just because it was so hard, but because success demands that we go beyond what seems possible and become more than we thought we could be. "It's all mine!" Chris Shalby told us. "It's like giving birth," Ellie Kahn claims. "I feel very lucky." Chellie Campbell puts it this way: "The best part is knowing that I'm totally the master of my own fate."

Success Is a Beginning, Not an End

We've found that once you begin to enjoy the sense of mastery success brings, you want to succeed all the more. You begin to have a sense of the magic you can make. It's the magic of life. It's the intoxicating force that has driven the creative powers of humankind throughout the ages. We all crave it, and as your own boss you're free to pursue it throughout your lifetime.

We urge you to let your natural desires direct and motivate you to increasing levels of success so that each day may become more rewarding and fulfilling. Each day can hold a new opportunity for you to participate in creating a world we'll all find more to our liking—a world in which all of us are free to pursue our creative talents and abilities to the fullest and to live well from them. We're delighted to be sharing this journey with you. Here's to your success!

RESOURCES

How Good People Make Tough Choices: Resolving the Dilemmas of Ethical Living. Rushworth M. Kidder. New York: Morrow, 1995. Offered are tools for careful deliberation of the ethical predicaments of daily living. Through self-reflection, Kidder provides an effective and applicable way to sort out ethical dilemmas from the most private and personal to the most public and global.

Lives Without Balance: When You're Giving All You've Got and Still Not Getting What You Hoped For. Steven Carter and Julia Sokol. New York: Villard, 1992. For those who work too much, owe too much, and worry too much, this book helps you step outside the limited idea that success has to be measured in terms of "money" and "things" and redefine your success to mean personal happiness and fulfillment.

The Paradox of Success: When Winning at Work Means Losing at Life. John R. O'Neil and Diana Landau. Los Angeles: Tarcher, 1995. A guide for those who are dissatisfied with what success has brought them and seek deep learning and renewal.

Appendix

Where-to-Get-Help
Resource Directory

WITH THIS DIRECTORY, you will be able to identify resources in your area that we have found serve the self-employed and home-based businesses. This directory differs from other compilations of small-business resources in that we have screened the entries to be certain that at the time of our research, they serve the very small business. Too often agencies that are listed as helping "small" businesses are only interested in larger small businesses and turn a deaf ear to the person wanting to start a business in his or her home or as a one-person operation.

We know these resources will change; many will be added; some will go out of existence or change their focus. With the cooperation of our publisher, future printings of this book will contain the updated information. We invite you to help us keep this information current.

Organized by state, the resources are divided into seven types. Not every state provides help for the very small business; and thus not every category is filled in each state at this time. Following is a description of the types of resources.

Information

Many states have an information number, usually provided by a Department of Commerce or Economic Development. The type of service varies. In some states, you may talk with a real person you can ask questions of; in others, you may make choices from a voice mail selection list for requesting material; in others a fax-back service may be offered. What a state offers in terms of information may cover only licenses and permits or be more comprehensive. The source of information may range from one person to an entire database of knowledge, contacts and referrals. Sometimes you will need to phone different phone numbers for start-up information versus information for existing businesses.

Small Business Administration (SBA)

The U.S. Small Business Administration offers assistance to small business in a wide variety of programs. Listed is the district office for each state. This office should be able to provide information on branch offices and Small Business Administration services throughout the state. The SBA also has an ANSWER DESK for the entire United States, reachable at (800) 8-ASK-SBA; (800) 827–5722. A listing of SBA services can be accessed on-line, on the Internet at **http://www.sbaonline.sba.gov** and without graphics at **gopherwww.sbaonline.sba.gov**

Small Business Development Centers (SBDC)

Both federal and state governments fund Small Business Development Centers. They are usually associated with universities or chambers of commerce. People get individual attention at SBDCs with counseling on matters ranging from business planning to identifying sources of funds. The lead office in each state can direct you to the SBDC nearest you.

Microloan Agencies

Microloan or microcredit agencies are a relatively newer type of lending institution that serves starting or expanding very small "microbusinesses," as they are called in microloan circles. Unlike conventional loans, microloans are not awarded primarily on collateral, credit histories, equity, or previous business success. Instead they are based primarily upon a belief in the borrowers' integrity and the soundness of their business ideas. The number of agencies in each state is provided. For the name and contact information for the microloan agency serving your area, contact the District Office of the Small Business Administration.

MINORITY ASSISTANCE

Every state has at least one office to help minority and women-owned businesses to become certified to bid on government work. Some provide assistance in getting technical and financial assistance.

UNIVERSITY COOPERATIVE EXTENSION

Extension is part of the land-grant university in each state, which has agents for each county. University extension programs have identified supporting and encouraging home-based businesses as a national priority. Although each state or county's program may differ, the county office can tell you if there is a home-based business specialist for your state or help you contact a specialist in a nearby state.

ASSOCIATIONS

Local and state home business associations are growing; however, the listings in this category change frequently as officers and leadership turn over.

Profile: DAVE CLARK
[Small Business Development Corporation]

In Homestead, Pennsylvania, three side-by-side homes house Rocky Mountain Enterprises. There for the past eleven years, fifty-four-year-old Dave Clark and his two younger brothers, Philip and Wayne, have crafted harps, lutes, zithers, lyres and other musical instruments. Dave jokes that his brothers keep him on because they prefer to be craftsmen rather than do the business development side of their business. In addition to working with his brothers, Dave commutes five miles to another town to help his fiancée with her home business, June's Homemade Fudge, which she makes from family recipes.

Dave has been self-employed for most of his adult life, most recently as a photographer. He has gone it alone without help until recently when he began using programs such as the SBDC to help with his business development. If Dave wants to investigate a business idea, he uses the SBDC out of Duquesne University in Pittsburgh to do market research. "They help me make intelligent decisions," he said. Once, he wanted to find out about the market for wood tobacco accessories, and the SBDC helped him gather information on the industry and products. Dave plans to continue using the SBDC for testing his ideas. In fact, now he also teaches classes at the SBDC.

Profile: LESLIE RIENZIE
[Home Business Association]

Leslie Rienzie is a single mother with a teenage son in Oak Park, Illinois. After seventeen years in management and human resources, she became self-employed in early 1995, starting her business, The Rienzie Group. Her primary focus is to provide human resources support in personnel. She writes policies and procedures and provides in-house training and interviewing. Leslie spent many hours at her local SBDC office at Triton College, using their computers, books, and SCORE counseling. She tested her presentations on her SCORE advisors, and they all celebrated when she got her first client.

Because she wanted to know more about business, Leslie applied and won an SBDC scholarship for an SBDC class. At the last class meeting, the president of Home Executives' National Networking Association (HENNA), a locally based home business association, was present and talked about the advantages of membership and the value of a support group.

She joined HENNA and especially enjoys the brown-bag lunches with other self-employed professionals that get her out of the house when she's working at home. She likes the businesslike atmosphere of the meetings and finds she always learns something new. She also gets to contribute her own expertise to the group. If she needs advice on a proposal she's drafting, she can fax it to another HENNA member and get feedback. She has gained clients, colleagues, and friends from her membership in this association. Now Leslie has started another HENNA chapter closer to her home.

Profile: JUDY AND LEONARD GREEN
[Assistance to Minorities and Women]

Judy and Leonard Green partnered to create a business they call Cowboy Contractors, Inc. Appropriately enough, it's located in Lovell, Wyoming. In the 1970s Leonard wanted a change from a job in sales, and so he and Judy went into business with his brother to provide fencing and seeding services to private and state contractors. In 1976, after buying out the brother, the couple got their business certified as a woman-owned business. Other contractors who wanted to contract with them encouraged Judy to get certified, saying it would help them out because they had to meet quotas. Prior to that, Judy and Leonard didn't know about certification; "We just fell into it," she said. After completing the required paperwork and being interviewed by both state and federal officers, the company was certified by the Department of Transportation. "Some men think they can just put their wives' names on the papers, and that would be enough, but it isn't. You have to be involved in the business and every year they must file for recertification."

Judy says that now 90 percent of their work consisting of fencing and ground work (seeding, mulching, fertilizing) comes from state bids. Because Judy has business experience, she runs the company and their twenty-five employees from their home. Because most of the jobs are done along highways and roads, the work takes their crews all over Wyoming.

Profile: FLOYD CULP
[Cooperative Extension]

In 1990 Floyd Culp's wife, Margaret, got him a new job. Floyd was a retired parks and recreation director who, with his wife, loved to repair airplanes. They were exploring ways to start a new business when she insisted they attend a workshop given by Oklahoma State University's Cooperative Extension Service's Home Economics Program. One of the speakers talked about defense contracting.

Within three months their new company, Aircraft & Industrial Services, Inc., had won its first bid on a government contract and the Culps were on their way. "Once people realized we were serious about doing this work, everyone went all out to help us and make this bid happen." Floyd said his experience drafting grants for parks and recreation prepared him for the paperwork involved in defense contracts. He also believes they have been able to compete with the big corporations because as a home-based business, their overhead is lower and they respond quickly to their customers' needs. Their family business has grown enough that they had their ten acres rezoned for light industrial use, and now have a separate building on their property to do their work.

The Culps continue to take extension classes. "Their only purpose is to help people like me, and I believe that. They tailor their programs around our needs." Another class brought the Culps in contact with a program that teamed large manufacturers, who normally send work out-of-state, with small manufacturers, who will do the work in the state. As a result, their small business now makes products for another company in Oklahoma which are sold in the United States, Canada, and Mexico.

His newest class is on computers. "The instructors wanted to know what software programs I use in my business, and then they got the same programs." This allows him to bring his work to the classroom for hands-on assistance.

Profile: CYNTHIA ELLIASON
[Microloans]

For the past five years, Cynthia Elliason has been taking people on dogsled tours. Her part-time business, Keewatin Sled Tours, is based in her home in Bartlett, New Hampshire. A few years ago she needed new harnesses, gang lines, and other equipment. And if her business was to grow she also needed money to do advertising and promotions.

By joining a Working Capital lending group, she was able to get a $500 microloan which she paid off in six months. The lending group consists of ten people. They didn't ask about her credit history, but they did want to know about her business, why they should make the loan, and what she would do to repay the loan if the business didn't do well. And there is considerable peer pressure because no one else in the group can get a loan if any member defaults on his or her loan. As a result, Elliason says, "Getting a microloan gives you a different kind of feeling than if you borrowed from a bank because it's your friends and colleagues you're letting down if you don't make your payments."

Elliason hasn't had problems making the loan payments, however. Her marketing efforts landed a contract with a ski area.

Profile: MELANIE CULLEN
[Small Business Administration]

RV Power Products, a business operated by Melanie and Rick Cullen, and Ford Motor Company have something in common. They both started in a garage. The Cullens' business grew from their enjoyment of RV traveling. Their enjoyment was interrupted, however, by discovering there was no way to monitor the RV's coach battery. Rick, an engineer, created a solution for this problem. The solution is a device that monitors battery life so that regeneration need only take half an hour. When other RV owners saw the mechanism, "they asked us where we could get one!" So the Cullens started RV Power Products to make and sell these devices.

Melanie decided to take classes offered by the Small Business Administration. "In their two-day workshop on writing a business plan, you work on a plan for your own business." She took several other SBA classes on marketing and advertising and on copyright, patents, and trademarks. Approximately thirty to fifty people attended each day-long class. "I enjoyed them," Melanie said.

In addition to operating their home-based business and raising two small children, Melanie is on the board of directors of the Association of Home-Based Businesses in Encinitas, California.

ALABAMA

	Agencies	Address	Phone Number	Fax Number
SBA	District Office	2121 Eighth Avenue N # 200	205-731-1344	205-731-1404
	Microloan Agencies: 1	Birmingham, AL 35203-2398		
SBDC	Lead Office	1717 11th Avenue S. #419 Birmingham, AL 35294	205-934-7260	205-934-7645
Assistance to Minorities	Office of Minority Business Enterprise Dept. of Economic & Community Affairs	401 Adams Avenue Suite 570 Montgomery, AL 36130	334-242-2220 800-447-4191	334-242-5099
University Extension	call county extension			

ALASKA

	Agencies	Address	Phone Number	Fax Number
Information	Department of Commerce Division of Trade & Economic Development	General Business Development Information-Network PO Box 110804 9th Floor, SOB Juneau, AK 99811-0804	907-465-2017	907-465-3767
SBA	District Office	222 West 8th Avenue #67 Anchorage, AK 99513-7559	907- 271-4022	907-271-4545
SBDC	Lead Office	430 W. 7th Avenue, Suite 110 Anchorage, AK 99501	907-274-7232	907-274-9524
Assistance to Minorities	Department of Transportation & Public Facilities DBE Office	PO Box 196900 Anchorage, AK 99519-6900	907-762-4260	907-762-4270
University Extension	call county extension			

ARIZONA

	Agencies	Address	Phone Number	Fax Number
Information	Business Connection	3800 N. Central #1500 Phoenix, AZ 85012	602-280-1480 800-542-5684	602-280-1339
SBA	District Office **Microloan Agencies:** 2	2828 North Central Ave. Suite 800 Phoenix, AZ 85004-1093	602-640-2316	602-640-2360
SBDC	Lead Office	Maricopa Community College 1414 W. Broadway #165 Tempe, AZ 85282	602-966-7786	602-966-8541
Assistance to Minorities	Arizona Minority & Women Owned Business Service	3800 N. Central #1500 Phoenix, AZ 85012	602-280-1476	602-280-1339
University Extension	call county extension			
Associations	Home-based Business Assoc. of Arizona	1432 W. Emerald #717 Mesa, AZ 85202-3209	602-464-0778	602-834-3432

ARKANSAS

	Agencies	Address	Phone Number	Fax Number
Information	Small Business Clearinghouse Arkansas Industrial Development Commission	One State Capitol Mall Little Rock, AR 72201	501-682-7782	501-682-1209
SBA	District Office **Microloan Agencies:** 3	2120 Riverfront Drive Suite 100 Little Rock, AR 72202	501-324-5277	501-324-5199
SBDC	Lead Office	Univ. Of Arkansas 100 S. Main St. #401 Little Rock, AR 72201	501-324-9043	501-324-9049
Assistance to Minorities	Arkansas Industrial Development Commission Minority Business Development Program	One State Capitol Mall Little Rock, AR 72203	501-682-1060	501-682-7394
University Extension	Arkansas Cooperative Extension Service	Univ. Of Arkansas PO Box 391 Little Rock, AR 72203	501-671-2000	501-671-2251

CALIFORNIA

	Agencies	Address	Phone Number	Fax Number
Information	Small Business Helpline		916-327-4367 800-303-6600 (CA only)	
SBA	District Offices Microloan Agencies: 4	2719 N. Air Fresno Dr. #107 Fresno, CA 92727	209-487-5791	209-487-5636
		330 N. Brand Blvd. #1200 Glendale, CA 91203-2304	818-552-3210	818-552-3260
		660 J Street, Rm. 215 Sacramento, CA 95814-2413	916-498-6410	916-498-6422
		550 W. C St. #550 San Diego, CA 92101	619-557-7252	619-557-5894
		211 Main St., 4th Flr. San Francisco, CA 94105-1988	415-744-6820	415-744-6812
		200 W. Santa Ana Blvd. #700 Santa Ana, CA 92701	714-550-7420	714-550-0191
SBDC	Lead Office	806 K St. #1700 Sacramento, CA 95814	916-324-1295	916-324-5084
Assistance to Minorities	Minority Business Development Agency	221 Main Street Suite 1280 San Francisco, CA 94105	415-744-3001	415-744-3061
University Extension	call county extension			
Associations	Assoc. Of Home-Based Businesses	140 Encinitas Encinitas, CA 92024	619-591-1151	

COLORADO

	Agencies	Address	Phone Number	Fax Number
Information	Small Business Hotline (Licensing, permits)	1560 Broadway Denver, CO 80202	303-592-5920 800-333-7798	303-894-7834
SBA	District Office **Microloan** **Agencies:** 2	721 19th Street 4th Flr. Denver, CO 80202-2599	303-844-3984	303-844-6490
SBDC	Lead Office	9905 E. Colfax Aurora, CO 80010-2119	303-341-4849	303-361-2953
Assistance to Minorities	State Office of Certification	1560 Broadway Suite 1530 Denver, CO 80202	303-894-2355	303-894-7834
University Extension	Colorado State University	1 Administration Building Coop. Extension Ft. Collins, CO 80523	970-491-6281	970-491-6208
Associations	Rocky Mt. Home Business Association	9905 E. Colfax Aurora, CO 80010-2119	303-367-1918	303-361-2953

CONNECTICUT

	Agencies	Address	Phone Number	Fax Number
Information	Business Resource Center	805 Brook St. Building 4 Rocky Hill, CT 06067-3405	800-392-2122	203-571-7150
SBA	District Office **Microloan** **Agencies:** 1	330 Main Street 2nd Flr. Hartford, CT 06106	860-486-4135	860-486-1576
SBDC	Lead Office	Univ. of Connecticut U-94, Bourn Place MTS Storrs, CT 06269-5094	860-486-1576	
Assistance to Minorities	Department Of Economic Development.	805 Brook St. Building 4 Rocky Hill, CT 06067-34054	800-392-2122	860-571-7150
	Department of Transportation	2800 Burlin Turnpike Newington, CT 06131-7546	860-594-2000	860-594-3066
University Extension	call county extension			

DELAWARE

	Agencies	Address	Phone Number	Fax Number
SBA	District Office **Microloan Agencies:** 1	824 Market #610 Wilmington, DE 19801	302-573-6295	302-573-6060
SBDC	Lead Office	Univ. of Delaware Purnell Hall, Suite 005 Newark, DE 19716	302-831-1555	302-831-1423
Assistance to Minorities	Department of Transportation	250 Bear-Christiana Rd. Bear, DE 19701	302-323-4494	302-323-4541
University Extension	call county extension			

DISTRICT OF COLUMBIA

	Agencies	Address	Phone Number	Fax Number
Information	Department of Economic Development	717 Fourteenth St. NW 12th Flr. Washington, DC 20005	202-727-6600	202-727-3787
SBA	District Office **Microloan Agencies:** 2	1110 Vermont Ave. NW Suite 900 PO Box 34500 Washington, DC 20005	202-606-4000	202-606-4225
SBDC	Lead Office	Howard University 2600 Sixth Street NW Washington, DC 20059	202-806-1550	202-806-1777
Assistance to Minorities	Department of Human Rights	441 Fourth Street NW Washington, DC 20001	202-724-1385	202-724-3786
University Extension	call county extension			

FLORIDA

	Agencies	Address	Phone Number	Fax Number
Information	Bureau of Business Assistance Department of Commerce	107 W. Gaines Room 443 Tallahassee, FL 32399-2000	904-488-9357	904-922-9596
SBA	District Office **Microloan Agencies: 2**	1320 South Dixie Highway 3rd Flr. Coral Gables, FL 33146-2911	305-536-5521	305-536-5058
SBDC	SBDC	Univ. of West Florida 11000 University Parkway Pensacola, FL 32514-5750	904-474-2908	904-474-2126
Assistance to Minorities	Commission on Minority Economic & Business Development	107 Gaines St. Tallahassee, FL 32399-2005	904-487-4698	904-922-6852
University Extension	University of Florida Extension	Orange Co. Coop. Service 2350 E. Michigan St. Orlando, FL 32806	407-836-7572	407-836-7578
Associations	American Assoc. of Home-Based Businesses-Tampa Bay, Inc.	8348 Somerset Dr., Largo, FL 34643	813-539-8384	
	SHIBA / Future Entrepreneurs' Network	PO Box 373229 Satellite Beach, FL 23937	407-779-9161	407-773-9557

GEORGIA

	Agencies	Address	Phone Number	Fax Number
Information	Georgia Chamber of Commerce	233 Peachtree #200 Atlanta, GA 30303	404-223-2264	404-223-2290
SBA	District Office **Microloan Agencies: 2**	1720 Peachtree Rd. NW Room 600 Atlanta, GA 30309	404-347-4147	404-347-4745
SBDC	Lead Office	Univ. of Georgia Chicopee Complex 1180 E. Broad St. Athens, GA 30602-5412	706-542-7436	706-542-6776
Assistance to Minorities	Minority Business Development Agency	401 W. Peachtree #1715 Atlanta, GA 30308	404-730-3300	
University Extension	call county extension			

HAWAII

	Agencies	Address	Phone Number	Fax Number
Information	Business Action Center (licensing only)	1130 N. Nimitz Highway Room A254 Honolulu, HI 96817	808-586-2545	808-586-2544
SBA	District Office Microloan Agencies: 1	300 Ala Moana Blvd. Room 2314 Honolulu, HI 96850-4981	808-541-2990	808-541-2976
SBDC	Lead Office	Univ. of Hawaii 200 W. Kawili St. Hilo, HI 96720-4091	808-933-3515	808-933-3683
Assistance to Minorities	Department of Commerce & Consumer Affairs	1010 Richards St. Honolulu, HI 96813	808-586-2727	808-586-2727
University Extension	University of Hawaii at Manoa College of Tropical Agriculture & Human Resources	3050 Maile Way, Gilmore 115 Honolulu, HI 96822	808-956-6755	808-956-2811

IDAHO

	Agencies	Address	Phone Number	Fax Number
Information	Idaho Department Of Commerce	700 W. State St. PO Box 720 Boise, ID 83720-0093	208-334-2470	208-334-2631
SBA	District Office Microloan Agencies: 1	1020 Main Street #290 Boise, ID 83702-5745	208-334-1696	208-334-9353
SBDC	Lead Office	Boise State University 1910 University Dr. Boise, ID 83725	208-385-1640 800-225-3815 (ID only)	208-385-3877
Assistance to Minorities	Idaho Department of Transportation DBE Support services	PO Box 7129 Boise, ID 83707-1129	208-344-8000	208-332-7812
University Extension	contact county extension			
Associations	Buy Idaho	PO Box 6016 Boise, ID 83707	208-343-2582	208-343-5231

ILLINOIS

	Agencies	Address	Phone Number	Fax Number
Information	First Stop Business Information Center	620 E. Adams Avenue Springfield, IL 62701	800-252-2923 (IL only) 217-785-8017	217-782-1963
SBA	District Office **Microloan Agencies:** 4	500 West Madison Street Suite 1250 Chicago, IL 60661-2511	312-353-4508	312-886-5688
SBDC	Department of Commerce & Community Affairs SBDC	620 E. Adams St. 3rd Flr. Springfield, IL 62701	217-524-5856	217-785-6328
Assistance to Minorities	Department of Central Management Services MASBE	100 W. Randolph St. #400 Chicago, IL 60601	312-814-4190	312-814-4190
University Extension	call county extension			
Associations	Home Executives' National Networking Association	PO Box 1054 Batavia, IL 60108-6223	708-307-7130	
	Home-Based Business Owners Northwest Suburbs	719 East Lincoln Avenue Belvidere, IL 61008	815-547-8833	815-547-8833

INDIANA

	Agencies	Address	Phone Number	Fax Number
Information	Inform Indiana Hotline		800-726-8000	
SBA	District Office **Microloan Agencies:** 2	429 N. Pennsylvania #100 Indianapolis, IN 46204-1873	317-226-7272	317-226-7259
SBDC	Lead Office	One N. Capitol #420 Indianapolis, IN 46204-2248	317-264-6871	317-264-3102
Assistance to Minorities	Indiana Department Of Admin.	402 W. Washington St. Room W474 Indianapolis, IN 46204	317-232-3061	317-233-5022
University Extension	Purdue University Cooperative Extension	1140 Agricultural Adm. Bldg. W. Lafayette, IN 47907-1140	317-494-8489	317-494-5876
Associations	Women's Home Business Network	2138 E. Broad Ripple Ave. #225 Indianapolis, IN 46220	317-251-1131 800-858-9426 (IN only)	317-823-5581

IOWA

	Agencies	Address	Phone Number	Fax Number
Information	Iowa Department Of Economic Development Small Business Helpline	200 E. Grand Avenue Des Moines, IA 50309	515-242-4750 800-532-1216 (IA only)	
SBA	District Offices **Microloan Agencies:** 1	215 4th Ave. Road SE #200 Cedar Rapids, IA 52401-1806	319-362-6405	319-362-7861
		210 Walnut St. #749 Des Moines, IA 50309	515-284-4422	515-284-4572
SBDC	Lead Office	Chamberlynn Building 137 Lynn Avenue Ames, IA 50010	515-292-6351	515-292-0020
Assistance to Minorities	Department of Inspection & Appeals	Lucas State Office Building Des Moines, IA 50319	515-281-7250	515-281-4477
University Extension	call county extension			

KANSAS

	Agencies	Address	Phone Number	Fax Number
Information	First Stop Clearinghouse	Kansas Department of Commerce & Housing 700 SW Harrison St. #1300 Topeka, KS 66603-3712	913-296-5298	913-296-3490
SBA	District Office **Microloan Agencies:** 2	100 East English St. # 510 Wichita, KS 67202	316-269-6566	316-269-6499
SBDC	College of Business Administration SBDC	2323 Anderson Avenue #100 Manhattan, KS 66502-2912	913-532-5529	913-532-5827
Assistance to Minorities	Office of Minority Business	Kansas Department of Commerce & Housing 700 SW Harrison St. #1300 Topeka, KS 66603-3712	913-296-3805	913-296-3490
University Extension	contact county extension			

KENTUCKY

	Agencies	Address	Phone Number	Fax Number
Information	KY Cabinet for Economic Development Business Information Clearinghouse	2200 Capital Plaza Tower 22nd Flr. Frankfort, KY 40601	800-626-2250 (KY only) 502-564-4252	502-564-5932
SBA	District Office **Microloan Agencies: 2**	600 Dr. Martin Luther King, Jr. Place #188 Louisville, KY 40202	502-582-5971	502-582-5009
SBDC	Lead Office University of Kentucky Center for Business Development	225 Carol Martin Gatton College of Business & Economics Lexington, KY 40506-0034	606-257-7668	606-323-1907
Assistance to Minorities	KY Cabinet for Economic Development, Small & Minority Business Div.	67 Wilkinson Blvd. Frankfort, KY 40601	502-564-2064 800-626-2250 (KY only)	502-564-9758
University Extension	Cooperative Extension Service University of Kentucky	205 Scovell Hall Lexington, KY 40546	606-257-3888	606-257-7565

LOUISIANA

	Agencies	Address	Phone Number	Fax Number
Information	The First Stop Business Shop (start-ups)	3851 Essen Lane Baton Rouge, LA 70809	800-259-0001	
	Business Services Division (existing)	PO Box 94185 Baton Rouge, LA 97004-9185	504-342-5893	504-342-5349
SBA	District Office **Microloan Agencies: 1**	1 Canal Place #2250 365 Canal St. New Orleans, LA 70130	504-589-6685	504-589-2239
SBDC	Lead Office Northeast Louisiana University	College of Business Admin. Room 2-57 Monroe, LA 71209-6435	318-342-5506	318-342-5510
Assistance to Minorities	Div. of Economically Disadvantaged Business Development	PO Box 94185 Baton Rouge, LA 70804-9185	504-342-5373	504-342-5926
University Extension	Call Parish Extension or Louisiana Cooperative Extension	Knapp Hall, LSU PO Box 25100 Baton Rouge, LA 70894-5100	504-388-4141	504-338-2478

MAINE

	Agencies	Address	Phone Number	Fax Number
Information	Business Answers	Department of Economic & Community Development State House Augusta, ME 04333	207-287-5701 800-872-3838 (ME only)	
SBA	District Office **Microloan Agencies:** 3	40 Western Avenue #512 Augusta, ME 04330	207-622-8378	207-622-8277
SBDC	Coastal Enterprises Inc. SBDC	Water Street Box 268 Wiscasset, ME 04578	207-882-4340	207-882-4456
Assistance to Minorities	Department of Transportation Div. of Equal Opportunity & Employee Relations	#16 State House Station Augusta, ME 04333-0016	207-287-3576	207-287-2083
University Extension	University of Maine	Cooperative Extension 5741 Libby Hall Orono, ME 04469-5741	800-287-0274	207-581-1387

MARYLAND

	Agencies	Address	Phone Number	Fax Number
SBA	District Office **Microloan Agencies:** 1	10 South Howard Street Suite 6220 Baltimore, MD 21201	410-962-4392	410-962-1805
SBDC	Lead Office	217 E. Redwood St. 10th Flr. Baltimore, MD 21202	410-767-6552	410-333-4460
Assistance to Minorities	Office of Minority Business Enterprise	10 Elm Rd. BWI Airport Baltimore, MD 21240	410-859-7327	410-850-9263
University Extension	call county extension			
Associations	American Assoc. of Home-Based Businesses, Inc.	PO Box 10023 Rockville, MD 20849-0023	800-447-9710	

MASSACHUSETTS

	Agencies	Address	Phone Number	Fax Number
	District Office **Microloan Agencies:** 4	10 Causeway St. #265 Boston, MA 02222-1093	617-565-5590	617-565-5598
SBDC	University of Massachusetts	Univ. of Mass., Amherst # 205 School of Management Amherst, MA 01003-4935	413-545-6301	413-545-1273
Assistance to Minorities	Office of Minority & Women Business Assistance	100 Cambridge St. #1303 Boston, MA 02202	617-727-8692	617-727-5915
University Extension	University of Massachusetts Extension	Tillson House PO Box 37605 Amherst, MA 01003-7605	413-549-8800	413-549-6337
Associations	Homebased Businesswomen's Network, Inc.	PO Box 681 Newburyport, MA 01950	508-462-2063	508-463-0241
	Women's Entrepreneur Homebased Support Group	24 Brayton Rd Boston, MA 02135-3015	617-254-1729	
	Boston Computer Society's Small and Home Office SIG	Boston Computer Society 101 1st Ave. Waltham, MA 02154	617-290-5700	617-290-5744

MICHIGAN

	Agencies	Address	Phone Number	Fax Number
Information	Michigan Jobs Commission Customer Assistance (Start-ups)	201 N. Washington Sq. Victor Office Center 4th Flr. Lansing, MI 48913	517-373-9808	517-335-0198
SBA	District Office **Microloan Agencies:** 4	477 Michigan Avenue Room 515 Detroit, MI 48226	313-226-6075	313-226-4769
SBDC	Lead Office	2727 Second Avenue #107 Detroit, MI 48201	313-964-1798	313-964-3648
Assistance to Minorities	Targeted Services Group Women/Minority Business Owner Services	Michigan Jobs Commission PO Box 30225 Law Bldg. Lansing, MI 48909	517-335-3099	517-373-9143
University Extension	contact county extension			

MINNESOTA

	Agencies	Address	Phone Number	Fax Number
Information	Small Business Assistance Office	121 Seventh Place E. 500 Metro Square St. Paul, MN 55101	612-297-2103	612-296-1290
SBA	District Office **Microloan Agencies:** 4	100 North 6th Street Suite 610C Minneapolis, MN 55403-1563	612-370-2324	612-370-2303
SBDC	Lead Office	121 Seventh Place E. 500 Metro Square St. Paul, MN 55101	612-297-5770	612-296-1290
Assistance to Minorities	Minnesota Department of Admin. Materials Management Division	Administration Bldg. 50 Sherburne Ave. #112 St. Paul, MN 55155	612-296-2600	612-297-3996
University Extension	call county extension			
Associations	Home-Based Business Association of Minnesota	5115 Excelsior Blvd. #211 St. Louis Park, MN 55416	612-361-3701	

MISSISSIPPI

	Agencies	Address	Phone Number	Fax Number
SBA	District Office **Microloan Agencies:** 2	101 West Capitol Street Suite 400 Jackson, MS 39201	601-965-4378	601-965-4294
SBDC	Lead Office	Old Chemistry Building Suite 216 University, MS 38677	601-232-5001	601-232-5650
Assistance to Minorities	Department Of Economic & Community Development	Minority Business Enterprise Division PO Box 849 1200 Walter Sillers Bldg. Jackson, MS 39205	601-359-3448	601-359-2832
University Extension	call local county extension			

MISSOURI

Agencies		Address	Phone Number	Fax Number
	First Stop Shop	PO Box 118 Jefferson City, MO 65102	800-523-1434 ext. 2 314-751-4892	314-751-7385
SBA	District Office **Microloan** **Agencies:** 1	323 West 8th Street #501 Kansas City, MO 64105	816-374-6708	816-374-6759
SBDC	Lead Office	300 University Place Columbia, MO 65211	314-882-0344	314-884-4297
Assistance to Minorities	Minority Business Assistance Program	PO Box 1157 Jefferson City, MO 65102	314-751-3237 800-523-1434 ext. 4 (MO only)	314-751-7258
University Extension	University of Missouri Extension	1901 NE 48th Street Kansas City, MO 64118	816-792-7760	816-792-7787
Associations	Home Business Connection	1901 NE 48th Street Kansas City, MO 64118	816-792-7692	816-792-7787
	Missouri Home-Based Business Assoc.	PO Box 105963 Jefferson City, MO 65110-5963	800-758-1888	816-436-0740

MONTANA

	Agencies	Address	Phone Number	Fax Number
Information	Business Licensing Center Department of Commerce Div. of Economic Development	1424 Ninth Avenue Helena, MT 59620	406-444-4109	406-444-1872
SBA	District Office **Microloan** **Agencies:** 2	301 South Park Room 334 Helena, MT 59626	406-441-1081	406-444-1872
SBDC	Montana SBDC	Department of Commerce 1424 Ninth Avenue Helena, MT 59620	406-444-4780	406-444-2808
Assistance to Minorities	Montana Office of Transportation Civil Rights Bureau	2701 Prospect PO Box 201001 Helena, MT 59620-1001	406-444-6337	406-444-7685
University Extension	call county extension			

NEBRASKA

	Agencies	Address	Phone Number	Fax Number
Information	One Stop Business Assistance Center	PO Box 94666 301 Centennial Mall S. Lincoln, NE 68509-4666	402-471-3782 800-426-6505	402-471-3778
SBA	District Office **Microloan Agencies: 2**	11145 Mill Valley Road Omaha, NE 68154	402-221-4691	402-221-3680
SBDC	NSBDC Lead Office	University of Nebraska, Omaha 1313 Farnam, Suite 132 Omaha, NE 68182	402-595-2381	402-595-2385
Assistance to Minorities	Department of Roads	P O Box 94759 Lincoln, NE 68509-4759	402-479-4531	402-479-4325
University Extension	University Cooperative Extension Hall County	3180 Highway 34 W. College Park Grand Island, NE 68801	308-385-5088	308-385-5092
Associations	Nebraska Home-Based Business Assoc.	208 E. 6th St. Ainsworth, NE 69210	402-731-6984	402-387-0636

NEVADA

	Agencies	Address	Phone Number	Fax Number
Information	Department of Business & Industry Center for Business Advocacy & Services	2501 E. Sahara #202 Las Vegas, NV 89104	702-486-4335	702-486-4340
SBA	District Office **Microloan Agencies: 1**	301 East Stewart Street Room 301 PO Box 7527 Las Vegas, NV 89125-7527	702-388-6611	702-388-6469
SBDC	University of Nevada-Reno	College of Business Admin. Business Bldg, Rm. 411 Reno, NV 89557-0100	702-784-1717	702-784-4337
Assistance to Minorities	Contracts & Compliance	1263 S. Stewart St. #210 Carson City, NV 89712	702-888-7497	702-888-7210
University Extension	call county extension			

NEW HAMPSHIRE

...es	Address	Phone Number	Fax Number
...ce of ...usiness & Industrial Development	PO Box 1856 Concord, NH 03302-1856	603-271-2591	603-271-2629
SBA District Office **Microloan Agencies:** 2	143 N. Main St. #202 Concord, NH 03301	603-225-1400	603-225-1409
SBDC New Hampshire SBDC	University of New Hampshire 108 McConnell Hall Durham, NH 03824	603-862-2200	603-862-4876
Assistance to Minorities Department Of Transportation, Labor Compliance Office	PO Box 483 Concord, NH 03302	603-271-6611	603-271-3914
University Extension	call county extension		
Associations New England Assoc. of Home-Based Businesses	P. O. Box 239 Rindge, NH 03461	603-899-3261	603-899-9887

NEW JERSEY

Agencies	Address	Phone Number	Fax Number
Information Division for the Development of Small Business, Women's Business & Minority-Owned Business	Department of Commerce & Economic Development 20 W. State, CN 835 Trenton, NJ 08625	609-292-3860	609-292-9145
SBA District Office **Microloan Agencies:** 4	2 Gateway Center Newark, NJ 07102	201-645-2434	201-645-6265
SBDC Rutgers University	Graduate School of Management University Heights 180 University Avenue Newark, NJ 07102	201-648-5950	201-648-1175
Assistance to Minorities Division for the Development of Small Business, Women's Business & Minority Owned Business	Department of Commerce & Economic Development 20 W. State, CN 835 Trenton, NJ 08625	609-292-3860	609-292-9145
University Extension	call county extension		

NEW MEXICO

	Agencies	Address	Phone Number	Fax Number
Information	Office of Enterprise Development	PO Box 20003 Santa Fe, NM 87504-5003	505-827-0300	505-827-0407 modem: 800-827-0285
SBA	District Office **Microloan Agencies:** 1	625 Silver Avenue SW Suite 320 Albuquerque, NM 87102	505-766-1870	505-766-1057
SBDC	Lead Office	PO Box 4187 Santa Fe, NM 87502-4187	505-438-1362	505-438-1237
Assistance to Minorities	General Services Department State Purchasing Agency	Joseph Montoya Bldg. 1100 St. Francis Dr. Room 2006 Santa Fe, NM 87503	505-827-0472	505-827-0499
University Extension	call county extension			
Associations	Rocky Mountain Home-Based Business Association	1925 Juan Tabo Blvd. NE B-275 Albuquerque, NM 87112	505-298-7112	505-292-3820

NEW YORK

	Agencies	Address	Phone Number	Fax Number
Information	Business Assistance Hotline	633 Third Avenue 32nd Flr. NY, NY 10017	800-782-8369	212-803-2309
SBA	District Offices	111 W. Huron St. #1311 Buffalo, NY 14202	716-551-4301	716-551-4418
	Microloan Agencies: 4	26 Federal Plaza #31-100 NY, NY 10278	212-264-2454	212-264-4963
		100 S. Clinton St. #1073 PO Box 7317 Syracuse, NY 13261-7317	315-448-0423	315-448-0402
SBDC	State University of New York	SUNY Plaza S-523 Albany, NY 12246	518-443-5398 800-732-SBDC (NY only)	518-465-4992
Assistance to Minorities	Department of Economic Development, Minority & Women's Business Div.	633 Third Avenue 32nd Flr. NY, NY 10017	212-803-2410	212-803-2309
University Extension	call county extension			

NORTH CAROLINA

		Address	Phone Number	Fax Number
	...ss License ...mation Office	110 S. Blount Raleigh, NC 27601	919-733-0641	919-733-0642
SBA	District Office **Microloan** **Agencies:** 1	200 N. College Street Suite A2015 Charlotte, NC 28202-2173	704-344-6563	704-344-6769
SBDC	Lead Office	333 Fayetteville St. Mall Suite 1150 Raleigh, NC 27601-1742	919-715-7272	919-715-7777
Assistance to Minorities	Department of Administration Division of Purchasing & Contracts	PO Box 29582 Raleigh, NC 27626-0582	919-733-3581	919-733-4826
University Extension	call county extension			

NORTH DAKOTA

	Agencies	Address	Phone Number	Fax Number
Information	Center for Innovation & Business Development	PO Box 8372 Grand Forks, ND 58202	701-777-3132	701-777-2339
SBA	District Office **Microloan** **Agencies:** 1	657 2nd Avenue North Room 219 PO Box 3086 Fargo, ND 58102-3086	701-239-5131	701-239-5645
SBDC	Lead Office	University of North Dakota 118 Gamble Hall PO Box 7308 Grand Forks, ND 58202	701-777-3700	701-777-3225
Assistance to Minorities	Department of Economic Development & Finance	1833 E. Bismarck Expwy. Bismarck, ND 58504	701-328-5300	701-328-5320
University Extension	call county extension			

OHIO

	Agencies	Address	Phone Number	Fax Number
Information	One Stop Business Permit Center	PO Box 1001 Columbus, OH 43266-1001	800-248-4040 (OH only) 614-644-8748	614-466-0829
SBA	District Offices **Microloan Agencies:** 4	1111 Superior Avenue #630 Cleveland, OH 44114-2507	216-522-4180	216-522-2038
		2 Nationwide Plaza #1400 Columbus, OH 43215-2542	614-469-6860	614-469-2391
SBDC	Lead Office	77 S. High St. 28th Flr. PO Box 1001 Columbus, OH 43266	614-466-2711 800-848-1300 (OH only)	614-466-0829
Assistance to Minorities	Office of Department of Development	Small Business Women &/or Minority Business 77 S. High St. Columbus, OH 43266	800-848-1300 614-466-2711 (Women Bus) 614-466-5700 (Minority Office)	614-466-0829 614-466-4172
University Extension	Ohio State University Extension	2120 Fyffe Rd. Columbus, OH 43210	614-292-6470	614-292-7341

OKLAHOMA

	Agencies	Address	Phone Number	Fax Number
SBA	District Office **Microloan Agencies:** 2	210 Park Avenue #1300 Oklahoma City, OK 73102	405-231-4494	405-231-4876
SBDC	Lead Office	Southeastern State University 517 W. University Durant, OK 74701	405-924-0277 800-522-6154 (OK only)	405-920-7471
Assistance to Minorities	(Women state & private procurement) OK Department of Commerce	PO Box 26980 Oklahoma City, OK 73126	800-879-6552 ext. 242 (OK only) 405-841-5242	405-841-5142
	(Minority-State Procurement) Department of Central Services	Room 5A State Capital Oklahoma City, OK 73105	800-213-9521 (OK only) 405-521-3875	405-521-4475
	(Minority Private procurement) OK Minority Supplier Development Council	PO Box 18228 Oklahoma City, OK 73154	405-528-6732	405-528-6733
University Extension	Cooperative Extension Service Oklahoma State University	Central Office for Home-Based Entrepreneurship HES 135 Stillwater, OK 74078-6111	405-744-5776	405-744-7113
Associations	Oklahoma Home-Based Business Assoc.	PO Box 1335 Durant, OK 74702	405-924-5094	405-920-2745

OREGON

	Agencies	Address	Phone Number	Fax Number
Information	Business Information Center	Public Service Building #151 255 Capitol St. NE Salem, OR 97310-1327	503-986-2222	503-986-6355
SBA	District Office **Microloan Agencies: 1**	222 SW Columbia Street #500 Portland, OR 97201-6695	503-326-2682	503-326-2808
SBDC	Lead Office	Lane Community College 44 W. Broadway #501 Eugene, OR 97401	503-726-2250	503-345-6006
Assistance to Minorities	Office of Minority & Women & Emerging Business	350 Winter St. NE Salem, OR 97310	503-378-5651	503-373-7041
University Extension	Oregon State University Cooperative Extension	Milam 161 Corvalis, OR 97331-5106	503-737-2713	503-737-4423
Associations	Association of Home Based Businesses	PO Box 82682 Portland, OR 97282-0682	503-795-7350	503-288-8488

PENNSYLVANIA

	Agencies	Address	Phone Number	Fax Number
Information	Small Business Office	404 Forum Building Harrisburg, PA 17120	717-783-5700	717-234-4560
SBA	District Offices **Microloan Agencies: 3**	960 Penn Avenue, 5th Flr. Pittsburgh, PA 15222	412-644-2780	412-644-5446
		475 Allendale Rd. #201 King of Prussia, PA 19406	610-962-3804	610-962-3795
SBDC	Duquesne University	Rockwell Hall #10 Concourse 600 Forbes Avenue Pittsburgh, PA 15282	412-396-6233	412-396-5884
Assistance to Minorities	Office of Minority & Women Business Enterprise	502 N. Office Building Harrisburg, PA 17125	717-787-7380	717-787-7052
University Extension	call county extension			
Associations	Pittsburgh Home Business Assoc. (PHBA) South	6535 Quaker Dr. Pittsburgh, PA 15236	412-655-7420	
	(PHBA) North Hills	PO Box 101181 Pittsburgh, PA 15237	412-931-1198 box 422	
	(PHBA) Downtown Pittsburgh	4019 Lydia St. Pittsburgh, PA 15207	412-521-0906	

RHODE ISLAND

	Agencies	Address	Phone Number	Fax Number
Information	RI Department Of Economic Development	1 West Exchange St. Providence, RI 02903	401-277-2601	401-277-2102
SBA	District Office	380 Westminster Mall Providence, RI 02903	401-528-4562	401-528-4539
SBDC	Lead Office	Bryant College 1150 Douglas Pike Smithfield, RI 02917-1284	401-232-6111	401-232-6933
Assistance to Minorities	Office of Minority Business Assistance	1 Capitol Hill Providence, RI 02908	401-277-6253	401-277-6391
University Extension	call county extension			
Associations	Home-Based Business Association of Rhode Island	Central Rhode Island Chamber of Commerce 3288 Post Rd. Warwick, RI 02886	401-732-1100	401-732-1107

SOUTH CAROLINA

	Agencies	Address	Phone Number	Fax Number
Information	Enterprise Development, Inc.	PO Box 1149 Columbia, SC 29202	803-252-8806	803-252-0056
SBA	District Office **Microloan Agencies:** 2	1835 Assembly St. Room 358 Columbia, SC 29201	803-765-5376	803-765-5962
SBDC	Lead Office	University of South Carolina College of Business Admininistration 1710 College St. Columbia, SC 29208	803-777-4907	803-777-4403
Assistance to Minorities	Gov. Office of Small & Minority Business Assistance	1205 Pendleton St. #418 Columbia, SC 29201	803-734-0657	803-734-0548
University Extension	call county extension			

SOUTH DAKOTA

	Agencies	Address	Phone Number	Fax Number
Information	Governor's Office of Economic Development	711 E. Wells Avenue Pierre, SD 57501-3369	800-872-6190 605-773-5032	605-773-3256
SBA	District Office **Microloan Agencies:** 1	110 South Phillips Avenue Sioux Falls, SD 57104-6727	605-330-4231	605-330-4215
SBDC	Lead Office	Univ. of South Dakota School of Business 414 E. Clark Vermillion, SD 57069	605-677-5498	605-677-5272
Assistance to Minorities	Department Of Transportation	700 E. Broadway Avenue Pierre, SD 57501-2586	605-773-4906	605-773-3921
	Bureau of Indian Affairs	Aberdeen Area Office Branch of Contracting 115 Fourth Avenue SE MC 206 Aberdeen, SD 57401	605-226-7426	605-226-7627
University Extension	call county extension			
Associations	South Dakota Marketing Alliance	76 Third St. SW #201 Huron, SD 57350	605-352-3413	

TENNESSEE

	Agencies	Address	Phone Number	Fax Number
SBA	District Office **Microloan Agencies:** 1	50 Vantage Way #201 Nashville, TN 37228-1500	615-736-5881	615-736-7232
SBDC	Lead Office	Univ. of Memphis State Memphis, TN 38152	901-678-2500	901-678-4072
Assistance to Minorities	Department of Transportation	505 Deaderick St. #400 Nashville, TN 37243-0347	615-741-3681	615-741-3169
University Extension	call county extension			

TEXAS

	Agencies	Address	Phone Number	Fax Number
SBA	District Offices	10737 Gateway W. #320 El Paso, TX 79935	915-540-5676	915-540-5636
	Microloan Agencies: 3	4300 Amon Carter Blvd. #114 Fort Worth, TX 76155	817-885-6500	817-885-6516
		222 E. Van Buren St. #500 Harlingen, TX 78550-6855	210-427-8533	210-427-8537
		9301 Southwest Freeway #550 Houston, TX 77074	713-773-6500	713-773-6550
		1611 Tenth St. #200 Lubbock, TX 79401-2693	806-743-7462	806-743-7487
		727 E. Durango, 5th Flr. San Antonio, TX 78206	210-229-5904	210-229-5937
SBDC	Lead Office	University of Houston 1100 Louisiana #500 Houston, TX 77002	713-752-8444	713-756-1500
Assistance to Minorities	Department of Commerce Minority Business Development Agency	1100 Commerce Room 7B23 Dallas, TX 75242	214-767-8001	214-767-0613
University Extension	Texas A&M University	Extension Service PO Box 38 Overton, TX 75684	903-834-6191	903-834-7140
Associations	Texas Home-Based Business Assoc. (THBBA)	Dept. 482 PO Box 19400 Austin, TX 78760	512-448-5664 800-460-9533	

UTAH

	Agencies	Address	Phone Number	Fax Number
SBA	District Office Microloan Agencies: 1	Small Business Center Salt Lake Community College 8811 S. 700 East Sandy, UT 84070	801-255-5991	801-965-4338
SBDC	Lead Office	University of Utah 102 W. 500 St. #315 Salt Lake City, UT 84101	801-581-7905	
Assistance to Minorities	Department Of Transportation	4501 S. 2700 West Salt Lake City, UT 84119-5998	801-965-4208	801-965-4338
University Extension	Utah State University Department of Economics	UMC 3530 Logan, UT 84322-3530	801-797-2310	801-797-2701

VERMONT

	Agencies	Address	Phone Number	Fax Number
SBA	District Office Microloan Agencies: 2	87 State St. #205 PO Box 605 Montpelier, VT 05602	802-828-4422	802-828-4485
SBDC	Lead Office	University of Vermont Extension Service Morrill Hall Burlington, VT 05405-0106	802-656-4479	802-656-3131
Assistance to Minorities	Office of Civil Rights & Labor Vermont Agency of Transportation	133 State St. Montpelier, VT 05633	802-828-2717 802-241-3600	802-828-8522 802-244-1102
	Agency of Natural Resources	103 S. Main St. Waterbury, VT 05671-0301		
University Extension	University of Vermont Extension System	Howe Center Business Park 1 Scale Ave, Unit 55 Rutland, VT 05701-4452	802-773-3349	802-775-4840

VIRGINIA

Agencies		Address	Phone Number	Fax Number
Information	Department of Economic Development, Office of Small Business	PO Box 798 Richmond, VA 23218-0798	804-371-8252	
SBA	District Office **Microloan Agencies:** 3	1504 Santa Rosa Rd. Dale Bldg. #200 Richmond, VA 23229	804-771-2617	804-771-8018
SBDC	Lead Office	Department of Economic Development 901 E. Byrd St., 19th Flr. Richmond, VA 23219-4068	804-371-8100	804-755-3384
Assistance to Minorities	Department of Minority Business Enterprise	200-202 N. Ninth St. 11th Flr. Richmond, VA 23219	804-786-5560	804-371-7359
University Extension	call county extension	call extension office for information		

WASHINGTON

Agencies		Address	Phone Number	Fax Number
Information	Community Trade & Economic Development, Business Assistance Center	906 Columbia Street SW PO Box 48300 Olympia, WA 98504-8300	800-237-1233 (WA only) 360-753-4900	
SBA	District Offices	1200 Sixth Avenue #1700 Seattle, WA 98101-1128	206-553-7310	206-553-7099
	Microloan Agencies: 2	Farm Credit Bldg. 10th Flr. East 601 W. First Avenue Spokane, WA 99204-0317	509-353-2809	509-353-2829
SBDC	Washington State University SBDC	501 Johnson Tower Pullman, WA 99164-4851	509-335-1576	509-335-0949
Assistance to Minorities	Office of Minority & Women's Business Enterprise	406 S. Water Olympia, WA 98504-1160	360-753-9693	360-586-7079
University Extension	Cooperative Extension	11104 149th St. Brush Prairie, WA 98606	360-254-8436	360-260-6161
Associations	Home-Based Business Network of So. King & Pierce Co.	PO Box 24384 Federal Way, WA 98093	206-927-9149	206-927-6513
	Olympic Home-Based Business Assoc.	1713 E. Third St. Port Angeles, WA 98362	360-452-2418	

WEST VIRGINIA

	Agencies	Address	Phone Number	Fax Number
SBA	District Office **Microloan** **Agencies:** 1	168 W. Main St. Clarksburg, WV 26301	304-623-5631	304-623-0023
SBDC	Lead Office	950 Kanawha Blvd. E. Charleston, WV 25301	304-558-2960	304-558-0127
Assistance to Minorities	Department of Transportation	Capitol Complex 1900 Kanawha Blvd. Bldg. 5, Room 925 Charleston, WV 25305	304-558-0444	304-558-4076
University Extension	call county extension			

WISCONSIN

	Agencies	Address	Phone Number	Fax Number
Information	Department of Development	Department of Development PO Box 7970 Madison, WI 53707	800-HELP-BUS (WI only)	
SBA	District Office **Microloan** **Agencies:** 4	212 E. Washington Ave. Suite 213 Madison, WI 53703	608-264-5261	608-264-5541
SBDC	University of Wisconsin at Whitewater	2000 Carlson Bldg. Whitewater, WI 53190	414-472-3217	
Assistance to Minorities	Bureau of Minority Business Development & Office of Women's Business Services	Department of Development PO Box 7970 Madison, WI 53707	800-HELP-BUS (WI only) 608-267-9550 608-266-0593	608-267-2829
University Extension	call county extension			
Associations	Home-Based Business Association	UW Whitewater Home Based Business Project 2000 Carlson Hall Whitewater, WI 53190	414-472-1917	414-472-5692

WYOMING

	Agencies	Address	Phone Number	Fax Number
Information	Division of Economic & Community Development, Department of Commerce	6101 Yellowstone Rd. Cheyenne, WY 82002	307-777-7284	307-777-5840
SBA	District Office	100 East B St. #4001 PO Box 2839 Casper, WY 82602-2839	307-261-6500	307-261-6535
SBDC	Lead Office	Univ. of Wyoming PO Box 3922 Laramie, WY 82071	307-766-3505	307-766-3406
Assistance to Minorities	Wyoming Department of Transportation	PO Box 1708 Cheyenne, WY 82003-1708	307-777-4375	307-777-4289
University Extension	University of Wyoming Cooperative Extension Service	412½ Gillette Avenue Gillette, WY 82716	307-682-7281	307-687-6376
		107 N. 5th #135 Douglas, WY 82633	307-358-2417	307-358-6703

Index

Do You Have Questions or Feedback?

The authors of this book, Paul and Sarah Edwards, want to answer your questions. They can respond to you directly, usually within twenty-four hours, if you leave a message for them on the Working From Home Forum on Compu-Serve Information Service. If you have a computer and access to CompuServe, simply type "GO WORK" at any "!" prompt; their ID is 76703,242. You can also visit Paul and Sarah's resources offered on the Internet's World Wide Web at **http://www.homeworks.com**

If you do not have a computer, you can write to Paul and Sarah in care of "Q&A," Home Office Computing magazine, 730 Broadway, New York, NY 10003. Your question may be selected to be answered in their monthly column or they may respond to it on their radio or TV show. However, they cannot respond to every letter.

Other Books by Paul and Sarah Edwards

Use the table below to locate other books that contain the information you need for your business interests.

Subject	Best Home Businesses for the 90s	Getting Business to Come to You	The Secret of Self-Employment	Making Money with Your Computer at Home	Working from Home	Finding Your Perfect Work
Advertising		Yes				
Business opportunities					Yes	
Business planning				Yes		
Children and child care					Yes	
Closing sales		Yes	Yes			
Credit					Yes	
Employees					Yes	
Ergonomics				Yes	Yes	
Failure			Yes			
Family and marriage issues					Yes	
Financing your business			Yes	Yes	Yes	
Franchise named					Yes	
Getting referrals		Yes			Yes	
Handling emotional/ psychological issues			Yes			
Housecleaning					Yes	
Insurance					Yes	
Legal issues					Yes	
Loneliness, isolation					Yes	
Managing information				Yes	Yes	
Marketing	Specific techniques by business	Yes Focus of book	Yes Attitude	Yes Technology tools	Yes	
Marketing materials		Yes		Yes		
Money			Yes	Yes	Yes	
Naming your business		Yes				
Networking		Yes			Yes	
Office space, furniture, equipment					Yes	
Outgrowing your home					Yes	
Overcoming setbacks			Yes			
Pricing	Yes Specific			Yes Specific	Yes Principles	
Profiles of specific businesses	Yes			Yes		
Public relations and publicity		Yes			Yes	
Resource Directory			Yes			
Selecting a business/career	Yes			Yes	Yes	Yes Focus of book
Software				Yes	Yes	
Speaking		Yes				
Start-up costs	Yes			Yes		
Success issues			Yes			
Taxes					Yes	
Time management			Yes	Yes	Yes	
Zoning					Yes	

Complete Your Library of the Working from Home Series by Paul and Sarah Edwards

These books are available at your local bookstore or wherever books are sold. Ordering is also easy and convenient. TO ORDER, CALL 1-800-788-6262, prompt #1, or send your order to:

Jeremy P. Tarcher, Inc.
Mail Order Department
PO Box 12289
Newark, NJ 07101-5289

For Canadian orders:
PO Box 25000
Postal Station 'A'
Toronto, Ontario M5W 2X8

		Price
_____ The Best Home Businesses for the 90s, Revised Edition	0-87477-784-4	$12.95
_____ Finding Your Perfect Work	0-87477-795-X	$16.95
_____ Getting Business to Come to You	0-87477-629-5	$11.95
_____ Making Money with Your Computer at Home	0-87477-736-4	$12.95
_____ Working from Home	0-87477-764-X	$15.95
Subtotal		_____
Shipping and handling*		_____
Sales tax (CA, NJ, NY, PA)		_____
Total amount due		_____

Payable in U.S. funds (no cash orders accepted). $15.00 minimum for credit card orders.
*Shipping and handling: $3.50 for one book, $1.00 for each additional book. Not to exceed $8.50.

Payment method:

☐ Visa   ☐ MasterCard   ☐ American Express
☐ Check or money order
☐ International money order or bank draft check

Card # _____ Expiration date _____

Signature as on charge card _____

Daytime phone number _____

Name _____

Address _____

City _____ State _____ Zip _____

Please allow six weeks for delivery. Prices subject to change without notice. Source key WORK